THE NEW NATURALI

A SURVEY OF BRITISH NAT

C000184708

GALLOWAY AND THE BORDERS

THE NEW NATURALIST LIBRARY

GALLOWAY
AND THE
BORDERS

DEREK RATCLIFFE

To Jeannette

This edition published in 2007 by Collins,
an imprint of HarperCollins Publishers

HarperCollins Publishers
77–85 Fulham Palace Road
London W6 8JB
www.collins.co.uk

First published 2007

A CIP catalogue record for this book is available
from the British Library.

Set in FF Nexus by
Rowland Phototypesetting Ltd
Bury St Edmunds, Suffolk

Printed in China by Imago
Reprographics by Saxon Photolitho, Norwich

Hardback
ISBN-10 0-00-717401-2
ISBN-13 978-0-00-717401-0

Paperback
ISBN-10 0-00-717402-0
ISBN-13 978-0-00-717402-7

Contents

In Memory of Derek Ratcliffe
1929–2005

Good prose is like a window pane
George Orwell, Why I Write

Derek Ratcliffe had a photographic memory of most of Britain, and certainly of the uplands. Name a location, and he could describe the habitats, the intricacies of their ecology, and especially the birdlife. He was an acute observer, with an enthusiasm for wild, open areas combined with a natural curiosity and an ability to think laterally. His industry and energy were remarkable, driven by a thirst for knowledge, an urge to understand what was happening around him, and the ability to reveal to others with straightforward clarity the hidden wonders of the natural world.

Born in London on 9 July 1929, Derek grew up in Carlisle, where he developed a keen interest in nature. His first step on the literary ladder was a school essay on peregrines and ravens for which he won a prize at Carlisle Grammar. As he describes in the New Naturalist *Lakeland: the wildlife of Cumbria* (2002), his parents 'made the wonderful decision to move from London to Carlisle when I was nine years old, and so paved the way for the eventual appearance of this book.' Indeed, that move was a blessing, for it has now also given us *Galloway and the Borders*, which is both a lament for the wealth of nature lost in our lifetimes and a celebration of one of Britain's neglected landscapes. In addition to writing these two volumes for the series, Derek was an enthusiastic supporter of the New Naturalist library, and a series editor for twelve years.

During six decades, from his early encounters with wildlife through to difficult and strained relations with politicians and senior civil servants, Derek always wrote lucidly about nature. He was one of the most distinguished conservationists in Britain, featuring once in *The Sunday Times* as one of the hundred people who had most influenced the twentieth century. He retired in 1989 as Chief Scientist of the Nature Conservancy Council (NCC), but went on to write several more books and articles. His publications list is unique for the breadth of subjects in which he had expert knowledge. Derek devised the modern framework for nature conservation in *A Nature Conservation Review* (1977), which he edited and largely wrote. He made the key discovery about the link between pesticides and eggshell thinning in raptors, producing in 1967 a paper in the prestigious scientific journal *Nature* which became what is now known as a 'citation classic'. Later, he published two classic bird monographs, *The Peregrine Falcon* (1980, 1993) and *The Raven* (1997), and a highly original book on *Bird Life of Mountain and Upland* (1990).

As a botanist, having taken his PhD on mountain vegetation at the University of Wales in Bangor, Derek went on to pioneer (with Donald McVean) the description and classification of upland vegetation in the Scottish Highlands, published in *Plant Communities of the Scottish Highlands* (1962). Later, he made pioneering studies of bryophytes, peatlands and mountain plants. He loved to write about his travels and experiences, and captured these first in *Highland Flora* (1977), later in his memoir of early years in the field, *In Search of Nature* (2000), and finally in the superbly illustrated book about his travels with his wife Jeannette in the far north of Europe, *Lapland: a natural history* (2005). Derek also wrote scientific papers, book chapters and articles which all had the hallmark of first-hand observation, clear analysis and fluent writing. Many of his photographs appear in his books, and even some of these have become conservation icons, such as the wave of conifers breaking over the uplands of Kirkcudbrightshire, Rannoch Moor with its pine stumps exposed, dotterel nesting on a Lakeland fell, and the great beeches of the New Forest.

He did not dress, speak or behave as if he was important. He was quiet – sometimes virtually silent; he was shy and unassuming; thoughtful, intense, brave and constitutionally sceptical; and at times outraged, especially over forestry and farming impacts on nature and the land. Derek thought critically about the plight of nature, wrote about its place in society, and constantly urged people, especially his colleagues, to rise up in its defence. He never ceased to be upset by the destruction of wild places, and in his writing you can hear his voice.

With his penetrating knowledge and understanding, and personal commitment, he effectively led the NCC in the 1970s and 1980s, laying the foundations for the wildlife legislation and protected areas we have today. It was an unorthodox style of leadership, founded on a first-hand understanding of the changing landscape, a capacity to analyse complex issues, an awareness of the political process, and the courage of his convictions.

In the field he was special company, and at his happiest. He rarely worked outdoors alone, instead enjoying company. There was a rhythm to his presence in the wilds, with which he always seemed so perfectly in tune. Of the many tributes to Derek written after his sudden death on 23 May 2005, few mentioned one of his sterling qualities – his capacity for friendship. He was not gregarious, and his many friendships were sustained by an immense capacity for letter writing, which he kept up throughout his life, and above all by comradeship in the field. Derek trusted his colleagues and friends, and this was returned in huge measure; he did not have much faith in humanity, but he did in his friends.

Derek inspired people; he breathed new life into them through his words, his photographs, his conduct, his humility – and his own idiosyncratic, understated greatness.

Des Thompson

Author's Foreword and Acknowledgements

T HE SOUTH OF Scotland has always suffered by comparison with the grander Highlands, and in natural history has been something of a Cinderella, relatively unknown and written about by a very few students of plants and animals. Galloway, in particular, comprising the twin counties of Kirkcudbright and Wigtown – the Stewartry and the Shire – has neither a full-blown flora nor a fauna to its publications credit, and the counties of Selkirk, Roxburgh, Peebles, West Lothian and East Lothian have little of recent literature. Yet this is a region rich in diversity of wildlife, with a range of habitat that spans nearly all the main types to be found in Britain. Parts of it still have the allure of the unknown, and there is still much basic recording to be done on the less popular groups of plants and animals.

I grew up only a short distance south of the Scottish border, and soon began to make forays in search of birds across it into neighbouring Dumfriesshire. Then I discovered the charms of Galloway, where from 1946 onwards I spent annual spring holidays exploring its hill country for peregrines and ravens, staying with shepherds and their families in out-of-the-way places. From 1956 to 1963, my first job with the Nature Conservancy was based in Edinburgh, and my work often took me south into the Borders and Galloway. Even though I have subsequently lived far away, there has not been a single year when I have failed to visit the region at least once.

This book is based especially on my own field experience, but supplemented by the observations and information of many others, from both personal contact and perusal of the literature. I have to thank first Donald and Joan Watson, warm friends for over forty years, whom I visited often in their charming home in Dalry, for their kindness and hospitality. Donald and I had many good days together in the field, looking for birds, and I learned much from his encyclopaedic knowledge of the Galloway scene and his artist's eye for it. His passion for the hen harrier was inspiring and his fieldcraft in finding their nests something to behold. Donald's books, *A Bird Artist in Scotland* and *One Pair of Eyes*, illustrated by his own superb pictures, wonderfully convey the character of the country in which he chose to make his career as a painter more than half a century ago. When Joan turned her attention to butterflies and their photography, our outings gained further in enjoyment.

Roderick and Jean Corner have hospitably welcomed me to their home in Penrith on numerous occasions, and Rod has given me the benefit of his profound knowledge of the flora of the Borders. His long-term fieldwork in Selkirk and Roxburgh has left few places unexplored botanically, and his discovery of the important fens in these hitherto little-known counties was a major find. I have greatly valued his information and advice on the botanical treatment, his comments on the text, and his companionship in the field. He kindly gave me copies of his historical review of botany in his two vice-counties, and of the bibliography for the Flora that he is compiling. Grant Roger was a colleague in the Nature Conservancy's Scottish headquarters in Edinburgh, and after his retirement to Melrose in the 1970s I visited him and his wife Jean regularly. The three of us had many days together in the field, botanising and taking pictures of plants, for Grant was a great photographer. Both he and Jean were the best of companions, with whom I shared happy times roaming the wilds.

I am extremely grateful to John Mitchell for his keen interest in the work, which, with his knowledge of the local literature and library researches on my behalf, has provided me with numerous references that I should otherwise never have known about. He has helpfully read and commented upon parts of the text. Humphrey Milne-Redhead, busy country GP, was always glad to talk botany and head for some unexplored corner of his territory. I thank him for company and hospitality.

My mentor Ernest Blezard first aroused my interest in the south of Scotland, by telling me of his experiences there, and this was the stimulus behind my early explorations of the Langholm, Galloway and Moffat hills. We had many memorable days together on the moorlands north of the border, and his description of changes seen within his lifetime gave an historical insight not otherwise available. Other Cumbrian friends, Ray Laidler and Peter Day, recounted their early times among the peregrines and ravens in Galloway, while Geoff Horne and Ralph Stokoe gave me detailed records of their golden eagle days in those rugged hills. I give special thanks to two bird of prey enthusiasts extraordinary, Dick Roxburgh and George Carse, who for over thirty years supplied me with precise data on the annual rounds of peregrine eyries which they made, with their helpers. Their lengthy epistles are minor masterpieces of literature, to be treasured for their vividness and passion, apart from the vital information. Chris Rollie has also kept me informed about golden eagles, peregrines, red kites, ravens and other birds in Dumfries & Galloway. In the Borders, George Smith, Malcolm Henderson and Chris Cameron have provided data on falcons and ravens. My thanks to them, too.

Not the least of the pleasures of my early days in the Southern Uplands were the good times I spent staying with shepherds and their families in lonely places among the Galloway and Moffat hills. They were some of the happiest days of my life, wandering over lonely uplands where the only souls I ever saw were other shepherds, and returning at night to wonderful suppers and good talk. I thank Will and Mary Murdoch of Dregmorn, Louisa McGarva of Craigenbay, and John and Elizabeth Borthwick of Polmoodie for their kindness to the young man with the bicycle and pack they welcomed to their homes year after year. All but Mary have passed away but my memories of them are evergreen.

I am grateful to my erstwhile colleagues on the South of Scotland regional staff of the Nature Conservancy, for help in various ways: Thomas Huxley, Langley Roberts (and Madeleine), Nancy Gordon, Joanna Robertson, Jim Lockie, Nigel Charles, Chris Badenoch, Vincent Fleming, John Young, Robin Payne. In the successor Scottish Natural Heritage (SNH), Chris Miles, Dianne Holman and Sarah Eno have been most helpful in giving me information about Sites of Special Scientific Interest (SSSIs) and reserves, and I am grateful to Heather Shirra for a copy of the SNH inventory of ancient and semi-natural woodlands. The list of SSSIs in Appendix 1 was taken from the SNH website (www.snh.org.uk). Des Thompson, Principal Uplands Adviser in SNH, has discussed the problems of upland and bird conservation over many years, and given me much valuable information and help, while days in the field with him have been a great pleasure. I have relied on Des to keep me informed about the Scottish conservation scene, which he observes with a perceptive and critical eye. Ian Newton has commented helpfully on the piece on sparrowhawks. Roy Watling very kindly wrote, at short notice, an account of fungi in the region, which is reproduced as Appendix 3.

Chris Rollie, the RSPB officer for southwest Scotland, has also been a mine of information and a stimulating field companion, with whom it is always a tonic to exchange the talk and put the conservation world to rights. He has very kindly read parts of the text and given me many valuable comments on it. Rob Soutar,

District Forest Manager for Forest Enterprise (i.e. the Forestry Commission) has brought me up to date on the changed policy of his organisation towards wildlife conservation. I thank the Forestry Commission for access to their vast estate in the south of Scotland, including some of the roads normally closed to the public, and acknowledge the help and interest of their field staff, even though we part company over the Commission's afforestation policy. Richard and Barbara Mearns have kindly given me notes on butterflies, moths and dragonflies, while David Clarke has also advised me on dragonflies and Graham Rotheray on Diptera. Other friends and contacts whose help and kindness I acknowledge are John and Hilary Birks, Elsie Gordon, Margaret Russell, Dorothy Blezard, Heather McHaffie, Stuart Illis, Tom Irving and George Trafford.

I am much indebted to Bobby Smith for letting me choose a selection from his fine collection of colour photographs of birds and habitats in southern Scotland. Norman Tait achieved a spectacular enhancement of some old and overexposed photographs that show pre-afforestation scenes, and I thank him also for the brown argus picture. Other photographs have been kindly supplied by David Clarke, Geoff Horne, John Mitchell and Philip Newman/Nature Photographers. Unattributed photographs were taken by me. Pradeep Sihota at the British Geological Survey kindly arranged permission for reproduction of the geological map.

As regards literature sources, I have drawn heavily from many of the works mentioned in the historical review in Chapter 2. Of the recent publications, I acknowledge particularly the annual bird reports for the Borders and Dumfries & Galloway, the various county botanical checklists, and the atlases of plants (Hill *et al.*, 1991–4; Preston *et al.*, 2002) and birds (Gibbons *et al.*, 1993; Murray *et al.*, 1998; Wernham *et al.*, 2002). The *Solway Firth Review*, compiled by the Solway Firth Partnership (1996), is also an important work of reference. I hope I may be excused for not giving the detailed references for these publications on every occasion when their information is used, but the value of the material is much appreciated. Ian Dawson and Lynn Giddings in the RSPB Library at Sandy have given valuable help over references, and I thank also Carol Showell in the BTO Library at Thetford.

British Plant Communities contains a classification of British vegetation types compiled by John Rodwell of Lancaster University under contract to the Nature Conservancy Council, and published in five volumes between 1991 and 2000. Where possible I have tried to relate southern Scottish plant communities to his types, by giving the reference code letter and number, but – to save space – without repeated acknowledgement of the source.

PUBLISHER'S ACKNOWLEDGEMENTS

To the great sadness of all who knew him, Derek Ratcliffe died just days after finishing the manuscript of this book. The publishers would like to extend their grateful thanks to all those who have helped make this publication possible. In particular, Des Thompson and Chris Rollie for checking facts, tracking down obscure references, and bringing rare-bird data up to date; Hugh Brazier for his superb editorial expertise; Jean Torrance of the Scottish Ornithologists' Club; Richard Mearns and Roy Watling; and all the photographers who have contributed their work.

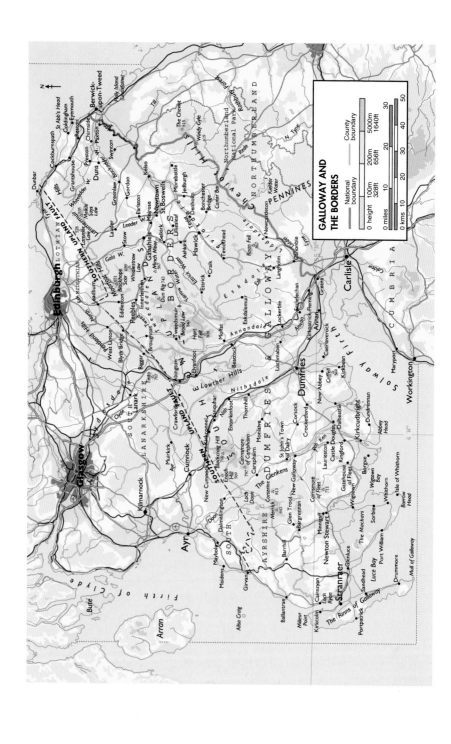

GALLOWAY AND
THE BORDERS

0 height   100m   200m   5000m
            328ft   656ft   1640ft
                                        National
                                        boundary
                                        County
                                        boundary

0 miles 10   20   30
0 kms 10   20   30   40   50

The Southern Uplands:
A Reminiscence

I T SEEMS WORTH attempting to convey what it was that first attracted me to this region. The hill country was the magnet – a wide panorama of lonely uplands forming the skyline to the north on clear days from near my home town of Carlisle. Not dramatic enough to have excited mountaineers, and hence to have become famous, it appeared little known outside its own residents, and neglected also by natural historians. As something of a *terra incognita*, it held prospects for exploration in search of wildlife, with possibilities for modest discovery in the wilds.

GALLOWAY

After an introduction to the Lakeland fells, the northern Pennines and the Border moorlands of north Cumberland in 1944–5, my thoughts turned to the more distant ranges of the Southern Uplands. Ernest Blezard told me about Galloway, a wild and little-known district of rocky hills, where three young friends of his had explored during short Easter holidays before the war and found several eyries of peregrine and raven in quite easy crags. I bought the maps and weighed the possibilities. A good many crags were shown, some in remote places devoid of tracks, and some of the hills had strange, romantic names – Cairnsmore of Fleet, Corserine, Millfire, The Dungeon, Mullwharchar and Curleywee. I read the Reverend C. H. Dick's book on Galloway and Carrick in the *Highways and Byways* series (1916), and was fired with enthusiasm by his vivid descriptions of the lonely hill country. Still more to the point, he mentioned the nesting of a pair of golden eagles in 1906. *The Birds of Ayrshire*

(Paton & Pike, 1929) added the information that the species nested in the Loch Doon hills in 1921, and I picked up rumours of more recent breeding.

This was good enough. I found that the Caldons farm in Glen Trool would put me up and this seemed a good central location within walking distance of much of the most interesting hill country. On 13 April 1946, I took an early train for Newton Stewart, intent on ten days' solitary exploration of the Galloway hills. My introduction to these wilds came as the train left New Galloway station. The journey had been through pleasant though tame country of green cattle pastures, with whitewashed farms and scattered woods, and some low hills behind. Across the River Ken, the scene changed suddenly and dramatically, as a great empty sweep of moorland marched into view. At the back of a large undulating plain along the course of the River Dee there rose strange rocky hills, with much higher tops more distantly behind them. The treelessness of the scene was striking (Figs 1 & 2). Distant patches of oakwood showed beyond the Dee, but otherwise the only trees were on a couple or so of birch-grown islands in Loch Skerrow. Two distant shepherds' cottages were the only sign of human presence. The imposing mass of Cairnsmore of Fleet presently loomed up to dominate the panorama, with a great slabby cliff in its eastern corries, and the craggy shoulder of Craigronald. This was truly a country fit for golden eagles. Then, swinging under a spur of the hill, the line ran beneath the finely sculpted

FIG 1. The Awful Hand range from Craignaw. Merrick, Kirriereoch Hill and Shalloch on Minnoch, with Loch Enoch. Kirkcudbrightshire – Ayrshire.

FIG 2. Muirburn on Cairnsmore of Fleet: before the trees came. April 1968, Kirkcudbrightshire.

escarpment at the Clints of Dromore, where grey granite buttresses rose with startling abruptness from the moor. Cairnsmore began to recede behind a further stretch of moorland before the track dropped to the Cree estuary with its woods, green fields and salt marshes.

That journey remains vividly imprinted upon my memory. These granite hills were different from those I knew in northern England. Their colours were drab at this time of year – grey or even white of exposed rock, pale bleached straw of flying bent grass, dark red-brown of heather and tawny bracken. The perfect day, with drifting masses of cumulus casting shadows widely, added to the rich tapestry of tone across the uplands. Later I realised that it is the flying bent (*Molinia*) that, as much as anything, gives the dominant visual character of these Galloway hills, through the huge areas occupied by this tough grass of wet ground, either in pure growths or variably mixed with heather and bog myrtle (Fig. 3). But this is the winter or early spring impression. In a few weeks time the scene is transformed as the new growth of *Molinia* appears and the hills flush with green. It is sometimes known also as purple moor-grass, and this colour refers to the inflorescences that come later still. The Galloway shepherds' name of 'white blaw grass' seems the best, for its long and pale dead leaves blow around and accumulate as a deep litter under the shelter of walls and rocks.

FIG 3. Galloway sheepwalks: flying bent on wet ground, fescue/bent on dry moraine knolls. Kells Range behind. Mackilston, north of Lochinvar, Kirkcudbrightshire.

From my base at the Caldons I trekked far and wide into the surrounding hills. One day I reached the pass known as the Nick of the Dungeon between the two hills, Craignaw and the Dungeon, in the central granite range, and gazed down on a scene of desolation surpassing even that of the Cairnsmore wilds. Within a kilometre radius or so much of the ground seemed to be bare rock: crags, slabs, pavements, boulder fields and block screes of grey granite, with a patchwork of heather and flying bent where peaty soil had managed to form (Fig. 4). The long slopes below the Nick dropped to the floor of a broad valley, the Cauldron of the Dungeon, with two bleak tarns, the Round and Long Lochs, in view and a third, the Dry Loch, hidden round the Dungeon shoulder. Confluent streams from the higher ground joined to form the Cooran Lane, which ran a sinuous course southwards to join the River Dee near Loch Dee. On broad flats, mostly on the nearer side of the Cooran Lane, was a chain of bogs, where the reflected light glinted from myriad pools and explained its name, the Silver Flowe, of sinister reputation in the writings of S. R. Crockett. Beyond the river, the ground rose, gently at first, then more steeply, into long, smooth grassy slopes to the broad, lofty ridge of the Kells Range, with the high summits of Corserine (813m), Carlin's Cairn, Meikle Millyea and other tops (Fig. 5).

Away in the middle of this broad strath was the wee shepherd's cottage at Backhill of the Bush, deserted for the past three years, when its occupants finally

FIG 4. The rugged summit of Craignaw, showing jointing of the granite. Kirkcudbright-shire.

FIG 5. The Loch Dungeon corrie and Corserine: a sheep-free summit with extensive woolly fringe-moss heath. Kells Range, Kirkcudbrightshire.

gave up this lonely existence, five long miles from the nearest road end (see Fig. 207). Apart from this, and the cairn beside me, there was no trace of human presence. There was no vestige of a track to the cottage, nor anywhere else. The smoke from a distant moor fire far down the valley told of shepherd activity, but I did not see another fellow human all day, and even sheep seemed to be thin on the ground. A few wild goats and red deer were more fitting occupants of the place, along with the ravens and peregrines that I had come to seek. It was the wilderness, quite treeless again, apart from two rowans by the empty cottage. In those days this condition had no message of past human impact for me and it appeared to be natural, unspoiled country.

This first visit to Galloway was not blessed with the best of luck as regards the birds. I walked hard and averaged 25 kilometres a day over seven days, mostly over trackless hill, but located only two nesting pairs of peregrines and seven of ravens. My best but frustrating find was an undoubted eyrie of golden eagles from which young had obviously been reared, evidently the year before. It seemed highly probable that there was an occupied nest not far away, but lack of time and mobility prevented an adequate search of possible alternative sites. Many years later I learned that there was indeed a nest in 1946, but it failed, and there was uncertainty about its exact location. Perhaps it had already come to nothing while I was there. By the following year the return of golden eagles to the Galloway Hills became well known, and two fine young in the nest were pictured by a local photographer.

With my appetite whetted by this challenging country, I was back the next year, this time with a bicycle and, working from both Glen Trool and Clattering-shaws, covered a wider area and had more success with my favourite birds. I continued to return every spring and before long had worked out the distribution of all the peregrines and most of the ravens in the higher Galloway Hills. I greatly enjoyed going the rounds of them each year, climbing to the nests that were accessible, recording the contents and making notes on their food and breeding habits. Their numbers seemed remarkably constant year by year. The golden eagles yielded some of their secrets and I watched their numbers slowly build up, from one pair during 1945–51 to four pairs by 1964. There were other birds of the moorlands, above all the curlews, and one of the abiding memories of those days on the wide open moors is of the haunting liquid bubbling calls of the display flight, as the 'whaups' rose on rapidly beating wings and then sank gracefully downwards. On still, sunny days, the smoke from the shepherds' moor fires rose high into the air from all quarters, and the freshly burned ground had a marvellously aromatic smell. Not the least of the pleasure was in staying with hill shepherds and their families in their sequestered dwellings deep among the hills, where I was welcomed back each year and partook of their simple and lonely life (Fig. 6).

In those early years I knew little about plants, but was aware that the granite Galloway Hills had little floral variety. The northern cliffs of the Merrick had a modest assortment of alpine plants, but the prevailing vegetation seemed to consist of about a dozen common plants of hill grassland, moorland and bog. A summer visit in 1949 brought the discovery of the azure hawker dragonfly, a boreal–arctic species previously unknown south of the Highlands. By fortunate chance I became a botanist at university, and learned about the nature of peat bogs. The Silver Flowe seemed to be an important and possibly unique system of bogs and, after a reconnaissance visit with my student colleague Donald Walker, the newly formed Nature Conservancy gave us funds to make a proper survey. This we did in the late summer of 1951, when we were joined by Richard West, and camped for two weeks, after carrying in a store of provisions, in the remote and empty cottage at Backhill of the Bush, which was conveniently close to the bogs. Our report formed the basis for the establishment in 1956 of a National Nature Reserve over the Silver Flowe, which became a major United Kingdom site for the study of peatland ecology (Fig. 7).

With my interest in peat bogs aroused, I realised the potential of the lower moorlands for other important sites. In Wigtownshire, especially, there were

FIG 6. The end of the road. Dregmorn cottage, where I stayed with Will and Mary Murdoch. 1955, Kirkcudbrightshire.

FIG 7. Northern end of the Silver Flowe, showing watershed bogs in 1956, before afforestation of the slopes behind. Round and Long Lochs of the Dungeon.

great areas of low-level peat moss, which seemed to be intermediate in character between the true raised bogs of the coastal plains and the typical blanket bogs of the uplands. I looked at some of these peatlands, fascinating of name: Tannylaggie Flow, Kilquhockadale Flow, Anabaglish Moss, Ink Moss, Gall Moss of Dineark and Dirskelpin. They had greater variety and number of birds than the typical higher hills of the district. I had always been struck by the numbers of curlews on some of the lower Galloway moorlands and, much later, turned my attention to those on the gentle *Molinia* sheepwalks northeast of Dalry. By this time, they had decreased greatly across the region, and the Galloway Hills had come to bear a very different appearance from that of my youth, as I shall relate.

MOFFATDALE

It was not until 1949 that I reached the hills of Moffat Water in the far north-eastern corner of Dumfriesshire. These, too, I first heard about from Ernest Blezard, but then read a fascinating account of them in a little book entitled *Birkhill: a Reminiscence*. Its author, C. R. B. McGilchrist, was a Liverpool merchant who spent holidays fishing for trout in the hill streams and lochs of the area.

He stayed with the shepherd and his family in the little cottage at Birkhill, at the very top of Moffatdale, where the pass goes through the hills to St Mary's Loch and Yarrow Water. His writing so beautifully captures the essence of the free and simple life among the hills, in company with the hardy folk who spend the whole year there. I read it again now and then, and recapture some of my own good times among these hills.

I was lucky to find accommodation at the sheep farm of Polmoodie, far up the valley, and arrived there early in April to prospect for ravens and peregrines. These sedimentary hills are very different from the granite uplands of Galloway. On both sides of Moffatdale, great smooth slopes soared high above, as steep as it is possible for hillsides to be, without breaking out into actual crag (Fig. 8). But in the heavily glaciated side glens of Black's Hope, Carrifran and the Tail there were extensive ranges of cliff, and in the last of these was the great waterfall gorge of the Grey Mare's Tail, with its stream issuing from the elevated Loch Skene under still higher scarps. Moffatdale was mainly green and grassy and, although there was patchy heather in places, it was clearly in retreat. On the northern side of the range, the similarly high hills of the Megget Water in Selkirkshire had more heather ground, but much less crag and, indeed, outside Moffat Water, rock outcrops of any size are few and far between in the central and eastern hills of the Southern Uplands. The smooth, rounded tops of Broad Law and Cramalt Craig above Tweedsmuir are, with Hart Fell and White Coomb on Moffat Water, of

FIG 8. A hill sheep farm. Polmoodie in Moffatdale, Dumfriesshire.

much the same height as the highest Galloway hills, and had sheltered hollows which sometimes held snow until late in the spring.

When I became a botanist and did postgraduate research on mountain vegetation in Snowdonia, my interest developed in the plants of other upland districts. *The Flora of Dumfriesshire* (Scott-Elliot, 1896) revealed that the base-rich rocks of the Moffat Hills were by far the richest area of the Southern Uplands for 'alpines', and in the early 1950s I systematically set to work searching the craggy glens to find them, again from Polmoodie as a base. I eventually found most of the recorded species, some of them hanging on in minute quantity in single localities, and even managed to discover a couple of new ones. Records of some other alpines have been judged erroneous, or the plants are long-lost and possibly extinct, but the possibilities of the area are perhaps not yet exhausted; and I still bear in mind things to look out for when I visit the Moffat Hills.

These Moffat and Tweedsmuir hills did not have quite the desolate character of the Galloway uplands, but they had their own distinctive charm, and became another favourite stamping ground, to which I paid at least one annual visit for many years.

THE LANGHOLM AND MOORFOOT HILLS

The nearest of the Southern Uplands to Carlisle were the unspectacular hills around Langholm, only 35km away, where the Malcolm Monument on Whita Hill was visible to the unaided eye as a distinctive feature in a massif of rounded tops reaching only 600m at their highest (Fig. 9). I first went there in 1945 in search of a pair of ravens nesting in one or other of two strange ravines, which had been occupied by the bird 'from time immemorial'; and subsequently followed them and their successors for many years, by annual visits. These were partly sheep hills but also grouse moors, dark and heathery in contrast to the green and grassy appearance of the former. They included moors famous for their record 'bags' of red grouse, especially on Tarras Water, but in the early years after World War II management had not returned to the intensity of the interwar period, and numbers of the bird seemed depressed. It was also an area that did not quite live up to expectations. Scarcity of decent rocks partly explained the lack of crag-nesting birds other than kestrels, but it did not account for the total absence of peregrines, which had been known to nest on minor outcrops in the past. And the single pair of ravens was puzzling, for the bird is quite common as a tree-nester in similar hill country in parts of Wales. Buzzards were hardly ever seen, yet many pairs bred on small rocks and in trees in Lakeland, not far to the south.

FIG 9. Heather in flower on the Langholm Moors, Dumfriesshire.

There were reports that golden eagles and hen harriers appeared in the area but soon vanished – victims of gun, trap or poison with which the grouse custodians soon put them down.

Later, when working in Edinburgh, I made the acquaintance of another grouse moor area on the Moorfoot Hills, not far to the south of that city. Here, too, was a scarcity of predators, except perhaps merlins, a single pair of ravens which presently dropped out, occasional nesting attempts by peregrines, and no sign of buzzards that I ever saw. Tidy lines of butts, heaps of white gravel and a neat patchwork of burned heather said it all. Yet this was great country for other moorland birds – even better than Langholm for golden plover, which I observed on the Moorfoots for some years, and with dunlin, curlew, snipe and lapwing. The broad watersheds, with their expanses of blanket bog, were fascinating as the British equivalent of tundra, and remarkable in their quantities of cloudberry, though dreary and featureless to many hill-walkers, so that they were usually lonely places where the day was passed in solitude.

THE REST

There are few more varied stretches of coastline in Britain than that of Dumfries & Galloway. Its chief glory is its long and diverse series of sea cliffs, which compare favourably with those of the better-known West Country and Pembrokeshire, ranging from broken scarps with wind-pruned oakwood to abrupt, bare bird-cliffs. The Mull of Galloway is a fine example of the last, a narrow and precipitous headland, forming the southernmost point of the region, on the latitude of Skiddaw in Cumbria. Off its point, the meeting of conflicting currents from Solway and Clyde creates an impressive tide-rip. It is now an RSPB reserve, where a good variety of seabirds can be viewed from the cliff tops. And if the seabird colonies of this coast are modest in size, those of the Berwickshire seaboard around St Abbs make up for any deficiency, with their teeming throngs of auks and kittiwakes. In the southwest, there are, besides, rocky shores, shingle beaches, sand dunes, estuarine flats and salt marshes to provide a wealth of maritime wildlife.

The woodlands of native broadleaved trees are the least well represented of the major habitats. There are plenty of them, but they are mostly small and scattered, and many of the best line the sides of steep glens and rocky ravines, so that their total area appears rather small. Many in Dumfries & Galloway have not been explored or documented as wildlife habitat. Plantation forest has, by contrast, become somewhat overwhelming in its scale and uniformity, as I shall discuss.

Lowland raised bog was, in my time, extensive, and the lower moorlands, especially in Wigtownshire, were one of the largest expanses of blanket and intermediate bog in Britain, outside the Flow Country of Sutherland and Caithness. Fens are numerous and interesting, though mostly rather small, while the lakes and rivers are delightful in their variety. The last include the great River Tweed, which gave its name to a whole industry based on the sheep rearing that became the principal use of the uplands over many centuries. This is not, otherwise, a region much disturbed by human activity such as the heavy industry of the Midland Valley. It is one of pleasant market towns, small ports and fishing villages; and in recent years has developed a flourishing tourist 'industry'.

LATER EVENTS

I count myself fortunate to have first seen the south of Scotland when I did. Britain was just beginning to recover from a great war, and there was a general quietness about the countryside. Few people had cars and many of the rural roads were almost deserted. Forestry was only in its infancy and the agricultural revolution had not yet taken off. Tourism was something hardly worth mentioning, and the only people to be seen about the hills were mostly shepherds, with a few gamekeepers. If this book could have been written when the New Naturalist series began – coincidentally, with my acquaintance with the Southern Uplands – it would necessarily have had a rather different emphasis than the one I have written, sixty years later. Someone writing at that time would have told a more straightforward tale of the plants and animals in a somewhat unchanging scene (Fig. 10). There would, no doubt, have been some mention of the relief experienced by persecuted predators through the absence of estate gamekeepers during two World Wars. The hydroelectric constructions of dams and reservoirs in Galloway and Carrick were the only serious developments during the first half of the twentieth century. It would probably have been a more generally positive

FIG 10. A Galloway scene that has hardly changed since I first knew it. Palnure Burn and Craigdews Gairy, near Talnotry, Kirkcudbrightshire.

celebration of the region's natural history, with few discordant notes. Such an emollient account today might read more comfortably, but it would – in my view – be false and dishonourable. I believe it necessary to write an honest warts-and-all version of what has happened to the wildlife of southern Scotland, especially over the last sixty years. If, at times, it seems to dwell on losses and failures, that is because I am trying to reflect reality. But I am also pleased to record gains and successes, some of which I had never expected to see.

The birds of prey are mostly a success story. After a worrying time in the 1960s, the peregrine has not only recovered but surged on to unprecedented numbers, with occupation of nesting places I would scarcely have thought possible. In 1946–7, while prospecting for possible peregrine and raven sites among the gentle hills across the border, in three glens I noted broken rocky banks that seemed suitable only for kestrels. Within the last ten years peregrines have bred regularly on two of these, and in the third locality a pair has nested more than once in a tree! The spread of the buzzard back across almost all the lowlands of the region is astounding. Golden eagles had re-established by 1945, and the subsequent period has seen the return as breeding species of hen harrier, goshawk, honey buzzard and, most recently, red kite and osprey. So, there is good news as well as bad.

One bright note is that there are now far more observers and recorders of wildlife than ever before. And, whereas in the earlier works on birds and mammals the entries for rarer species tended to be dismal catalogues of creatures shot or trapped, modern records are mostly of the living animal. The growth of enthusiasm for wildlife is a very positive trend, provided always that the enthusiasts are prepared to stand up and be counted, when their support is most needed. There will be no shortage of issues to be fought over in the defence of this interest in the years ahead.

CHAPTER 1

Environment

TOPOGRAPHY AND GENERAL FEATURES

THE BOUNDARIES defining this region are partly geological and partly topographical/political. It lies to the south of the Southern Uplands Fault, and extends to the coast of the Solway Firth and outer Clyde in the west, and to the border line between Scotland and England in the east. It includes the whole of the counties of Wigtown, Kirkcudbright, Dumfries (the small area north of the Fault on the Spango Water is included), Roxburgh, Selkirk and Berwick, most of Peebles except its northern tip, and the southern parts of Ayr, Lanark, Midlothian and East Lothian (Fig. 11). The southwest part is mostly in the new (1975) region of Dumfries & Galloway, while the northeast sector is mostly in the Borders region. South Ayrshire and south Lanarkshire belong to Strathclyde, and the bits of the old Lothians to the new Lothian. I have ignored the new districts defined in the administrative reorganisation of 1975, as they do not correspond to any previous boundaries. And I have used the term *region* as applying to the whole of the area dealt with in this book.

Geologically the south of Scotland is the massive block of Ordovician and Silurian strata, interrupted by granite intrusions, and merging into the series of Carboniferous and Permo-Triassic rocks which occupy large areas of Cumbria to the south. Some geographers refer to it as 'the Southern Uplands', in the wider sense, and although there are substantial areas of lowland, in both the southwest and northeast, the numerous ranges of hills give its dominant character.

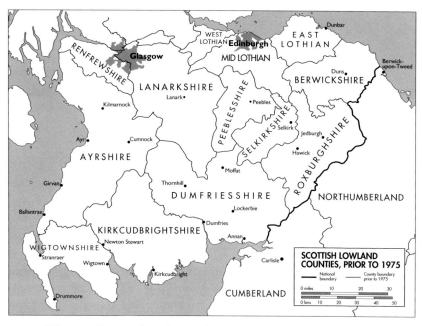

FIG 11. Galloway and the Borders, showing the traditional counties (pre-1975), as used in this book.

CLIMATE

There is a pronounced climatic gradient across the region, from west to east, and superimposed on this are local gradients according to altitude. The main contrast is between the oceanic west, influenced by the North Atlantic currents, and the more continental east. This is expressed in the heavier rainfall, higher atmospheric humidity, greater windiness, smaller temperature range, with milder winters and cooler summers, of Galloway and Carrick, compared with conditions in Berwickshire and Roxburghshire. Yet the southwest is sheltered by the mass of Ireland against the full influence of the Atlantic, with frequent gales and mountainous seas, and does not have the extreme oceanic climate of the exposed Highland coast farther north. Marked differences in climate also occur between both coasts and the lowlands generally, compared with the uplands of the centre. The southwestern coastal areas have a notable mildness, while the northeastern lowlands are dry and sunny. Conditions deteriorate with increasing altitude, as rainfall, cloud cover, snowfall and wind increase, while temperature and sunshine diminish. The hill climate of the Borders can be bleak and inhospitable, and spring slow to arrive, as Abel Chapman (1907) pointed out:

> *The months of March, April and May include some of the crudest and most inclement periods of the year, as regards weather, on the northern hills. Up to the end of May snowfalls may occur, and the highlands, at times, lie as white as in December. If one of these months chances to be bright and fine, the others do extra penance to the Nimbi.*

Rainfall

While annual rainfall over the highest Galloway hills is only some 2,300mm, compared with well over 4,000mm over the western Lake Fells in Cumbria, both districts lie within the zone of 200–220 annual 'wet days'. A 'wet day' in meteorology is a period of 24 hours with one millimetre of rain falling and, when totalled for 12 months, is a measure of rainfall *distribution* over the year, and gives a more telling index of climatic wetness for soils and plants than total amount of rain. This explains the tendency to peatiness of soils in the Galloway and Carrick uplands, and the large extent of peat bog at low levels on level or gently inclined moorland in Wigtownshire. It also accounts for the fairly rich assemblage of Atlantic mosses and liverworts within the western half of the region. It does not, however, reach the extreme wetness of the western Highlands, with well over 220 annual 'wet days' in the mountainous areas. Annual precipitation falls to 1,800mm over the Lowther, Moffat and Hermitage hills, and then to 1,250mm on the Cheviots and Moorfoot Hills, and 1,020mm on the Lammermuirs. Lowest rainfall in the west is 890mm at the Mull of Galloway, and in the east 635mm at St Abbs and Dunbar, while 'wet days' fall to 140–169 over the Solway lowlands of Dumfries & Galloway and 120–140 over the lower Tweed valley and Berwickshire coast. 'Cloudburst' deluges occur randomly anywhere at any time, and can cause scouring of stream ravines, as they did behind Creetown some years ago.

Temperature

Southwestern coastal districts are relatively mild, especially in Wigtownshire, where the growing of warmth-loving exotic plants in the gardens at Castle Kennedy attests to the low incidence of damaging frost. There are also in the southwest a number of native plants associated with mild winter climate. To show comparative geographical trends, the Meteorological Office has corrected all figures for mean daily maximum, mean daily minimum and mean annual temperatures to mean sea level, using the standard lapse rate of 1°C for every 150m change in altitude. They are also based on screen or shade temperatures. Mean annual temperatures in the southern half of the Rhins of Galloway, the western peninsula of Wigtownshire, are 9.4–10°C, while daily temperature range (DTR) here is 5.4–6.0°C. This compares with 8.3–8.9°C and 7.2–7.8°C, respectively, for the Berwickshire coast. In the central zone of the Southern Uplands, mean temperatures are in the range 7.8–8.3°C, indicating the trend to continentality with distance inland.

The average number of days with frost increases from 25–50 in coastal parts of the southwest to over 100 over a large part of the central Southern Uplands, and days when temperature never rises above freezing increase from one to five or more along the same geographical gradient. In frost hollows and at higher levels on the hills, there is a marked increase in subzero temperatures in the central district and also in the number of months with recorded frost. High summer temperatures show nearly the same tendency, with mean daily maxima for July of 17.8°C along the outer Rhins coast, rising to 19.4°C or more in a central area which extends south of the English border. Summer temperatures at high altitudes are much lower (by a mean 5°C at 750m, according to the standard lapse rate), and this accounts for the survival there of cold-adapted montane plants, which are damaged by critically high summer temperatures at low elevations (Conolly and Dahl, 1970). The isotherm maps suggest a winter climate slightly colder than that of northern England, except the northern Pennines, but much

FIG 12. Snow cover on the hills is usually intermittent during winter. Carewoodrig and Frodaw Height, Ewes Water, Dumfriesshire.

less severe than that of the central and eastern Highlands in terms of absolute minimum temperatures (Fig. 12).

Wind

Coasts in general are windy, and those of both the Solway and the North Sea experience over 20 days annually on average with gale-force winds, compared with under 10 days for much of the interior farthest from the sea. Wind speed tends to rise with altitude and the highest and most exposed summits are the windiest of all. There are no measurements for these places and extreme wind speeds can only be inferred by reference to the nearest high-altitude recording stations. That closest to the Southern Uplands tops is on the northern Pennines, where observations were made by Gordon Manley on Great Dun Fell at 825m. He recorded an average of about force 5 (30–38km/hr), with extremes of an hourly wind of 158km/hr and a gust of 214km/hr. Wind-blasting is sufficient to cause ablation on some exposed summit fell-fields, and produces unidirectional growth away from the prevailing winds (west-south-west) in plants such as woolly fringe-moss, crowberry and heather.

Snow

The coldest, central part of the Southern Uplands is the snowiest. An area from the higher Nithsdale and Annandale hills to the Lammermuirs has an average of over 30 days a year with snow falling on ground below 61m, and over 50 mornings with snow lying (Meteorological Office, 1952). Because frequency of snowfall increases with altitude, the data for recording stations at higher elevations were corrected to values for 0–61m, giving a common basis for comparisons, to show geographical variations in snowfall frequencies. A day with snow lying is one on which more than half the ground representative of the recording station is covered with snow at the morning observation hour. The data are thus strongly influenced by the altitude of the station and the surrounding land, and the resulting map tends to be a reflection of both altitude and winter cold/ precipitation. While snowfall is generally more frequent and lasts longer in the hilly centre and east of the region than in the Galloway uplands, long-lasting snow beds occur up to mid-June on the Merrick and Corserine as well as on the Cramalt Craig, Broad Law, Hart Fell and White Coomb. These late snow patches are characteristic of elevated hollows on north to east aspects just below high summit plateaux, which act as gathering grounds for snow that is then blown off and accumulates on sheltered ground beneath. Characteristic plant communities have developed in some of these situations. Snow also accumulates in the lee of walls running across some of the high tops, and in places lasts long enough to

FIG 13. Late snow-lie in the shelter of a wall across high ground, showing debris accumulation. A *Nardus* strip marks its occurrence after snow-melt. Merrick, Kirkcudbrightshire.

affect the vegetation beneath (Fig. 13). If climatic warming intensifies, these late snow patches of early summer could become a thing of the past in the Southern Uplands.

GEOLOGY

This account of rocks and substrates is written from the viewpoint of someone trying to explain the diversity of terrain and habitat for plants and animals by looking at the factors controlling topography and soil conditions. Those concerned with geology per se should consult the last edition of *The South of Scotland* in the British Regional Geology series (Greig *et al.*, 1971), and the fourth edition of Sheet 1 of the British Geological Survey's geological maps of Britain at the scale of 1:625,000. The first is a work I have drawn upon heavily in writing this account, though it is not easy going for a non-geologist. The earlier and more popularised account for the Merrick district by R. J. A. Eckford (1932) is also a valuable source of information. Table 1 summarises the geological formations present in the region, and Figure 14 is adapted from the British Geological Survey map.

TABLE 1. Geological formations present in Galloway and the Borders. (From Greig *et al.*, 1971. Reproduced by permission of the British Geological Survey, NERC. All rights reserved. IPR/63–37C)

RECENT AND PLEISTOCENE	Soils, blown sand, peat, river and lake alluvia. Raised beach deposits. Solifluction deposits. Fluvio-glacial sand and gravel. Glacial moraines and boulder clay.	
TERTIARY	Tholeiite dykes.	
NEW RED SANDSTONE	Trias. Annan Series: red sandstones, shales and marls. 'Permian'. Red desert-sandstones and breccias. Lavas and agglomerates.	
Unconformity		
CARBONIFEROUS	Coal Measures	Sandstones, shales, mudstones, coal seams and seat-earths. Some thin marine mudstones in Canonbie area. Late quartz-dolerite dykes.
	Non-sequence or unconformity	
	Millstone Grit Series	Upper beds mainly sandstones with many seat-earths and thin coals, bauxitic clays at Thornhill. Some thin marine shales and limestones. Lower beds of Yoredale facies, sandstones, mudstones, limestones, coal seams and seat-earths. Thin basaltic lava at Loch Ryan.
	Carboniferous Limestone Series	Upper beds of Yoredale facies, sandstones, mudstones, limestones, coal seams and seat-earths. Lower beds mainly sandstones, with mudstones and thin cementstones. Basaltic lavas and tuffs, volcanic vents and acidic and basic intrusions, especially near base
OLD RED SANDSTONE	Upper Old Red Sandstone	Conglomerates, sandstones, marls, corn-stones.
	Unconformity	
	Lower Old Red Sandstone	Conglomerates, sandstones, cornstones, lavas, agglomerates, acid intrusions.
Unconformity		
SILURIAN	Wenlock	Riccarton and Raeberry Castle beds: greywackes, shales and fossiliferous grits. Upper part of Dailly Series near Girvan: shales and fossiliferous grits.

TABLE 1. – *cont.*

SILURIAN	Llandovery	Birkhill Shales in Moffat area. Gala Group: greywackes, flags and shales, with bands of conglomerate and grit. Dailly Series (lower part) and Newlands Series in Girvan area: greywackes, flags, shales, limestones and conglomerates.
ORDOVICIAN	Ashgill	Upper Hartfell Shales in Moffat area. Shales and greywackes with limestones and conglomerates elsewhere, e.g. upper part of Portpatrick Group. Upper part of Ardmillan Series of Girvan: sandstones and shales, with limestones and conglomerate.
	Caradoc	Lower Hartfell Shales and Glenkiln Shales in Moffat area. Shales, greywackes and conglomerates elsewhere, e.g. lower part of Portpatrick Group and Kirkcolm and Corswall groups. Lower part of Ardmillan Series and Barr Series of Girvan: conglomerates, sandstones, shales, limestones and greywackes. Lavas, tuffs and intrusions.
	? Llandeilo	Lavas, cherts and mudstones.
	Unconformity	
	Arenig	Lavas, pyroclastic rocks, cherts and mudstones: basic and acid intrusions.

Sedimentary rocks

The region is defined to the north by the geological boundary of the Southern Upland Fault, which separates it from the Midland Valley, though the southern limits are drawn by the geologically arbitrary border line between Scotland and England. The bulk of the region is composed of the oldest rocks, sedimentary deposits formed beneath ancient seas of the Ordovician and Silurian periods of the Lower Palaeozoic era, from 500 to 350 million years ago (Fig. 15). The Ordovician Series forms a northern band which increases in width from its beginning, on the coast just east of Dunbar, southwestwards to the Firth of Clyde in Wigtownshire and south Ayrshire; while the Silurian formation adjoins it as a broader band to the south. The Southern Upland Fault running through the Ordovician Series divides near its southwest end towards Girvan and this area is

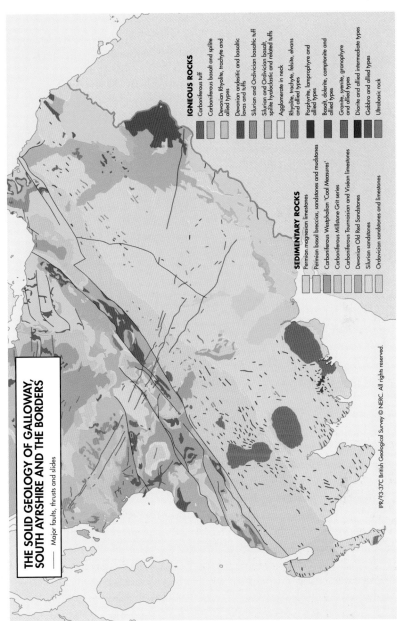

THE SOLID GEOLOGY OF GALLOWAY, SOUTH AYRSHIRE AND THE BORDERS

— Major faults, thrusts and slides

IGNEOUS ROCKS

Carboniferous tuff

Carboniferous basalt and spilite

Devonian Rhyolite, trachyte and allied types

Devonian andesitic and basaltic lavas and tuffs

Silurian and Ordovician basaltic tuff

Silurian and Ordovician basalt, spilite hyaloclastic and related tuffs

Agglomerate in neck

Rhyolite, trachyte, felsite, elvans and allied types

Porphyrite, lamprophyre and allied types

Basalt, dolerite, camptonite and allied types

Granite, syenite, granophyre and allied types

Diorite and allied intermediate types

Gabbro and allied types

Ultrabasic rock

SEDIMENTARY ROCKS

Permian magnesian limestones

Permian basal breccias, sandstones and mudstones

Carboniferous Westphalian 'Coal Measures'

Carboniferous Millstone Grit series

Carboniferous Tournaisian and Viséan limestones

Devonian Old Red Sandstones

Silurian sandstones

Ordovician sandstones and limestones

FIG 14. Geological map of southern Scotland. (Based on British Geological Survey)

FIG 15. The smooth and rounded sedimentary hills. Hart Fell, near Annan Head, Dumfriesshire.

geologically complex, with various igneous masses. I have taken the northern limit of the main mass of the Ordovician Series, which reaches the coast immediately south of Girvan, as the definitive boundary west of the Nick of the Balloch road. This choice thus excludes the complex of igneous and sedimentary rocks south of Maybole, but includes the contemporaneous and intrusive igneous rocks between Girvan and Ballantrae. Ordovician sedimentary rocks occur north and south of the Fault in this area.

The sediments which formed the Ordovician and Silurian rocks vary from fine material of clay and silt (giving shale and mudstone, and, where calcareous, limestone) through sand with a matrix of fine material (greywacke), to coarse sand (gritstone) and pebbles with sand (conglomerate). They are dated by their often numerous fossils, especially graptolites, primitive coelenterates evidently related to the Hydrozoa, which had developed by those far-off times and lived as plankton in the sea, but became extinct towards the end of the Silurian (Fig. 16). Their hard horny or chitinous exoskeletons are well preserved within black shales and have a characteristic, often serrated form, which changed markedly as they evolved over many millions of years. The significance of graptolites to the geological record was first realised by Professor Charles Lapworth, who in 1878, by working out the evolution of the different forms in time, was able to sequence the different Lower Palaeozoic strata exposed in the ravines of Hartfell Spa and Dobb's Linn in the Moffat Hills (Fig. 17). Faulting had here caused both the Ordovician and Silurian Series to be visible together. His chronology then became a set of benchmarks for dating comparable fossiliferous beds elsewhere, including in other parts of the world. Graptolite-bearing shales of both Ordovician and Silurian age also have numerous outcrops in the Galloway Hills (Eckford, 1932). The shepherd's cottage close to the classic graptolite locality of Dob's Linn has a plaque commemorating Lapworth's achievement.

The next oldest sedimentary rocks are Devonian Old Red Sandstones, of which the Lower occurs as a smaller block south from St Abbs Head, and as a larger but discontinuous belt north of the Southern Upland Fault (and thus outside our region) from near West Linton to Girvan. The Upper Old Red Sandstone occurs as a north-to-south band extending from south of Dunbar to the Langholm area. It is widest in the middle section, around Jedburgh, and becomes attenuated towards both northern and southern limits. From around Greenlaw to the Jedburgh area, it gives rise to a stretch of undulating lowland country. This rock also reaches the Berwickshire coast at Siccar Point, where it appears as the famous unconformity above Silurian rocks.

FIG 16. Fossiliferous Silurian shales at Craigmichan Scaurs, Moffat Water, Dumfriesshire.

FIG 17. The steep, smooth slopes of Moffatdale, from near Dobb's Linn, Dumfriesshire.

Then come Lower Carboniferous strata, forming the end of the massive extent of this series in northern England, and running along the western Cheviots to west of Annan and along the Galloway coast to near Kirkcudbright Bay, with a large separate block north of Kelso, mainly in Berwickshire, and another outlier along the coast between Dunbar and St Abbs. Although known as the Carboniferous Limestone Series, this is confusing to the ecologist, as they are chiefly shale, mudstone, sandstone and only thin or impure limestone. Purer limestone of commercially usable quality occurs locally, near Canonbie and southeast of Dunbar, but it is scarce in the region as a whole. The northern zone of these Carboniferous rocks within Scotland (and also northern Northumberland) was formerly distinguished as the Scottish Calciferous Sandstone Series, but this distinction has been dropped in more recent years. The more limited occurrence of Upper Carboniferous rocks is of Millstone Grit near Loch Ryan, Thornhill, Sanquhar and Canonbie; and at the last two localities there are also substantial beds of Coal Measures, forming the upper- most Carboniferous strata, which gave rise to local coal mining. Finally are New Red Sandstones of Permian and Triassic age, around Stranraer, along the valleys of the Nith and Annan, and between Gretna and Annan. These form a northwards extension of the larger area of these rocks occupying the south Solway Plain and Eden valley in Cumbria.

Igneous rocks

This basic pattern (Fig. 18) is greatly complicated by numerous igneous intrusions and extrusions, of varying extent, belonging to each of the main geological periods, either formed contemporaneously or emplaced later. Eckford (1932) notes that the basement beds of the Ordovician in the region are lavas of Arenig age, well exposed in the Ballantrae area and along the northern margin of the system, and probably underlying most of southern Scotland. The Ballantrae Igneous Complex is described by Greig *et al.* (1971) as comprising 'a group of spilitic lavas and pyroclastic rocks, with associated cherts and fossiliferous shales, and a number of major and minor intrusions'. These are exposed at Bennane Head and form low inland hills, notably the broad ridge from Pinbain Hill to Byne Hill, where the occurrence of large masses of serpentinite is of particular interest. These volcanic formations produce a knobbly landscape of low hills, south and east of Girvan.

The largest and most significant of these igneous plutons to topography and landscape are the Devonian granite intrusions of Galloway and Carrick, of Lower Old Red Sandstone age. That running for 20km south of Loch Doon forms a central ridge of rugged hills, with Mullwharchar, Dungeon Hill and Craignaw

FIG 18. A granite landscape: the junction with the Silurian follows the crag on the skyline to the left. Craigdews Gairy, near Talnotry, Kirkcudbrightshire.

all exceeding 600m, and covers 122km². This coarse-grained acidic biotite granite is surrounded by a mass of finer-grained and intermediate tonalite (quartz mica diorite), with two southern and northwestern outer marginal blocks of basic norite, before the Ordovician country rocks take over. The igneous magma created a metamorphic aureole in which the surrounding sedimentary rocks of the Merrick and Kells ranges became somewhat altered by heat. The Cairnsmore of Fleet granite is an oval mass of both biotite and muscovite-biotite granites covering 148km², and intruded into mainly Silurian rocks but with some Ordovician. The Criffel granite is the largest at 194km² and consists mainly of granodiorites emplaced within the Silurian system. The Cairnsmore of Fleet and Criffel plutons also created metamorphic aureoles in the surrounding sedimentary rocks. The altered rocks are greywackes, grey and black shales, cherts, Ordovician igneous materials and dykes of Old Red Sandstone age. Smaller granitic intrusions occur at Cairnsmore of Carsphairn, Afton Water, Spango, the Knipe, Creetown and Portencorkrie just northwest of the Mull of Galloway.

In the east of the region, the mainly andesitic and basaltic lavas of the Cheviot Volcanic Series have largely replaced the Lower Old Red Sandstone, and form the northeastern end of the Cheviot range. They are also exposed along the fine range of sea cliffs on the Berwickshire coast between Eyemouth and St Abbs Head. Numerous remnants of volcanoes regarded as active in Carboniferous times form intrusions both within this series and in strata of Silurian and Upper Old Red Sandstone age, between Lockerbie and Duns. They are mostly basalts and tuffs, sometimes in volcanic vents and plugs, which give rise to distinctive features such as the prominent though low hills of Burnswark (Birrenswark), Tinnis Hill, Arkleton Hill, Ruberslaw, the Eildon Hills and Minto Hills. These more basic igneous rocks also give rise to a smooth and rounded hill topography, and are mostly not much exposed as outcrop, though they form the abrupt and impressive escarpment of Minto Craigs (Fatlips Crags) west of Jedburgh.

Igneous dykes are numerous across the region, and in Galloway are especially abundant around the Loch Doon and Criffel granite intrusions, where they cut both the plutonic rocks and surrounding sediments. In Wigtownshire, both Ordovician and Silurian rocks are cut by many dykes. In the Borders, dykes are often associated with major intrusions, as at Cockburn Law and Priestlaw in Berwickshire. The dyke rock is variable and includes granophyre, porphyrite, diorite and lamprophyre.

Earth movements and landforms

The predominant Ordovician and Silurian rocks of the region are intensely folded by lateral compression from earth movements, as exposed strata both inland (e.g. at Penton Linns) and on the coast (e.g. at St Abbs Head) reveal (see Fig. 51). The predominant trend of the structures is between northeast and east-north-east. They are also much faulted, besides the major fault which separates them so definitively from the younger rocks of Old Red Sandstone and Carboniferous age along the edge of the Midland Valley. The main period of folding was at the end of the Silurian, and these Caledonian movements produced an anticlinal tract of Ordovician strata along the northern margin of the region (the Northern Belt), and a synclinal zone mainly of Silurian rocks along the central part (the Central Belt). Eckford suggested that the Northern Belt of older rocks be regarded as the tectonic axis of the Southern Uplands. Greig et al. (1971) note that the Southern Upland Fault itself may not have originated until the Lower–Upper Old Red Sandstone interval.

Following the Caledonian period of folding, the entire Southern Upland region was uplifted from the sea to form a land mass of plateau-like form, higher in the north and with a slope to the south or southeast. Erosion, especially by water-carving, then began to sculpt the great plateau into hills and valleys (Fig. 19). Some part of the present main drainage system may have been established, and some folds of the northern belt were denuded to their cores of

FIG 19. Water-sculpted Silurian hills near Billhope, head of Hermitage Water, Roxburghshire.

Arenig rocks, before the Old Red Sandstone was deposited. Eckford believed, accordingly, that the Southern Uplands were submerged several times, and received later cappings of sediment after their first uplift.

Denudation has left the highest summits of the Southern Uplands, in the Galloway–Carrick and Moffat–Tweedsmuir hills, with an elevation of about 825m above sea level, though a more usual figure in some massifs is closer to 610m. For the most part these uplands have the characteristic form of relatively soft rocks eroded mainly by water: smooth and often impressively steep slopes which soar into rounded summits or plateaux, and are drained by deep, branching valleys with very little exposed rock, except sometimes along the actual water-course, where ravines have been cut. The general absence of major rock outcrops is noteworthy, though areas of unstable debris (scree) are more frequent, and may sometimes represent weathered-down crags. Only among the highest hill ranges is there dramatic evidence of ice-carving during glaciation, yet the great crag-girt hollow of Loch Dungeon in the Kells Range is one of the finest corries in Britain (Fig. 20). The three lateral valleys of Moffatdale also have impressive examples of crag-lined U-shaped or hanging valleys (Fig. 21), with extensive moraine systems. The only narrow mountain ridge in the Southern Uplands is here, on the Saddle Yoke between Carrifran and Black's Hope. These features showing the effects of ice action are believed to have formed gradually during the successive glaciations of the Quaternary period. Corrie glaciers evidently developed in the higher hills of Galloway and the Moffat–Tweedsmuir massif during the Loch Lomond Readvance that saw a return of arctic conditions to Scotland around 11,000–12,000 years ago (Fig. 22). Morainic features occur very widely over the region (Fig. 23), and much of the lower hill slopes, as well as the lowlands generally, are covered with a layer of glacial drift.

The Loch Doon and Cairnsmore of Fleet granite intrusions in Galloway have given rocky terrain which contrasts sharply with that of the sedimentary hills. While the hills are still generally rounded, they are flanked in many places by ranges of high cliffs, of up to 200m, and by massive 'boiler plate' slabs, and covered with block screes and boulder fields. In places on flat summits and spurs are bare granite pavements with scattered erratics or residual boulders, such as the quaintly named 'Deil's Boolin Green' on Craignaw (Fig. 24). The granite is a hard, coarsely crystalline rock, splendid for climbing upon, from the roughness and reliability of its often rounded hand- and footholds. In this it contrasts with the friable shales and the none-too-reliable sandstones of the sedimentary formations. Even where the mica of the granite is black (biotite) instead of white (muscovite), the colour of the rock is predominantly a pale grey. This is where it

FIG 20. The fine ice-carved corrie of Loch Dungeon in the Kells Range, Kirkcudbright-shire.

FIG 21. Waterfall below a hanging valley. The Grey Mare's Tail, Moffatdale, Dumfriesshire.

FIG 22. Corrie wall at the head of Carrifran Burn. Raven Craig, Moffatdale, Dumfriesshire.

FIG 23. Moraines below the Clints of Dromore, picked out by snow, sunshine and shadow. Kirkcudbrightshire.

FIG 24. The Deil's Boolin Green, Craignaw: granite pavement with loose blocks. Kirkcudbrightshire.

is weathered and lichen-grown: newly broken surfaces or faces where the lichens have been destroyed by recent fire are almost white.

Solifluction

Patterned ground features caused by alternate freezing and thawing of moisture in the substrate are less well developed than on the hills of northern England. On the higher hills of Galloway and the Moffat–Tweedsmuir ranges there are striped screes in places, with lines of stones about 30cm apart alternating with finer, soily material parallel to the slope, which is usually of only moderate angle. Good examples occur high on the Corserine. Lobed block screes and terraces occur in places, with the latter most visible in evening light, when shadows pick out the changes in slope angles. Perhaps the best-developed frost–thaw features are the systems of soil hummocks present over many hectares of certain summit plateaux above 700m in the Moffat and Tweedsmuir hills, especially the Carrifran Gans, White Coomb, Broad Law, Cramalt Craig, Dun Law and Dollar Law (see Fig. 148). The average size of these hummocks is rather less than one metre, and their centres rise 15–23cm above the intervening hollows, which are 15–30cm wide, so that the hummocks appear fairly closely spaced. They evidently represent fossil features that have persisted long after their original formation, which may have been under a more severe climate. Up to the early 1950s they showed a marked vegetational pattern, but this has largely disappeared under heavy sheep grazing and treading. There may be an underlying stone network but, if so, it is quite deeply buried under a layer of soil. Rock is little exposed at the surface of this hummocky ground, and on rocky stretches of summit, the hummocks disappear.

The soil hummocks occur on level to slightly inclined ground (0–5°), and where the slope steepens (5–10°) they elongate into ridges: this again suggests the similarity with stone nets, which change into stone stripes with increase in gradient. Soil hummocks are less well developed on the Galloway Hills, but a small area was noted near the summit of Cairnsmore of Fleet, and a more extensive system on the high western spur of the Merrick. Both hummocks and ridges are more pronounced (wider and taller) in the extensive systems on summit plateaux of the Drumochter Hills and Ben Wyvis in the Highlands. Bare stone networks have not been noticed in the Southern Uplands, and exposed rock debris is mostly irregularly distributed.

Minerals

The Criffel granite is quarried near Dalbeattie, and an outlying mass of this rock was formerly worked on the coast near Creetown. Another localised granite at Cockburn Law in Berwickshire has been extracted since 1965. Many small quarries in dykes and other local intrusions of basalt and dolerite have operated but some are now closed. Porphyrite is worked near Kirkcudbright. Of the sedimentary rocks, New Red Sandstone has been much quarried in Dumfries-shire, and greywacke more widely across the region. These materials are used as building stone, roadstone, aggregate and for monumental work. Limestone of both Ordovician and Carboniferous age has been worked in its widely scattered localities, and is used especially for cement making and fertiliser. Dolomite was also mined near Thornhill.

Coal has been mined from the Dumfriesshire fields at Sanquhar and Kirkconnel, and near Canonbie, but the only active mines now are opencast workings to the north of our boundary, around Muirkirk in Ayrshire. Clays have been worked at Newton Stewart, Langholm and elsewhere for making agricul-tural drain tiles, while shales have been quarried in various places for roofing slates. Sand and gravel have also been extracted in various places for use especially in the construction industry. The most recent of the superficial deposits, peat, has been cut on a commercial scale for horticultural moss litter at Nutberry Moss, near Annan, and very widely used as a local source of fuel from small-scale peat cuttings. Peat bogs have also been extensively used for the establishment of coniferous forests since around 1960, to the point where some are now largely inactive as regards further peat formation, as at the Lochar Mosses near Dumfries.

Of the metallic minerals, lead and zinc have probably been the most important commercially. The large deposits of galena (lead sulphide) at Leadhills and Wanlockhead were first mined at least 700 years ago, and associated zinc blende (zinc sulphide) at Wanlockhead since 1880. The ores occur in veins of brecciated Ordovician greywacke and, although the mines are all now closed, considerable reserves of galena remain. Both minerals have also been mined in the Gatehouse of Fleet, Newton Stewart and Carsphairn areas. Silver was an important by-product of the galena mining and smelting at Leadhills and Wanlockhead. The Glengaber Burn on Megget Water was a sixteenth-century source of alluvial gold, as was Leadhills, where a gold-bearing quartz vein was also reported. Several small copper mines were formerly active, mainly in Galloway: the usual ores were chalcopyrite (copper iron sulphide) and malachite (copper carbonate), which were also associated with the lead–zinc veins at Leadhills and near Newton Stewart. Iron was obtained in the nineteenth century from haematite (ferric oxide) veins associated with the Loch Doon and Criffel granites and the Wanlockhead–Leadhills lead–zinc veins. Another deposit near Lamancha, Peeblesshire, contained a good deal of pyrolusite (manganese oxide). Near Bentpath in lower Eskdale, the Glendinning Burn had a vein with stibnite (antimony sulphide) which was mined up to 1920 for this metal, and there was another antimony mine at the Knipe, near New Cumnock. Nickel, arsenic and barytes have also been worked on a small scale within the region.

Soils

The terms acidic and basic, as applied to rocks by geologists, are defined strictly by the silica content of the material. Soil scientists use them in a different way, as forming the parent materials of soils which are either deficient in base cations and with a pH below about 5.0, or with base cation saturation of the soil exchange complex and pH above 6.0. In Britain, calcium is the predominant base cation, usually forming at least 80 per cent of the total, but magnesium some-times replaces it to a large extent, as on rocks such as dolomite and serpentine. Rocks which yield large amounts of these two elements are thus regarded as basic in soil-forming properties, while those with only low content of available calcium or magnesium are considered acidic. The granite of Galloway and Carrick is the poorest of the soil-forming parent materials in the region. It is not only deficient in base minerals, but also hard and resistant to weathering, so that it only slowly yields a coarse, porous sand with little capacity for holding the chemical elements that contribute to developing soil fertility. In contrast, many strata of the Lower Palaeozoic and Carboniferous formations not only consist of fine clayey or silty materials with good base-exchange properties, but also contain considerable amounts of calcium carbonate. Some of them are, indeed, limestones which form calcareous soils, and even the more acidic types often have numerous veins of calcite. While the general run of Lower Palaeozoic rocks contain a good deal of fairly acidic beds, they typically vary so much within a short space that basic material is usually present not far away, and shows its influence in the effects of the water draining from it on the flora. The contrast in soil quality in passing from the granite areas to the sedimentary formations, shown by vegetation changes, is immediately apparent to a botanist.

This tendency to produce fertile soils is less true of the later sandstones, especially those of Permo-Triassic age. The difference is shown by the contrast between the flora of the South Solway Plain and St Bees Head in Cumbria and that of the Galloway lowlands and sea cliffs to the west. The absence of rock-rose from the first district, compared with its frequency in the second, is a good example. The other igneous rocks of southern Scotland vary greatly in their pedogenic properties. Some are markedly acidic, such as the trachytes and felsite of the Eildon Hills, whereas the basaltic outcrops around Langholm and Newcastleton are often quite strongly calcareous. Perhaps through the meta-morphic alteration of the sedimentary rocks that form the highest hills in Galloway, the Merrick and Kells ranges have little basic rock exposed in their cliffs, to provide good alpine plant habitat, and it is only in the Moffat Hills where calcareous materials in the Silurian rocks occur widely at high altitudes.

In the lowlands, most soils are derived from the thick deposits of glacial drift (boulder clay) covering most of the landscape, in which the original parent materials are usually much mixed and weathered chemically, reducing or removing any earlier differences in soil-forming properties. Most of these soils are of good agricultural potential, though this has been much enhanced by the long-continued addition of fertilisers, once organic and mineral, but latterly largely inorganic. Clayey materials impede drainage, especially on level ground, but extensive draining – latterly using drain-tiles – has greatly dried out many areas of once waterlogged soil. Many areas of fen with underlying nutrient-rich peat have been drained out of existence or severely modified, but in deep hollows and channels with internal drainage, numerous pockets of fen have survived, especially in the Borders. The deep and acidic peat of raised and blanket bogs is a more intractable material for cultivation, and many of these had survived relatively unscathed until recent years, though repeated fires had often dried out their surfaces, and peat cutting or local reclamation had nibbled away at the shallower edges.

Superimposed on the raw soil materials have been the other factors that determine soil development, notably ground water and the drainage regime. In well-drained situations, under the prevailing cool and humid oceanic conditions across the region, there is a tendency for soil nutrients to be washed out from the upper layers faster than they can be replaced. This leaching leads generally to the process of *podsolisation*, with a characteristic colour gradient in the exposed soil profile, resulting especially from the movement of iron. Typically, there is a dark thin surface layer of acid humus, then a grey or even white layer from which the iron has been leached. This tends to darken with depth and is sometimes abruptly replaced by a narrow band of dark red-brown, where this element has been precipitated out. Sometimes this forms a hard, compacted and somewhat impermeable layer, and is then termed an iron pan. Below this the colour of the lower layer is warmer, a fawn to orange-brown which may intensify with depth, as the zone of more general iron deposition. At greater depth this passes into the unmodified parent material of the soil. While these podsols are acid soils, the acidity decreases down the profile: the A horizon typically has pH 3.8–4.5, whereas the B horizon is usually 4.0–5.0.

On steep hillsides, the shallow soils often have the colour and other properties of the B horizon, and some soil experts formerly regarded them as truncated podsols which had lost their upper layer through erosion. They are now more generally believed to be immature or skeletal podsols which have not developed the typical profile under conditions of slope instability. And while deep podsols have often developed beneath coniferous forest, broadleaved woodlands often have deep brown soils in which leaching has been incomplete and, although acidic, B-horizon characteristics again prevail.

On less well-drained sites, the B horizon is paler, inclining to a greyish-fawn or clay colour, but flecked throughout with spots of rust-red. This is the result of alternate reduction of the iron to the ferrous state (grey) under wet conditions which exclude oxygen, and its oxidation to ferric iron (rust-red) during periods of drying out. The reduction process is called gleying and the soil a gley. As the soil becomes more continuously waterlogged, the rusty flecks disappear, and the whole profile becomes a clay-grey colour with a cheesy texture, under continuously reducing conditions. The layer of surface humus also deepens and begins to represent a shallow peat. This type is a true gley soil, though now distinguished as a stagno-gley. There is a continuum in the sequence as waterlogging and peat depth increase, but degree of humification (decomposition) of the peat decreases. Under the high rainfall of the uplands, peat formation is general on all but the steeper ground and often reaches a depth of at least three metres on poorly drained plateaux; but the deepest peat of all (up to 10m) occurs where raised bogs have developed in the flat lowlands.

VEGETATION HISTORY

Knowledge of the sequence of vegetation changes during the last 15,000 years or so, since the last Ice Age came to an end and the glaciers melted, is somewhat incomplete, as relatively few deposits containing a record have been studied within the region. Tipping (1997) has given a useful summary of work on vegetation history in the south of Scotland. The earliest study was that by Mitchell (1948) at Whitrig Bog in Berwickshire. Birks (1972) lists ten sites in Dumfries & Galloway where Post-glacial pollen diagrams have been prepared. Examination of Late-glacial muds and clays beneath some of the Borders fens has shown that, as elsewhere in Britain, the early phase of warming climate, with spread first of tundra and steppe vegetation, and then birch forest and juniper scrub, was interrupted by a return to cold conditions and renewal of glaciers in the mountain regions. This Loch Lomond Readvance saw the return of treeless conditions to the adjoining lowlands for around 1,000 years, but climate warming was eventually resumed and forest gradually spread back. During the open tundra phases, a rich arctic–alpine flora was present, but eventually became depleted through competition from taller woody growth (Webb & Moore, 1982).

Evidence for the vegetation of this Post-glacial time in Galloway comes from a pollen diagram made by Hilary Birks (1972) from lake mud on the floor of Loch Dungeon in the Kells Range. This deposit evidently dates from the end of the Devensian (Late-glacial) or beginning of the Flandrian (Post-glacial) periods, some 10,000 years before the present (BP). The earliest pollen shows abundance of grasses, sedges and willows, probably representing open and marshy ground, crowberry and juniper probably from heaths on drier areas, and birch, which increasingly invaded to form early woodland. Other herbaceous pollen is from associated communities and includes common sorrel, meadowsweet and meadow-rue. Spores of fir clubmoss are particularly abundant, suggesting that extensive open heaths were present.

There was later change to dominance of birch and hazel or bog myrtle pollen (the last two pollens are not distinguishable with certainty and so are lumped). There was much reduced abundance of herbaceous types, indicating a general woodland cover, but moderate amounts of ling heather point to open tree growth in places, or to areas of treeless heath. This phase formed the basal zone of a peat profile on the Silver Flowe a few kilometres west of Loch Dungeon, and has been found in pollen diagrams throughout Scotland to the north, as well as the Cumberland lowlands to the south, where its lower boundary has been radiocarbon dated to 8900 BP. The abundance of elm pollen rises throughout this zone and its upper boundary is marked by the increasing amount of oak and the decline of birch. During the next phase of woodland development birch remains the most abundant tree, with oak and elm constant (pollen at 15–20 per cent of total tree pollen), willows plentiful, and Scots pine and alder appearing increasingly. Heather increases markedly and the spores of *Sphagnum* reach a peak, suggesting development of treeless bog on flatter ground. A peat sample slightly above the base of this zone from the Cooran Lane was dated at 7541 BP.

Over the next few hundred years alder pollen rises to become the most abundant tree pollen type, while birch and pine decline. Oak and elm remain at their earlier frequency but fluctuate, and ash appears. Pine stumps of this phase preserved in the base of peat deposits at Loch Dungeon and the Cooran Lane have been dated at 7471 and 7165 BP, while another from the upper boundary of the zone at Clatteringshaws Loch had a radiocarbon date of 5080 BP. The evidence suggests that pinewood was patchy in the district and probably occurred mainly on the most acidic upland soils, such as those on the granite areas, but that this tree was also widespread in mixed woodland. At the beginning of this period it expanded on dry peat surfaces, but by the end it was becoming eliminated by the generally increased wetness and bog growth. Heather remained plentiful but *Sphagnum* declined. Pine was present but infrequent through the succeeding period up to recent times, when it again became abundant through deliberate planting in the re-forestation programme.

Elm pollen subsequently declined sharply, while oak became the most abundant tree type at 35–40 per cent frequency in the total tree pollen. Alder remained at 15–25 per cent and ash increased towards the top of this zone, but birch and hazel/bog myrtle remained abundant throughout, as did heather. Birks believed that an overall equilibrium existed between the forest components from about 7000 to 5000 BP. The evidence is for a mixed broadleaved forest, of elm, oak, alder, birch and hazel on the better, brown earth soils of the valley floors. Holly was plentiful in the understorey, and ivy flowered in the canopy, while bluebells, cow-wheat and bracken were important in the field layer. Alders and willows occupied wetter sites, with alder buckthorn and guelder rose, and tall herbs such as meadowsweet, globeflower and thistles. On low ground birch was probably restricted to acidic, peaty sites, but at higher altitudes it may have grown with pine, aspen and rowan on rocky ground with shallow and acidic soils. At the Nick of Curleywee, 152m above the sites studied by Birks but in the same area, a pollen diagram constructed by Moar (1969) indicated a general cover of birchwood at 460m. Birks suggests the treeline ran almost to the hill summits, at 700–800+m, but that severe exposure on the highest plateaux probably inhibited tree growth. Doubtless there was a gradient of decreasing stature of the trees with altitude, with the upper limits of woodland represented by low scrub, until they disappeared altogether.

After 5,000 years ago, elm pollen declined markedly, as elsewhere in Britain, and some ecologists believe this was the result of an earlier epidemic of disease affecting this tree, in a way similar to the recent outbreak. Pine also decreased, while oak, alder and ash increased, though the last was a small proportion of the total tree pollen.

Yet, from this time onwards, the most important change was not so much further change in the tree composition of woodland as the increasing loss of woodland cover, from the activities of early human colonists. The first signs of clearance were during the appearance of Neolithic people, and show by a reduction in tree pollen and an increase in that of weeds of cultivation, notably ribwort plantain, common sorrel and mugwort. Bracken also shows marked increases. By 4000 BP and the entry of Bronze Age people, the evidence of forest clearance became stronger, and when the Celtic people known as the Gaels came to Galloway and cultivated the lowlands, around 2450 BP, the forests were in full retreat. The pollen record shows a large increase in ling heather, evidently as this dwarf shrub flourished on cleared areas of the upland, which became the heather moorland of more recent times (Fig. 25). Clearance steadily depleted the forest cover, and a great deal had been lost by the Middle Ages, though the loss evidently reached its nadir by the late eighteenth century. Dick (1916) noted the presence of tree remains exposed in eroding bogs on the Loch Enoch plateau at 505m, and deduced that 'at one time the country was densely wooded wherever trees could grow'. He adduced the former occurrence of alders, willows and hawthorns from certain place names, and quoted from old texts to show that some at least of the then treeless uplands were thickly wooded at the time of Robert the Bruce (1274–1329), who fought the English occupiers among these hills.

Even the woods of native trees have mostly been replanted, though on the sites of original forest, and the most natural remnants are probably the relatively inaccessible wooded sides of steep and rocky gorges, where extraction of timber was most difficult. Across the region are many other planted woods, of both broadleaves and conifers, or mixtures of the two. Some have been managed for game and some of the smaller plantations were intended as shelter woods for

FIG 25. Heather moorland at the Craig of Grobdale, with drystane dyke, near Gatehouse-of-Fleet, Kirkcudbrightshire.

domestic stock. The planted trees are of both native and non-native species: oak, wych elm, beech (not native here) and sycamore among the broadleaves, and Scots pine, Norway spruce, Douglas fir and larch among the conifers.

LAND USE

The varied geology of the uplands has had a considerable influence on land use there. Virtually the whole of the Southern Uplands became a vast sheepwalk (Fig. 26). For hundreds of years, the flocks founded by the Cistercian monasteries of the Tweed valley supported a woollen industry that took its name from the great river. The rich soils and good grazings of the central and eastern sedimentary hills supported a higher stocking density of sheep than the more acidic substrates of the Galloway uplands. Although the woollen industry of the Tweed valley is now in decline, with closure of many mills at Hawick, Selkirk, Galashiels, Jedburgh and Kelso, more sheep farms have survived here than in the west, which suggests a greater viability for this land use in the east. From the Middle Ages to the early eighteenth century, the sheep evidently shared their range with large numbers of cattle and goats, and the scattered groups of feral goats across the region may well be the survivors of these earlier herds. The extensive peatlands of Wigtownshire and south Ayrshire supported only a low stocking density of sheep, while on the Galloway granite and associated metamorphic rocks, where carrying capacity was low, the higher hills with red deer had some affinity to Highland deer 'forest'.

There was, in fact, a long tradition of deer hunting in the Galloway Hills, according to Dick (1916), who referred to a late fourteenth-century nobleman known as the 'Ranger of the Forest of Buchan', and described the location of three of his hunting lodges along the foot of the Kells Range. The name Polmaddy meant 'the stream of the dogs', and Mullwharchar was 'the hill of the hunting-horn'. In the early eighteenth century, very large red deer were said to occur in Minnigaff parish, but they were alleged to be hunted to extinction by the end of that century. The red deer which have lived wild on these hills in more recent times were said by some to be descendants of animals that escaped from the deer park established at Cumloden, just northeast of Newton Stewart, but they could also have come from survivors of that ancient native stock.

Where heather-dominated ground was extensive, early nineteenth-century landowners followed the later fashion of creating red grouse preserves, especially

FIG 26. Black-faced sheep: they are responsible for the loss of heather moorland, seen on the slopes behind. Grobdale Hills, near Laurieston, Kirkcudbrightshire.

on gently contoured moorland where the birds could be driven over butts. Grouse moors became established on suitable uplands right across the region, though the best shoots were in the centre and east. These moorlands were managed to maximise the numbers of this bird for sport. Gamekeepers were employed to burn the heather on a ten- or twelve-year rotation, so that there was always a good extent of the nutritious younger growth at any one time – this dwarf shrub being the principal food of the grouse. The keepers also waged war on any animal suspected of being a competitor with the grouse-shooters, and the onslaught on the various forms of 'vermin' led to a serious ecological imbalance in the moorland ecosystem, as predators were wiped out on a large scale. With this destruction extending also to the lowland pheasant and partridge preserves, some birds of prey became extinct or extremely localised well before 1900. The red kite and hen harrier were lost altogether, while peregrines, buzzards and ravens hung on in craggy mountain fastnesses away from the grouse moors. Golden eagles were confined to the hills but fell foul of the sheep graziers there and were extinct by around 1875. Fishermen also removed the few ospreys as undesirable competitors. Grouse moors reached their zenith during Edwardian times, though some flourished again between the two World Wars. After 1945 there was a marked decline and this sport is now only a shadow of what it was a hundred years ago. But it generates more controversy now than it ever did in its heyday, as I shall discuss later.

When the Forestry Commission was expanding its programme of state afforestation, the uneconomic and struggling sheep farms of the Southern Uplands became a focus for its land acquisitions. In Galloway one estate or farm after another was bought up and planted, with the result that by 2000 this district was one of the most heavily wooded in Britain. Many sheep farms in other districts were also turned over to trees – on the Water of Ae north of Dumfries, Kershope and Wauchope on the Border, around Innerleithen in Peeblesshire, and Craik and Eskdalemuir in Selkirk and Dumfries. New forests were created all over the region's uplands, and even some grouse moors which had deteriorated through carrying too many sheep were turned over to the plantations. The only hill areas which have escaped afforestation are the most productive sheepwalks and cattle pastures, the best grouse moors, and moorlands which nature conservationists have defended against this destructive influence.

The fairly heavy rainfall has led, in modern times, to the creation of numerous reservoirs in the hill country, both for water supply and, in Galloway and Carrick, for hydroelectric power generation. Freshwater angling is an important sport, with the Tweed rated as one of the best salmon rivers in

Britain, but some of the western rivers and lochs have declined as fisheries, mainly through pollution of one kind or another, but especially the effects of extensive afforestation in the catchments.

In the farmed lowlands, there has been a broad division between predominance of permanent grassland for cattle and sheep in the west and a much larger proportion of land under arable crops in the east, especially on the Merse of Berwickshire. The grassland is of hay meadows and grazed pastures, while the arable is mainly of barley, wheat, potatoes and swedes. Oats have declined and oilseed rape has become important on arable land. Many farms are held under tenancies from the large estates into which much of the region is divided, this being the long-established pattern of land-holding in Scotland. Game-shooting and fox-hunting are traditional sports of the aristocracy and landed gentry who own much of the land, and a large part of the whole region has long been under the surveillance of their gamekeepers.

When I first knew the Southern Uplands, tourism hardly existed. In my hill wanderings I seldom met another fellow walker for a good many years. There was, however, a deliberate attempt by local authorities after 1950 to promote tourism and attract visitors to the region, and this has had considerable success. Hill-walking in the higher ranges, old architecture such as the Cistercian abbeys of the Tweed valley, castles and manor houses with their gardens open to the public, and the literary associations of famous poets and writers such as Robert Burns, James Hogg, Sir Walter Scott and Thomas Carlyle, have drawn people in increasing numbers to holiday in these parts. The opening of a signposted coast-to-coast walk, the Southern Upland Way, in 1985, and of a National Trust visitor centre at the Grey Mare's Tail in Moffatdale, were expressions of this growth of interest in enjoying the countryside. Caravan parks have multiplied, especially on the coast, and the provision of accommodation, food and gear boosts the local economy. Bird-watchers and anglers flock to the region in due season, and the tourist trade is increasingly becoming a year-round business.

CHAPTER 2

The Naturalists

N O HISTORY OF wildlife survives from the Middle Ages, which was a turbulent period in southern Scottish history, with the clan feuds of the 'raiders and reivers' over territory and livestock, and then the vicious persecution of the Covenanters for their religious beliefs. As Chapman (1907) well put it, 'The Borderers had sore shift to keep their own lives – let alone keeping field-notes!' The region has never been well endowed with resident naturalists, and at any one period the job of natural history compilation has fallen largely on the shoulders of a few key individuals. The fact that, for many groups of plants and animals, it is now fairly comprehensively recorded is a tribute to their dedication, energy and expertise. Despite the great increase in botanical recording in recent years, a recent map of the distribution of members of the Botanical Society of the British Isles shows a total of 11 in Dumfries & Galloway (three vice-counties) and 20 in the Borders (four vice-counties), compared with 40–140 for many individual English vice-counties. Ornithology is now much better served than in earlier years, especially in the Borders, but there are few devotees for most of the other groups of animals.

There have been a good many books dealing with the history, countryside and human affairs of southern Scotland. Few of them, however, have taken an interest in its wildlife, apart from passing references to rarer birds such as ravens and peregrines, and comments on the aesthetic value of certain plants. Many of these works, from Harper's *Rambles in Galloway* (1908) and Dick's *Highways and Byways in Galloway and Carrick* (1916) (Fig. 27) to Clavering's *From the Border Hills* (1953), are much more preoccupied with the bloody deeds of the Reiver and Covenanter times. There is a disappointing lack of interest in our concerns. Sir Herbert Maxwell, historian and angler, also wrote a good deal

FIG 27. Stream flowing from granite hills. Eglin Lane, with Merrick range behind, Carrick, south Ayrshire. The Reverend C. H. Dick wrote evocatively about these hills.

in a general way about the wildlife of southern Scotland in the early 1900s (e.g. in *Memories of the Months*, 1901), but it was unsystematic and does not give an ordered picture.

FAUNA

Probably the earliest historical reference to animals is the oft-quoted allusion by A. Symson in 1684 to eagles, ospreys and ptarmigan in Galloway (see Chapter 8). The *Statistical Account of Scotland* (Sinclair, 1791–9) and the *New Statistical Account of Scotland* (1834–45) contain scattered and erratic mention of wildlife, mainly animals, but until late in the nineteenth century there is little in the way of organised publication on fauna. Evans (1911) has given a valuable summary of earlier faunal sources. The first relevant work appears to be that of John Wallis (1719–93) in 1769, mainly about Northumberland but with some material referring to the Tweed. In 1831, George Johnston (1797–1855) founded the Berwickshire Naturalists' Club, and operated widely over the Tweed area. His own writings included manuals on zoophytes, lithophytes and sponges, worms and snails, and two volumes on flora. Evans (1911) notes that 'Berwickshire' in this context was practically equivalent to the Tweed faunal area, and described Johnston as 'the father of natural history in the eastern Borders'. William MacGillivray in his *History of British Birds* (1837–52) made some observations on the region's birds, such as peregrines in the Moffat Hills. Prideaux John Selby (1788–1867) was concerned primarily with Northumberland, but contributed papers on the birds of the Tweed area and St Abbs Head to the first volume of the *History of the Berwickshire Naturalists' Club* in 1832. He also engaged in frequent correspondence with the Dumfriesshire ornithologist Sir William Jardine, who published his now sought-after *Naturalists' Library*, including the four-volume *Birds of Great Britain and Ireland* (1838–43), which contains some information relating to the region.

Sir Walter Elliot (1803–87) wrote papers on the birds of the Hawick district and the first Borders vole plague of 1876–7. This last, and the still larger peak of 1892–3, caused great concern and were the subject of investigations and reports, such as that by Harvie-Brown *et al.* (1893). The parallel increases in vole predators, notably short-eared owl and kestrel, and the subsequent crash in numbers of rodents and predators, were described by P. Adair (1892, 1893). The banker Robert Gray (1825–87) produced the first work referring to the southwest district with his *Birds of the West of Scotland* (1871), which has many items concerning Galloway and Ayrshire. The first publication dealing wholly with our region was, however, the two-volume *Birds of Berwickshire* by George Muirhead in 1889–95, which gave a valuable historical account of many species. Andrew Brotherston (1834–91) was in charge of natural history at the Kelso Museum, where he practised taxidermy and was known as a reliable observer of birds and also a considerable botanist. The hunter–naturalist Abel Chapman, who lived on the North Tyne, wrote a general work on *The Bird-Life of the Borders* in 1889, but it dealt mainly with the Northumbrian side. The completely rewritten second edition (1907) and his later *Borders and Beyond* (1924) described the breeding of wigeon, tufted duck, pochard and great crested grebe on the Scottish Borders, which he claimed was a new event.

Around the turn of the century, the Galloway naturalist Robert Service, a nurseryman by profession, contributed over 200 papers to scientific journals, on subjects ranging from aculeate Hymenoptera to birds, which were his main interest. He reorganised the Dumfries & Galloway Natural History and Antiquarian Society and became its secretary, as well as honorary curator of the Dumfries Museum. Under the pen name of Mabie Moss, he also wrote numerous articles for the local press, but never achieved a work of any great substance. John Harvie-Brown, creator of the inspired *Vertebrate Faunas* of Scotland, had intended the last remaining gap in the series, the Solway, to be filled with a volume written by Service, but the prospective author sadly died before the project saw fulfilment. The other gap in Harvie-Brown's series was filled in 1911 with the publication of *A Fauna of the Tweed Area* by A. H. Evans. This was a milestone in the natural history of the region, and is of considerable historical value, especially in reporting the contemporary status of species. It was followed in 1912 by the Borders naturalist George Bolam's *Birds of Northumberland and the Eastern Borders*, another scholarly work which overlapped somewhat with the previous one in geographical scope.

In the southwest, Sir Hugh Gladstone of Capenoch produced *The Birds of Dumfriesshire* (1910), another extremely informative tome. Gladstone was one of the first ornithological writers to give population figures for some species, such as peregrines and ravens, and he took a particular interest in the rookeries and heronries of his county. His account of the late-Victorian vole plagues on the Southern Uplands and their effects on predatory birds is also extremely interesting. In 1912, Gladstone published *A Catalogue of the Vertebrate Fauna of Dumfriesshire*, which was a kind of annotated checklist of all the groups, including the birds. He followed with a supplement to his first work, bringing the bird record up to date, in 1923. Sir Hugh was also a bibliophile and assembled what was described at the time as the finest ornithological library in Britain, containing a copy of every book published on British birds, as well as many original letters and manuscripts. His contribution to the region's natural history was very considerable, but I cannot forbear to mention that he also wrote what, to me, is about the most bizarre work in the whole of our field of interest, *Game Bags and Shooting Records* (1930), a meticulous catalogue of the slaughter of sentient creatures by 'sportsmen'. From this, we learn *inter alia* that the record one-day bag of red grouse in Scotland was made on 30 August 1911, when 2,523 birds were shot by eight guns on the Tarras Moors at Langholm in his own county (see Chapter 8).

Entomologists R. S. Gordon and J. G. Gordon wrote on the Lepidoptera of Wigtownshire in 1913 and 1919. Their records included several butterflies no longer present in south Scotland, in brimstone, large tortoiseshell, silver-washed fritillary, silver-studded blue and grizzled skipper, and also the broad-bordered bee-hawk moth. These old butterfly records have been accepted by Asher *et al.* (2001) as authentic. Bertram McGowan also published a three-part list of beetles of the Solway area from 1912 to 1921.

Ornithology in the southwest received further attention with publication of *The Birds of Ayrshire* (1929) by E. R. Paton and Oliver Pike, and the Reverend J. M. McWilliam's *Birds of the Firth of Clyde* (1936), though our region lays claim only to the southern part of this area. Galloway failed to receive corresponding treatment, though J. G. Gordon and Adam Birrell wrote locally about birds during the 1920s. Although the Dumfries & Galloway Natural History and Antiquarian Society was founded in 1862 and its *Transactions* became the main vehicle for wildlife papers in the district, the predominant interests of members – as reflected in its publications – have always appeared to be antiquarian rather than natural history. The list of Galloway birds published there by Sir Arthur Duncan in 1947–8 had only brief annotations on distribution and status. O. J. Pullen wrote on the rarer birds of Galloway in the *Gallovidian Annual* for 1936–7.

The expanding afforestation of moorlands in the 1930s led to marked increases in numbers of field voles, and revived interest in the effects of these on predatory birds and mammals. The pioneer animal ecologist Charles Elton visited the Southern Uplands to observe the phenomenon, which led him to seek – somewhat inconclusively – an explanation of the underlying causes of the great vole explosions in Dumfriesshire and the Borders towards the end of the nineteenth century. He devoted a whole chapter to the subject in his monumental *Voles, Mice and Lemmings* (1942). During the 1930s, the flats and saltings of the Nith and Lochar estuaries became a celebrated haunt of wildfowlers, drawn by the numbers of geese, greylag, pinkfeet and barnacle, though little was written about these. In the late 1930s, three young Carlisle birders, Raymond Laidler, Peter Day and Sandy Bannister, began to explore Galloway for ravens and peregrines, but their efforts were interrupted by the outbreak of war. I continued their work in 1946 and paid annual visits to the Stewartry hills to learn about the nesting habits of these birds, especially the role of territory in limiting their numbers. From 1949 I extended my fieldwork with annual visits to the Moffat Hills.

In 1951, Donald Watson settled at Dalry in Galloway to make his career as a painter of wildlife and landscape (Fig. 28). He diligently observed and recorded the birds of Galloway and became the leading authority on them – a walking encyclopaedia, in fact. With information from his growing network of local contacts, and the many visitors to Galloway – including myself – who made their way to his door, he became the clearing-house for bird news across the district. For many years Donald compiled the Bird Report for Dumfries & Galloway, and was the local recorder for the district. He wrote two fascinating books containing much material on his experiences of Galloway wildlife, *A Bird Artist in Scotland* (1988) and *One Pair of Eyes* (1994). The first contains a diary of a typical Galloway year, which gives a vivid impression of the charms of the district to the naturalist, and has an annotated checklist of the birds which updates that of Duncan (1947–8). Donald watched the return of the hen harrier as a breeding bird to southwest Scotland from 1959 and paid special attention to its nesting and

FIG 28. Donald and Joan Watson.

roosting habits, leading to his important monograph *The Hen Harrier* in 1977. His book *Birds of Moor and Mountain* (1972) drew especially on his experiences in Galloway. Donald Watson was one of the few people able to stand up for nature conservation in this part of Scotland, which he did frequently and to good effect, and during his long residence he witnessed, with some misgivings, the transformation of his chosen country by afforestation. His wife Joan developed an enthusiasm for butterflies and added greatly to knowledge of their distribution in Galloway.

Other ornithologists were active in the southwest from the 1950s onwards, including Willie Austin in Dumfries, Langley Roberts, warden at the Caerlaverock reserve, and Dumfriesshire farmers Bobby Smith and Jim Young, who became enthusiastic and able bird photographers, along with Dumfries medic Dr Edmund Fellowes. In Wigtownshire, Bert Dickson became the local bird expert and compiler of records, and published a valuable book on *The Birds in Wigtownshire* in 1992. Commander Geoffrey Hughes-Onslow was a leading figure in south Ayrshire ornithology. John Young, who replaced Roberts at Caerlaverock, wrote interesting papers on the Wigtownshire gannetry (Fig. 29) in 1968 and greylag geese (Fig. 30) in 1972, and, with the help of various friends, began to monitor the Dumfries sparrowhawk population. During this postwar period, various egg-collectors became active in the district, most of them

FIG 29. Big Scare Rock with gannet breeding colony. Luce Bay, Wigtownshire. (Bobby Smith)

FIG 30. Feral greylag geese nest widely on the islands of lochs in the southwest. (Bobby Smith)

Ayrshire men, and severely depressed the breeding success of ravens and peregrines, in particular. The clutch data of Donald Cross and John Hutchinson eventually became available, but those of the others have never surfaced.

Thomas Huxley was the Nature Conservancy's Regional Officer for the south of Scotland from 1956, concerned with the establishment and management of National Nature Reserves and the notification of Sites of Special Scientific Interest. He developed the permit system to regulate shooting pressure at Caerlaverock, and oversaw management also at the Silver Flowe, Tynron Juniper Wood and Kirkconnell Flow Reserves. A serious conservation problem of this time was the impact of agricultural pesticides on birds of prey, notably the peregrine. The importance of long-term monitoring of populations was clear, and southern Scotland became a key area for such work, through the dedication of certain people. In the southwest, ex-coal miner Dick Roxburgh at Catrine developed a passion for the peregrine, and spent much of his time checking known eyries and prospecting the hills for new ones (Fig. 31). He also enthused

FIG 31. Dick Roxburgh, beside a ground nest of peregrine in south Ayrshire.

a band of helpers, including Chris Rollie, Charlie Park, Richard Gladwell and Ian Millar. In the northeast, George Carse, in Edinburgh, developed a similar enthusiasm for peregrine monitoring and annually, with helpers, covered the nesting places in the Moffat Hills and the Borders. Together, these two leaders, whose comprehensive annual surveys covered a period of over 30 years, made the peregrine population of southern Scotland one of the best documented in Britain, and charted the recovery in numbers from the trough of 1963–4 to the unprecedented peak of the 1990s.

From this start, bird of prey studies 'took off' during the 1970s. In 1971, Ian Newton, assisted by Herman Ostroznik, Willie Murray and later Mick Marquiss, began an intensive study of sparrowhawks in Annandale, and extended this next year to Eskdale. The work led to his classic book *The Sparrowhawk* (1986) and to another important monitoring baseline. Ian also promoted the programme of goshawk reintroduction to Britain and, with Mick Marquiss, followed the increase and spread of the species in southern Scotland. With Richard Mearns he developed a ringing and marking study of breeding peregrines in the Southern Uplands, to examine the rates of turnover in the population. Mick Marquiss investigated the decline in raven breeding population that had become apparent during the 1970s, and which was partly the result of afforestation. With Dick Roxburgh, who had followed the golden eagles of Galloway and Carrick with great commitment, and myself, he studied the parallel decline of this bird from the same cause. Richard Mearns continued to work on peregrines and also made a repeat raven survey that showed further decline.

In 1991 Chris Rollie became the RSPB's officer for southwest Scotland, based in Dalry, and soon organised bird of prey efforts under a Dumfries & Galloway Raptor Study Group, which meets regularly under his chairmanship and publishes a journal covering monitoring and other studies on all species. In particular, they have monitored the remarkable recovery of the breeding peregrine and raven populations to unprecedented levels in the late 1990s. A comparable Borders Raptor Study Group was set up by Dave Dick, covering the north and east of southern Scotland.

Work on other birds has developed also. The Forestry Commission's Wildlife Officer in Galloway, Geoff Shaw, has focused especially on barn owls, and boosted the population considerably by nest-box provision. His studies include other forest birds and his surveys of dippers gave valuable help to Juliet Vickery when she examined the effects of stream water acidification on this bird during 1987. A major project developed with the study of predation on red grouse by birds of prey on the Langholm Moors on the borders of Dumfries and Roxburgh. Conducted by Steve Redpath and Simon Thirgood, and supervised

by Ian Newton, it was funded by several parties with an interest in grouse management and bird conservation, in an attempt to provide facts on the simmering
controversy over illegal raptor persecution by game-preservers. The report on
the study (Redpath & Thirgood, 1997) showed that hen harriers and peregrines in
this area did indeed appreciably reduce the shootable stocks of grouse, but the
underlying conservation issue appears no nearer to resolution.

Bird-watching and recording have a vastly greater following across the region
than fifty years ago, and it becomes increasingly difficult – and invidious – to
single out individual efforts. Both the Borders and Dumfries & Galloway now
produce annual Bird Reports, compiled by Ray Murray and Peter Norman, which
are an invaluable source of information, though the former is perhaps the better
supported in terms of contributor numbers. This has led to the production of
a bird breeding atlas for southeast Scotland (Murray et al., 1998). Ornithology is
flourishing, and underpins the efforts on bird protection and conservation
across the region.

Work on the other animal groups has flagged by comparison. Forestry Commission staff, including Judy Rowe, have made studies of red deer in Galloway
and undertaken practical work such as reintroduction of the pine marten, which
Geoff Shaw and J. Livingston have monitored. David Bullock and colleagues
surveyed the feral goats on Cairnsmore of Fleet in 1976, and John Mitchell
investigated the minor vole plagues following afforestation in Eskdalemuir
during 1970–2. Peter Maitland wrote a valuable paper on the fish of southwest
Scotland in 1970.

Study of invertebrates has been patchy. Sir Arthur Duncan was an expert on
Diptera and Hymenoptera, and took a general interest in other groups, including
butterflies and moths, on which he and D. Cunningham wrote in the *Transactions*.
His collections are in the National Museums of Scotland, Edinburgh. Professor
Frank Balfour-Browne, the authority on water beetles, lived in Dumfries and
published frequently on this group. Roy Crowson, the beetle taxonomist of
Glasgow University, carried out some of his field work in the region. Dragonflies
have received periodic attention from various entomologists, and most recently
from Bob and Betty Smith, Barbara and Richard Mearns and David Clarke.
Joan Watson's work on butterflies has been mentioned, and George Thomson's
Butterflies of Scotland (1980) and *The Millennium Atlas of Butterflies in Britain and
Ireland* by Jim Asher et al. (2001) are important sources for this group. Richard
and Barbara Mearns have also taken up study of the butterflies and moths to
good effect, and there is now a thriving local group of entomologists making
many contributions to the study of the region's biodiversity.

FLORA

Knowledge of the botany of the south of Scotland accumulated quite slowly. The Reverend Dr John Walker, man of many parts, was appointed minister in Moffat in 1762, and proceeded to record the local flora. One of his important finds was whortle-leaved willow, growing some way above downy willow on the White Coomb. This is the most southerly station for this montane willow, which has scattered localities on calcareous soils around the Highlands, but has not been found elsewhere in the Southern Uplands. He also discovered the Scotch argus butterfly, new to science, in Dryfesdale in the late 1770s and found the holly blue at Moffat. Walker did not hit it off too well with the locals, perhaps through seeming more enthusiastic about 'weeds' and other products of the countryside than about his flock, and earned himself the title of the 'mad minister of Moffat'. A parishioner remarked that 'he spent the week hunting butterflies and made the cure of the souls of his parishioners a bye-job on Sunday' – but he evidently found the parish something of an intellectual desert. Walker was appointed Regius Professor of Natural History at Edinburgh in 1779, though he retained his ministry in Moffat until 1783.

Braithwaite and Long (1990) record that brief notes on Berwickshire botany by a Dr Parsons were published in Lightfoot's *Flora Scotica* in 1777. Surgeon John V. Thompson published *A Catalogue of Plants Growing in the Vicinity of Berwick upon Tweed* in 1807, and this provided a basis for Dr George Johnston to widen the scope in compiling his two-volume *Flora of Berwick on Tweed* (1829–31). Johnston founded the Berwickshire Naturalists' Club in 1831, the first local natural history society in Britain, which prospered greatly and published a journal entitled its *History*. Johnston continued to botanise and enthused others, such as Dr James Hardy (1815–98), who became extremely active in the district and wrote both lichen and moss floras of the eastern Borders, in 1863 and 1868. Additions to the vascular flora were published in the *History*, and Johnston included botany in his subsequent *Natural History of the Eastern Borders* (1853), an accomplished work which remained the standard reference flora until only 15 years ago. Hewett C. Watson, father of plant geography, visited the region in the 1830s and made new discoveries.

Other botanists who contributed significantly to knowledge of the Borders flora during the nineteenth century included Archibald Jerdon near Jedburgh, Andrew Brotherston in Kelso (both Roxburghshire) and Dr Charles Stuart at Chirnside, Berwickshire. Brotherston (1834–91) was the most consistent and productive of all the Border botanists in the nineteenth century, and one of the outstanding early local botanists. Stuart was the first to take an interest in the numerous introduced plants of the Tweed valley around Galashiels. Jerdon was a keen mycologist and also interested in mosses and liverworts. The Reverend James Duncan of Denholm contributed an annotated list of plants to the flora section in Volume 4 of Jeffrey's *History of Roxburghshire* (1864), though James Murray, of *Oxford English Dictionary* fame, later claimed that – apart from a few additions – this list was made by him, and had not been acknowledged by Duncan. The Reverend James Farquharson published an unannotated list of Selkirkshire plants in 1877, and W. B. Boyd of Faldonside contributed botanical notes to the *History of the Berwickshire Naturalists' Club* between 1872 and 1914.

The Moffat Hills in the northeast corner of Dumfriesshire were first put on the botanical map by the discovery there of the very rare little fern oblong woodsia around 1840, when the Victorian fern craze was just taking off (Fig. 32). This drew many fern-hunters, including John Sadler from the Royal Botanic

FIG 32. Oblong woodsia, the most famous mountain plant of the region, almost exterminated by Victorian fern maniacs. A reintroduced tuft from cultivation. Moffat Hills.

Garden in Edinburgh, who published his *Narrative of a Ramble Among the Wild Flowers of the Moffat Hills* in 1857 and described its botanical interest more widely, showing it to be an important area for montane plants. Sadler dug up four of five tufts of woodsia that he found, but a few years later was hypocritically castigating 'an English nurseryman' for similar rapacity (Fig. 33). The redoubtable John Hutton Balfour, Professor of Botany in Edinburgh, also took parties of his students to the Moffat Hills. It was *de rigueur* for botany students to make a personal herbarium in those days (and the practice is not all that long discontinued in Edinburgh) and all would be intent on filling their vasculums: the damage they inflicted on the rarer species has to be left to the imagination. A number of rather dubious plant records for the Moffat Hills were attributed to the Reverend Dr J. Singer, incumbent of a nearby parish, who compiled a plant list for the *New Statistical Account* in 1843.

The Reverend William Little made a collection of pressed plants from Dumfriesshire which included woodsia, yellow star-of-Bethlehem and narrow-leaved helleborine, the last two being unreported from the county in recent years. In 1863, Dr William Carruthers, also of Moffat, produced *The Ferns of Moffat*, an album of pressed ferns with accompanying text, published in book form. He later became Keeper of Botany in the London Natural History Museum. Good finds,

FIG 33. The Raven Craig, head of Carrifran Burn and White Coomb, Moffatdale, Dumfriesshire. Where John Sadler collected oblong woodsia.

FIG 34. Alpine saxifrage, probably the rarest plant in southern Scotland. Moffat Hills, Dumfriesshire.

including holly fern, alpine saxifrage (Fig. 34) and pyramidal bugle (Fig. 35), were later made here by another Moffat botanist, J. Thorburn Johnstone, who published botanical notes in 1891 and 1893 in the *Transactions of the Dumfries & Galloway Natural History and Antiquarian Society*. The Society was established in 1862 and its *Transactions* became the main vehicle for papers on flora and fauna in the southwest.

Botanical knowledge of the southwest of the region lagged somewhat behind that in the northeast, though good finds had been reported sporadically, such as the discovery of the southern small restharrow near West Tarbert by Professor Graham in 1835 and the northern purple oxytropis at the Mull of Galloway in 1848 by Dr Walker Arnott. Professor Balfour also visited the Galloway coast in 1843 and 1868 and found it botanically productive (Stewart, 1987). In 1896, at the age of 34, African explorer and, later, Great War soldier George Scott-Elliot published his *Flora of Dumfriesshire*, which remains the definitive work for the county up to this day. He was greatly interested in the pollination of flowers and their insect visitors and his *Flora* contains much information on the species of both. Scott-Elliot helpfully included some of the more notable plants for the adjoining counties of Kirkcudbright and Wigtown. His *Flora* contains many records made by James M'Andrew, headmaster of Kells School at New Galloway, who

FIG 35. Pyramidal bugle, another contender for rarest plant. Moffat Hills, Dumfriesshire. (John Mitchell)

assiduously studied Galloway plants and made many interesting discoveries, such as cowbane (Fig. 36), brown beak-sedge, upright bitter-vetch, lovage and alpine hawkweed. He published numerous notes and short articles on his finds, and in 1893–4 produced *A List of Wigtownshire Plants*, a checklist with localities mentioned for most species. M'Andrew also studied cryptogams and did good work on the mosses, liverworts and lichens of Dumfries & Galloway, which he reported in the *Transactions*.

Botanical work in the region flagged somewhat after 1900. The hawkweed specialists W. R. Linton and E. S. Marshall visited the Moffat area, and published an article in 1908 which included a list of *Hieracia* as well as many additions to Scott-Elliot's *Flora*. George C. Druce was in the Moffat Hills in 1910, by which time the oblong woodsia was supposedly reduced to a single plant, which he was shown. Druce botanised in the Borders and took an interest in the numerous alien plants which had arrived in the Tweed valley through the importation of sheep's wool from overseas to the woollen mills. He was joined in this by an enthusiastic mill-owner's relative, Ida Hayward, who did most of the fieldwork, resulting in a joint publication, *The Adventive Flora of Tweedside*, in 1919.

In the wider world, plant ecology 'took off' in the early 1900s, and one of the early developments was the Botanical Survey of Scotland, launched by the brothers Robert and William Smith in 1897. This involved the description and mapping of the vegetation of the area around Edinburgh, including the Pentland Hills. A map of this district (and one of Perthshire) was published, but the project stalled through the death of Robert Smith, aged only 26, in 1900, and then the move of his brother William to Leeds. The geographer F. J. Lewis, who had been mapping vegetation in the northern Pennines, extended his work to Scotland, mainly the Highlands, but visited some of the Southern Uplands. Lewis was especially interested in peat deposits and the record of Post-glacial history that their profiles contained, including the preserved remains of ancient trees at various depths (Lewis, 1905). When the technique of pollen analysis evolved later, it became the principal means of investigating Quaternary vegetation history, though studies in our region mostly began much later, in the 1960s. Ecological research included study of mat-grass colonisation of downwashed peat in the Moorfoot Hills by Donald Macpherson (published by W. G. Smith in 1918, after

FIG 36. Cowbane: a rare and poisonous plant of rich fens.

Macpherson's death in the Great War), and salt-marsh succession in the Nith
estuary by W. L. Morss (1927). The interwar period saw something of a hiatus in
botanical work, with little activity reported, though the bryologist J. B. Duncan
settled in Berwickshire and published on this group.

After World War II, the creation of the Nature Conservancy (1949) gave
impetus to ecological, biological and geological surveys to find notable wildlife
areas and earth science locations to notify as National Nature Reserves (NNRS) or
Sites of Special Scientific Interest (SSSIS). In Galloway, Donald Walker, Richard
West and I reported to the Conservancy our 1951 survey of the Silver Flowe, a
unique bog system hitherto unknown to peatland ecologists; the site was
declared an NNR in 1956. Botanical recording in the region also began to look up.
Between 1951 and 1956 I explored the Moffat Hills and published a paper on the
mountain flora in 1959. Effort was mustered around this time to give a reasonable
picture of species' presence and distribution across the region in the landmark
Atlas of the British Flora (Perring and Walters, 1962). In Galloway, Dr Humphrey
Milne-Redhead settled as a country GP at Mainsriddle near Carsethorn, and
began exploration of the district, and also the western Borders, for bryophytes as
well as vascular plants. An energetic and tireless fieldworker, he was impervious
to adverse conditions and often ended the day soaked to the skin, after the
investigation of some dank ravine or remote hill crags. He had a keen eye for
plants and made many interesting finds in the region, such as holy grass, tall
bog-sedge and alpine rush. He published a paper on plant distribution in
southwest Scotland (1963) and another on the liverwort flora of Dumfries and
Kirkcudbright (1964). His main contribution was a checklist of the flowering
plants of Dumfries, Kirkcudbright and Wigtown (1972), the areas for which he
was botanical Recorder. This fruitful period was brought to a close in the early
1970s by Milne-Redhead's early death.

In the Borders, medical student Roderick Corner from St Boswells began
exploring the hitherto little-known counties of Selkirk and Roxburgh, and in the
late 1950s discovered the florally rich fens known as the Whitlaw Mosses near
Selkirk town and other productive wetlands near Hawick, which later became a
focus of attention for research into fen ecology and Quaternary history. They
have proved to have many rarities such as alpine rush, holy grass, coralroot and
round-leaved wintergreen. Although a busy GP living in Penrith, Cumbria, Rod
Corner continued diligently to return over the border in his capacity as Botanical
Society of the British Isles (BSBI) Recorder for his two home counties, and
worked every nook and cranny of their varied habitats. Now retired, he is
presently distilling his encyclopaedic knowledge into a first-time Flora of
Roxburgh and Selkirk.

Michael Braithwaite published on the railway flora of Teviotdale in 1975 and on the Eildon Hills in 1976. He had also been studying the vascular flora of Berwickshire since that time, and *The Botanist in Berwickshire* (1990) contains two annotated checklists for the county, the first on flowering plants and ferns, compiled by himself, and the second on bryophytes, compiled by David Long. David McCosh, BSBI Recorder for Peeblesshire, has studied the flora of that county for many years. Also in the Borders, Arthur Smith in Selkirk was an active local botanist during this period, and Olga Stewart and Mary McCallum Webster renewed the search for wool aliens at Galafoot with some success in the 1960s and 1970s. Roderick Corner notes (personal communication) that these plants have nearly all since disappeared, and pirri-pirri bur from New Zealand is the only species that has become naturalised in any quantity along the Tweed.

In Dumfries, Mary Martin at Lochmaben published a checklist of plants of Dumfriesshire (1985), which brought the county flora further up to date. Plant recording in the Stewartry was taken over by Olga Stewart at New Abbey, and culminated in her annotated checklist of the flowering plants of Kirkcud-brightshire (1990), the nearest to a Flora that the county has so far had. Allan Stirling lived for some years at Kirkcudbright from 1960 and was an active surveyor of the local flora who contributed many records to Stewart's lists, and later became BSBI Recorder for Ayrshire. In Wigtownshire, county Recorder Alan Silverside privately circulated *The Flowering Plants and Ferns of Wigtownshire* (1990), which he modestly described as a very provisional checklist, though it is well annotated with information on status and distribution.

Mosses and liverworts in the region have been fairly well covered, both by resident bryologists and by visitors, including three field visits by the British Bryological Society in 1961, 1971 and 1994. Lichens have received attention from Roderick Corner, Brian Coppins, Francis Rose and Peter James, and are reason-ably well known. The fungi are perhaps the most neglected group, though Professor Roy Watling has distilled current knowledge into a contribution included as an appendix to this book.

The peatlands have received attention from research ecologists, studying the fine-scale differentiation of plant communities and their successional relationships. David Goode studied the hydrology and plant ecology of the Silver Flowe in Galloway and Derek Boatman and his postgraduate students used this as a site for long-term research into vegetation pattern and bog development. In the Borders, Rosalind Tratt studied the factors differentiating plant communities on 68 different mire sites in the Hawick–Selkirk area.

Historical ecologists have also been active in the region. Frank Mitchell (1948) and Ann Conolly (1961) examined the macroscopic plant remains in the

Late-glacial deposits of Whitrig Bog, an ancient but degraded fen adjoining Bemersyde Moss in Berwickshire. Using pollen analysis, Hilary Birks (1972) studied forest history and especially the role of Scots pine by examination of Post-glacial blanket bog peat in the Galloway Hills, while Neville Moar (1969) looked at peat profiles in both upland and lowland Post-glacial sites in the southwest. In the Borders, J. A. Webb and P. D. Moore (1982) analysed older, Late-glacial lake sediments and fen peats in the Whitlaw Mosses, to give a detailed picture of the sequence of plant communities that held sway during the long development of these rich fens. Julie Tight (1987) made a similar investigation of Branxholme Wester Loch and Kingside Loch in the Borders. In Galloway, Rick Battarbee and his colleagues (1985, 1989) applied the techniques of lead and diatom analysis, as well as pollen analysis, to lake sediments in tracing the insidious process of acidification of unbuffered waters that began with the Industrial Revolution and the outpouring of sulphur dioxide in smoke. They found that most hill lochs on the granite had become markedly acidified.

Field meetings of the BSBI in the region over the last half-century or so, usually led by local experts, have helped to boost information on the vascular plants. Yet, despite the great increase in field botanising in the region since 1950, and the good knowledge of plant distribution in all the vice-counties, there has not yet been another full-blown Flora within the region since Scott-Elliot's of Dumfriesshire in 1896. The various checklists show the species present and, with the *New Atlas of the British and Irish Flora* (Preston *et al.*, 2002), give a general idea of distribution, status and abundance; but it would be good to have fuller and more informative accounts for each county.

CHAPTER 3

The Coast

THERE ARE TWO coastal sections, one in the southwest, bordering the north side of the Solway Firth and the North Channel, and the other in the northeast, from Dunbar to Berwick-on-Tweed, fronting the North Sea. The first is much the longest and most varied, and will be considered first.

DUMFRIES, GALLOWAY AND AYR

The coast of Dumfriesshire is flat and bordered with a variable width of salt marsh and sand flats, but that of Kirkcudbrightshire to the west soon rises into long lines of sea cliff. Wigtownshire also has extensive sea cliffs, especially on the west side of the Rhins, but it also has shingle beaches and salt marsh, while at the head of Luce Bay is the large sand dune system of Torrs Warren. That part of the Ayrshire coast within our region has mostly sea cliffs and rocky shores. Steers (1973) has pointed out the large extent of ancient raised beach platforms backed by fossil cliffs along this coast, especially in Wigtownshire. In places there are two series of raised beaches, a higher (15m) and a lower (7.5m). Unlike the Cumbrian coast opposite, there has been no major industrial development, apart from the ordnance factories between Gretna and Annan (of which that at Eastriggs remains), and the Scottish Solway is a largely unspoiled coastline scenically (Fig. 37). Until fifty years ago it could also have been called unpolluted, but there has since then been insidious contamination of the marine sediments by radionuclides released from the nuclear developments at Sellafield in Cumbria and Chapelcross near Annan, the second close to the Solway shore. On the

FIG 37. Mudflats at the mouth of the River Annan at Waterfoot, looking to Blackshaw Bank and Criffel. Scottish Solway. (Bobby Smith)

north Ayrshire coast, Hunterston nuclear power station must contaminate the Clyde littoral.

In the early twentieth century the Reverend Dick portrayed the northern Solway as an enchanting coast, in its variety of scene, with ever-changing vistas of sands, bays, coves, cliffs and headlands, interspersed with quiet old-world fishing villages. It retains much of this original charm, though scattered caravan parks are a modern intrusion that speak of its present popularity with holidaymakers. This is a fascinating coast to the naturalist, especially rich in its wild flora, and parts of it are still incompletely explored botanically. In autumn and winter its abundant and varied wildfowl and wader populations excite and draw birders from far and wide. In summer, the warm, sun-exposed cliff slopes with their abundance of flowers are probably the best single haunt of butterflies in the region.

Sand flats

The waters of the inner Solway are under 10m deep for most of the stretch above a line from Balcary Point to Maryport, and those of Kirkcudbright Bay and at the head of Wigtown and Luce Bays on the outer Solway are similarly shallow (Rowe, 1978). The only deep water close inshore lies off Burrow Head and the Mull of

Galloway, where the 20m depth contour is less than two kilometres offshore (Solway Firth Partnership, 1996). Large sandbanks have built up on the inshore sea-bed here: they are submerged during most high tides, but exposed extensively at low tide. The inner Solway as a whole has the third largest area of intertidal estuarine flats in Britain, covering 26,000ha, and half the total area lies below high water mark (Fig. 38). They can be very mobile, eroding in one place and building up in another, and the fresh river channels running through them are constantly changing position. The sediment is mostly relatively coarse, with finer silt and clay plentiful only in rather few places, and it is believed to be mainly of marine origin, rather than river-borne (Solway Firth Partnership).

Apart from algae such as *Enteromorpha* spp. and *Ulva lactuca*, and scattered colonies of three species of eel-grass (dwarf, narrow-leaved and common) (salt-marsh community SM1; Rodwell, 1991–2000), there is little vegetation on these sand flats. They are, however, important for their intertidal fauna, which is a vital food source for the large flocks of wintering and passage waterfowl. In general, the diversity and abundance of invertebrate species increase away from sources of freshwater inflow, but the fauna is rather limited everywhere.

Areas of muddy sand between high and low waters have dense beds of the lugworm, polychaete worms such as common ragworm, catworm and *Pygospio*

FIG 38. Sand flats and salt marshes of the north Solway. Mersehead from Lot's Wife, Caulkerbush, Kirkcudbrightshire.

elegans, and the bivalves Baltic tellin and cockle. In especially sheltered conditions, with fine sediments, ragworms may be especially abundant, with a more diverse fauna including the mud snail and a burrowing amphipod, *Corophium volutator*. Slightly muddy, medium to fine sand has cockle populations and other bivalves such as the thin tellin, sometimes in large numbers. Where beds of eel-grass occur on lower-shore fine and muddy sand, in sheltered bays, as at Rough Firth and Auchencairn Bay, they form a habitat for other species such as cockles and burrowing sea urchins. In large bays such as Luce Bay, or in the entrances to the large estuaries of the outer Solway, there is a rich community of at least eight polychaete worms and several bivalves.

In places on the sand flats are patches of raised rocky ground known as scaurs (scars in England), which are the pebbles, cobbles and boulders eroded from boulder clays and other glacial deposits. They are more frequent on the south Solway, but occur at Powfoot, Hestan Island, Wigtown Bay and the east side of Luce Bay. Scaurs are important habitats with a rich community of algae and invertebrates, including brown fucoids and red algae, mussels, barnacles, periwinkles and the breadcrumb sponge (Solway Firth Partnership, 1996).

Salt marshes

Burd (1989) has identified 19 sites on the Scottish Solway with areas of salt marsh greater than 10ha in extent. From Gretna to Powfoot there are only five small areas of fringing merseland, and inland boulder clay runs down to the Solway edge or to raised beach. Until recently, government explosives factories sealed off much of the foreshore here. West of Powfoot a 4km strip of salt marsh extends seawards into the sand flats of Priestside Bank. They are divided by the estuary of the Lochar Water from the much larger Caerlaverock Merse and Blackshaw Bank, which stretch another 10km to the Nith estuary. This is the largest salt-marsh system in the region, covering about 5,500ha, but there is a moderate area at Kirkconnell Merse west of the Nith, and two smaller patches higher up the estuary towards Dumfries. Farther south, towards Southerness Point there is a small area near Carsethorn, and then westwards are patches at Mersehead, Rough Firth, Auchencairn Bay, Manxman's Lake, Kirkcudbright and Fleet Bay. The second large system is at the head of Wigtown Bay, around the estuaries of the Cree and Bladnoch, and there is a final patch at the head of Luce Bay.

The vegetation of these saltings is much the same as that of the south Solway marshes, such as Rockcliffe, Burgh and Longnewton. The main pioneer sand and mud coloniser is the common saltmarsh-grass, which forms individual radiating patches from establishment of seeds. These grow centrifugally, trapping increasing amounts of sediment as they expand, and gradually coalesce to form a continuous sward at a higher level (community SM10). Where there is a higher proportion of clay and silt compared with sand, as in the estuaries west of the Nith, glassworts and common and lax-flowered sea lavenders also act as pioneer colonists of the bare sediment (SM8, SM10). Perhaps because of these finer sediments, the invasive cord-grass of southern England has appeared in the early stages of marsh formation on these estuaries (SM6), and now occupies over half the salt-marsh area in Rough Firth, Auchencairn Bay and Fleet Bay (Solway Firth Partnership, 1996). It is a vigorously competitive plant which soon suppresses other salt-marsh pioneers, and its spread on the north Solway is a matter of some concern.

The early stages – where not dominated by cord-grass – are then invaded by sea arrow-grass, sea milkwort, thrift, sea plantain, annual sea-blite and sea-spurrey, to form an increasingly dense sward of salt-loving (halophytic) or salt-tolerant plants (SM13). As the ground level rises still higher through deposition of sand and silt during tidal inundation, red fescue, creeping bent and Gerard's rush colonise, and some of the earlier species in the succession decline (SM16). In places, hollows and channels are left amongst the developing marsh, and tend to deepen by water erosion of the sediment, to form salt-pans and creeks. Where grazing is light or absent, fleshy herbs such as scurvy-grass, sea-aster and, more locally, sea purslane form part of the marsh community (SM12, SM14), but where grazing is heavy they are mostly confined to the sides of creeks and ditches. Micro-successions may be renewed around these depressions and channels, which are the habitat of other species such as sea club-rush, common club-rush and saltmarsh flat-sedge (SM19). The inner marsh has abundant sea rush in places (SM18) and in Galloway, the blunt-flowered rush of fens is locally plentiful here in somewhat brackish conditions.

In places, as on Caerlaverock Merse, there are up to three banks, usually sloping and vegetated, and from 35 to 45cm high, forming distinct steps in the marsh level. These are repeated on the south Solway marshes across the estuary. They point to past cycles of erosion and renewed marsh-building, with the ground raised during the intervening period by the tilting of the land in relation to sea level – the isostatic changes which represent readjustments of the land surface following release from the massive load of ice during de-glaciation. The result of this elevation is that the recently accreted marsh never reaches the height of the old marsh, and the intervening bank is the worn-down remains of the erosion face, showing the change in levels. In other places, erosion is active again, destroying the newly formed marsh and eating back into the more mature stages, while yielding up the stabilised sediment to the estuary again. It caused the net loss of 93ha of merse at Caerlaverock between 1946 and 1973 (Rowe, 1978), and erosion has continued to exceed accretion in the subsequent period. Erosion tends to occur where the river channels move landwards and steepen the gradient between water and land. Above the old erosion banks are more mature grassland swards, in which some of the halophytes have been replaced by less salt-tolerant plants such as autumn hawkbit, smooth hawk's-beard, white clover, bird's-foot trefoil, meadow buttercup, glaucous sedge, common sedge, common and velvet bents (MG11). Red fescue usually remains abundant. Depending on the precise height of the ground above sea level and, hence, the frequency of tidal inundation, the halophytes extend a variable distance landwards; and they often occur towards the inner edge of the marsh along creeks.

The final stage in the succession, in which the mature marsh becomes invaded by scrub and trees to form woodland, does not really occur on this coast, for sea-wall construction has usually created an artificial inner margin to the salt marshes, beyond which is enclosed farmland 'reclaimed' from former merseland. Most of Preston Merse has been lost in this way. Perhaps the thickets of gorse that have colonised the inner edges of some marshes are the closest to this final stage. Places showing a transition to oakwood represent topographic gradients in which the land rises into higher, often steep ground, which has never in recent times been within the direct influence of the sea. Marshy ground and ditches sometimes occur at the inner marsh edges, and these tend to show brackish conditions, reflected in the presence of plants such as sea rush, sea club-rush, brooklime, hemlock water-dropwort, parsley water-dropwort, brackish water-crowfoot, beaked tasselweed, distant sedge, long-bracted sedge and false-fox sedge (S21). The common reed is a plant of brackish conditions, and beds of it flank the flats of the Nith estuary and the inner zone of salt marsh below Southwick Heughs, where the saline influence becomes reduced by freshwater inflows (S4). Prickly restharrow is a distinctive plant of the highest marsh and sea walls very locally.

The larger salt marshes are used as year-round grazings for cattle and sheep, which keep the sward mostly short or tussocky and tend to suppress taller plants, and floristic diversity is lost through dominance of grasses. Rotational turf-cutting to supply recreational greens is another activity on the more mature successional stages of saltings, where the vegetation approaches a neutral grassland.

Sand dunes

There are minor sand-dune ridges at Southerness Point and Sandyhills Bay, but by far the largest dune area is that at Torrs Warren (formerly sometimes known as Loddanree) at the head of Luce Bay, which extends over a 9km front, with a maximum width of 2km, and covers 800ha. This is a 'hindshore' dune system, developed above a beach well supplied with sand, and an onshore prevailing wind which drives the sand inland as a series of dune ridges or crescent-shaped dunes (Solway Firth Partnership, 1996). The sand is mainly siliceous and derived from windblow of fluvioglacial and marine beach deposits, but there is a small amount of shell sand towards the east end. The northern inner zone of the Warren was planted with Corsican, Scots and lodgepole pines by the Forestry Commission in the 1950s, and the rest is a Ministry of Defence weapons testing area, so that it is not a place where the public can wander at will.

The vegetation of Torrs Warren has been described by Idle & Martin (1975). At the seaward side there is a colonising fringe of oraches, especially frosted, followed by abundant sea rocket, with lesser amounts of prickly saltwort, sea sandwort, sea bindweed and sand couch, which build up a sandbank on the shore (SD2). This rises into the first dune ridge, thickly grown with marram tussocks (SD6), beyond which there is a complex of further unstable marram dunes (yellow dunes) with blow-outs, and stabilised sand of gentler relief with herbs, mosses and lichens (grey dunes). These contain series of hollows of varying wetness (slacks). The vascular flora is quite rich, with at least 260 species.

With its mainly non-calcareous sand, Torrs Warren is one of the largest acidic dune systems in Britain. While there is local abundance of moderately base-demanding plants such as bloody cranesbill (Fig. 39) and carline thistle

FIG 39. Bloody cranesbill, locally abundant on sand dunes and cliff slopes. Near the Mull, Wigtownshire.

where shell sand occurs, the bulk of the flora is composed of calcifuge or tolerant species. The closed communities have dense, tall red fescue, common bent, lady's bedstraw, restharrow, germander speedwell, bird's-foot trefoil, wood sage and creeping thistle. Sand sedge is locally plentiful. In places the sward is more open, with wild thyme, English stonecrop, sheep's fescue, sand sedge and the dune form of wild pansy; and mosses are important in stabilising the sand – *Tortula ruraliformis*, *Rhytidiadelphus triquetrus*, *R. squarrosus*, *Racomitrium canescens*, *Pseudoscleropodium purum* and *Dicranum scoparium*. These are replaced locally by lichens, notably *Cladonia arbuscula*, *C. portentosa* and *Peltigera canina*. Communities SD7, SD8, SD9 and SD12 cover these types. With increasing maturity of the dunes there is change to ling and bell heather dominance, often with dense lichen carpets, but also varying amounts of bracken, giving a type of lowland heath (H20). Stag's-horn clubmoss and shepherd's-cress are two characteristic plants of the acidic sand of these inner dunes, some of which reach a height of 15m.

The slacks vary from seasonally moist hollows to permanently wet pools, and the Clayshant Pools at the southwest end are two metres deep with emergent and fringing vegetation. The driest types have Yorkshire fog, creeping and common bents, vernal grass, tormentil, creeping buttercup and silverweed. Creeping willow is abundant in many as a low shrub layer (SD15), and sand sedge acts a slack pioneer in places. Uncommon herbs are lesser wintergreen, lesser twayblade and coralroot orchid. With increasing moisture, marsh pennywort, marsh cinquefoil, lesser spearwort, marsh St John's-wort, greater bird's-foot trefoil, flying bent, bulbous rush, common spike-rush, common sedge and cross-leaved heath appear (SD17). The more permanent pools, which occur especially towards the southwest end of the Warren, have poor fen communities with bottle sedge, white sedge, star sedge, bogbean, skullcap, marsh St John's-wort, lesser marshwort, sharp-flowered rush and jointed rush (M6). Shore-weed is an unusual dune plant, growing in the shallow water of pool edges. Plants of richer fen appear in places, such as bladder sedge, bulrush, common club-rush, mare's-tail, hemlock water-dropwort, parsley water-dropwort, cowbane, lesser water parsnip, nodding bur-marigold, water dock and greater tussock sedge (S27). The yellow water-lily grows in permanent pools. Bog myrtle is locally abundant and there is patchy invasion of grey and eared willows to give patches of tall scrub, in which royal fern grows (W1).

Uncommon plants of Torrs Warren, mostly in unstable sand or grey dunes, are sea spurge, Portland spurge, lesser meadow-rue, fleabane, heath pearlwort, bird's-foot, spring vetch, smooth cat's-ear and sticky storksbill (the only southern Scottish locality for the last two).

Shingle beaches

These occur widely around the flatter shores of the Galloway coast, especially in Wigtownshire, but the pebbles commonly have some admixture of sand. Raised shingle beaches occur along much of the east shore of Luce Bay, from Burrow Head to Auchenmalg Bay. There are also good examples at Myroch Point on the east side of the Rhins, where the characteristic flora is well developed. Close to tide level there may be much sea sandwort, sea campion, thrift, sea mayweed and oraches – spear-leaved, Babington's, frosted and common. Higher up the beach is a non-halophyte community, with mats of English stonecrop and wild thyme colonising the stones (Fig. 40), along with taller plants such as lady's bedstraw, rock-rose, bird's-foot trefoil, kidney vetch and wild onion. Communities SD1, SD2 and SD3 are represented here. At Myroch Point there is abundant spring squill and compact low patches of wood vetch in an unusual habitat (Fig. 41), and meadow saxifrage is occasionally present. Burnet rose is an attractive feature of the upper shingle, with its nearly prostrate carpets studded with creamy-white flowers in late spring (Fig. 42). Sea cabbage is widespread, though in varying quantity, and in places there is abundance of sea radish and sea beet. A plant which is surprisingly scarce on the Scottish Solway shore, considering its abundance along most of the Cumbrian coast opposite is the Isle of Man cabbage.

FIG 40. English stonecrop, common on shore shingle and maritime rocks on both the southwest and northeast coasts. Monreith, Wigtownshire

FIG 41. Wood vetch forming tight prostrate patches on shingle, at Myroch Point, Wigtownshire.

FIG 42. Burnet rose forms dense patches on coastal shingle, as at Myroch Point, Wigtownshire.

Sea holly and horned poppy are also less plentiful than on the Cumbrian beaches.

An uncommon species of these shores is the handsome oyster-plant, with its blue-grey leaves and deep blue flowers. It is known from several places in Galloway and Ayrshire, having evidently recovered ground after earlier decline. A northern strandline species, it flourishes on the shores of the Arctic Ocean, and its recovery has been linked to a period of colder springs which began around 1960, but has since fizzled out. Winter storms can destroy colonies by shifting the beach material, so that it has to be able to re-establish from seed. Whether it will manage to cope with warming climate in this region will be interesting to see.

Some shingle beaches have flat, dwarfed patches of blackthorn, and thickets of the plant with normal tall shrub stature (w22) occupy the tops of some sites. There are also thickets of gorse and bramble (w23), and at Rascarrel Bay is a tall scrub of hazel and grey willow. The north Solway shingle beaches are a significant part of the British total, and an important conservation feature.

Rocky shores

Intertidal rocky shores are extensive on the outer north Solway between Southerness Point and the Mull of Galloway, and occur around Loch Ryan and between Ballantrae and Girvan, but much of the west coast of the Rhins is sea cliff falling into fairly deep water. The shores are usually of boulders with occasional bedrock outcrops, and their exposure to wave action varies greatly according to situation. There is usually a clear vertical zonation of communities according to the gradient of submergence. The *Solway Firth Review* (Solway Firth Partnership, 1996) recognises six main zones. Beginning with the maximum inundation by the tides is a floating kelp canopy with the rock beneath encrusted with coralline red algae, and plentiful barnacles. Other red algae are frequent among the kelp, and brown seaweeds occur on the more exposed shores. Rock-pools occur frequently, and their surfaces are encrusted with coralline algae and grown with a turf of other red algae, both filamentous and foliose, while animals include periwnkles, top-shells and limpets. The beadlet anemone is often common in pits and crevices.

On moderately exposed shores the next zone is one with floating growths of serrated wrack, with coralline red algae forming crusts over much of the rock surface, and overlying this a turf of red algae extending up the shore under overhangs and in crevices. Associated animals are barnacles, dog-whelks and limpets, while crevices have small mussels and molluscs. Mid-shore bedrock and boulders have some of the preceding species, but bladder wrack and knotted

FIG 43. Lichen community on shore rocks at Myroch Point, Wigtownshire.

wrack become abundant, with the green algae *Ulva lactuca* and *Enteromorpha* spp. Barnacles *Semibalanus balanoides* are dominant and edible mussels common. Above this, at the top of the intertidal zone, are growths of the brown seaweeds channelled wrack and spiral wrack, with periwinkles and the lichen *Verrucaria maura*. With increased exposure to wave action, *Verrucaria* and the periwinkle *Littorina saxatilis* increase and the wracks decrease. On exposed shores, a band of the barnacle *Chthamalus montagui* is present. Finally, above high-tide level is a splash zone, which widens vertically as the exposure to wave action increases. It is characterised by the colourful lichens *Verrucaria maura* (black), *Caloplaca marina* (orange), *Xanthoria parietina* (yellow) and *Lecanora atra* (grey) (Fig. 43).

Sea cliffs and slopes

Starting at the eastern end, the cliffs begin across the Southwick Burn at Caulkerbush, overlooking the RSPB reserve at Mersehead. They are at first low, rather broken and well wooded with rather scrubby oaks (Fig. 44), though the detached stack known as Lot's Wife is a distinctive feature along the section called Southwick Heughs. Southwest of Sandyhills Bay there are higher and steeper faces at Port Ling and Port o' Warren. Then, across Auchencairn Bay, the abrupt 70m headland of Balcary Point begins a long line of sea cliff that extends to the eastern entrance to Kirkcudbright Bay, with a few breaks in its continuity where inland streams have cut valleys down to the coast. West of the bay the cliffs resume again at the island of Little Ross and the mainland peninsula of Meikle Ross, and there is another section between Brighouse Bay and Meggerland Point. West of Fleet Bay there is a final Stewartry line of cliff, partly grown with wind-pruned oakwood at Ravenshall, but beyond this the coast flattens into the Cree estuary, with flats and salt marshes, at the head of Wigtown Bay.

The east side of the Machars in Wigtownshire has low wooded coastal scarps from Innerwell to Eggerness Point, but sea cliffs begin south of Sliddery Point and stretch with a few breaks round the tip of the peninsula at Burrow Head to St Ninian's Cave. There is then a stretch of mainly broken slopes to Cairndoon, but another cliff section occurs from there to near Monreith, while near the head of Luce Bay the Mull of Sinniness forms an isolated cliff headland. On the east side of the Rhins of Galloway fronting Luce Bay, sea cliffs do not begin until 2km north of the Mull of Galloway, but they occupy almost the whole length of the west side from the Mull to Milleur Point in the north, and broken rocks extend round into Loch Ryan, with a further cliff at Clachan Heughs. From the boundary at Galloway Burn, most of the south Ayrshire coast up to Ardwell Bay is bounded by sea cliffs or rocky slopes, though with a sizeable break at Ballantrae Bay.

FIG 44. Hanging oakwoods, willow scrub and shore habitats at Southwick Heughs, near Caulkerbush, Kirkcudbrightshire. Scottish Wildlife Trust reserve.

FIG 45. Steep sea cliffs falling into deep water at the Mull of Galloway, Wigtownshire. RSPB reserve.

In Galloway these cliffs are mostly formed of sedimentary Ordovician or Silurian rocks, with an outcrop of Scottish Calciferous Sandstones from Rascarrel to Netherlaw Point, but in Ayrshire they are composed mainly of lavas and other igneous rocks. The result is to produce substrates that tend to base-richness, as shown by the plant communities that have developed. Many of the sea cliffs drop into deep water and on exposed headlands such as the Mull of Galloway are subject to strongly saline conditions, with spray-influenced crests (Fig. 45). Elsewhere, they have a shore exposed at low tide or a permanent undercliff, which may be walked, to view them from below. In places they are relatively sheltered, especially in deep inlets and bays, and here woodland or scrub may occur close to sea level, with herbaceous vegetation showing little influence of salt water. Many have caves, and some of those accessible from land were once noted smugglers' hideaways, such as Dirk Hatteraick's Cave at Ravenshall.

Steers (1973) uses the term fossil cliff for many of those which lie above raised beach platforms and are set back landwards at varying distances from the present sea. In common with many of our cliff coasts elsewhere, agricultural intensification has pushed the enclosed farmland ever closer to the edge, and in many places there is only the narrowest of uncultivated cliff-top zones along which one can walk. Extensive areas of heath are few and mostly found on steep slopes rising above the sea.

Cliffs washed by the sea have salt-tolerant plants, at least along their lower parts. Above the level of the algal communities within the uppermost splash zone are those of lichens, showing the colourful zonation described under rocky shores, above. There is then a zone of vascular halophytes with thrift, sea campion, common scurvy-grass, red fescue, sea plantain and stag's-horn plantain (MC1, MC2). This extends over the top of spray-drenched headlands, to form a colourful display in the spring (Fig. 46). Sea spleenwort is plentiful in sheltered crevices and caves. Within this zone are rarer plants such as rock samphire, rock sea-spurrey and rock sea-lavender. Golden samphire grows on the upper rocks of the Mull of Galloway, its most northerly British station. Ground much affected by seabird droppings has rather few species, but abundant scurvy-grass, sea mayweed, spear-leaved orache and sorrel (MC7). Sheltered faces are often grown with sheets of ivy.

On the tops of exposed headlands such as the Mull, the halophyte swards pass into heath of short ling and bell heather with bracken (H20), or dense grassland with cock's-foot, Yorkshire fog, red fescue, bents, perennial rye-grass, bearded couch, timothy and mat-grass and a variety of dicotyledonous herbs, including yarrow, sorrel, cat's-ear, smooth hawk's-beard, white clover, lady's bedstraw,

FIG 46. Dense beds of thrift and sea campion on spray-washed headland at the Mull of Galloway, Wigtownshire.

devil's-bit scabious and ribwort plantain (MC9). Where the soil is thinner there is a shorter turf with red and sheep's fescues, wild thyme, bird's-foot trefoil, harebell, sea mouse-ear, and often some of the cliff-face halophytes. In some localities this sward is coloured blue at the end of May with abundance of spring squill (MC8) (Fig. 47). Bare, soily places and dry rocks have abundant English stonecrop and on basic substrates there are also biting and white stonecrops. Where sheltered slopes occur above the cliffs or between buttresses, halophyte swards with thrift and sea campion (MC10) give way to a taller herbaceous community with wild carrot, burnet saxifrage, lady's bedstraw, yarrow, kidney vetch, agrimony, restharrow, carline thistle, common centaury and bloody cranesbill (MC11). The pretty purple milk-vetch (Fig. 48) is plentiful in this community or in the cliff-edge grass heaths in several places, in one of the few western occurrences of an otherwise markedly eastern British plant. Meadow saxifrage grows profusely on steep faces and banks on some cliffs, and rock-rose is often plentiful, while other local plants of the sheltered cliff slopes are columbine, long-stalked cranesbill, wood vetch, narrow-leaved everlasting-pea and wild liquorice. Professor Balfour found the last species, wild basil, gromwell, sea wormwood, sand-leek and crow garlic on the rocky coast of Kirkcudbright in 1843: all still occur there sparingly (Stewart, 1987). Wet seepages down steep

FIG 47. Spring squill is a notable plant of grassy shores and cliff tops on the Galloway coast. Myroch Point, Wigtownshire.

FIG 48. Purple milk-vetch is abundant in the cliff-top turf of some Galloway headlands. (John Mitchell)

slopes and broken rocks have tussocks of black bog-rush, with a variety of sedges and rushes, grass of Parnassus and bog pimpernel.

Several markedly southern plants have unexpected occurrences in these semi-maritime habitats on sheltered Galloway sea cliffs. The very rare small restharrow of limestone headlands in Devon and south Wales grows in two places on the rocky western side of the Rhins of Galloway, in by far the most northerly of its very few British localities. During survey for the first Botanical Atlas the Bithynian vetch was found in two places on rocky bluffs near Burrow Head, again its most northerly and quite isolated station. Wild celery reaches its northern limit in the Mull area, and ivy broomrape does likewise as a native at Burrow Head. Perennial flax has long been known from the cliff coast of Brighouse Bay near Kirkcudbright. It is otherwise an eastern plant with its nearest localities on the Shap Carboniferous limestone in Cumbria, and then the Magnesian Limestone of County Durham, where it reaches a limit slightly farther north. Yellow vetch occurs in at least five places on sheltered sea cliffs along the north Solway coast, far from its nearest native colonies on shingle beaches of the Essex–Suffolk coast, though supposedly alien inland occurrences bridge the gap (Preston *et al.*, 2002). At the base of sea cliffs and in the brackish transition zone below are several colonies of the rare dotted sedge. A surprising find in 1976 was the thin-spiked wood-sedge growing near Lot's Wife, presumably in the wind-pruned woodland there. Pellitory-of-the-wall has a cliff station hereabouts.

There are also a few northern plants on the sea cliffs. Roseroot is mainly a mountain plant, but commonly descends almost to sea level on sea cliffs in the Highlands, and does so at several places on the Galloway and Ayrshire coast. Lovage, a more widespread coastal plant in the Highlands, also reaches its southern British limit on the Galloway coast. The most notable northerner is the rare purple oxytropis which, with its purple-red flowers and silky, silvery leaves, is one of our most beautiful wild plants. Only known in Scotland, mostly on coastal scarps and cliffs in Ross-shire and Sutherland, but also on a few inland mountains, the Mull of Galloway is its most southerly British locality. Formerly recorded from several sites in this area, it is said to be only just hanging on here. Heathy ground above the cliffs at Dunman has an isolated colony of chickweed wintergreen, a plant of boreal woodland and upland heaths in the Highlands. Spring sandwort is a plant of upland limestone and lead-mine spoil in northern England, while sticky catchfly occurs on scattered outcrops of basic igneous rock at low levels in Scotland and Wales. Both grow on the screes and cliffs of the Colvend coast, but also have inland stations in the region (Chapter 5). The rare holy grass grows below cliffs on the Stewartry coast where freshwater seepages flow into fringing salt marsh.

As a point of phytogeographical interest, none of these southern and northern rarities occurs on sea cliffs of the Cumbrian coast, which also lack more salt-tolerant species such as golden samphire, rock sea-spurrey and spring squill. The Galloway sea cliffs where most of these plants occur tend to face south, which may give a warmth factor, as well as favourable geology and soils, to account for this floral richness, at least as regards southern species. Navelwort has a curious distribution: it occurs on the south Ayrshire coast and is abundant on Ailsa Craig, but is otherwise only on a wall near Balcary Point (where it has been known for many years), and far inland in two localities in the far west of Dumfries, one of which is not regarded as native (Preston *et al.*, 2002).

In many places, especially in sheltered situations, vegetation development has progressed to scrub or woodland. Gorse and blackthorn are the most notable tall shrubs, forming thickets locally along the upper part of cliff slopes, though hawthorn and hazel are quite common also. Semi-prostrate growths of juniper fringe the top edge along many of the cliffs and scarp slopes on the Rinns (Mearns, 2001). The woodland is especially of oak, and often shows marked wind-shaping of the trees by the fierce blasts that sweep up from the sea. Good examples occur at Southwick Heughs and Ravenshall, but there are oakwood fringes along the lower coastal scarps in several places, such as that between Innerwell and Garlieston. The oaks are often thickly grown with ivy, marking the absence of grazing. The field layer is usually dominated by great woodrush, with abundant bluebells and red campion (w11), but the full range of communities of the inland oakwoods is to be seen, in one place or another. Where the soil is more basic, ash–hazel stands with their richer field layer take over, and on moist clayey soils there is locally a distinctive community with hemp agrimony, pendulous sedge, great horsetail, hart's tongue and soft shield-fern (w9). A notable fern of steep, rocky banks in these woods is southern polypody, the rarest and most base-demanding of the three *Polypodium* species now recognised. It is the one most prone to variation, with forms once recognised as varieties *serratum* and *cambricum*.

Shady rocks and rills on the Galloway coast support some of the distinctive Atlantic mosses and liverworts that otherwise belong mainly to inland woods and ravines (Chapter 4). The calcicole *Marchesinia mackaii* has several localities, and other noteworthy species are *Frullania tereriffae, F. microphylla* and *Lophocolea fragrans*, while *Porella obtusata* grows on dry, sun-exposed rocks. Quite recently the moss *Fissidens rivularis* was found on wet rocks near Creetown: it occurs mainly in southwest England and Wales.

There are other coastal habitats which are difficult to classify. One such is the small and low offshore islands in Kirkcudbright, usually with a rocky or even cliff-girt shore but a grassy or scrubby centre. Rough and Hestan Islands south of Dalbeattie, the Little Ross in Kirkcudbright Bay, and Barlocco and Ardwall islands off Gatehouse of Fleet are all much of a size, in the range 15–25ha. The many lengths of raised beach platform and their variable fringe of fossil cliffs should perhaps be considered as another habitat, of only semi-maritime type. The main road along the west side of the Machars runs along one such platform for about 15km. Some mainly western plants flourish in these semi-maritime situations, such as sheep's-bit and English stonecrop.

THE FAUNA OF SOUTHWEST COASTAL HABITATS

Breeding birds

The larger salt marshes at Caerlaverock, Kirkconnell and Wigtown are important for their nesting birds, though some of these have declined in numbers in recent years. Oystercatchers varied in numbers, but lapwings and redshanks bred at fairly high density, and there were breeding dunlin up to at least 1960. The first two species make quite open nests on the short, close-cropped turf, and the second two in taller grass tussocks where the nests are well hidden. Lapwings were once far more numerous than today and, even by 1910, Gladstone said the bird was decreasing all over Dumfriesshire. In 1888, Robert Service recorded that one person had collected 'to his own hand in one day, forty-eight dozen Lapwing eggs [i.e. c. 145 clutches] on Blackshaw [Caerlaverock].' There were scattered pairs of snipe. Small numbers of lesser black-backed gulls bred at Caerlaverock up to at least 1960, along with a few pairs of herring gulls, the odd pair of great black-backed gulls, and small numbers of black-headed gulls. There was also a small colony of common terns. Of these species, only oystercatchers, lapwings, redshanks and snipe remain, in reduced numbers, at Caerlaverock: in summer 2000 there were 19, 40, 33 and 4 pairs, respectively, of these species. The propensity of the Merse here to flooding by high tides in the breeding season may have had a discouraging effect on some birds. Skylarks remain numerous (121 pairs in 2000) though less so than formerly, and there are a few meadow pipits. A full count of the breeding birds of the Dumfries & Galloway merselands in 2000 gave oystercatcher 126 pairs, lapwing 74, redshank 85, curlew 13, snipe 7 and skylark 358 (SNH & RSPB unpublished reports).

The breeding birds of sand dunes and shingle beaches are rather few. Ringed plovers are widespread and even cling to beaches that are constantly disturbed by passers-by. The New Atlas (Gibbons et al., 1993) shows a rather low breeding density and there is not a large population, but probably at least 100 pairs attempt to breed annually. Oystercatchers are similarly widely spread and also nest on rocky coasts, where outcrops and little stacks provide nesting places safer from trampling human feet than on the level shore. On my first visit to Southerness, in 1947, both oystercatchers and shelduck were numerous in the area, with many of the 'sea-pies' nesting on coastal farmland and pairs or singles of the ducks continually flying to and fro between the sands and their inland nesting places in rabbit burrows. I believe there are fewer shelduck these days, though it remains a common species along the Solway coast.

The terns are notable birds of the low coasts, but with the habit of capriciously shifting their breeding places in an unpredictable way between years. Common terns have bred in many places along the coast of southwest Scotland, but in fluctuating numbers. Thom (1986) gave 350 pairs for Kirkcudbright and 50 pairs for Wigtown in 1969–70, but 250+ and 200 pairs during 1975–83. The Kirkcudbright figure included an unknown group breeding inland, while Wigtown had an additional 150+ inland pairs during the later period. R. Stokoe, A. Barton and E. Blezard saw several hundred pairs nesting on the top of Hestan Island in 1956, but recent colonies are of only modest size, with up to 50 pairs. Paton & Pike (1929) said that several hundred pairs bred near Ballantrae on the south Ayrshire coast. Much smaller numbers of arctic terns are often associated with the other species, but sometimes they breed in separate groups; Loch Ryan is one of their best stations.

Sandwich terns shift around this coast: the history of an earlier colony known to J. G. Gordon on the dunes of Torrs Warren is now lost, and recent breeding records have been elsewhere. In 1956 about 40 pairs nested amidst the large common tern colony on formerly cultivated ground on top of Hestan Island. The 1968–72 Atlas (Sharrock, 1976) showed breeding in four 10km squares, but the New Atlas in only two, one in Wigtown and the other in Ayr. The Scottish Bird Report for 1999 notes that 70 pairs were at Loch Ryan, though only 28 nests were seen and few young were reared. A few pairs of little terns have long had a tenuous foothold on this coast, but were fairly constant to their chosen haunts. The New Atlas showed them down to a single square from the previous three. A pair or two of roseate terns have been suspected of nesting now and then, but breeding has never been proved, and the species is regarded as only a rare summer visitor to the Galloway coast.

All six of our breeding gulls are well represented on the southwest coast. The herring gull is the most numerous, with the sea cliffs as its main habitat, and breeds along almost all of the cliff coast. It nests most numerously on the more broken upper sections, but spills over onto the grassy cliff tops in places. Thom (1986) gave 5,200 pairs for the Stewartry and 1,070 for Wigtown in 1969–70, but probably most of the Ayrshire figure of 1,160 pairs belonged to Ailsa Craig. Lesser black-backed gulls prefer less precipitous situations and one of the two largest recent colonies, numbering 1,500 pairs in 1987 (Watson, 1988) is on the promontory of Almorness Point south of Dalbeattie, which is rocky in places but has no real cliffs (Fig. 49). Herring gulls also breed there, mixed with the lesser black-backs, in smaller numbers. The other large colony of these two species, which also has great black-backs and common gulls, to a total approaching 2,000 pairs, is on the Murray Isles in the entrance to Fleet Bay. The much smaller colony of lessers on the saltings of Caerlaverock Merse also had a few herring gulls for company. Both of these species have taken to nesting on rooftops in Dumfries (Norman, 2001). Great black-backed gulls are widespread along the rocky coasts, occurring in scattered pairs which prefer rock stacks for nesting places but will also breed on grassy islands and saltings. Thom gave 60 pairs for Kirkcudbright and 45 for Wigtown and Ayr combined in 1969–70. The common gull is not a cliff-nester and prefers the grassy offshore islands for its breeding sites. These have long included the Isles of Fleet, where numbers had built up to over 100 pairs by 1986 (Watson, 1988). On the coast, black-headed gulls have nested only on the salt marshes at Caerlaverock, Mersehead and elsewhere, in widely fluctuating numbers.

FIG 49. Mixed colony of lesser black-backed and herring gulls at Almorness Point, Kirkcudbrightshire.

Considering the extent of sea cliff on the Galloway and south Ayrshire coast, it is perhaps surprising that breeding seafowl colonies are not larger and more numerous than is the case. The relatively shallow waters of the Solway Firth may not give an optimum food supply, while in the Firth of Clyde the great island rock of Ailsa Craig draws the bulk of the population. The biggest cliff-nesting colony in our district is on the bare, conical 20m rock of the Big Scare (Scar) in Luce Bay, some 10km east-north-east of the Mull of Galloway (see Fig. 29). This is the only breeding place of gannets in the region, where Robert Service first found two nests in 1883. There was then a lapse until 1939, when six pairs were found nesting by J. M. McWilliam and Lord David Stuart. The colony then grew steadily, to 40–50 pairs in 1943, 134 in 1953, 240–300 in 1965 and 437 in 1968 (Young, 1968). The latest count is for 770 pairs in 1984 (Thom, 1986). Kittiwakes nest on the Big Scare (175 pairs in 1968) and the Mull of Galloway (a peak of 577 nests in 1984, followed by decline). There are smaller numbers at Port Mona, Balcary Head, and several other sites. Guillemots have a similar distribution, with the biggest colonies at the Mull (2,140 birds in 1999) and Big Scare (1,505 pairs in 1943, 15,000 birds in 1983, 3,000 in 1987, but only 700 in 1989: Dickson, 1992), and smaller colonies at Meikle Ross, Balcary and Port Ling. With them are razorbills in smaller numbers (358 birds at the Mull in 1999), nesting singly in crevices and crannies instead of in jostling throngs on open shelves. Black guillemots are scattered and usually in isolated pairs, preferring the shelter of slabs on undercliffs, though there was formerly a group nesting in drain-holes of the Portpatrick harbour. Puffins have a rather tenuous foothold on this coast now, perhaps still breeding at the Mull and Big Scare. Fulmars have spread all along the main cliffs, but are not in large numbers.

The southwest coast is a breeding stronghold of the cormorant, though the species moves about and fluctuates in numbers, sometimes as a result of persecution by fishermen. In Kirkcudbright a favourite breeding cliff at Port o' Warren was known locally as 'the dookers' bing', but the site was deserted for many years. The birds have been present again in recent years, with numbers varying between 100 and 200 pairs. Another colony of up to 100 pairs has moved between Balcary Point and the Orroland cliffs while, farther west, the Meikle Ross and Little Ross are alternative locations for another group of up to 50 pairs. The Isles of Fleet have a fourth colony, with 46 nests in 2000. In Wigtownshire, World War II Mulberry Harbours at Rigg Bay near Garlieston were colonised: 160 nests were seen in 1959 and 61 in 1967, with another 47 on adjoining low cliffs. A similar structure in the Piltanton estuary had 29 nests in 1968. The Big Scare colony declined from 71 nests in 1939 to 10 in 1968, as the gannets took over their ground. Smaller numbers, from 5 to 30+ pairs, have bred at Cruggleton cliffs, Burrow Head, the Mull, Killantringan near Portpatrick and Currarie Port near Ballantrae. Data are from Smith (1969) and Norman (2001). The inland nesting colony at Castle and Mochrum Lochs is mentioned in Chapter 6. Shags nest widely along the cliff coast of the southwest (Fig. 50), with a total of around 150 pairs in 1970, mostly in Wigtown (Thom, 1986). There were 24 pairs on the Big Scare in 1968, but a large colony at the Mull, with c. 150 pairs in 1953, had declined seriously by 1970.

Ravens breed widely on the cliffs of the southwest coast, though the population has fluctuated during the last half-century. Lot's Wife at Southwick has occasionally had nesting pairs, but Douglas Hall is usually the eastern limit. In the Stewartry there have probably been at least 11–12 territories, with pairs spaced at a minimum distance of 2.5km. Wigtown has more scope for the species, in its long frontage of cliff on the west side of the Rhins, and a total of 29 territories is a fair estimate – 20 in the Rhins, 9 in the Machars (Dickson, 1992). The south Ayrshire cliffs have held at least another five, giving a total of 45–46 pairs. During the peregrine survey of the southwest coast in 1961–2, raven pairs were seen in at least 27 territories, and of these, 21 certainly bred (R. Stokoe). But at least ten formerly regular territories were not examined, so that the population could have numbered up to 37 pairs. In 1974–5 all but four territories

FIG 50. Shag: a widespread breeding bird of cliff coast in the southwest; also numerous at St Abbs Head.

were visited, and at least 19 were found occupied, with 13 definite nests, so that the maximum population was no more than 23 pairs (M. Marquiss). The decline had deepened by 1981, when all but one territory was examined and only 12 pairs located, of which 10 may have bred. This represented a drop of at least 50 per cent since 1961–2, and was accompanied by a decrease of 66 per cent in breeding success of the remainder (Mearns, 1983). There has since been a recovery, with 33 pairs holding territory in 1994, of which at least 18 bred successfully (C. Rollie, unpublished). The causes of this population fluctuation are discussed in Chapter 8.

While there are historic breeding places of peregrines on this coast, there was never a reliable survey to determine the total population before this crashed during the organochlorine pesticide episode of 1956–63. Service (1901) said that 8–12 pairs usually nested on the Scottish side of the Solway Firth. If he meant from Port Ling to the Mull of Galloway, his figure agrees closely with the pre-1960 estimate of ten pairs for this stretch of the coast. There would then be another ten or so for the Rhins and three more for the Ayrshire section: a total of 23 pairs for the whole southwest seaboard – roughly half the number of ravens. In 1961–2, survey was incomplete, but only four pairs were found in 16 territories, and only one of these was successful (R. Stokoe). Numbers picked up slowly from 1970, and by 1978 there were ten pairs, eight of them successful, in 17 territories (R. Mearns). By 1981 the population was almost back to normal, with 21 territories occupied, and by 1991 there were no fewer than 32 pairs, the highest number ever known on the coast of southwest Scotland (South-west Scotland Raptor Study Group).

The individual pairs of ravens and peregrines tended to move their nesting places within their territories over a period of years. The bigger rock faces were preferred, but some nests were on cliffs of less than 30m, in sheltered places protected from heavy seas. Both species were subjected to keeper persecution in places adjoining lowland pheasant and partridge shoots. After the female parent was shot at the Balcary eyrie in 1922, the male peregrine successfully reared the three young to flying age on his own, but all the eyases were taken into captivity (E. Blezard). These coastal falcons fed especially on pigeons, including those breeding on the same cliffs, and on birds from the farmed hinterland, but some of them took a good many seabirds.

The cliff-nesting pigeons originally were rock doves, but these were increasingly diluted in stock by homing pigeons gone feral and returned to the haunts of their ancestors – the one was derived from the other by breeding in captivity, and both share the same scientific name. Ernest Blezard noted numerous stray homing pigeons were noted with the rock doves at Balcary even in 1922. Birds showing the plumage typical of the true wild rock dove were still to be seen on this coast up to at least 1956, but in more recent times virtually the whole population has become mongrel. Ledges in deep caves are the nesting places of these assorted rock pigeons, which have an extended breeding season. Stock doves nest in small numbers on some of the sea cliffs.

Jackdaws have cliff-breeding colonies in many places, and forage mainly on the adjoining farmland. There is no evidence that they were responsible for the disappearance of the chough, which once had a stronghold on the Wigtownshire coast, as has sometimes been asserted. Gray (1871) named the Mull of Galloway and Burrow Head as 'at one time inhabited by considerable numbers of these birds', but said that they were currently much reduced there, though still around Portpatrick and on the south Ayrshire coast. He mentioned that five broods were seen on cliffs to the north of Portpatrick and two to the south, but did not give the year. Breeding by choughs continued well into the twentieth century, and in 1907 J. G. Gordon saw a nest with five eggs in the roof of a cave near Dunskey old castle, with another four birds in the area and a further nine in the Portpatrick area. They were believed to nest along the Rhins into the 1930s before finally fading out (Watson, 1988), and a pair or two still bred on the south Ayrshire coast shortly before this (Paton & Pike, 1929). In 1988 a pair returned to nest in a typical cave site on a Galloway cliff (Fig. 51), and they have bred successfully in most years since then (C. Rollie, RSPB). This is the only mainland breeding pair in Scotland. Their disappearance from many earlier haunts is probably connected with the 'improvement' of farmland right up to the cliff edges, which has spoiled their feeding habitat.

Rock pipits remain widespread breeders along the southwest coast, where some nests are on sheer faces, but habitats on lower shores are also occupied. The twite is as much a bird of the south Ayrshire and Wigtown seaboard as of the inland moors nowadays, and Dickson (1992) reported several coastal breeding groups along the Rhins. Stonechats are frequent in the cliff-top heaths and steep vegetated slopes running down to the sea (Fig. 52). Small numbers of eiders nest along the rocky shores of the Firth of Clyde in Wigtown and South Ayrshire.

In 1922 Ernest Blezard was told by one of the Balcary gamekeepers, Peter Fitzsimon, that a pair of ospreys had nested (or attempted to nest) on a rock stack farther west along that coast a few years previously. As Ernest said, with the description of 'a white heid and blue legs', what else could it have been? Service (1901) said there were eyries of sea eagles at Burrow Head and the Mull of Galloway at the beginning of the nineteenth century, and Gray (1871) implied that this species still bred on the Wigtownshire coast when he wrote, but did not give details.

FIG 51. Nesting place of chough in cave of Wigtownshire sea cliffs. Shows folding of the Silurian strata.

FIG 52. Stonechat: a frequent bird of coastal heaths. (Bobby Smith)

Mammals, amphibians and reptiles

Many of the mammals present in inland areas also occur on the coast. Probably the most important is the otter, which has a major coastal niche on the upper Solway, and ranges the salt marshes. The *Solway Firth Review* states that this animal decreased on the inner Solway during the widespread crash in population during the 1960s and 70s, but remained widespread and little changed in numbers in the west. It is now generally numerous along this coast, and 97 per cent of sites surveyed in Dumfries & Galloway showed its presence. Breeding is known in Wigtown Bay, Luce Bay and at the Mull of Galloway, as well as at a variety of freshwater habitats within the coastal zone. Most of these Solway otters evidently move between the shore and the hinterland. On the coast, they hunt especially over rocky shores with a well-developed seaweed zone, extending down into kelp beds where there are fish and crustaceans. In freshwater habitats bordering the coast, otters concentrate on eels and coarse fish, plus salmonids, amphibians and birds. Holts on the coast are usually spaced 2–3km apart, and are in tree roots, reed-beds, rabbit holes, boulder crevices, wood piles, breakwaters, field and road drains. This southern Scottish otter population is an important source of animals re-colonising depleted areas of northern England.

Escapes from Galloway mink farms were one of the sources of the colonisation of Britain by this unwelcome predator. Mink spread all along the Scottish Solway and reached high density in places. It remains to be seen whether the flourishing otter will cause a decline in numbers and distribution of mink, as has been claimed elsewhere in the country. On the coast they hunt especially over rocky shores with boulders and rock-pools, backed by grassland, rough ground and woodland, and take a wider selection of prey than otters – though again mainly fish, crustaceans and birds. Foxes have dens on the inner reaches of the saltings, raised beaches and cliff slopes, and work the marshes for birds crippled and lost by wildfowlers. Rabbits occur on the inner parts of salt marshes and brown hares are sometimes frequent there. Water voles occur in some of the freshwater streams entering the Firth, and water shrews are also known here.

The natterjack toad (Fig. 53) is a notable amphibian of the inner Solway shore, where it breeds in freshwater pools and ditches either above high tide level on the merse hinterland and grazing marsh or where there is slight brackish influence. These are its most northerly occurrences in Britain, and the only ones in Scotland. Bridson (1978) gave population figures for 1976, but the Solway Firth Partnership (1996) have given a more recent detailed account of the animal here. The largest population is at Caerlaverock, where there are from high hundreds to low thousands of adults. Priestside Merse, Southerness, and the old ordnance factory at Powfoot also each have hundreds, the last site being heathland with ponds. These are larger than the several colonies on the Cumbrian Solway, but the combined Solway population amounts to about 10 per cent of the British

FIG 53. Natterjack toad in a Solway locality. (Bobby Smith)

total. The great crested newt, an Annex II species under the EU Habitats and Species Directive, also has important colonies in pools and ponds at the old explosives factory at Powfoot and elsewhere towards Gretna. It occurs also to the west at Southerness, Kirkcudbright, and several places on the Wigtown Machars (Beebee & Griffiths, 2000). The abundance of adders in Galloway extends to the sea cliffs, both on the crests and on the rough slopes running down to the shore. They are fond of basking on rocks, walls, ledges and banks in sunny places here, and it is as well to watch where you put your hands when venturing onto these places. Adders occur also on the inner parts of sand dunes, shingle beaches, and upper salt marshes. Common lizards are to be found frequently in this range of habitats.

The grey seal has hauling-out sites along the Scottish Solway, on rocky platforms and beaches in quiet places, especially on islands, and up to 150 animals have been counted at one time. The Scar Rocks are a regular haunt. Grey seals also frequent the Berwickshire coast, the animals coming from their breeding stronghold on the Farne Islands not far to the south. Of the cetaceans, only 12 species have been recorded since 1980 within 60km of the coast in the eastern Irish Sea (Solway Firth Partnership, 1996). Only three species are present throughout the year or recorded as annual visitors in the Solway Firth: harbour porpoise, bottlenose dolphin and common dolphin. The first two are, along with the grey seal and otter, Annex II species under the Habitats and Species Directive of the European Union, requiring special protection measures.

Fish and fisheries

Sea fishing is one of the oldest human activities on the Solway, and 130 marine fish species are recorded in the whole area (Solway Firth Partnership, 1996). The main fishing ports are at Annan, Kirkcudbright, the Isle of Whithorn and Drummore. Fish of commercial importance taken by inshore trawlers are demersal (living at or near the bottom of the sea) species: cod, whiting, plaice, dover sole, turbot, rays and dogfish. Shellfish fishing has become increasingly important, the main species being scallops, queen scallops, nephrops (scampi prawns), lobsters, brown shrimps, cockles and mussels. The pelagic fish herring, mackerel and sprat are also caught, but the landings include fish taken farther out in the Irish Sea. The largest tonnage in the total Solway catch (5,145 tonnes in 1991) was the cockle, but this huge increase from 1987 was the result of mechanical fishing, which was banned in 1994 to allow recovery of the depleted cockle stocks. The catch then declined to very low levels. The largest catch of fish by weight is of plaice (466 tonnes in 1987), but the high-value dover sole (41 tonnes in 1987) is an important item (*Solway Firth Review*). Kirkcudbright is the most important of the Scottish Solway ports in terms of catch value, though this has declined since 1991. Other marine fish include the flounder, sea bass, common goby, thick-lipped mullet and thin-lipped mullet.

The migratory salmon and sea trout are also caught by fixed stake nets and other kinds close inshore, but drift-netting has been banned on the Scottish side. Catches of both have declined in recent years, and the coastal fishery is blamed by freshwater anglers for reducing the numbers of these fish found in the rivers of southern Scotland. Both species occur in all the main rivers of the region, and penetrate to the headwaters unless access is prevented by insurmountable waterfalls or dams without fish passes. The Tweed is an especially famous salmon river, and rated among the best in Britain by anglers. The Atlantic salmon is now regarded as a threatened fish on the European scale, and is on Annex II of the Habitats and Species Directive. Also listed there are rare and endangered marine fish: the allis shad, twaite shad, river lamprey and sea lamprey, the first two occurring especially in the Cree estuary and Wigtown Bay. The sparling in the River Cree is one of only two Scottish populations, but is taken commercially and not regarded as endangered.

A potential conservation problem on the mud and sand flats is the digging out of invertebrates such as lugworms and ragworms for use as bait by shore anglers, as these are the important food items of some of the autumn and winter birds of the estuaries. Wildfowling is a major activity on the Solway shore, though the number of bird species which may be legally shot has been reduced considerably over the years, and the sport is quite heavily regulated both under the law and through voluntary arrangements between the shooters, most of whom belong to the British Association for Shooting and Conservation.

Insects

The coast, with its mild, sunny climate and prevalence of sun-exposed aspects, is the most productive of the major habitats for butterflies. The immigrant red admirals and painted ladies often turn up there in numbers, while most of the recent records of the clouded yellow are coastal (17+ on 17 June 2000, Richard and Barbara Mearns). The resident peacocks, small tortoiseshells, large, small and green-veined whites take advantage of the abundant flowers of the ungrazed maritime habitats. Sand dunes and cliff slopes, with their abundant violets and pansies as larval food-plants, are important for dark-green and small pearl-bordered fritillaries, while the luxuriant grassland beyond the last farm walls and fences provides the browns with plentiful breeding habitat. Cunningham (1951) said that half the female dark-green fritillaries in the Solway area were the dark form, subspecies *scotica*. The meadow brown, ringlet and small heath are widespread and common, while the grayling and wall brown are largely confined to these coastal locations in this region. Large skippers are widespread in grassy places by the sea and the much more local dingy skipper has its main occurrences there. Sheep's sorrel is common on acidic substrates, and accounts for the frequency of small coppers. Common blues are numerous wherever bird's-foot trefoil is abundant and many of the females have the beautiful deep blue uppersides typical of the subspecies *mariscolore*, which occurs in northwest Scotland and western Ireland. Another 'blue', the northern brown argus (Fig. 54) is widespread, with some large colonies, following the distribution of rock-rose, on which the larvae feed. The most elusive species is the small blue, and although there are several earlier coastal records, there are none after 1995. Its larval food-plant, the kidney vetch, is widespread along the shore, though seldom abundant. Some of the sheltered but sunny inlets and bays on the west side of the Rhins of Galloway are especially good habitat for these coastal butterflies.

Coastal habitats are quite productive for moths. Although its larval food-plant, ragwort, is common across the region, the cinnabar is confined to coastal localities here. The lime-speck pug is frequent at coastal sites, and the

FIG 54. Northern brown argus: its local distribution follows that of the larval food-plant, rock-rose. (Norman Tait)

chestnut-coloured carpet and juniper pug occur where there are cliff-top junipers, but the juniper carpet is rarer and not seen recently. The nationally scarce thrift clearwing moth, whose larvae mine the roots of thrift, is now known to be widespread along rocky sections of the Galloway coast, from Port o' Warren to the Mull and west side of the Rhins. The crescent dart has proved to be widespread and sometimes abundant on rocky sections of the Galloway coast, and the same is true of the scarce footman in similar places, pebbly shorelines and even salt marsh. Moths from three localities were identified as the northern footman. The northern rustic has several stations in rocky places and the least yellow underwing has been found at seven localities on the Dumfries & Galloway coast in open grassland with some scrub. Most of these records come from Richard and Barbara Mearns, who found the Rhins a good place for observing migrant butterflies and moths, including hummingbird hawks (at least 13 on 17 June 2000), silver Y and rush veneer. Half a century ago and more, Cunningham (1951) said the hummingbird hawk was common on the coast every year.

Torrs Warren is notable for its diverse insect fauna, especially Diptera and Coleoptera, and rates as a nationally important site for its water beetles, woodlice and grasshoppers. Nelson (1980) surveyed the invertebrates of Caerlaverock Merse and found that while these were quite diverse, they were mostly species widespread around the British coasts.

THE BERWICKSHIRE COAST

The northeast coast of the region is much shorter and less varied, lacking the flats, saltings and dunes of Aberlady Bay to the west and Holy Island to the southeast. Most of it is rocky, and its main feature is the fine range of cliffs extending, with a few breaks, from Lamberton just beyond the border to near Cockburnspath. Along the most spectacular section, from St Abbs Head to Fast Castle, the cliffs rise to 150m. From Siccar Point to Bilsdean they are lower and more broken, and from Torness Point to our boundary near Dunbar the coast is mostly flat, though with raised beach rock platforms, often sand-covered and cut in the Carboniferous Series. The geology of this cliff coast varies, with Scottish Carboniferous Limestone Series between Berwick and Burnmouth, then predominance of Silurian sediments, but with Lower Old Red Sandstone at Callercove and St Abbs village, and extrusive felsite of the same age at St Abbs Head. At Siccar Point is the famous unconformity between the Silurian and Carboniferous, first described by the pioneering geologist James Hutton in the late eighteenth century. The Silurian strata between Petticowick and Fast Castle show spectacular folding. Steers (1973) notes that all along this coast the shore platform is well developed, and the cliffs here are fossil, but in some places, as at St Abbs Head, they fall into deep water and are again under attack from the sea.

The rocks of this North Sea seaboard give mostly basic substrates, and the vegetation and flora of the cliffs and cliff tops is remarkably similar to that of the Galloway coast, though it lacks most of the rarities. The total vascular flora of the St Abbs nature reserve is rich, with over 360 species, though this includes wetland and other inland habitats besides the strictly maritime ones. The thrift and sea campion communities are well represented, and there are spring squill, purple milk-vetch and rock-rose in local abundance in the cliff-top grasslands and heaths. Northern plants include lovage, roseroot and spring sandwort, and species occurring only on this northeast coast of the region are hound's-tongue and fern-grass. The oyster-plant formerly had localities here and horned poppy still survives. Scrub woodland on steep slopes again has the typical bluebell/great woodrush/red campion community.

The populations of breeding seabirds on the Berwickshire sea cliffs have been counted at intervals since 1958, and were censused fully in 2000 (Murray, 2002). They far exceed those of the southwest coast in size, with 44,636 guillemots, 3,533 razorbills, 18,739 pairs of kittiwakes, 1,146 pairs of fulmars and 349 pairs of shags in 2000. The main concentrations of the auks are at St Abbs Head, where some of the guillemot colonies on stacks near the lighthouse are quite spectacular

FIG 55. Sea cliffs with guillemot stacks at St Abbs Head, Berwickshire.

(Fig. 55). Numbers of both guillemots and razorbills have risen markedly since counting began, and were at the highest levels known in 2000. By contrast, kittiwakes, which breed along several cliff sections but are again concentrated at St Abbs Head, were down in 2000 from the peak of 23,094 pairs in 1987 (Fig. 56). Fulmars began to prospect the Berwickshire coast from 1910 and were found breeding in the 1920s. They increased steadily, with 536 birds counted in 1957, but appeared to level off by 1978, with numbers remaining at around 1,100–1,200+ up to 2000. The main breeding area is around the Brander, east of Fast Castle. Cormorants maintain a moderate population of 20–60 pairs on stacks west of Fast Castle, while shags are scattered all along the Berwickshire sea cliffs, with a main concentration at St Abbs Head. In 1987, 660 pairs bred, 396 of them at St Abbs Head. Herring gulls have declined along the Berwickshire cliff coast over the last fifty years, from 3,635 pairs in 1958 to only 945 in 2000. This decrease has been offset in some degree by the rise of nesting on the roofs of buildings close to the sea, with up to 170 pairs on Eyemouth factories. There is also a modest colony of puffins, but breeding places are inaccessible and difficult to view, so that counts of birds on the water (79 in 2000) are only of possible breeders. Black guillemots do not breed on this coast, and nesting by great black-backed gulls is somewhat uncertain. Eiders are rare and nest only as a few scattered pairs.

One of the earliest British records of peregrine breeding haunts is for St Abbs Head, where in 1298 two eyries figured in the rental of Coldingham. Four pairs were known to nest on this coast in 1850 (Muirhead, 1889–95) and this was the regular number until the pesticide years from 1961, when there was a virtual absence until a single pair reappeared in 1981. The old haunts were then steadily reoccupied until four pairs were again regularly in residence, with a fifth in some years. Two pairs of ravens still cling to their former breeding places, the same number as was known to Muirhead (1889–95), this being the only extant east-coast haunt of the bird in Britain south of the Black Isle (New Atlas). Evans (1911) documented the history of the chough as a breeding bird on the St Abbs–Fast Castle cliffs, noting that Selby said it was 'not uncommon' in 1841, which he suggested might have meant three or four pairs. Evans also gave records that indicated it bred here up to 1866. Thereafter, choughs appeared only sporadically on this coast, though Bolam was told that a pair bred near St Abbs Head in 1895. There are no recent records, and for over a century the chough has been known only as a west-coast breeding species in Britain.

In the mid-1960s, I collected samples of guillemot, razorbill, kittiwake and shag eggs from both the Mull of Galloway and St Abbs Head for Norman Moore's studies of toxic chemical pollution at Monks Wood Experimental Station. The levels of organochlorine insecticide residues were generally quite low, though all

FIG 56. Guillemots and kittiwakes breeding on the sea cliffs of St Abbs Head, Berwickshire.

contained DDT and its derivatives, and HEOD (dieldrin). All eggs also contained the industrial pollutant polychlorinated biphenyls (PCBS), sometimes in moderate amounts (up to 8 parts per million, wet weight (Prestt & Ratcliffe, 1972). These last substances were implicated as probable contributory agents in the great Irish Sea bird disaster of autumn 1969, in which 17,000 guillemot corpses were washed up on the surrounding shores (Moore, 1987). Of these four species whose eggs were studied, only the shag showed the significant eggshell thinning (12 per cent in this case) that came to be associated with contamination by DDT and its metabolite DDE, and with population declines of many of the affected species. While the undoubted decrease in auk populations around 1960–70 was never shown beyond doubt to be the result of toxic chemical pollution of the sea, the recovery in numbers of guillemots and razorbills at many British colonies since around 1975 has been a marked trend that needs some explanation. Improving food supply has been suggested (RSPB et al., 2004), though this seems to be based on conjecture rather than hard evidence. The efforts to restrict the use of persistent organochlorines (including PCBS) have certainly reduced environmental contamination by their residues during the last three decades or so, and allowed recovery of birds known to have declined through their influence, with the peregrine leading the way.

Examination of the egg contents showed that in 1967 guillemots and razorbills had laid about two weeks earlier at St Abbs than at the Mull, while kittiwakes were at least a week earlier, though shags were no different. This was presumably a food difference, and may have been caused by weather conditions peculiar to that year. There is presently concern about the dramatic fall in breeding success of seabirds such as guillemots and kittiwakes in northern Scotland, attributed to a severe decline in sand-eels, their principal food. Previous sand-eel collapses were blamed upon over-fishing, but the latest decline has occurred after bans were imposed on the taking of the species, and it is now conjectured that rising sea temperatures may be having an adverse effect on the plankton which form the food of this small fish.

AUTUMN AND WINTER BIRDS

Geese and swans

The upper (or inner) Solway flats and marshes are of international importance for their passage migrants and wintering waterfowl, though the Scottish and English sectors are best treated as a single unit for conservation purposes. Prater (1981) has summarised the importance of the north (Scottish) Solway for wildfowl and waders for the earlier period 1969–75, and the more recent annual reports on birds in Dumfries & Galloway (Norman, 2001, 2002) bring the population figures up to date. Prater identifies the key areas as the merselands of the Nith (especially Caerlaverock), to the west of Southerness Point at Mersehead, Rough Firth/Auchencairn Bay, Kirkcudbright Bay, Fleet Bay, Wigtown Bay, Luce Bay and Loch Ryan.

Caerlaverock Merse is the outstanding site, famous for its wintering flock of barnacle geese (Fig. 57). This flock represents the entire Svalbard population, which had long become attached to the place through the relative security afforded by controlled shooting under private ownership. The numbers have steadily increased since the species was given full legal protection in 1954, and the National Nature Reserve was established at Caerlaverock in 1957. Thom (1986) gave figures for five-year intervals, as shown in Table 2. Numbers have continued to build up, and the flock has divided between Caerlaverock and the more recent RSPB reserve at Mersehead, west of Southerness. Total Solway numbers were estimated at over 24,100 in 1999–2000 and 22,290 in 2000–01.

The barnacle flock originally fed exclusively on the short grass of the saltings, but as it expanded the geese increasingly took to feeding on adjoining farmland, where they caused damage to young crops. There was controversy when a complaining farmer was given a licence to shoot birds on his land, and compensation

FIG 57. Barnacle geese on Caerlaverock Merse, Dumfriesshire, their main Solway wintering ground. (Bobby Smith)

TABLE 2. Numbers of barnacle geese at Caerlaverock, 1955/56 to 1983/84. (From Thom, 1986)

PERIOD	AVERAGE	RANGE
1955/56–1959/60	1,190	810–1,650
1960/61–1964/65	3,330	2,800–4,250
1965/66–1969/70	3,860	3,700–4,200
1970/71–1974/75	4,320	3,200–5,200
1975/76–1979/80	7,300	6,050–8,800
1980/81–1983/84	8,930	8,300–10,500

payments were arranged. The problem was resolved in 1970 when the Wildfowl Trust acquired the nearby Eastpark Farm and established a refuge which included 96ha managed primarily for the benefit of the geese. Latterly the flock has tended to disperse during the winter, some going westwards to the Mersehead area (where the RSPB have also acquired a farm), and some to Rockcliffe Marsh at the head of the Solway in Cumbria. Most of the population now ends up on Rockcliffe Marsh in April and May prior to its departure for the arctic breeding grounds (Owen, in Wernham *et al.*, 2002).

Other geese find a congenial winter haunt at Caerlaverock, principally pinkfeet. The numbers of this species vary, but they have tended to increase as the species has withdrawn from the more heavily shot marshes of the Cumbrian Solway. Over 8,000 birds were counted on the adjoining Priestside area in January 2001. Greylags, to the number of several hundreds, and rather smaller numbers of Canada geese also frequent these coastal saltings. Small numbers (up to c. 30) of light-bellied brent geese appear regularly at Loch Ryan on the Clyde coast of Wigtownshire. Caerlaverock is a major wintering haunt for whooper swans, with 379 present in December 2001. Smaller numbers of mute swans occur there, and a few Bewick's swans also sometimes appear, this species having declined over the last century. The whoopers, in particular, are another source of complaints from farmers when they take to feeding on the young grain crops of arable land. The next most important area for wintering geese and swans is the salt marshes and flats at the head of Wigtown Bay, where 5,000 pinkfeet, 560 greylags and 102 whoopers were recorded in 1999.

Ducks, divers, grebes and seabirds

Shelduck tend to be scattered in groups all along the upper Solway coast, as far east as Gretna, but the largest numbers have been reported at Caerlaverock, with 3,060 birds in October 2001. Averages in 2000 were 559 in the Caerlaverock–Carse

Bay area, 184 at Powfoot and 209 from Browhouses to Redkirk Point. Wigtown Bay had a maximum of 529 in January 1999. Wintering wigeon flocks on the inner Solway at Caerlaverock and Mersehead usually number 500–1,000 birds, and those at Kippford and Auchencairn Bay are similar. Wigtown Bay has had larger gatherings (up to 1,600+ in 2001) and Loch Ryan also attracts up to 1,400 fairly regularly. Teal reached a maximum of 4,180 birds at Mersehead in December 2000, considerably more than at Caerlaverock (1,420) the previous month. Both merses can hold up to 500 mallards, while Caerlaverock is the top site for pintail, with the huge population of 6,700 birds in December 2001. Pintail have scattered sites where up to several hundreds gather elsewhere along the Solway shore, including Wigtown Bay. Shovelers are in much smaller numbers at a similar variety of locations, but with the favourites, Caerlaverock and Mersehead, holding up to a hundred or so birds each. Goldeneye are usually in only small numbers along the inner Solway, being mainly birds of the freshwater lochs, but low hundreds occur at times on Loch Ryan. Around 50 or so tufted ducks appear at Caerlaverock in winter, but this is even more a species of inland lakes.

The sea-ducks appear to favour deeper inlets, and Loch Ryan is one of their important areas. A maximum of 2,037 eiders were seen there in late July 2000, and only much smaller numbers elsewhere. This is the most regular haunt of long-tailed ducks, though only a few birds (<10) are usually seen there; and it is also the best place for red-breasted mergansers, with autumn flocks of over 100 birds. Common scoters favour the part of the Solway south of Hestan Island and Balcary Point, where 5,400 were counted on 22 May 1999 and 5,800 on 4 September 2001. Other important scoter areas are off the mouth of Luce Bay, Wigtown Bay, Auchencairn Bay and Rough Firth, but it is unclear how much interchange within the total flock occurs between all these places. Scaup are spread around a number of different areas as far east as Carsethorn. Loch Ryan regularly holds from one to several hundreds, and in December 1999 a mixed flock with scoters numbering 2,500 birds was seen off Corsewall Point. The Carsethorn area can also hold this number.

Loch Ryan is also favoured by the divers, with up to 50 red-throated and sometimes one or two black-throated and great northern. Great crested grebes congregate here, with a maximum of 212 birds in November 2001, but Carsethorn/Southerness is even more favoured, with up to 378 in 2001. The rarer grebes, Slavonian, red-necked and black-necked, also visit Loch Ryan – the first in modest numbers (up to 42), but the others usually as singles. Corsewall Point, at the western entrance to Loch Ryan, has become a favourite place for sea-watching of passage migrants, with good numbers of Manx shearwaters (up to

1,700 in one hour in July 2000), much smaller numbers of Leach's petrel, and occasional storm petrels.

Waders

The number of lapwings wintering on the saltings and adjoining farmland of the Solway is much less than a century ago. Gladstone (1910) said that a flock estimated at 50,000 birds was seen in a modest-sized field in lower Nithsdale in 1900. In December 1999, a count of 4,185 birds was the largest recent total for the inner north Solway. Golden plover in these same habitats have shown a parallel decline. The recent highest figure was 4,500 birds on Baldoon airfield, Wigtown Bay, in October 2000, but 1,500–2,000 are more usual Solway maxima. Curlew numbers are probably smaller than hitherto, and recent maxima for the inner north Solway were 2,500 in both September 1999 and February 2000. Redshanks (Fig. 58) winter all along the coast, with local concentrations in the hundreds, and a maximum total on the inner north Solway of 3,641 in December 1999. Oyster-catchers have increased and are the most numerous autumn and winter waders of the Solway. A maximum total of 37,707 birds was reported in September 2000, and each of the main estuaries usually holds several thousand. Ringed plovers reach their highest numbers in May, presumably as late-nesting Fennoscandian

FIG 58. Mixed wader flocks: curlew, redshank and grey plover on the north Solway. (Bobby Smith)

birds assemble before migration: a total of 1,537 birds was counted on the inner north Solway in May 1999.

Of the more obvious visitors from the far north, the dunlin is probably the most numerous, with maximum totals of around 10,000 birds in most recent years. This number can occur at Caerlaverock alone. Knots are the next most abundant migrants wintering on the inner Solway, with recent counts of 7,500 in January 1999 and 5,394 in February 2000 (Fig. 59). The area south of Carsethorn is a favourite, with up to 4,800 birds. All the other visiting waders occur in much smaller numbers. Bar-tailed godwits are up to 400 strong and favour the Annan–Powfoot area, while grey plovers reach 190 and may be concentrated anywhere between Annan and Carsethorn. The turnstone prefers stonier shores, with Loch Ryan (a favourite area) holding up to 110 birds, though the inner Solway total reaches 210. Purple sandpipers are even more constant to rocky shores, and the best localities for them are the rocky platforms along the coast between Southerness and Carsethorn. Besides the waterfowl, the Solway merselands are quite important for wintering twites.

The remaining waders are mostly passage migrants in autumn and spring, though a few individuals of any of them may spend the winter on the Solway. Black-tailed godwits are in modest flocks of up to 80 birds, with Caerlaverock and Browhouses as favourite areas, but whimbrels are mostly in parties of less

FIG 59. Wintering flocks of knot and oystercatcher on the north Solway. (Bobby Smith)

than 30. Sanderlings are variable, often in small groups but exceptionally up to 300, as at Caerlaverock on 4 October 2001. Loch Ryan is the strongest draw for greenshanks, with a remarkable 85 birds on 10 January 2001, but daily parties of less than ten passage birds are more usual elsewhere in July and August. Green sandpipers pass through regularly in still smaller numbers, mostly in late summer. The rest are irregular, and their occurrences are mostly in ones and twos a year: curlew sandpiper, wood sandpiper, ruff, spotted redshank, little stint and Temminck's stint. Rare vagrants such as the pectoral sandpiper and long-billed dowitcher turn up now and then.

On the Berwickshire coast, small numbers of some of the above waders appear in autumn and/or winter, with purple sandpiper and turnstone the more constant visitors to these rocky shores. Some species, such as greenshank and ruff, are more often seen at inland wetlands.

Gulls and skuas

Moderate numbers of black-headed gulls roost in autumn and winter on the Solway saltings and flats, with around 2,600 on the Nith in September 2000. Common gull roosts are bigger, with up to 12,800 at Mersehead in February 2000. Lesser black-backs are fewer (up to 300 in spring or autumn), and roosts of herring gulls are largest in summer or early autumn, with 1,500–1,700 birds in the Nith area between June and September. Great black-backs numbered up to 140 at Caerlaverock in November 2000. Occasional individuals of the rare gulls – Iceland, glaucous, Mediterranean, little, Sabine's and ringed-billed – can appear at various places on the southwest coast. The skuas, arctic, pomarine and great, are rare offshore visitors in spring and autumn.

CHAPTER 4

Ancient and Semi-Natural Woodlands

S OUTHERN SCOTLAND has suffered even more than most parts of Britain from deforestation, and its semi-natural broadleaved woodlands are reduced to scattered small remnants mostly of under 100ha. The maps of ancient and semi-natural woodlands produced by Scottish Natural Heritage show just how fragmentary the distribution of these types is, with parts of Dumfries and Kirkcudbright the best endowed, while Wigtown, south Ayr and the Borders counties have very little indeed.

OAKWOOD

In the western hills the prevailing type is sessile oakwood on acidic brown soils (Fig. 60), with the best examples in the Fleet valley at Castramont and Killiegowan; the Wood of Cree, Knockman, Garlies and Corwar near Newton Stewart; the Glen Trool woods of Caldons, Buchan and Glenhead (Fig. 61); and the Glenkens series at Hannaston and Garroch, Kenmure High Wood and Airds of Kells. Most of these have well-grown 'maiden' trees, of up to 22 metres, but the Wood of Cree has mostly spindly multiple-stems that have regrown as coppice after clear-cutting of the main woodland block. Downy birch is plentiful in some woods and has evidently replaced oak on some sites that were felled and not replanted. There is seldom much of a tall shrub layer but some woods have scattered rowan, holly and hazel, and these were probably once more abundant – all grow commonly on rocky glen sides and lower hill crags. These woodlands are represented by communities w11 and w17.

Some of these oakwoods are grazed by sheep only lightly or not at all and

FIG 60. Sessile oakwood. Glenhead, Glen Trool, Kirkcudbrightshire.

FIG 61. Remnant hill oakwoods at the Buchan and Glenhead, Glen Trool, Kirkcudbrightshire.

have wonderful carpets of bluebells. Castramont and Wood of Cree in particular are delightful in late May, with sheets of blue and rich fragrance from the myriad flowers (Fig. 62). Both are included in the list of the ten best bluebell sites in Britain compiled by Plantlife. This is a floral feature for which Britain and Ireland are distinguished in Europe, for the bluebell is an oceanic plant and soon fades out on the continental mainland, away from the Atlantic seaboard. Ungrazed sites have local dominance of great woodrush and bilberry, but the second is not – for whatever reason – abundant as a Galloway plant. Grazed woods mostly have a grassland floor of sheep's fescue, wavy hair-grass, bents, soft fog and vernal grass, variably invaded by bracken. Honeysuckle is common in places, both on the woodland floor and as a climber; and ivy clothes many of the trees in ungrazed woods but is largely absent from those to which sheep have had free access. Other typical herbs are wood sage, wood sorrel, common cow-wheat, tormentil, golden-rod and heath bedstraw. Where soil conditions are a little richer, there are also red campion, greater stitchwort, pignut, celandine, heath violet, bitter-vetch, wood anemone and three-nerved sandwort.

Rocky woods with litters of blocks usually have abundant ferns besides bracken: male fern, Borrer's male fern, broad buckler fern, lady fern and hard fern. The blocks are also covered with luxuriant cushions of moss and leafy

FIG 62. Bluebell glades in the Castramont Woods, Fleet Valley, Kirkcudbrightshire. Scottish Wildlife Trust reserve.

FIG 63. Waterfall ravine of Buchan Burn. Habitat of Wilson's filmy fern. Glen Trool, Kirkcudbrightshire.

liverwort, which flourish under the wet climate. Mostly they are of species which grow in drier parts of the country, such as *Pleurozium schreberi, Hylocomium splendens, Hypnum cupressiforme, Thuidium tamariscinum, Dicranum scoparium, Leucobryum glaucum* and *Diplophyllum albicans,* but there are also kinds found mainly in the wetter west, including *Rhytidiadelphus loreus, Bazzania trilobata, Scapania gracilis* and *Plagiochila spinulosa.* The moss-like Wilson's filmy fern grows in some rocky woods and waterfall glens but is quite local: the Buchan Falls are one of its best localities (Fig. 63). It fades out eastwards as rainfall decreases, and is confined to the western glens of the Borders. Cascading streams within woodland also have certain bryophytes of markedly western distribution.

Galloway is, however, not as rich in the more exacting Atlantic ferns and bryophytes as Lakeland to the south. While its rainfall is not quite as extreme, this less prominent presence of plants loving a humid atmosphere is more probably the result of lack of suitable habitat. Some of the notable species are present, but in very small quantity and in only one or two localities: the hay-scented fern (two extant locations) and Tunbridge filmy fern (only in Dumfriesshire); and the liverworts *Adelanthus decipiens, Radula voluta, R. aquilegia, Plagiochila tridenticulata* and *Jubula hutchinsiae*, in particular. There is a lack of deep waterfall ravines or good block litters and rock outcrops in native woodland, and especially of these features with a north to east aspect. While some woods look promising at first sight, such as Garlies Wood near Newton Stewart, closer inspection suggests that they have at some point been clear-felled and, although they have been replanted, this clearance exposed the more sensitive species to fatal desiccation. They died out, and when suitable conditions returned again, with redevelopment of the woodland cover, only the more robust and successfully reproducing bryophytes were able to recolonise the vacant habitat. The rarities, almost by definition, were unable to spread back again from their tiny remaining populations, though most of them were probably once more widespread in the original forests of the Sub-Atlantic period. The moss *Sematophyllum micans*, which grows in some Lakeland and west Highland woods, has never been found in Galloway – it could have been there in the original forests but later extinguished by loss of favourable habitat. There is an old and unlocalised record of the Killarney fern for Ayrshire, and this fern could occur within the region, but it is again limited by lack of good habitats. Even its more widespread, thread-like gametophyte stage has not yet been found in southern Scotland.

The robust moss *Isothecium holtii* grows abundantly on rocks within the flood zone of streams in several shady wooded glens. Other noteworthy Atlantic species with several localities are the liverworts *Lophocolea fragrans, Frullania teneriffae* and *F. microphylla*. Some of these oceanic bryophytes occur also on coastal rocks, which may be wooded, and a few are on treeless mountain cliffs. A few Galloway woodlands have mosses which are distinctly western in Britain but somewhat boreal in Europe as a whole, such as *Hylocomium umbratum* and *Hypnum callichroum*. The lower trunks of many trees in the western woods are thickly clothed with the mosses *Isothecium myosuroides* and *Hypnum mammillatum*, and some have dark red sheets of the liverwort *Frullania tamarisci*. Rotting logs are frequently grown with another red liverwort, *Nowellia curvifolia*.

With distance east, the remaining patches of semi-natural woodland change mainly in decreasing luxuriance of moss growths and the presence of oceanic species, while the communities of vascular plants stay much the same. Examples

are the oakwoods at Elibank, east of Innerleithen, and those on the flanks of the
Lammermuirs at Abbey St Bathans in Berwickshire. Many woodlands in the
region, and probably most of those in the east, have become modified from their
original state, by the introduction, at the replanting stage, of non-native trees
such as beech, sycamore, Scots pine, Norway spruce, Douglas fir and larch. There
are many plantations of spruce, larch and Scots pine all over the region, and they
are mostly botanically dull.

The native status of Scots pine here is questionable, except perhaps on some
of the lowland peat mosses, such as Kirkconnell Flow, though the pinewood at
Rachan, Drumelzier (felled in the 1950s) had a suite of boreal pinewood plants in
twinflower, creeping lady's tresses, lesser wintergreen and the moss *Ptilium crista-
castrensis*. Creeping lady's tresses survives in a few Borders woods or perhaps
reappears with the replanting of pinewoods, but twinflower is now known only
in a birchwood near Mellerstain in Berwickshire. Braithwaite & Long (1990) say
that both have perhaps been unintentional and only temporary reintroductions
in several pine plantations established on the site of former native [*sic*] pinewoods
in the county. In the hill country, many shelter woods with the four above-
mentioned conifers were created in the years before the great twentieth-century
wave of afforestation, and the woods around the mansion houses of the large

FIG 64. The stand of fine old Scots pines near Tarras Lodge, Langholm, Dumfriesshire.
The trees have been fenced to promote regeneration, albeit by orthodox planting. The
birchwood also needs a helping hand. Tinnis Hill behind.

estates are mostly diversified by a variety of introduced tree species. Some of these are of great stature, and the famous Shambellie Wood near New Abbey contains some magnificent 30m beech and oak as well as scattered tall Scots pine and larch. The Scots pine clump near Tarras Lodge, Langholm (Fig. 64), has some splendid trees, rivalling the finest in the country.

MIXED BROADLEAVED WOODLAND

As usual, woods on basic substrates with brown soils of pH more than 5.5 have a greater variety of trees and other vascular plants, and a rather different moss flora. Many of the best examples overlie Ordovician and Silurian rocks, but basic woodland soils also occur on the Carboniferous formations, Old Red and Permian Sandstones, and igneous intrusions. Ash is nearly always an abundant tree, and on calcareous Ordovician rocks in the Ayrshire valley of Glen App there were, up to 1960, stands of almost pure ashwood resembling those on limestone in parts of northern England. They were then mostly felled before any conservation measures could be applied to save them. There are still patches of ashwood in places, but more usually there is a mixture of trees. Wych elm was formerly a constant species, until it was virtually wiped out in the great disease epidemic of the 1980s: Cragbank Wood near Bonchester Bridge in Roxburgh is an example of a wood that was spoiled by loss of its numerous elms. Typically there is a scattering of oak, which can be either sessile or pedunculate, and birches of either species – downy or silver – are usually present. Hazel forms a denser understorey than in the oakwoods and may be dominant on its own in places. Other less constant or abundant trees and shrubs are wild cherry (gean), bird cherry, rowan (Fig. 65), sallow, hawthorn, blackthorn and elder. Community W9 represents these types.

The herbaceous field layer of these base-rich woods has higher species diversity than that of the acidophilous oakwoods. Communities dominated by dog's mercury and wild garlic are usually present, but there is also commonly a mixture of species with primrose, wood avens, water avens, herb robert, bugle, sanicle, wild strawberry (Fig. 66), barren strawberry, enchanter's nightshade, woodruff, wood speedwell, heath speedwell, yellow pimpernel, moschatel, self-heal, nipplewort, ground-ivy and wood-sedge. Prickly shield-fern (Fig. 67) is widespread and often abundant but hart's tongue is less common. More local woodland herbs of basic soil are wood cranesbill, wood vetch (Fig. 68), stone bramble, wood forget-me-not, goldilocks, alternate-leaved golden saxifrage, toothwort, bird's nest orchid, early purple orchid, twayblade, giant bell-flower,

FIG 65. Rowans by the Buchan Burn, Glen Trool, Kirkcudbrightshire.

FIG 66. The wild strawberry is still a common plant of open woodland, and of dry waysides and banks.

FIG 67. Prickly shield-fern, a frequent fern of basic rocks in shady, wooded glens. Fairlie Glen, Ayrshire.

FIG 68. Wood vetch, an uncommon plant of woodland on basic soils. Yester woods, near Gifford, East Lothian.

wall-lettuce, great horsetail, smooth-stalked sedge and pendulous sedge. The characteristic grasses of these woods are false brome, wood melick, tufted hair-grass, wood meadow-grass and hairy brome: they tend to increase at the expense of dicotyledonous herbs under grazing of the woodland floor. Wood millet is uncommon. Soft shield-fern and hemp agrimony occur in milder districts, especially near or along the coast, and a few rocky glens have tutsan and wood fescue. Broad-leaved helleborine and rough horse-tail are rare, and narrow-leaved bitter-cress has a single extant locality in the Borders, on the outskirts of Hawick; it was formerly in the Garpol and Beldcraig ravines near Moffat.

Deeper and moister soils with 'mull' humus have meadowsweet, angelica, valerian, marsh hawk's-beard, and, more locally, globeflower, large bitter-cress and wood stitchwort. Wet clayey soils typically have creeping buttercup, remote sedge and golden saxifrage. Common mosses of woods on base-rich soils include *Brachythecium rutabulum*, *Eurhynchium praelongum*, *E. striatum*, *Hylocomium brevirostre*, *Ctenidium molluscum*, *Thuidium tamariscinum*, *Atrichum undulatum* and *Mnium undulatum*, while liverworts are *Porella platyphylla*, *P. arboris-vitae*, *Plagiochila asplenioides* and *Pellia endiviifolia*.

These mixed woods on base-rich soils are widely distributed across the region, though seldom extensive, and most are under 50ha in area. Examples from west to east are at Garchew near Bargrennan, Blackcraig near Newton Stewart, Chanlock on the Scaur Water and Stenhouse on the Shinnel Water, Cragbank near Bonchester Bridge and Minto Craigs near Jedburgh. Stands of hazel wood with scarcely any other trees are found at Henderland above St Mary's Loch. Species-rich woods are especially characteristic of steep-sided glens where the streams have cut rocky sections that have discouraged the complete clearance of trees, so that they include examples probably showing the nearest approximation to natural woodland now left, especially where they are fenced against stock. They occur at Dunskey Glen at Portpatrick, Moneypool and Balloch Burns at Creetown, Kirkdale Glen near Ravenshall, Ness Glen near Dalmellington, Glenhoul Glen on the upper Ken, Raehills Glen on the Kinnel Water, Hermanlaw and Muchra Cleuchs near St Mary's Loch, Tarrasfoot near Langholm, Tinnis Burn near Newcastleton, Langton Lees Cleuch near Duns and Pease Dene near Cockburnspath. Partly wooded rocky stream ravines with crags, waterfalls and cascades include the Buchan Falls and Caldons Burn in Glen Trool, Buck's Linn at Glenlee, Black Linn near Ae, Crichope Linn near Thornhill, Garpol Linn and Beldcraig near Beattock, Black Burn at Newcastleton and Sundhope Linn near Hermitage.

OTHER WOODLAND TYPES

Alder-lined streamsides are very typical of southern Scotland, and especially the Borders (Fig. 69), but the tree is usually confined to the alluvial banks which receive periodic flooding, and woods of alder are somewhat fragmentary. There is one at the base of an open slope at the Scrogs of Drumruck in the Fleet valley, but they are more typical of the carr woods found around the edges of lowland fens and lakes, where they may represent the late stage of hydroseres (w5 and w6) (see Chapter 6). There are examples at the head of Loch Ken and at Woodhall Loch (see Figs 115 & 117). Scattered bushes of juniper are quite widespread, especially in the northeast, but the region contains rather few good stands of this shrub. The best known is the Tynron juniper wood on a slope above the Shinnel Water in Dumfriesshire. Spread over five hectares, it contains finely grown junipers in a wide variety of form, averaging over three metres tall, mixed with scattered ash trees and geans (w19). The isolated occurrence of this juniper scrub, the only notable stand in the southwest, is unexplained, but presumably it results from some chance of management. Smaller stands occur at several places in the Borders, such as at Colmsliehill between Galashiels and Lauder.

In unmanaged places, scrub composed of tall shrubs has developed widely,

FIG 69. Alder fringe to upland stream. Hermitage Water, near Newcastleton, Roxburghshire.

though it is seldom extensive. Even-aged stands of hawthorn (w21) are seen in various places, mainly in the marginal land, and there is one I have known for nearly sixty years near Crofts between Crocketford and Corsock. It has been suggested that they date from a period of agricultural depression (probably in the late 1800s) when grazing animals were removed for long enough to allow seedlings of hawthorn to become well established. Mixed scrub with hawthorn, blackthorn, rowan and elder is widespread (Fig. 70) and thickets of gorse (w23) occur in many coastal and inland situations. Gorse and broom rapidly invade road banks and produce luminous yellow displays in spring that add colour to the countryside (Fig. 71). Western gorse is widespread in the lowlands of the Stewartry and often forms dense patches, sometimes with the common species, on knolls in ordinary sheep and cattle pastures. Wild roses are also an attractive feature of hedgerows and scrubby places, with dog-rose, glaucous dog-rose, soft downy-rose and Sherard's downy-rose the principal species. Hedges are predominantly of hawthorn, with varying presence of other tall shrubs, but beech hedges are especially common in eastern areas.

Woodland fungi of the region (Fig. 72) are described by Roy Watling in Appendix 3.

FIG 70. Scrub of hawthorn and blackthorn. Townhead, near Crocketford, Kirkcudbrightshire.

FIG 71. Thickets of broom on roadside banks make displays of luminous yellow during the spring. Near Dalry, Kirkcudbrightshire.

FIG 72. Honey fungus, parasitic on trees. Canonbie, Dumfriesshire

LICHENS

Southern Scotland is disappointing for its arboreal lichens. Perhaps the most important site is the stand of ancient pollarded oaks at Lochwood Tower, 8km south of Moffat, where there is an assemblage of southern species. These strange trees have assumed a rather baobab-like form and are over 400 years old. Besides the lichens, they have mossy trunks with masses of polypody on the lower parts (Fig. 73). The Lochwood oaks also played an important part in the development of dendrochronology, and allowed the construction of a tree ring sequence from 1571 to 1970 (Rodger *et al.*, 2003).

The Lobarion community of large, foliose lichens in the genera *Lobaria* and *Sticta* has only the most fragmentary occurrence, and is represented mainly by infrequent and scattered patches of tree-lungwort *L. pulmonaria*, usually on ash but sometimes oak. The southwest, where even most ash trees have a very limited lichen flora, is especially poor in these plants, and the best area is in Dumfries and the west of Roxburgh and Selkirk, where sheltered glens have retained old trees. Some of the other characteristic species occur, but only rarely, such as *Lobaria laete-virens*, *L. amplissima*, *L. scrobiculata* (now known on a single tree), *Sticta sylvatica*, *S. limbata*, *Nephroma laevigatum*, *N. parile*, *Peltigera collina*, *Parmeliella triptophylla* and *Thelotrema lepadinum* (Corner, 1981). There is little doubt that most

FIG 73. Intermediate polypody, a local fern of wooded banks. Southwick, Kirkcudbright-shire.

of these species were once more widespread and have declined seriously. M'Andrew (1891) said that in Dumfries & Galloway *L. pulmonaria* was common, while *L. scrobiculata*, *S. limbata* and *N. laevigatum* were frequent.

The explanation for their present scarcity is the acidification of tree bark by atmospheric pollution from emissions of sulphur dioxide and nitrogen oxides, which began with the Industrial Revolution and has continued ever since. The poverty of Galloway and Carrick for these tree lichens is explained by proximity to the major pollution source of the Clydeside industrial conurbation, while the east of the region is affected by emissions from the Edinburgh and Tyneside areas. The centre, though more distant from these sources, probably receives acid deposition from both. While the prevailing winds are west to southwest, they can blow from almost any quarter of the compass. Lichens moderately tolerant of bark acidity, such as *Evernia prunastri*, remain fairly common generally.

Government figures show that sulphur emissions have declined over the last two decades, while those of nitrogen have increased, so that the overall picture is of no improvement. I have observed a single large ash tree with patches of tree lungwort beside the New Galloway–Mossdale road for nearly forty years. The growth was originally healthy-looking and covered a large part of the lower trunk, but within ten years patches had begun to peel off, reducing its extent. After another ten years the growth had separated into upper and lower patches, and the lower continued to contract and to look unhealthy. In 2004, the lower patch has almost gone, while the upper hangs on in reduced amount – perhaps stabilised, but much poorer than when I first knew it. Nor is there any sign of recovery of this and other lichens of the Lobarion anywhere in southern Scotland. Unless or until there is a significant fall in output of acidity, these plants will have no chance of ever again attaining the abundance and luxuriance still to be seen in the western Highlands, and which they must once have shown across much of our region.

MAMMALS

Service (1901) said that the roe deer (Fig. 74) became extinct in the Solway district in the late Middle Ages and was probably quite absent during the eighteenth century. It reappeared in Annandale around 1850, and reintroductions to the estates of Drumlanrig and Culzean Castle probably led to its recolonisation of Nithsdale and the west of Carrick and Galloway. By 1870 it was widespread over Galloway, and numerous in suitable habitats by 1900. The new forests have greatly expanded the area available to it, and the roe remains plentiful in most parts of the southwest. In the Borders, Evans (1911) reported a similar earlier

FIG 74. Roe deer buck: it finds shelter in conifer plantations, but has to feed outside. (Bobby Smith)

history, but with reappearance in smaller numbers than in the southwest by 1900. It is now constantly present in the woods of the Borders. With the great expansion of forest over the region, red deer have again become woodland animals in the southwest, though they forage mainly over open ground outside, as food is mostly lacking within the dense stands of trees. The forest stags reach a much larger stature and carry heavier heads of antlers than those found on the open hills.

Red squirrels (Fig. 75) were also alleged by Service (1901) to have become extinct in the Solway district and, following unspecified reintroductions, to have re-established by 1837 in upper Eskdale. They then spread westwards into the Stewartry around 1860, where they reached the River Cree by 1873, and through Wigtownshire by the early 1980s. Evans (1911) gave a similar account for the Borders, of earlier extinction, reintroduction to Dalkeith around 1772, and subsequent spread throughout the Borders woodlands by the time he wrote. Although the grey squirrel has reached many parts of the region, the vast conifer forests provide the red with an extensive refuge from its competition, and the native species remains common also in many of the broadleaved woodlands.

The badger (Fig. 76) is primarily a woodland animal and has become widespread across most parts of the region. It is here as in parts of England being made a scapegoat for the spread of bovine tuberculosis, and there have

FIG 75. Red squirrel: still widespread in the region and a beneficiary of conifer plantations. (Bobby Smith)

FIG 76. Badger: a widespread woodland animal across the region. (Bobby Smith)

been clamours for a general cull. As usual, some of the outbreaks of the disease are attributed to movement of infected cattle into the affected areas. It is also suggested that some farmers need to show rather more concern for the welfare of their animals by greater attention to hygiene. The feeding of cattle with hay in metal baskets, while they stand in a slough of mud (Fig. 77), is all too common nowadays, but gives little confidence that their health is considered paramount.

The wild cat was said by Service (1901) to be long extinct in the Solway region, the last record for Dumfries being one shot near Middlebie in 1813, and in the Stewartry one killed near Balmaghie in 1820. Evans (1911) notes that it was mentioned for Castletown and Saughtree in Roxburghshire in the old *Statistical Account of Scotland* (1791–9) but that the *New Statistical Account* (1834–45) gave no record for any part of the Tweed area. Evans quotes Berwickshire records for Old Cambus, Monynut and Coldingham from 1834 to 1849, but even by that time there was suspicion that wild cats had so interbred with domestic cats that the true native species was becoming a rarity, including in the Highlands. This hybridisation is now considered to threaten the survival of the real wild cat in Scotland.

The pine marten is a rather similar case, although it hung on a little longer. Evans (1911) gave Berwickshire records for the woods and denes around Pease Bridge, near Cockburnspath, from 1834 to 1879, and for Lauderdale in 1848. There were no others, and the animal had presumably died out before the end of the nineteenth century. Gladstone (1912) said that it was formerly not uncommon in

FIG 77. Cattle (Black Galloways) create a slough of mud by congregating around hay-feeders.

Dumfries, but probably extinct when he wrote. It was gone from Galloway by 1850 and Ayrshire by 1882. Pine martens were reintroduced to the Galloway Forest Park by the Forestry Commission in 1980–81, when 12 animals were released at Backhill of the Bush and the Caldons in Glentrool. Apart from occasional sightings in the area, the first group is not known to have established, but the second led to a small breeding population, with subsequent records of animals within a radius of 12km south and west of the Caldons release site. Dispersal tended to be to lower and more productive ground, whilst remaining in or close to conifer forest. The view that modern Galloway forests can support the pine marten thus appears to be upheld (Shaw & Livingstone, 1992). Both this animal and the wild cat are regarded primarily as denizens of woodland, but both range out onto open moorland and mountain, and some evidently live in these treeless habitats.

Bats are not well represented in Scotland, and even the southern part has fewer species than Cumbria, just across the border. They belong primarily to woodland as natural habitat, but need open ground over which to feed, either wide glades or farmland beyond the woodland edge. When Evans (1911) and Gladstone (1912) wrote, only three species were certainly known in the region – pipistrelle, long-eared and Daubenton's bats – though the presence of noctule and Natterer's bat was suspected. All five of these species are now known to occur, plus two more, Leisler's bat and the whiskered bat (Altringham, 2003). The last was only separated fairly recently from Brandt's bat, which occurs in Cumbria but is not known north of the border. The noctule appears to be widespread though sparse throughout the southern part of the region, but Leisler's bat is confined to the southwest. The other five bats are all widespread through southern Scotland, though in varying numbers. Daubenton's bat is especially associated with rivers and lakes. Tree-holes and rock caves and crannies are the natural roosting, breeding and hibernation sites of bats but some of them have found congenial habitats in buildings.

BIRDS

The vast coniferous plantations of southern Scotland support large breeding populations of the widespread and common woodland birds: blackbird, song thrush, mistle thrush, chaffinch, wren, willow warbler, robin, goldcrest, dunnock, coal tit, treecreeper, wood pigeon, pheasant, jay, carrion crow, tawny owl and sparrowhawk. Blue tits and great tits breed in the plantations mainly where nest-boxes are provided. The new conifer forests have become attractive to crossbills and siskins, two once-rare birds which now breed widely across the region, though in extremely variable numbers, depending on annual variations in cone and seed production. Other species prefer the more open broadleaved woods: blackcap, garden warbler, whitethroat, chiffchaff, wood warbler and long-tailed tit. Hole-nesters need older trees or dead ones, as do redstart, pied flycatcher (Fig. 78), starling and great spotted woodpecker. Willow tits occur especially in damp birchwoods where rotting stumps allow them to excavate nest cavities. Nest-boxes will induce the smaller hole-nesters to breed in almost any kind of woods, and partly compensate for the lack of old trees with natural holes. The three *Sylvia* warblers and chiffchaffs are mostly in ungrazed lowland broadleaved woods with a good undershrub layer, especially of brambles. Wood warblers prefer the open grassy floor of grazed oakwoods, particularly in upland areas.

Rather patchy in occurrence but in a variety of woods are greenfinch, bullfinch, redpoll, long-tailed tit and spotted flycatcher, the last having declined considerably of late. Linnet, yellowhammer and lesser whitethroat can breed in woodland, especially in young growth, though they belong more to scrub and field hedges; and the goldfinch more typically uses scattered hedgerow trees, gardens and parks. The hawfinch is a rare breeder in lowland woods and large gardens in the Borders, preferring the surrounds of stately homes, but most of the nesting records for the southwest are pre-1973. Grey herons use woodland exclusively for nesting but are otherwise wetland birds. Rooks are also birds of

FIG 78. Pied flycatcher: a woodland bird which has increased in Galloway. (Bobby Smith)

the trees only for breeding, and are dealt with under farmland (Chapter 5). Their colonies are in tree clumps and open shelter woods more often than closed woodland. Jackdaws favour large tree-holes where these are available, but will use other nest sites: a colony was found breeding in rabbit holes within woodland on a steep slope at Abbey St Bathans. Magpies are equally at home in hedgerow trees and thorns, and have a patchy distribution across the region, with some surprising gaps.

Green woodpeckers first appeared in the south of Scotland during the 1940s, but the main wave of colonisation was in the 1950s. They became widespread by 1970, and their ringing call was a familiar sound across the region. More recently they have thinned out and are much less often heard, especially in Dumfriesshire, though they still occur widely in both lowland and upland woods and open stands of trees. A still more recent colonist is the nuthatch, which, after expanding through Cumbria and Northumberland in the 1970s and 80s, reached the lower Tweed valley by 1988–91. The first successful nesting in the Borders was in

1989, and numbers are now estimated at about 50–60 pairs. Birds have also been seen increasingly in Dumfries & Galloway, and small numbers are known to breed as far west as the Ken valley. Woodcock are fairly constant in woods across the region, but mostly at rather low density, and may have declined in recent decades: there was a loss of at least thirty 10km squares for confirmed breeding between the two Bird Atlases (1968–72 and 1988–91). Murray (2002) believes they are under-recorded at the recently mapped presence of 12 per cent of tetrads, with 29 roding birds seen at 17 sites. The woodcock's breeding status in the southwest is unclear at present; it was described as a 'scarce resident' in 2000 by Norman (2001). As in other regions, the winter population is evidently boosted by immigrant birds from Fennoscandia. Woodcock prefer woods on basic, clayey soils with good earthworm populations, and trees not too densely stocked, and so are sparse in the coniferous plantations of the uplands.

The gorgeous golden pheasant from China was introduced to the Newton Stewart area around 1895 (Sharrock, 1976), and established itself in woodland there. When the expansion of coniferous plantations took off, the bird readily spread into the young thicket stages. In the 1950s its distinctive, harsh call was frequently to be heard – much more often than the secretive bird itself was seen – in Kirroughtree Forest and the lower Cree valley. Yet its expansion did not keep pace with that of the forests, and it has become rarer in recent years, for reasons that are unclear. Another group became established after 1976 in the area around Moffat (Gibbons et al., 1993), presumably as the result of a further introduction. The related Lady Amherst's pheasant was also introduced to Galloway but did not establish permanently.

The tawny owl is the commonest owl, and present in woods throughout the region. It has evidently maintained a fairly stable population, though with variations in breeding performance according to changes in small rodent numbers. Barn owls (Fig. 79) include woodland as a habitat, though they hunt mostly outside or in open places within, and have been encouraged in the vast conifer plantations of the southwest by provision of nest-boxes. Numbers are good in the Borders also, and the bird is no longer regarded as threatened by organochlorine pesticides. In 2000, 258 breeding sites were checked in Dumfries & Galloway, and produced at least 444 young, the success being attributed to high numbers of voles (Norman, 2001). In the Borders that year, breeding-season records came from 51 sites (breeding was proved at only eight) and non-breeding-season records from another 41 (Murray, 2002). The long-eared owl is scattered and rather unpredictable in distribution, though it is difficult to locate and numbers may be underestimated. The New Atlas shows a loss of thirty 10km squares for confirmed breeding across the region and, though present in only

FIG 79. Barn owl with field vole: a predator that maintains good numbers across the region. (Bobby Smith)

4 per cent of tetrads, it is now more widespread in the Borders than in the south-west. The rather bare shelter belts of conifers widely planted on the sheepwalks early in the twentieth century were once regarded as favourite nesting places of the long-eared owl, and Paton & Pike (1929) said it was 'fairly common . . . where there are fir plantations of suitable size' in Ayrshire. Yet it is unclear whether the recent conifer plantations have been attractive to the bird. Unlike the tawny owl, which can nest also in tree-holes, rocks or even on the ground, this species uses only the old tree-nests of other birds – crow, magpie, sparrowhawk or buzzard.

The sparrowhawk (Fig. 80) was known from earlier observations to be a widespread woodland raptor across southern Scotland, though much subject to gamekeeper persecution, during the first half of the twentieth century. After 1956, its population collapsed over much of England and Wales and some parts of Scotland, through secondary poisoning by the organochlorine pesticides used extensively as agricultural seed-dressings, and by 1964 it had almost disappeared from heavily intensive arable farming areas. Yet it responded quite rapidly to the early restrictions on use of organochlorine seed-dressings, in 1962 and 1964, and on the Cumbrian Solway Plain just to the south some reoccupation of deserted territories had occurred even by 1966. In the late 1960s, John Young, with Herman Ostroznik and other friends, followed the recovery of sparrowhawks from this depression in Dumfriesshire and found them relatively numerous by

1970. Although breeding failure was still frequent, the group ringed a consider-able number of nestlings during this period. From 1971 Ian Newton developed an intensive study of the sparrowhawks of Annandale and Eskdale, which is described in detail in his monograph on the species (Newton, 1986). Interested readers should obtain this work, which is the most thorough account of the biology of any raptor in Britain.

The Annandale study area of some 700km² included the large (55km²) coniferous Forest of Ae, but also had a good deal of agricultural land, both pastoral and arable, with scattered smaller woods. The Eskdale area was smaller at around 200km², and less intensively farmed, with smaller fields, little arable, and woodland in valley strips or scattered small blocks. In the earlier years, Annandale had up to 110 known sparrowhawk nests in one year, and Eskdale up to 39. Breeding density was similar in both areas, when measured as the average distance between each occupied nest and its nearest neighbour – 0.60km in Annandale and 0.62km in Eskdale. The Eskdale population remained fairly stable over the period 1972–84, with fluctuations of only 16 per cent either side of the mean of 35 pairs. Some of this variation was attributed to cold and wet weather in March–April, when small-bird populations were at their lowest and food supply for the hawks was at its most critical. By contrast, the Annandale sparrowhawk population declined markedly between 1971 and 1980, from 110 to 61 pairs. This decline was not related to pesticide contamination, which

FIG 80. Female sparrowhawk at nest with young. (Bobby Smith)

decreased during the period, but to land-use trends that led to reduction in food supply. In Annandale there was decline in woodland area through felling, replacement of broadleaves by conifers, loss of hedgerows and scrub, draining and improvement of wet pastures, cultivation of rough ground and conversion of some grassland to arable – all adding up to adverse change for populations of small birds, which decreased accordingly. In Eskdale there was continuing stability in habitat and hence in food supply, although widespread field drainage occurred in the early 1980s.

Even within the Annandale study area there were differences in breeding density which related to local variations in food supply. In the Forest of Ae, nest spacing became progressively farther apart from the lowest and richest ground on the south and east to the highest and poorest ground on the north and west, the range being from 0.8km to 2.7km. The Eskdale population remained relatively constant, with a mean of 33 pairs annually, from 1985 to 1994, but by 1997 it had fallen to only 21 pairs (Newton & Rothery, 2001). By way of explanation, many former nesting sites had been clear-felled, while most remaining woods were no longer being thinned, so that the area of suitable nesting habitat had probably declined. Decreases in farmland birds had also become noticeable, so that reduction in food supply was probable. A third factor was the establishment of three pairs of goshawks in the area from 1995, this larger relative being a dominant competitor with the sparrowhawk.

Numbers of breeding sparrowhawks obviously depend on the amount of woodland in an area, but it must be suitable woodland: fairly dense but open enough for the bird to fly through. Newton (1991) found that in conifer plantations in south Scotland, stands 20–35 years old were favoured for nesting. Younger stands had usually not been thinned and so were too thick, while beyond 35 years repeated thinning tended to make them too open. The short rotation of conifer crops, with felling and replanting of some areas every year, ensures a continuity of suitable habitat, but in ever-changing locations, so that the hawks have to move around accordingly. Woodland does not have to exist in the form of extensive forests, and a good frequency of scattered small to medium blocks can support a high breeding density of sparrowhawks. Where there are only a few large blocks of forests in generally non-wooded countryside, a certain amount of clumping of active nests may occur, with normal spacing between pairs much reduced.

Sparrowhawks breed at lower density in the huge conifer forests of Galloway, to the west of the Dumfries study areas. These plantations are mostly on acid moorland, with little in the way of adjoining farmland, and so have a low density of prey. They are also mostly unthinned plantations and large areas are unsuitable as nesting habitat. Newton found evidence of local variations in the habitat quality of individual sparrowhawk territories, which were reflected in frequency of use for nesting, nest success, age of the occupying female and its fidelity to the location. In the areas he studied the known territories were never all occupied in any one year. Favoured territories were occupied every (or almost every) year, and others more sporadically. Annual nest success was highest in the favoured territories, but even in these the turnover in occupants was high. This was partly due to high annual mortality (about 34 per cent per year), but even more to frequent territory changes by individuals. About a third of all surviving sparrowhawks changed territories one year to the next, and many moved from poor to good territories during their lives (Newton, 1991). The implication is that the most important aspect of habitat quality for the sparrowhawk is its food value.

The earlier history of the goshawk in the region is obscure, because of the name confusion with peregrines. It most probably bred, but was exterminated not long into the nineteenth century, and remained absent until falconers' birds escaped in the 1960s, followed by a deliberate and approved introduction of Finnish birds from the early 1970s. The 1968–72 *Atlas* showed a handful of probable breeding records, mostly in Dumfries & Galloway, but by 1988–91 there was certain breeding in ten 10km squares, mainly in the Borders. In 2002, 55 occupied Borders home ranges were monitored and 29 nests found, of which 26 were successful – a slight reduction on 38 nests (29 successful) in 1999 (Murray, 2003). In Dumfries & Galloway in 2000, 16 sites were checked and ten found occupied, eight successfully (Norman, 2001). This bird spends much of its time in woodland and breeds nowhere else. It is elusive and some pairs may be overlooked, but its increase has been hindered by persecution, and its stronghold is in the state forests (Marquiss, in *New Atlas*). Able to take prey as large as blackcock and hare, it is one of the few predators of its smaller relative the sparrowhawk (Newton, 1986). It often feeds outside the nesting woods, and birds from some upland forests take a good many red grouse on adjoining moorland (Marquiss & Newton, 1982).

The kestrel breeds in woodland, but hunts mainly outside, and so is regarded more as a bird of other main habitats (see Chapter 5). The same is true of the buzzard, although this bird is more reliant on woods as nesting habitat, and also feeds to a greater extent within woodland, especially where this is open, with low stocking density of trees. The spread of the buzzard as a lowland tree-nester during the last twenty-five years is one of the most remarkable features in the birdlife of southern Scotland in recent times (Fig. 81). The spread has been particularly in the east, where the bird was scarce or absent up to the 1950s, but

FIG 81. Buzzard at tree-nest with young. This bird has made a spectacular increase across the region. (Bobby Smith)

it has filled in previous gaps over most of the southwest. The 1988–92 *New Atlas* showed a gain of almost thirty 10km² squares for confirmed breeding, and the increase has continued apace since 1992. Buzzards now nest almost continuously through the lowlands of Dumfries & Galloway, and the northern half of the Borders, but are more scattered in the southern half (map in Murray, 2002). The Borders population was estimated at 1,000 pairs in 2000 (Holling, in Murray, 2002). There are no figures for the southwest district, but the breeding population there probably exceeds that of the Borders.

With the inclusion of Galloway in the red kite reintroduction programme, this bird is now once more established in the woodlands of the region. During 2001–04, 100 young birds were released in the Stewartry. First breeding occurred in 2003, and nine nests were found in 2005, despite the loss of 13 birds to illegal poisoning – though none since April 2004. Up to thirty birds are often seen together during the winter in the Loch Ken area. A feeding station has been set up at Bellymack Hill Farm near Laurieston, and a Galloway Kite Trail is boosting tourism by attracting the attention of both local and visiting birdwatchers (Rollie, 2004).

BUTTERFLIES AND MOTHS

The purple hairstreak was found to be quite widespread in the oakwoods of
Galloway by Joan Watson in the 1980s, but there are only a few pre-1970 records
for the Borders. It is, however, an easily overlooked insect, from its habit of
remaining mostly high in the canopy of oak trees, where its presence is best
detected through binoculars, so that it could be more frequent than is realised.
The speckled wood is the only other strictly woodland butterfly in the region,
known before 1970 in scattered places mainly in the northeast, but recently
seen only in the Wigtownshire Rhins. The small pearl-bordered fritillary is
widespread in Dumfries & Galloway, but scarce in the Borders. While woodland
glades, rides and edges are a favourite habitat, this species is widespread also on
moorland, wet grassland, coastal dunes and cliff-slopes. Its relative, the pearl-
bordered fritillary, is much scarcer, and is now found in open broadleaved
woodland or woodland edges, especially where recent felling has created clear
areas where the violets on which the larvae feed can flourish. Its few extant
localities are in the neighbourhood of Dumfries, though it was previously
scattered in Galloway, where Cunningham (1951) recorded five new sites, and
had still earlier stations in the Borders. The dark-green fritillary is not really
a woodland species, but is often seen along forest rides and roads, where
ungrazed flowering herbs give good nectar sources.

Green hairstreaks are surprisingly rare – or, more probably, overlooked –
and there is only a handful of recent records, mainly from Wigtownshire. They
frequent open woodland, especially of birch with bilberry, or scrubby places with
gorse and other shrubs. Another butterfly of open places with scattered scrub is
the holly blue, recorded around Dumfries in 1970–82, but only from near Annan
after 1995. Holly and ivy are not its only larval food-plants, for bramble and gorse
are recorded also. After a lapse from earlier presence in the Borders, during
1850–70 (Thomson, 1980), the comma has again spread northwards to recover its
former distribution, besides appearing also in Galloway. It is a butterfly of the
woodland edge and open scrub.

Several other butterflies often frequent the sheltered glades, rides or edges
of woodland, such as the small tortoiseshell, peacock, red admiral, painted lady,
orange-tip (Fig. 82) and the three common whites. Thomson (1980) gives three
nineteenth-century records of the Duke of Burgundy, a butterfly of open
woodland, for Dumfries and Roxburgh, but there have been none since 1900.

For many moths, woodland is only one of various lowland habitats in which
they live (Fig. 83). Among the more notable, several narrow-bordered bee hawks

FIG 82. Male orange-tip: a butterfly which has spread recently in southwest Scotland. (Bobby Smith)

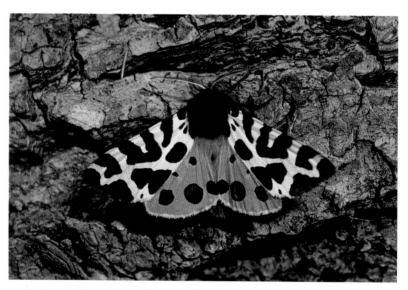

FIG 83. Garden tiger moth: an insect seen less frequently now than in earlier years. (Bobby Smith)

were seen feeding at bluebell flowers in a Galloway woodland in 1977 and a single one similarly engaged in a Dumfries wood in 1978. Cunningham (1951) described the red sword-grass as common, the peach blossom as locally common, the pale prominent as rare but scattered, and the early grey, sword-grass and clouded silver as all rare. The saxon, a northern moth, is known from at least two recent sites in the southwest, while the southern buff arches was rediscovered in Galloway near Gatehouse of Fleet in 1999, after a lapse of 64 years. Richard and Barbara Mearns have reported an increase in the red-necked footman in Dumfries & Galloway, mostly in low-altitude commercial conifer plantations. They note that bird photographers Brian Turner and Rab Smith found a pair of pied flycatchers near Penpont feeding their young almost exclusively on this species. There has been a recent increase in the copper underwing, especially in woodland near the coast, and there is one record of the barred tooth-striped from Nithsdale. Juniper pug and chestnut-coloured carpet have been found at inland juniper scrubs.

CHAPTER 5

Lowland Farmland, Grassland and Heath

T HIS GROUP OF habitats essentially comprises the dry lowlands, where agriculture is the predominant land use, and countryside used for other purposes has survived somewhat erratically.

FARMLAND

Most of the agricultural land in southern Scotland is under permanent grass, and used for grazing cattle and sheep, or for growing hay with which to feed them at other times. That included in this chapter is the *enclosed* land, with fields bounded by hedges, fences and walls (Fig. 84). Its soils have mostly been improved in fertility in some degree, and often over a long period of enclosure, by the addition of animal manures, seaweed, lime and modern inorganic fertilisers with nitrogen, phosphorus and potassium (NPK). A recent feature is the brilliant emerald-green pastures of the upland valley bottoms, of bowling-green smoothness, and stocked with high densities of sheep or cattle. Yet, on many damp pastures, improvement has been either a complete failure or only partly successful, leading sometimes to almost total dominance of common rush or to dense and luxuriant patches of this plant, sharply delineated from the green grass sward. This results, apparently, from failure to treat the rush growths with herbicide.

Arable crops cover a more limited area, mainly in the drier east, in the lower Tweed valley (the Merse) and the coastal lowlands of Berwickshire and East Lothian. The breeding of modern varieties to cope with the more humid and cooler conditions in the west has also allowed an expansion of arable

FIG 84. Border foothill country with improved pasture and planted woodland in the Wauchope Valley, south of Bonchester Bridge, Roxburghshire.

farming in Dumfries & Galloway. The chief crops are barley, wheat, oilseed rape, potatoes and swedes. Oats are little grown now and even barley has declined in preference to grass. Much of the grassland grown for hay could be considered a form of arable, for it has mostly been created by ploughing the earlier grass and re-seeding with commercial strains, particularly rye-grass, to give high-production swards which are now usually converted to silage. Stacks of the large black bags of big-bale silage are a feature of the modern British countryside, here as elsewhere.

Modern farms mostly contain little habitat of value to wildlife, except where a few concerned farmers deliberately forgo maximising production in order to support the presence of wild plants and animals (Fig. 85). For the most part, it is a matter of scattered fragments that have survived by accident, as uncultivated corners and patches of waste ground, or as the unimproved meadows of old-fashioned and usually elderly farmers. Hedges and hedgerow trees are important, but they have lost ground also. Railway embankments and cuttings were valuable linear habitats, but with line closures many sections have been sold off and become incorporated into the adjoining farmland. Road verges have become regarded as a last refuge of semi-natural herbaceous communities in heavily agricultural areas (Fig. 86), but they, too, can be improved, to add to the intensive

FIG 85. Foxglove is one of the most spectacular wild plants of acid soils in a variety of lowland habitats. It is highly poisonous.

FIG 86. Lowland roadsides and unimproved grasslands provide refuges for plants such as rock-rose, but this once-common plant has lost much ground in recent years.

grass production. This has happened in Cumbria, not far away, and could do so in Scotland, though I have not been aware of any instances yet.

The arable crops have, in common with those throughout the rest of Britain, lost most of the colourful weeds that once relieved their monotony, especially in cereal fields. The cleaning of seed crops and heavy use of herbicides have eliminated most of them. Hutton Balfour noted corncockle as common in Galloway in 1843; it is now extinct. Cornflower was always uncommon in southern Scotland but survives in Wigtownshire and the Borders, while corn marigold is more widespread but decreasing. There are occasional brilliant displays of common poppies in cereal fields, especially in the Borders.

HERB-RICH GRASSLANDS

The old-style hay meadows, rich in attractive and colourful flowers, were once widespread, but have lost ground on an enormous scale since 1940, and very few survive today. Those rich in tall herbs of ungrazed subalpine birchwoods (e.g. wood cranesbill and melancholy thistle), which still survive in places in the north of England, were probably once widespread in southern Scotland, but have virtually disappeared. Sometimes lightly grazed and enclosed pastures were similarly rich: I noted one at the south end of Woodhall Loch near Laurieston in 1956, with globeflower, burnet saxifrage, dyer's greenweed, rock-rose, greater butterfly orchid, fragrant orchid, whorled caraway, mountain everlasting, sea plantain and pale sedge. Most of these plants have since been 'improved' out of existence. The majority of the surviving herb-rich grasslands are pastures grazed by cattle or sheep in some degree, and have survived purely by chance, in escaping heavy treatment with the NPK fertilisers which have reduced so much of the former semi-natural grasslands to dull, species-poor uniformity.

Surveys by SNH have identified 56 grassland sites of importance in the Borders (Lusby, 1992). They are generally small, in the range 5–30ha, but that at Greenlaw Dean covers 63.6ha. They are mostly on moderately lime-rich substrates derived from the prevailing sedimentary rocks, but a few are on basic igneous materials. While outcrops of limestone and calcareous basalt occur in scattered places, there is nothing to match the large expanses of limestone grassland of the Carboniferous formation in northern England, and the flora is more limited. Probably because of the wetter climate, with heavier leaching and widespread peat formation, these grasslands of base-rich soils are scarcer in the southwest, but they occur in scattered patches on the same substrates. They are, again, mostly small, but the complex at Feoch, near Barrhill in south Ayrshire, extends over 83ha, and that at Cleugh, above Carsfad Loch in the upper Ken Valley, covers 54ha.

There is a good deal of floristic similarity between the swards of well-drained situations. Sheep's and red fescues, bents, cock's-foot, vernal grass, crested dog's-tail, heath grass, crested hair-grass and Yorkshire fog are the characteristic grasses of the dry swards, while mat-grass, tufted hair-grass and flying bent are typical of damper and more acidic situations. Carnation, glaucous and spring sedges are usually present, while common and constant herbs include yarrow, white and meadow clovers, harebell, meadow and creeping buttercups, self-heal, wild thyme, common milkwort, eyebright, ragwort, knapweed, bird's-foot trefoil, mouse-ear hawkweed, ribwort plantain, heath violet, fairy flax, lady's bedstraw, devil's-bit scabious and meadow vetchling. Some sites show signs of incipient acidification, in the presence of plants such as tormentil, pignut, cat's ear, heath bedstraw, bitter-vetch, beautiful St John's-wort, common sorrel and sheep's sorrel. On moister, deeper soils water avens, lady's mantle, hogweed, angelica, sneezewort and meadowsweet form a taller herb community.

More local but still widespread species are rock-rose, burnet saxifrage, common spotted orchid, fragrant orchid, zigzag clover, perforate St John's-wort, rough hawkbit, cowslip, field scabious, kidney vetch, annual knawel, autumn gentian, mountain pansy and wood anemone. Less common grasses are yellow oat-grass, smaller cat's-tail, quaking grass, downy oat-grass and meadow oat-grass. Whorled caraway is a common plant in damp pastures of enclosed and marginal land in Kirkcudbrightshire, which forms one of its three main centres of distribution in Britain, the other two being southwest Wales and the southwest Highlands. Sometimes with it is spignel, another characteristic umbellifer of the Stewartry, though much less common. This flourishes best in drier, ungrazed situations, on roadside banks or neglected corners near farms, where its feathery dark green foliage is quite distinctive (Fig. 87). It is a strongly aromatic plant, formerly used as a herb, but it is regarded as native, and has been found high on ledges at the Grey Mare's Tail and White Coomb in Moffatdale.

Globeflower is quite widespread in damp southwestern pastures which have escaped serious 'improvement', and along riversides, but usually as scattered patches, and it is still declining (Fig. 88). Its frequent hay-meadow associates in northern England, wood cranesbill and melancholy thistle, are more frequent in the northeast of the region. In places where grazing is slight or absent, such as road verges, false meadow-grass may be dominant, with a variety of the herbs of the previous grassland communities. Bush vetch and tufted vetch are still common grassland plants in the less-grazed places, but the handsome upright bitter-vetch is now rare, having lost much ground in recent times (Fig. 89). It has

FIG 87. Spignel is one of the most distinctive plants of roadside banks and unimproved grassland in the Galloway lowlands. Milnmark, Kirkcudbrightshire.

FIG 88. Globeflower is a plant of old meadows and streamsides, but has become much rarer through farming 'improvements'.

FIG 89. Upright bitter-vetch is now a rare herb of old meadows and uncultivated places, mostly in the Galloway lowlands.

scattered localities in Galloway, in rough uncultivated places, including an old railway line, and Stewart (1992) notes that a colony on a promontory of Loch Ken is intermingled with spignel. The cliff ledges of Cairnbaber have patches in unusual habitat. In the northeast its only known surviving station is on a steep bank of the Yarrow Water. Of the various lady's mantle micro-species, *Alchemilla glabra* is common and widespread, *A. xanthochlora* and *A. filicaulis* ssp. *vestita* more local, and *A. filicaulis* ssp. *filicaulis* rare. Roderick Corner found the northern *A. glomerulans* in hay meadows and roadside verges in upper Ettrickdale, but the population has since been severely reduced by modern farming practices, and survives in just three sites.

Rarer herbs with no particular geographical orientation are field gentian, knotted clover, heath pearlwort, meadow saxifrage, common restharrow, betony, sand-leek, twayblade, early purple orchid, frog orchid, lesser butterfly orchid, small-white orchid, moonwort and adder's-tongue. Of the other uncommon meadow plants, great burnet, maiden pink, pepper saxifrage and soft hawk's-beard are rare and only in the northeast; while dyer's greenweed, saw-wort and greater butterfly orchid are confined to the southwest. Sea plantain appears in some coastal sites, and common fleabane is largely confined to the actual coast of the southwest. Nearly all these species have declined seriously over the last few decades through pasture improvement. For instance, small-white orchid, once recorded from at least twenty-one 10km squares across the region, is now known from only three. Some grassland species well known in Cumbria or Northumberland, such as bee orchid and ploughman's spikenard, fail to cross the border. A few that occur farther north in Scotland are also absent from the region, such as blue moor-grass, so abundant on the Pennine limestone.

An interesting example of the basiphilous grassland occurs on the serpentinite of Pinbain Hill south of Girvan, where magnesium-rich soils have outlying occurrences of spring sandwort and alpine pennycress, two plants especially associated with lead-mine debris in the Pennines. A herb-rich grass heath occurs there, with ling, bell heather, rock-rose, red and sheep's fescues, bents, meadow oat-grass, spring sedge, wild thyme (Fig. 90), kidney vetch, lady's bedstraw, mountain everlasting, heath violet, bird's-foot trefoil and sea plantain. Ground with slightly impeded drainage has flying bent and mat-grass, with associated small herbs in places, and there is an isolated population of junipers. On other basic igneous rocks at Bennane Head, not far to the south, there is a remarkable disjunct occurrence of green-winged orchid, in its only extant Scottish locality and the most northerly now known in Britain; the nearest stations are on the Morecambe Bay limestone of south Cumbria.

Situated as they usually are on uneven morainic ground, many of these dry

FIG 90. The aromatic wild thyme is common in dry, open places wherever the soils incline to base-richness.

swards grade into wet flushed grassland and then shallow marsh in poorly drained hollows and channels, and where lateral drainage water emerges as springs and flushes at the ground surface. There is a marked change in flora, with the appearance of moisture-loving plants typical of damp, base-rich conditions, such as carnation, yellow, long-stalked yellow, dioecious, flea and tawny sedges, few-flowered spike-rush, jointed rush, black bog-rush, grass of Parnassus, common butterwort, marsh valerian, northern marsh-orchid and cuckoo flower. More local species include broad-leaved cotton-grass, early marsh-orchid and flat sedge. Where conditions are more permanently waterlogged, approaching fen, there are kingcup, bogbean, marsh cinquefoil, marsh woundwort and bog pondweed. Good examples occur on the serpentinite of Pinbain Hill, where there is a profusion of black bog-rush along moist seepages. In the west, transitions to more acidic conditions are shown by the presence of bog myrtle, bog asphodel, marsh violet, common cotton-grass, flying bent, common and sharp-flowered rush. These communities and habitats grade into the fens of permanently waterlogged ground, which are dealt with in Chapter 6. Grasslands dominated by flying bent (purple moor-grass) are extensive in the Galloway lowlands, but they belong more particularly to the uplands and are dealt with there (Chapter 7).

Roadside and railway verges support linear remnants of grassland, often rich in herbs. The quantities of knapweed, ox-eye daisy, ragwort, rosebay willowherb, bush vetch, tufted vetch, yellow-rattle and creeping thistle growing on roadside verges are an important nectar source for insects (Fig. 91). The larger ferns also find a major niche on road verges, in particular male fern, scaly male fern, lady fern, lemon-scented fern and bracken (Fig. 92). Towards the coast, especially in Wigtownshire, roadside banks and verges have abundant bluebells, red campion and greater stitchwort, representing a fragmentary woodland community. Disused railway lines that have remained closed to livestock have some good

FIG 91. Rosebay willowherb grows densely on roadside verges, as well as where woodland has been felled and the brushwood burned.

FIG 92. Scaly male fern forms vigorous clumps along roadsides and on lower hill slopes.

herbaceous communities in places, and damp spots have some fine colonies of northern marsh-orchid on the old tracks. There are a few rare calcicoles also. A cutting on the disused Waverley line at Hummelknowes has a northern colony of torgrass, a typical plant of chalk downs, with other calcicoles such as small scabious and hoary plantain. The only extant Borders site for pyramidal orchid is on an old railway bank in Selkirkshire, but sand-leek is probably extinct in its Roxburgh railway site. Roadside banks in the Borders, and some woodlands, are increasingly being invaded by the alien few-flowered garlic.

A recent phenomenon has been the colonisation of road verges by halophytic (salt-loving) plants in response to the growing use of road-salt for de-icing roads in winter. The trend has been studied by Roderick Corner, who has found the reflexed saltmarsh-grass, lesser sea-spurrey and spear-leaved orache widespread, but greater sea-spurrey and grass-leaved orache rare so far. All are characteristic salt-marsh plants.

The most important grassland sites in the region, under management as SSSIS, are listed in Appendix 1. Much of the dry grasslands belong to one or other sub-communities of the Rodwell types MG5 and MG6, but on the richer sites CG10 is well represented, while those at the acidic end belong to U1 and U4. M1 is also well represented. Moist grasslands mostly fall within mire types M23–25. Flush communities belong to M10, and incipient fens are close to M26 and M27.

DWARF SHRUB HEATHS

The semi-natural grasslands as a whole are still widespread within the farmland scene, but lowland heaths, as communities dominated by dwarf shrubs and with southern rather than northern features, are decidedly local. The best example is probably the coastal dune heath at Torrs Warren, described in Chapter 3. Other heaths of ling and bell heather (Rodwell H10) are quite widespread in coastal areas of Galloway, and occur on the basic igneous rocks of the Lendalfoot complex in south Ayrshire. They occur at the upland fringe and well into the submontane zone. The dry, heathery and bracken-grown edges of peat mosses, such as Kirkconnell Flow, probably qualify, but the kind of southern heaths with western and dwarf gorse, represented by surviving fragments in Cumbria, across the Solway, hardly exist north of the border. Wet grass heaths are, however, widespread in the humid southwestern district. The type dominated by a mixture of cross-leaved heath and deer sedge (M15) is the most extensive, especially in the submontane upland zone. Flying bent and ling are typically present, with tormentil, heath milkwort, lousewort and carnation sedge. Moisture-loving plants such as bog asphodel, common cotton-grass and bog-mosses in wetter sites mark the intermediate position of this community between heath and bog.

ROCK HABITATS

Rock outcrops at low elevations are an interesting plant habitat, especially where they are of basalt or other basic igneous material. The most famous is at Minto Craigs (Fatlips Crags) west of Jedburgh, where a volcanic vent filled with a basalt plug has given rise to an impressive escarpment with faces of 30 metres or more, feeding block screes below. This lies within a woodland setting, albeit a somewhat secondary one with abundance of sycamore, beech and spruce, and is otherwise surrounded by farmland. The rock is evidently both acidic and basic (in the soil-forming sense) in different places, with a mixture of plants such as ling, wood sage, red campion, shining cranesbill, meadow saxifrage and thale-cress. The most notable plants are the forked spleenwort fern, surviving here in its only locality in the region, and the sticky catchfly, present also on the Galloway coast (both grow on Arthur's Seat and Salisbury Crags in Edinburgh). The catchfly also grew on a riverside rock at Corbie Linn above Selkirk, but became shaded out by luxuriant gorse. An attempted reintroduction from seed previously collected from the locality is doubtfully viable (R. Corner). The hybrid between forked spleenwort and the diploid form of maidenhair spleenwort (*Asplenium* × *alternifolium*) formerly grew at Minto Craigs, but has not been seen for many years. Smailholm Craigs are ribs and slabs of basalt on the flat with a patchy vegetation cover which includes a profusion of wild pansy and *Cladonia* lichens, with maiden pink and rock-rose. Another basalt outcrop, Craigturra above Tynron in Dumfries, looks promising but has mostly common plants of dry rocky places, with rock-rose, sheep's-bit and burnet saxifrage as the only ones with a less continuous distribution. The heath dog-violet is now rare in the Borders and found mainly on riverside rocks. The lack of limestone outcrops, especially pavements, explains the absence of a whole group of calcicole plants present on the Carboniferous rock habitats in Cumbria.

Walls, bridges and man-made cliffs such as disused quarries and railway cuttings are another rock habitat. Drystone walls have a selection of common ferns including ordinary polypody, but also the more local parsley fern towards the hills, and they hold a variety of mosses and lichens (Fig. 93). Mortared walls offer suitable conditions for lime-loving species, and maidenhair spleenwort and wall-rue are often in profusion (Fig. 94), with black spleenwort less common. Scaly spleenwort has a patchy distribution and a generally precarious existence as its wall habitats are periodically re-pointed – or demolished. For a

FIG 93. Stag's-horn clubmoss grows in dry heathy places, but is not common. Near Stroan Loch, Kirkcudbrightshire.

FIG 94. Maidenhair spleenwort is a common fern of mortared walls across the region.

Mediterrean–Atlantic species, some of its Borders localities are surprisingly far inland. Probably its finest colony in the southwest was lost, along with the other wall ferns, when the disused Little Water of Fleet viaduct was blown up by British Rail. Ivy-leaved toadflax is a fairly common plant of mortared walls, though absent from parts of the interior. The introduced fairy foxglove is widely scattered on old walls, including those of buildings, but pellitory-of-the-wall is mainly in Berwickshire.

MAMMALS

Many of the woodland mammals, including fox, badger, stoat, weasel, hedgehog, wood mouse, bank vole and common shrew, also have a niche in the farmlands and grasslands. The mole is one of the most constant mammals of the grasslands across the region, though unwelcome to farmers and gardeners. Rabbits also remain widespread, though numbers tend these days to cycle, as recurrent myxomatosis cuts down populations building up to peaks after periods of low numbers. Brown hares remain widespread, though less numerous than in years before the agricultural revolution (Fig. 95). The bats described under woodland (Chapter 4) mostly feed over farmland as well, and some of them, such as

FIG 95. Brown hare: still relatively numerous on farmland across southern Scotland. (Bobby Smith)

pipistrelle, long-eared and whiskered bats, roost and breed in buildings. The decline in some species is attributed to the effects of modern agriculture on insect populations. Herbicides destroy the weeds that are insect food-plants, and insecticides can adversely affect bats directly (Altringham, 2003).

BIRDS

In common with the farmlands elsewhere in Britain, those of southern Scotland have declined greatly in their bird interest (Wright, c.1990). The once common corncrake (Fig. 96) was recorded breeding in only five 10km squares in the *New Atlas*, while another casualty of modern farming, the formerly widespread corn bunting, survives in very few localities, mainly on the coasts. The yellow wagtail never had more than a foothold, and that only in the northeast, for it seemed, like some plants, to find its northern distribution limit at the border. It is still rarer now but present in a handful of 10km squares (*New Atlas*). The common birds of hedgerow and wayside, chaffinch, greenfinch, goldfinch, linnet, yellowhammer, blackbird, song thrush, mistle thrush, great tit, blue tit, dunnock, house sparrow, robin, wren, skylark, pied wagtail, have nearly all declined, some of them seriously. For some, gardens have become relatively a more important habitat than farmland (Fig. 97). More local species, such as tree sparrow, whinchat, redpoll, bullfinch and reed bunting are fewer also. Of the waders, the snipe and redshank have become uncommon breeders as the damp meadows and other marshy grasslands have been drained and converted to commercial leys on a massive scale. While they favoured the old wet pastures with scattered rush clumps, the dense rush growths of failed attempts at 'improvement' seem unattractive to birds generally. Lapwings remain widespread but erratic in occurrence and their former population has been decimated (Fig. 98); while the curlew, which expanded onto the drier farmland and even arable after 1940, has thinned out and retreated towards the peat mosses, marginal lands and uplands. Only the oystercatcher has benefited from the agricultural revolution, and now breeds quite widely in the farmed lowlands across the whole region. An unusual concentration of 21 pairs was reported at the Beattock gas station in the summer of 2001 (Norman, 2002).

Rook populations in the Borders and Dumfriesshire had a lean time between 1944–6 and 1975, decreasing by 33–73 per cent (Brenchley, 1986). In Dumfriesshire the number of nests declined from 10,964 to 7,252, in Roxburgh from 29,785 to 8,149, and in Berwickshire from 20,809 to 8,336. The 1960s and 70s were a period when the organochlorine pesticides were causing considerable damage among

FIG 96. Corncrake: a casualty of the farming revolution, now virtually extinct across the region. (Bobby Smith)

FIG 97. Mistle thrushes often nest in trees in gardens, and around isolated shepherds' cottages. (Bobby Smith)

FIG 98. Incubating lapwing on ploughed field: a bird which has declined seriously across the region. (Bobby Smith)

wild birds, and it is suspected that they may have affected rooks adversely, since this species was so directly in contact with them. That problem has largely passed away, and the present heavy use of fertilisers on farmland may favour rooks by boosting invertebrate populations. A survey in Peeblesshire showed an increase from 1975 to 1990 of 59 per cent, and from 1990 to 1998 of 97 per cent, to 8,370 nests. Numbers in Dumfriesshire had recovered, for censuses in 1973, 1975 and 1993 showed a gradual increase, to 50 per cent by 1993, when the population was similar to that of 1963 (Griffin *et al.*, 2004). Yet the 2003 census showed a fall in the number of nests in Dumfriesshire from 25,489 in 1993 to 17,853, a 30 per cent decline, so that the overall picture is mixed (Fig. 99).

Favourite rook nesting places are in clumps of trees near farmhouses, but sometimes in shelter belts and bigger woods, so that they have some claim to be considered as woodland birds. The very largest colonies in Peeblesshire have disappeared since 1990, while those of under a hundred nests have increased, producing an overall decrease to 122–4 nests per colony. Counts of 13 rookeries in other parts of the Borders averaged 55 nests (10–160).

Carrion crows are ubiquitous across the farmlands, and in winter are – with rooks – often the most commonly seen larger bird there. They maintain their numbers despite the war waged against them by gamekeepers, though numbers

FIG 99. Even common species such as rooks have declined in some places, such as this fringe of trees in an upland valley. Milnmark, Dalry, Kirkcudbrightshire.

and breeding density vary according to this control. The output of young from areas with little or no keepering keeps the numbers up generally, and may account for the apparent non-breeding surplus present in some areas in the spring. Nests are placed especially in hedgerow trees and tall hedges, but sometimes in woods. Jackdaws are common farmland birds and usually colonial, nesting in holes of hedgerow trees, buildings, chimneys and, occasionally, rabbit burrows on hillsides. Magpies are surprisingly erratic in occurrence, perhaps as a result of gamekeeper persecution, from which few parts of this region are free. They nest in places in the last scattered thorns and crab-apple trees on the lower moorlands.

Several of the raptors feed on farmland a good deal: the buzzard on rabbits and young corvids, the sparrowhawk on birds up to wood pigeon size and the goshawk on medium-sized birds and mammals. The kestrel (Fig. 100) is the most familiar bird of prey of the lowland countryside, and has become especially well known through its habit of hovering in search of food over the verges of main roads, where the often rank vegetation harbours good numbers of the small rodents that are its favourite prey. Two major studies of the kestrel have recently been made in the region. One was by Andrew Village in the Dumfries valley of Eskdalemuir, where, over the last forty years, extensive afforestation with conifers has increasingly altered the character of the marginal land and lower upland

FIG 100. Male kestrel with mouse on a tree-nest: the most widespread raptor. (Bobby Smith)

sheep pastures, and provided an important opportunity for following the fortunes of animal populations. The second study – still ongoing – is by Gordon Riddle and colleagues in southern Ayrshire, beginning on the coast at Culzean, just north of our boundary, and extending south through farmland into the recent conifer forests of the Carrick uplands.

Both researchers have pointed out that, while small rodents form the main diet of kestrels, other items are important at times or in some places. On the rich pastures of farmland, earthworms are eaten a good deal, along with other invertebrates such as large beetles, whose wing-cases frequently appear among the undigested remains in the raptor's castings. Small birds are also eaten quite commonly, and Riddle (1992) gives an impressive list of 58 species taken as prey including – exceptionally – quite large birds such as pheasant, wood pigeon and moorhen. Kestrels will, however, feed on birds found recently dead. Village (1990) found that meadow pipits, skylarks and starlings were frequent prey on Eskdalemuir farmland. Much depends on opportunity: at a nest near Langholm I found that the young had been reared largely on newly fledged starlings from nearby farms, with 39 pairs of wing-girdles left in and around the nest-ledge.

Woodland is important to the kestrel, both in providing nest sites in the form of old crow and magpie nests, or tree-holes, and through the afforestation of sheepwalks, which brings a great increase in its food supply. The removal of sheep from the planted ground allows the grasses to become much more luxuriant and to build up a deep layer of dead leaf litter. This in turn provides the short-tailed field vole with plentiful food and excellent cover, thus favouring its breeding; and with up to several litters a year, the numbers soon multiply. The kestrel was one of the predators that increased greatly in numbers during the late-nineteenth-century vole plagues on the Scottish Borders and then declined again when the rodent numbers fell away (Adair, 1892, 1893). While numbers of neither have reached these levels in more recent years, Village found in the young Eskdalemuir forests that voles fluctuated in abundance from a peak in autumn 1975 to a trough in spring 1977 and then recovered somewhat in the next two years, but his study was not long enough to discover whether a regular four- to six-year cycle (regarded as the norm in northern Britain) was established in this habitat. And, while there was a general correlation between density of territorial kestrel pairs and spring index of vole numbers, this was not statistically significant over the four years of the study. By contrast, vole populations on grazed sheepwalks remained at consistently lower levels and showed little annual variation, and kestrel numbers followed suit.

Breeding density of kestrels was also higher on the Eskdalemuir grasslands than on lowland English farmlands, where vole numbers were consistently lower (means of 32 pairs per 100km² and 12–19 pairs per 100km²).

Breeding territories varied from an average of one square kilometre during vole peaks to several square kilometres during troughs, but dispersion of nests was mostly irregular because suitable nest sites (old crow nests in scattered trees or clumps) were unevenly distributed. In some areas nests were clumped because that was the pattern of nest-site distribution, and in some parts of Eskdalemuir availability of nest sites limited the population, as Village proved by providing numerous nest-boxes in strategic locations, which allowed many more pairs to move in and breed. In Ayrshire, Riddle distinguished between traditional territories, occupied annually, and secondary territories used only when food was abundant and the population high. During the early stages of afforestation both were occupied, but when the canopy closed the secondary territories were increasingly deserted and the population declined: in one area from fifteen pairs in the 1970s to only two or three in the 1990s. In some lowland farming areas of Ayrshire the breeding population was stable and nesting pairs were evenly spaced.

After the newly fledged young kestrels part company from their parents, in July, they disperse randomly from the breeding areas, mostly to within a few kilometres of their birth-place, but a few travel much farther afield. Then, in September–October, there is a more general though variable migration, of both young and adults, from southern Scotland. Both Village and Riddle found that their ringed kestrels moved away in autumn, in all directions, but mainly south and southeastwards, to southern England and the fringes of mainland Europe between the Netherlands and Spain. A few marked birds were seen within or not far from their breeding areas but, since there was a winter population occupying individual territories in the marginal land and valley bottom grasslands, there was clearly also an influx of new birds from elsewhere. The new arrivals in southern Scotland were probably mostly birds from Fennoscandia, escaping the rigours of the northern snowy winters. Winter density was generally lower than in summer and autumn, reflecting the poorer food supply, and upland birds had to move to lower ground during prolonged periods of snow cover. The breeding birds and locally reared young returned the following March and April to occupy spring territories again. Turnover in the breeding population was high in both Ayrshire and Eskdalemuir, with often a new bird in any territory each year. Sometimes this was because individuals had moved elsewhere or changed mates. Mortality of southern Scottish kestrels was quite high in their first year, at 60–70 per cent, but lower in adults (2+ years) at 30–40 per cent.

Winter birds

Many of the smaller passerines flock together in autumn and spend the winter thus, roving around or staying in one place as food supply dictates. Formerly, when corn stacks were a regular feature of farmyards, the mixed flocks included a variety of finches, buntings and others – chaffinch, greenfinch, brambling, yellowhammer, reed bunting, blue and great tits, skylark, dunnock and a few pied wagtails and meadow pipits (Watson, 1988). Larger birds also joined in, including partridge, wood pigeon, mallard and pheasant, and predators such as sparrowhawk, kestrel and merlin followed them for easy pickings. With the disappearance of stackyards and the decline of winter stubbles, such diverse flocks are less often seen, but a large flock of chaffinches (3,500), greenfinches (500) and linnets (1,500) was reported on a turnip field in the Cree valley in 1987 (Watson, 1988), and moderate numbers of many species have been reported across the region in many recent years. Immigrant flocks of fieldfares and redwings work the hedgerows for berried plants (Fig. 101). The winter of 2004–5 saw a major waxwing invasion of Britain, with hundreds seen in southern Scotland, though they were often feeding on the berries of shrubs in suburban areas as well as on farmland (Fig. 102).

The problem of wild geese and swans feeding on farmland crops in winter is discussed in Chapter 3.

FIG 101. Flocks of fieldfares roam the lowlands in winter, seeking a variety of berries. (Bobby Smith)

FIG 102. Waxwing: an irregular winter visitor that comes from Fennoscandia in search of berries. (Bobby Smith)

FIG 103. Adder basking in the sun. Galloway is a great stronghold, from the coast and lowland peat mosses to the hill sheepwalks and moorlands.

REPTILES AND AMPHIBIANS

The Biological Records Centre map in Beebee & Griffiths (2000) shows that the adder is more continuously distributed across the south of Scotland than any other region of comparable size in Britain (Fig. 103). It occupies a wide range of habitats but is less often seen in the generality of farmland than in extensive uncultivated ground such as peat mosses, rough grassland and heath. Adders are also more frequently encountered in Galloway than Dumfriesshire and the Borders. The grass snake is recorded in two 10km squares covering lower Eskdale, but the habitat is unclear; these are the only occurrences in the region. Lizards are fairly common on uncultivated ground, and the slow-worm is widespread in Galloway, but more scattered in the Borders.

BUTTERFLIES

The three whites, large, small and green-veined, with caterpillars feeding on the Cruciferae, are all common across the farmlands. Though varying in numbers from year to year, the vanessids are often abundant also: small tortoiseshell, peacock, red admiral and painted lady, of which the last two are mostly immigrants that may breed in favourable years. Nettles are the main larval food-plant for the first three and thistles for the last. Grassy field margins and other uncultivated places, including road and railway verges, have the browns, with meadow brown, ringlet and small heath widespread and generally common, but wall brown local and now mainly along the southwest coast. There is a post-1970 record of the gatekeeper for Galloway, and a warming climate could encourage the northward spread of this species. The large skipper is frequent in the same grassy habitats in the southwest, but less so in the Borders, while the dingy skipper is mainly on grassy shores in Galloway. The dark-green and small pearl-bordered fritillaries were often to be seen at the flowers of tall herbs on the ungrazed banks of railways in Galloway but, after the incorporation of many disused sections of line within farmland, they have declined in this habitat. Cunningham (1951) said that the marsh fritillary was still on the Lochar Moss at that time – presumably in a marginal grassland community. It was also formerly in a number of Borders localities, but the only recent record was for the Southerness area during 1970–8 (Asher *et al.*, 2001). When clovers and lucerne were widely cultivated, the clouded yellow turned up sporadically on inland fields, but most of its recent occurrences have been on the coast.

On unimproved short grassland in the lowlands, especially on roadside and railway banks, the common blue is locally plentiful where there is abundant bird's-foot trefoil, but the northern brown argus is limited to the more scattered occurrences of rock-rose, on which its larvae feed. The small blue is now a rarity, with only a single post-1995 record, though it was once more widespread. The larval food-plant, kidney vetch, has declined greatly through grassland reclamation and improvement. Small coppers are locally common on rather acidic habitats where sheep's sorrel is plentiful, though it is also associated with other *Rumex* species on more neutral soils.

MOTHS

The hawk moths are not well represented in southern Scotland. The large elephant is the most frequently seen: its larvae feed on rosebay willowherb, which is common in waste places and occurs in dense stands on the site of cleared woodland. The small elephant is recorded from a number of localities across the region, and poplar hawks turn up now and then, mostly where there are poplars and aspens. Duncan & Cunningham (1953) trapped 157 species of moth in Dumfriesshire and eastern Kirkcudbright in 1951, and described the poplar hawk as common and the small elephant as frequent then. The eyed hawk is uncommon and perhaps sporadic in occurrence; it is a species found mostly south of the border: Richard Mearns trapped several near Dumfries, but only in one year. The hummingbird hawk appears in some years, but other immigrant hawk moths such as the death's-head, convolvulus and striped occur more rarely. Drinker moths are perhaps less frequent on grassy roadside verges than in earlier years, but the chimney sweeper is still quite common. The herb-rich grasslands produce some local species, such as the mother shipton, burnet companion and six-spot burnet. More rarely seen are the forester and narrow five-spot burnet.

CHAPTER 6

Wetlands: Rivers, Lakes, Fens and Bogs

THESE CONSIST OF the open waters (rivers and lakes), and the peatlands or mires (fens and bogs) of the lowlands.

RIVERS

The main rivers of Dumfries & Galloway all drain south to the Solway Firth. Beginning in the east, the Liddel is shared with Cumbria along the border and rises on the moorlands where the Cheviots become the Southern Uplands. Next to the west is the Esk, which is fed by the Ewes Water at Langholm and the Tarras Water (Fig. 104) lower down, but after collecting the Liddel near Scotsdike loses its lower course to Cumbria. The Sark forms the border south of the Scotsdike and reaches the Solway just east of Gretna, while the Kirtle Water enters the Firth immediately to the west. Moffat Water is the principal head-stream of the River Annan, which has lower tributaries in the Kinnel and Dryfe Waters and Water of Ae. The Nith rises on the moorlands of south Ayrshire close to Dalmellington and first flows east, but after entering Dumfriesshire it gradually turns southwards, and picks up many side-streams – the Mennock and Carron Waters from the Lowther Hills, and the Kello, Euchan, Scaur, Shinnel and Dalwhat Waters from the hills bordering the Stewartry (Fig. 105). Beyond Dumfries town it forms the important Nith estuary, with the huge sand flats of Blackshaw Bank.

The first major river of Kirkcudbrightshire is the Urr, which flows past Dalbeattie to enter the Solway at the inlet of Rough Firth near Kippford. The River Dee rises in the high hills of Minnigaff and is joined by the combined Ken

FIG 104. Cascading moorland stream, haunt of dipper, grey wagtail, common sandpiper and goosander. Tarras Water, near Langholm, Dumfriesshire. (Bobby Smith)

FIG 105. A lowland river: the Nith near Dumfries. Kingfisher habitat. (Bobby Smith)

and Deugh at New Galloway, reaching the sea past Kirkcudbright town. From Cairnsmore of Fleet issues the river of that name, to run past Gatehouse and enter the deep Solway inlet of Fleet Bay. The Waters of Minnoch and Trool join as the River Cree, which forms the county boundary with Wigtownshire and becomes estuarine past Newton Stewart, feeding another large system of sand flats at the head of Wigtown Bay.

Wigtownshire has two main rivers: the Bladnoch, which is joined by the Tarf Water from the northern moors and, after draining the Machars, discharges into the west side of Wigtown Bay; and the Water of Luce, flowing from the moors farther west, and in south Ayrshire, into the head of Luce Bay. In south Ayrshire the main stream is the River Stinchar, flowing southwest from the Carrick Hills into the North Channel at Ballantrae. The River Doon from Loch Doon soon leaves our area beyond the Ness Glen, and only the head of the Afton Water lies south of the Southern Uplands Fault. Various headstreams of the Clyde drain west and north from the Culter Fell massif and the Lowther Hills, but beyond Lamington the river belongs to the Midlands Valley.

Almost the whole of the Borders is drained by the great River Tweed, which, along its 155km course from source in the Tweedsmuir Hills to mouth at Berwick-upon-Tweed, gathers several main tributaries. In the west, the Yarrow Water issues from St Mary's Loch after entry of the Megget Water (Fig. 106), and

FIG 106. A fast-flowing upland river with few higher plants. Megget Water, Selkirkshire.

is joined just above Selkirk by the parallel Ettrick Water from the hills bordering Moffatdale and Eskdalemuir. The River Teviot collects other streams from along the watershed with Dumfriessshire, flows past Hawick and meets the Tweed at Kelso. From the north run numerous smaller streams, including the Gala Water from the Moorfoot Hills, the Leader Water from the western Lammermuirs, and the Blackadder and Whitadder (Whiteadder) Waters from the south and east of those uplands.

None of these rivers has remained unaltered by human hand from its pristine state. All suffered first the general disturbance of deforestation and wetland drainage that must have profoundly affected stream flows and sedimentation patterns. All have more recently experienced the disruptive effects of afforestation (see Chapter 9) in their upper catchments, sometimes extensively, as in the case of the upper Tweed, Liddel, Esk, Ken, Dee, Cree and Bladnoch. Most are affected along their lower courses by the excesses of modern agriculture, with topsoil, fertiliser and pesticide runoff, and some receive urban pollution from sewage and industrial chemicals as well. Some have been altered by drainage schemes intended to alleviate flooding of alluvial plains. Many have been dammed to create water-supply reservoirs, and virtually the whole lengths of the Galloway Ken and Dee have been modified by the grandiose hydroelectric scheme of the 1930s.

LAKES

Southern Scotland has numerous lakes, but the largest are either man-made or modified by raising their water levels, involving damming in both cases. Loch Doon in Carrick is the biggest (area 5.3km², maximum depth 30.5m). It is the enlarged successor to a natural lake, part of the hydroelectric project that created Clatteringshaws Loch on the upper course of the River Dee and the chain of lochs along the Water of Ken. In the south, a dam at Glenlochar caused the combined Ken/Dee to expand into a shallow lake of variable width (up to 1km) along the 18km stretch up to New Galloway. North of Dalry, further dams impounded the waters of Earlston, Carsfad and Kendoon Lochs. The region also contains numerous water-supply reservoirs, mostly created in upland valleys where no lakes existed previously: the biggest are Talla, Fruid and Megget, all in the Moffat–Tweedsmuir Hills (Fig. 107); Daer in the Lowther Hills; Camps in the Culter Fells; Black Esk in Eskdale; Afton in the New Cumnock Hills; Penwhirn northeast of Stranraer; Gladhouse on the north side of the Moorfoots; and Watch Water in the Lammermuirs.

FIG 107. Part of the Edinburgh water supply. Talla Reservoir from above the Linns, Peeblesshire.

The largest unmodified natural lake is St Mary's Loch in the upper Yarrow Valley (Fig. 108). In the southwest, most of the important original lowland lochs are in Galloway, but Dumfriesshire has one at Castle Loch by Lochmaben. In Kirkcudbright, the most notable are Lochs Kindar, Arthur and Lochrutton under the Criffel massif; Milton and Auchenreoch Lochs near Crocketford; Carlingwark Loch at Castle Douglas; Bargatton and Glentoo Lochs, Woodhall Loch and Loch Mannoch in the area of Laurieston. The Wigtownshire lowlands have the Black and White Lochs, and Soulseat Loch at Castle Kennedy; Whitefield Loch southeast of Glenluce; and Lochnaw and Loch Connell in the north of the Rhins.

In the Galloway Hills are numerous natural moorland lochs (Fig. 109). In the Cairnsmore of Fleet massif are Lochs Grennoch, Fleet, Skerrow and Stroan; under the Kells Range, Lochs Dungeon and Harrow; and in the central granite hills, Loch Dee, the two Glenhead Lochs, Loch Valley, Loch Neldricken and the three small Lochs of the Dungeon. In the Carrick Hills immediately north are Lochs Macaterick, Riecawr, Finlas and Bradan, the last with its level now raised by a dam. Wigtownshire has several lochs in a peatland setting, such as Castle and Mochrum Lochs in the Machars, and Lochs Eldrig, Ronald, Maberry and Ochiltree on the Moors. In the east of the Stewartry are Loch Howie, Lochinvar

FIG 108. The largest natural lake. Morning reflections at St Mary's Loch, Selkirkshire.

FIG 109. A moorland loch – now surrounded by forest and accessed by a road. Black Loch, Talnotry, Kirkcudbrightshire.

and Loch Urr, the last shared with Dumfries. The Moffat Hills have the high-lying Loch Skene at 510m, while the lower moorlands of Selkirk to the east have a series of small lakes, of which the largest are Alemoor Loch (now dammed), Hellmoor Loch, Akermoor Loch, Shaws Under Loch, Branxholme Easter and Wester Lochs, Crooked Loch and Kingside Loch, plus a number of smaller tarns. In the east of Roxburgh are Yetholm and Hoselaw Lochs, and in Berwickshire the tarns on Hule Moss and Coldingham Loch near St Abbs Head.

WATER CHEMISTRY

The waters of rivers and lakes are characterised according to their feeding value (or trophic level) for aquatic plants, which is largely a matter of content of dissolved nutrients, especially calcium carbonate. This lime content also determines water softness or hardness, in common parlance. The levels of nitrogen, phosphorus and potassium are also important. Nutrient content depends largely on the geology of the catchment, and its secondary effects on land use. Water draining from hard, acidic and base-poor bedrocks, superficial glacial materials and derived soils has a low content of the dissolved compounds necessary for plant growth, and is termed *oligotrophic*. Pools and tarns on peatlands, especially blanket bog, which receive their nutrients largely from the atmosphere, are similarly nutrient-deficient, and often have water stained brown by peat acids: they are called *dystrophic* (Fig. 110). Both these categories of nutrient-poor waters are typical of upland areas: oligotrophic streams and lakes are found especially on the Galloway granite, while dystrophic types occur on flat peatlands (flows) across the region.

Where nutrient status of the drainage water is rather higher, usually in lowland situations and often in agricultural settings, with fertility enhanced through chemical additions, the term *mesotrophic* is applied. A good many of the lowland rivers and lakes across the region fall into this category. A few, in places receiving drainage from calcareous substrates, and located within farmland, reach the highest nutrient status and are *eutrophic*. A good example of the last category is Carlingwark Loch at Castle Douglas. The agricultural enrichment of drainage water has become increasingly marked over the last fifty years, through the continual addition of inorganic fertilisers, to the extent that the increments of soluble nitrogen and phosphate to streams and lakes have come to be known as eutrophication and are regarded as having undesirable effects on aquatic life. These elements are also added in quantity through pollution by untreated sewage, from farms, villages and towns. An excess of these nutrients leads to

FIG 110. A dystrophic moorland tarn lying amidst blanket bogs. Loch Eldrig, Wigtownshire.

population explosions of microscopic photosynthetic organisms, known as algal blooms, which cause deoxygenation of the water and death of higher plant and some animal life, especially fish.

The other important change has been the increased acidification of oligotrophic waters by gaseous atmospheric pollutants from urban–industrial sources, especially sulphur dioxide and nitrogen oxides, which become converted to sulphuric and nitric acids. This process began with the Industrial Revolution and the huge outpouring of smoke from the burning of coal in large quantities. It has continued up to this day, and though efforts to reduce sulphur dioxide emissions have diminished the contribution of this gas to acidification, those of nitrogen oxides have increased, so that there is little if any lessening of the overall level of acid deposition. The nitrogen oxides also undergo partial conversion to ammonia, and then to nitrate, and so add to the eutrophication that is so widespread, on land as well as in water.

The acidification of lake waters has been particularly marked in the lochs of the Galloway granite, which were originally moderately acidic and are naturally susceptible (unbuffered is the technical term) to change in pH. Studies by Rick Battarbee and his colleagues of changes in diatom deposits (which indicate varying levels of acidity) in some of these lochs (the Round Loch of Glenhead and Loch Enoch) have shown decreases of around one pH unit, from 5.7 to 4.3–4.7. Most of this increase in acidity occurred after 1840, and was correlated with a marked increase in sediment levels of the trace metals lead, copper and zinc, supporting the hypothesis that much-increased atmospheric contamination from the Industrial Revolution was responsible (Battarbee *et al.*, 1985).

A similar study of lake cores at Loch Grennoch on the Cairnsmore of Fleet granite showed that similar acidification occurred here well before the advent of afforestation (Flower & Battarbee, 1983). When the catchment was subsequently extensively afforested from 1962, there was an initial rise in water pH to 5.0, probably caused by soil erosion and sedimentation from catchment ploughing and also the downwash of calcium phosphate applied to the tree seedling roots (Fig. 111). After another fifteen years there was a further drop in pH, to 4.3 by 1979, suggesting that acidification processes had overridden this brief improvement in lake conditions. There is evidence that the trees themselves can enhance the acidification of drainage waters by 'scavenging' the pollutants concerned from the atmosphere via their dense foliage (Harriman & Wells, 1985).

In attempting to reverse the relentless process of acidification, some lochs have had substantial amounts of lime (calcium carbonate) added to their surfaces and catchments. Loch Fleet in the Cairnsmore of Fleet massif has been treated

FIG 111. A moorland loch with water chemistry altered by afforestation in its catchment. Loch Grennoch, Cairnsmore of Fleet, Kirkcudbrightshire.

as an experimental site, with the treatments and results carefully recorded. While successful in some people's eyes, it does not restore the treated lochs to their original condition, but to a somewhat different chemical state, with an altered fauna and flora, especially of microscopic organisms.

The mesotrophic lake waters, and even more so those of eutrophic types, are mostly well buffered against acidification, and little if any change has been detected in those which have been studied.

VEGETATION

Rivers

The hill streams are fed at their sources by springs and rills dominated by mosses and liverworts, and these plants form the main vegetable growth on rocks in the mainly fast-running upper watercourses (Fig. 112). Different species are adapted to varying degrees of submergence. The mosses *Fontinalis antipyretica*, *F. squamosa*, *Rhynchostegium riparioides* and liverworts *Jungermannia exsertifolia* ssp. *cordifolia* and *Nardia compressa* grow mostly submerged under average stream-flow conditions, while *Hygrohypnum luridum*, *H. ochraceum*, *Hyocomium armoricum*, *Heterocladium heteropterum*, *Thamnobryum alopecurum*, *Brachythecium*

FIG 112. A rocky upland stream draining from a hanging valley. The Buchan Burn, with Benyellary and the Merrick behind, Kirkcudbrightshire.

plumosum, Racomitrium aciculare, Scapania undulata and *Marsupella emarginata*
occur on rocks mainly within the intermittent flood zone.

The lower courses of the rivers draining the lowlands flow more slowly
and have usually built up alluvial deposits, which form soft banks. While some
would qualify as flood plains, they have mostly been drained for agriculture,
and farmland reaches almost to the watercourses. The open water has locally
developed aquatic plant communities, and Dr Nigel Holmes found that the
Tweed and its tributaries have a greater number of submerged vascular plants
than any of the comparable rivers he has examined in northern England
(Corner, 1979a, 1979b). The more upland tributaries in Selkirkshire have
plentiful alternate-flowered water-milfoil, while spiked water-milfoil and several
pondweeds are found only in the Teviot and downstream from its confluence
with the Tweed (A11–13). Stream water-crowfoot is the most abundant of the
submerged higher plants (A17). Monkeyflower and its various hybrids colour
shingle and gravel beds yellow in places, and the true *Mimulus luteus* is common
on Caddon Water. Tree bases within the flood zone have mosses such as *Leskea
polycarpa*, and the rare *Myrinia pulvinata* occurs in this habitat beside Loch Ken.

The richer lowland river banks have luxuriant growths of aliens, with
'jungles' of giant hogweed and Indian balsam, and less robust species such as
leopard's-bane, few-flowered garlic and Russian comfrey (Corner, 1979a, 1979b).
The Adventive Flora of Tweedside (Hayward & Druce, 1919) recorded numerous alien
plants deriving from the woollen industry of the Tweed valley, which had
established themselves along the banks of the river and its lower tributaries,
especially the Gala Water at Gala Foot. They originated especially from the
imported fleeces of Merino sheep in Germany and Australia but also from other
parts of the world. In earlier years woollen-mill effluents carrying the seeds after
cleaning the fleeces washed into the rivers. These aliens have dwindled over the
ensuing decades and only a relatively small number remain today, the most
prominent being the pirri-pirri bur from New Zealand (R. Corner). Native plants
of the river banks include butterbur, whose large rounded leaves form
conspicuous growths, giant bellflower (Fig. 113), wood stitchwort, green figwort
and wood club-rush. Rarer plants of Borders riversides are pendulous, water and
slender-tufted sedges, lesser meadow-rue, northern bedstraw, round-fruited rush
and great horsetail.

The rivers of Dumfries & Galloway have less well-developed aquatic
communities, but the lower reach of the Nith has growths of pond and stream
water-crowfoots.

FIG 113. Giant bellflower, a local plant of river banks (and open woodland) on basic soils. Gifford, East Lothian.

Lakes

The oligotrophic lochs, often with inflows of peaty water, typically have a clean margin of sand, gravel and boulders, with an open growth of plants. The leaf rosettes of shoreweed, quillwort and water lobelia form a green fringe submerged in the shallow water (A22), and the last produces delicate stems with pale blue flowers that rise above the surface in summer. In the same habitat, awlwort is more scattered and spring quillwort is rare. On Loch Ken, where fluctuating water levels periodically expose sand and mud along the shore, are six-stamened waterwort and mudwort, two uncommon annual aquatics confined to the southwest district. Floating but rooted plants are alternate-flowered water-milfoil, common and intermediate water-starwort, floating bur-reed and the charophyte *Nitella opaca* (A13). Intermediate bladderwort occurs only in the southwest, but is quite widespread in peaty waters there. Within the zone of fluctuating water level are bryophytes such as *Fontinalis antipyretica* and *Jungermannia exsertifolia* ssp. *cordifolia*, while bulbous rush, creeping buttercup and bog pondweed are often exposed in a shore community (A24). Open growths of bottle sedge are frequently rooted in the shallow water and form a sparse fringing swamp along some loch edges.

The first signs of slightly more nutrient-rich water are the water-lilies, both white and yellow (Fig. 114), which form floating mats of leaves in rather deeper water, especially in sheltered bays (A7). They are both much more plentiful in Galloway than in the Borders, where Roderick Corner considers most occurrences to be introductions. In 1995, Olga Stewart (1996) confirmed the presence of the more northerly lesser yellow water-lily, along with the ordinary yellow species and the hybrid between the two, at Stroan Loch on the River Dee. G. T. West, who first found all three yellow water-lilies here in 1905, also recorded all three in Loch Ken, but the lesser species has not been re-found there. Pondweeds also increase in variety with rising nutrient content of lake waters: first the broad-leaved, perfoliate, long-stalked and red (A10), and then various-leaved, lesser, small, fennel, curled, blunt-leaved and flat-stalked (A11). Rigid hornwort occurs mainly in the richer waters of the Borders, but horned pondweed, mare's-tail, amphibious bistort and water-plantain are in eutrophic

FIG 114. White and yellow water-lilies, bottle sedge and wooded islands. Loch Skerrow, Kirkcudbrightshire.

lakes and tarns in both districts. Common water-crowfoot is widespread, but greater bladderwort rather uncommon, and lesser water-plantain now only in the southwest. Lesser water parsnip is mainly in the northeast, but greater water parsnip – formerly in Berwickshire – is considered extinct. The rare slender naiad has been found in the open water of Loch Kindar in Galloway. Introduced aquatics have spread: they include Canadian and Nuttall's waterweeds, and more recently the aggressively invasive New Zealand pygmyweed of lake shores has appeared in the region.

Fringing growths of reed are frequent around the edges of mesotrophic and eutrophic lakes (Fig. 115), and sometimes form quite dense reed-beds (s4). Sometimes, reed-grass is abundant or dominant (s28). Other emergent plants at lake margins in the richer waters are bulrush, common club-rush, branched bur-reed, bottle sedge, water sedge, bladder sedge, greater and lesser tussock sedges (s3, 7, 9, 10, 14). Of the rare species of *Carex* in these habitats, slender tufted sedge is scattered across the region, great fen-sedge and tufted sedge are only in Galloway, while greater pond sedge is confined to the Borders. Great fen sedge is still in at least two Galloway localities, but Silverside (1990) said it was once known around a number of Wigtown lochs, mostly in the Machars, and grew abundantly at some of these. He suggests that its evident disappearance may be connected with the widespread acidification of lake waters in this district. The nationally rare and declining pillwort, an unlikely-looking

FIG 115. Reedswamp and alder carr beside Woodhall Loch, Laurieston, Kirkcudbrightshire.

fern-ally, occurs all round the edges of Loch Ken below the viaduct, in one of the largest populations in Britain (Stewart, 1990, 1992). Small water-pepper, of pond edges and marshy places, is scattered over the southwest of the region.

Organic muds accumulate beneath these swamp communities at lake margins, and then become peat as the vegetation closes and consolidates in hydroseral development towards fen and carr. In oligotrophic waters, the progression is to 'poor' fen with carpets of *Sphagnum* bog-mosses and bottle, star, common and white sedges. Bog-sedge grows in several poor fens but is also in several richer sites. At mesotrophic and eutrophic sites the comparable development is of carpets of 'brown mosses' and rich fen meadows with the bryophytes and vascular plants listed below.

An important addition to the flora of the region was made in 1999 with the discovery of the Esthwaite waterweed in Bargatton Loch, Kirkcudbrightshire, by R. Lansdown (Farrell & Miles, 2003). Although known still in a lough in County Galway, Ireland, this aquatic plant has been regarded as probably extinct in its previously only known locality in Esthwaite Water, Cumbria, evidently as the result of eutrophication. Bargatton Loch is a mesotrophic site with clear water and has a rich aquatic flora with several pondweeds, and an extensive though sparse stand of water lobelia. Search of other lochs in the same district has not revealed any further populations of the Esthwaite waterweed.

Peatlands

The less well-drained parts of the lowlands were once covered with mires that developed during the period after the end of the last Ice Age. These probably all originated as fen, where the vegetation, dominated by monocotyledonous plants (especially sedges), was influenced by ground water containing dissolved mineral nutrients in varying quantity. On flood plains drained by rivers and where water drained from base-rich substrates, to accumulate in hollows and valleys, there was eutrophic or rich fen, but acidic catchments had oligotrophic or poor fen, and intermediate types were mesotrophic. The peat deposits built up by the undecomposed or only partially oxidised dead plant remains reflected these chemical characteristics of soil and water. In many places, upward growth of the peat body through accumulation of plant remains was followed by increasing acidification at the surface, with colonisation by calcifuge plants, especially the bog-mosses (*Sphagnum*). Some of these are capable of rapid upward growth and can raise the living surface above the water table, so that the mire becomes independent of ground water and dependent on the atmosphere as its source of nutrients. Most of the input comes in precipitation, and the mire has become *ombrotrophic*, so that it qualifies for the designation bog instead of fen.

In the lowlands, and especially where they have formed over estuarine sediments which were later raised above sea level, these mires have a character-istic profile as a lens, thickest in the middle, becoming shallower towards the edges and then sloping quite steeply to a well-defined perimeter. They can be up to ten metres higher in the middle than the surrounding land, and are, in consequence, known as *raised bogs*, though the term peat-moss is the usual local name. Typically, raised bogs have formed under annual rainfall in the range 500–1,200mm, and they occur as fairly discrete peatland units. In the uplands, where rainfall is higher (>1,200mm) and temperatures lower, under the oceanic British climate, acidic peat formation is not limited to individual mires, but occurs generally, wherever flat or gently sloping ground has caused marked drainage impedance. It has often formed without any intervening stage of fen, and may have replaced woodland, as buried stumps and logs at the base of the deposit reveal. Such peatlands tend to occur in large continuous masses, grading indistinctly into non-peat-forming vegetation over mineral soils on steeper ground. From the way in which they often smother the landscape with a mantle of peat, they have been termed *blanket bog*.

Fens

Of the extensive fens that survived long enough to enter the historical record, Billie Mire in Berwickshire was the largest and most famous. Muirhead (1889–95) describes it as 'a deep and extensive morass which lay along a narrow valley from the vicinity of Ayton to the neighbourhood of Chirnside, a distance of five miles [8km].' Draining began in 1801 and was completed by about 1830. Helpfully, a list of plants compiled before draining suggests that it was a eutrophic to mesotro-phic valley fen, with perhaps acidic nuclei, similar to such mixtures occurring in the Norfolk Broads. There were beds of common reed, bulrush, yellow flag, sedges, hemlock water-dropwort, water-cress, fool's water-cress, marsh ragwort, kingcup, brooklime, marsh forget-me-not, angelica, bogbean, marsh cinquefoil, marsh pennywort, marsh violet, and several species of rush, cotton-grass and pondweed (M27). The presence of willows indicates that there was some hydroseral development to carr, probably along the mire edges.

There are still a good many surviving rich fens across the region which have most or all of these species, though they are all much smaller than Billie Mire. The Borders are one of the most important parts of Britain for this mire type, as Dr Roderick Corner's explorations and discoveries in Roxburgh and Selkirk first revealed. Rosalind Tratt (1997) later surveyed 68 different mires in this district, mostly small, with only 11 sites covering more than five hectares, and lying between 150 and 300 metres above sea level. All were on Silurian greywackes, and in basins or valleys of glacial drift. Eutrophic fens also occur in glacial hollows and channels in the southwest district, but these have not been studied in detail.

In the Borders, good rich fens occur in the vicinity of Hawick at Branxholme Wester Loch, Alemoor Loch, Blind Moss at Ashkirk Loch and the nearby Long Moss, but there is an important group at the Whitlaw Mosses east of Selkirk, with the five separate sites of Murder, Blackpool, Beanrig, Nether Whitlaw and Over Whitlaw Mosses. These Borders fens are all different in detail, but have common features, first in occupying troughs and hollows in glacial morainic country. At Branxholme Wester, Alemoor and Ashkirk Lochs they adjoin open water and show hydroseral development from this, but little open water remains in the other fen sites. The successional sequence is from sedge swamp with bottle, bladder, brown, lesser pond, greater and lesser tussock, and slender sedges, branched bur-reed, bogbean and common reed to herb-rich fen meadow with most of the Billie Mire species, such as meadowsweet, angelica, ragged robin and sharp-flowered rush, plus greater spearwort and cowbane (M26 and M27). Some sites have abundant reed-grass. The fibrous tussock-sedge, a plant mainly of East Anglian fens, has been found in several of the Selkirk–Roxburgh sites, growing in sedge fen or carr. Narrow small-reed is another rare plant of sedge fen or carr, while purple small-reed is not confined to fen but grows also on road verges.

Tratt (1997) recognised 24 National Vegetation Classification communities and variants in the Borders fens, under the broad categories of rich fen, poor fen, bog, tall herb fen, fen meadow, rush pasture, species-rich flushes and sedge swamp. She found that peat fertility depended on the surrounding agricultural influence, but was not correlated with any water chemical variables. Despite the application of NPK fertilisers to the land surrounding most fens, the concentrations of these elements were generally low compared with some UK sites. The recent intensity of surrounding land use is, in turn, correlated with fertility of peat at the edges and nutrient content of water inflows to the fens. Species richness was negatively related to peat fertility, and the most species-rich communities, with the greatest number of rare plants, were confined to low-fertility sites. Branxholme Wester Loch was the most species-rich site (144 species, with 28 rare species), while Beanrig Moss had 88 species and 22 rarities. Values for pH ranged from 5.29 for acidic bog to 6.03 for poor fen, 6.43–6.76 for meadowsweet fen and flying bent wet grassland, to 7.04–7.74 for rich fens.

These fens around Selkirk and Hawick were distinguished up to at least 1960 by open carpets of 'brown mosses' with *Scorpidium scorpioides, Cratoneuron filicinum, Campylium stellatum, Drepanocladus revolvens, D. cossonii, Calliergon giganteum* and *Bryum pseudotriquetrum*, and vascular plants such as grass of Parnassus, northern marsh-orchid, long-stalked yellow sedge, tawny sedge, broad-leaved cotton-grass and dioecious sedge (M9 and M10). The rare alpine rush and holy grass were discovered here by Humphrey Milne-Redhead in this type of vegetation. The alpine rush has been found by Roderick Corner to have a wider distribution in this district, in calcareous flushes on the lower uplands as well as in fens, but holy grass has only three localities. Dr Corner also found the liverwort *Leiocolea rutheana*, once believed to be restricted to the Norfolk fens in Britain, in these habitats. The 'brown moss' carpets have increasingly been invaded by the common moss *Calliergonella (Acrocladium) cuspidata*, marking the onset of eutrophication caused by fertiliser addition to the dry farmland of the immediate catchments; and at Beanrig Moss the uncommon moss *Tomentypnum nitens*, which was abundant in 1957, has virtually disappeared. It appears to be especially sensitive to N and P enrichment, but survives in other fens and is still in remarkable quantity with *Cinclidium stygium* in a series of calcareous springs and flushes at Whithaugh Moor, near Hawick. As well as *Calliergonella* the moss *Rhytidiadelphus squarrosus* is now conspicuously abundant on rather drier ground: both have become indicators of high nitrogen and phosphorus levels.

Poor fens in southern Scotland typically have *Sphagnum* carpets with *S. recurvum*, *S. palustre*, *S. fimbriatum*, *S. subnitens* and *S. squarrosum*, grown with bottle sedge, common sedge, common cotton-grass, marsh cinquefoil, bogbean, marsh marigold, common spike-rush, water horsetail, floating sweet-grass and the moss *Aulacomnium palustre* (M4). Some of the vascular species, such as bottle sedge, tolerate a wide range of water or peat nutrient levels and pH, and so have little or no value as indicators of base status. The mosses are more reliable indicators of such conditions, with *Sphagnum teres*, *S. contortum*, *S. subsecundum* and *S. warnstorfii* pointing to subtle increases in base status within communities which can still be regarded as poor fen (M8).

Some rich fens have developed nuclei of acidic bog among the mesotrophic or eutrophic communities, with carpets or hummocks of *Sphagnum* (*S. papillosum*, *S. rubellum*, *S. plumulosum*), cross-leaved heath, bog asphodel (Fig. 116), round-leaved sundew, cranberry, common and hare's-tail cotton-grasses, bog myrtle, flying bent and tormentil (M18 and M25). They occur among the borders fens, and a good example occurs at Heart Moss near Dundrennan in Galloway, where there is also rich fen with long-stalked yellow sedge, lesser tussock-sedge, blunt-flowered rush, common bladderwort and the moss *Scorpidium scorpioides* (M10). Swamp with reed, bottle sedge, slender tufted sedge, bogbean and marsh cinquefoil (S8) is also present, and there is grey willow carr of the more acidic type, with abundant broad and narrow buckler ferns and hummocks of *Sphagnum*

FIG 116. Bog asphodel, a common bog plant which flowers freely when ungrazed, as in this picture.

palustre (w1). In the Borders, fens adjoining Kingside and Clearburn Lochs are mesotrophic, with mud sedge. Adderstonlee Moss, near Hawick, is a mesotrophic site in which succession has gone through willow carr to birchwood with remnants of reed and greater tussock sedge, and it may be acidifying, as *Sphagnum palustre* hummocks are locally dominant (w2). The adjoining but separate Buckstruther Moss is closer to poor fen and has an abundance of the rare *Sphagnum riparium*. Lesser twayblade grows in some of the more acidic communities.

Southern Scottish willow carr (Fig. 117) is usually dominated by grey willow, but other species are bay, dark-leaved and tea-leaved willows. Goat willow is less in fen carr than in open woodland and scrub, while purple willow is mostly on riversides. An extensive willow carr has developed on alluvial flats at the confluence of the Tima and Ettrick Waters, and another good example is at Riskinhope by Loch of the Lowes, Little Yarrow. Patches of willow scrub have developed in the Whitlaw Mosses, and have local abundance of round-leaved wintergreen and coralroot orchid. Many of the willows here and at Adderstonlee Moss are densely grown with witch's-beard lichens, giving them a shaggy appearance (Fig. 118). Elongated sedge is a characteristic plant of alder–willow carr, sometimes growing on the bases or fallen trunks of alders, but is known

FIG 117. Complex of fen and willow carr at the head of the mesotrophic Loch Ken, Kenmure Holms, near New Galloway, Kirkcudbrightshire.

FIG 118. Witch's-beard and other lichens on willows in fen-carr woodland. Blackpool Moss, near Selkirk.

only from a few fens in Galloway, beside Loch Ken and a sluggish section of the River Cree. Near Kirkcudbright, a fen at Newlaw which has developed almost entirely into grey willow carr has a residual flora of more open fen, including an abundance of marsh fern in one of its few Scottish localities.

Raised bogs

Raised bogs are best developed in the wetter southwest of the region. The complex known as the Lochar Mosses, southeast of Dumfries, covered over 18km² of the North Solway Plain, and was thus approximately the same size as the more famous Thorne and Crowle Moors east of Doncaster, claimed as the largest raised bog system in Britain. No other raised bog in the region was nearly as large. Also in Dumfriesshire were Priestside Flow, Nutberry Moss, Gillshaw and Bonshaw Flows near Kirtlebridge, and a smaller, separate Lochar Moss, northeast of Dumfries. The Stewartry has fewer raised bogs, with Kirkconnell Flow north of New Abbey, Auchencairn and Rascarrel Mosses, and possibly Aucheninnes Moss near Dalbeattie. In Wigtownshire the Moss of Cree, with the adjoining Carsegowan and Borrow Mosses, was an important raised bog, but in the lowlands of this county were extensive areas of bog of a type intermediate between raised and blanket bog in their topographic features (Fig. 119). These were

FIG 119. Western flows, intermediate between raised and blanket bogs. Extensive afforestation has taken place. Challochglass Moors, Wigtownshire.

especially in the northern part of the Machars, between the roads from Newton Stewart to Glenluce and from Wigtown to Garheugh Port. North of the first road the low, flat moorlands of northern Wigtownshire (known as the Moors) and Carrick were probably best regarded as blanket bog. In the Borders, raised bogs are few and smaller, with Dogden Moss at the southeast edge of the Lammermuirs adjoining Greenlaw Moor, Threepwood Moss south of Lauder, and Din Moss adjoining Hoselaw Loch near Town Yetholm. Fala Flow, at 325m on the western flank of the Lammermuirs, is described as blanket bog, but could also be regarded as an intermediate between this and raised bog.

Raised bogs are the simplest type of mire to describe as regards botanical character, because of their uniformity and lack of floral diversity. The most actively growing stage is dominated by bog-mosses, but has an undulating surface structure, with shallow hollows, flat lawns, and both lower and higher hummocks. The hollows are typically filled with the semi-aquatic *Sphagnum* species, usually *S. cuspidatum*, but locally *S. pulchrum* (M2), while Racks Moss (part of the Lochar Moss complex) had an abundance of the rare *S. balticum*. Lawns and low hummocks are typically dominated by *S. magellanicum* and *S. papillosum*, while some taller hummocks are of these two species, though more often of *S. rubellum/capillifolium*, with scattered mounds of *S. fuscum* and *S. austinii*. *S. subnitens* is a less abundant member of the bog-moss community (M18). Towards the drier edges or on disturbed ground *S. tenellum* and *S. compactum* are often plentiful, and *S. molle* occurs more sparingly (M16). The vascular plants of hollows or lawns are common cotton-grass, white beak-sedge, round-leaved and great sundews, bog asphodel and cranberry. Others that come in slightly higher above the water table are bog rosemary (Fig. 120), cross-leaved heath, ling heather, hare's-tail cotton-grass, deer sedge and, on the driest hummocks, crowberry. Bog myrtle is locally abundant but usually towards the bog edges. Oblong-leaved sundew occurs locally in the southwest, usually on shallow and rather bare peat of wet heath, rather than on deep bog, and is sometimes associated with pale butterwort.

The sequence from wet hollow to dry tall hummock may to some extent represent a mini-succession, but sometimes upward growth of the bog surface takes place with the undulations remaining more or less in their same positions. These active, *Sphagnum*-dominated raised bogs are now rare in the region, and probably the best remaining example is in the centre of Kirkconnell Flow. Many of the others have been afforested with conifers after deep ploughing, and, of the huge Lochar Moss complex, only the eastern area known as Longbridge Muir remains free of these plantations. The Moss of Cree still has an active area which could be extended by removal of the trees. Nutberry Moss, near Eastriggs,

FIG 120. Bog rosemary, a typical plant of lowland raised bogs such as the Lochar Mosses, Dumfriesshire.

has been scalped into a bare, dried surface by horticultural peat extraction. An industrial estate has intruded onto the smaller part of the Lochar Moss northeast of Dumfries, and landfill is taking over the remainder. The rest are mostly degraded by repeated fires, which have dried their surfaces and caused heather, cotton-grasses and deer sedge to become dominant, with only the few bog-mosses of disturbed ground left. Where birch and pine invasion have occurred on these modified peat mosses (Fig. 121), *Sphagnum fimbriatum* and *S. palustre* become abundant (w4), and in old peat cuttings or wet disturbed edges *S. recurvum* is the characteristic species.

Of the rarer plants, mud sedge once grew on Lochar Moss and brown beak-sedge on Auchencairn Moss, but both have evidently been eliminated by afforestation. Royal fern was once scattered over the region, especially in the lowland peat mosses of the southwest, but was much reduced by collecting in Victorian times. Silverside (1990) quoted an earlier statement that 'it was carried off in cartloads by fern-vendors' in that period, but it survives in several Galloway localities. The distinctive tall hummock moss *Dicranum bergeri* was once present in fair amounts on several of the raised bogs of the Cumbrian Solway, and is likely to have been on the Lochar Moss, but its only known southern Scottish locality was at Din Moss in the northeast. Kirkconnell Flow has the rare *Cladonia*

FIG 121. A raised bog showing invasion by Scots pine from surrounding woodland. Kirkconnell Flow National Nature Reserve, Kirkcudbrightshire.

stygia in lichen communities, and the uncommon moss *Dicranum undulatum* in the birchwood fringe. *Sphagnum austinii* has lost ground but still grows in its most easterly outpost at Dogden Moss and, while *S. balticum* was lost to afforestation on Racks Moss, it could possibly occur on remaining unplanted parts of the Lochar Mosses.

From records of such plants as greater spearwort, mare's-tail, cowbane and nodding bur-marigold (Scott-Elliot, 1896), the Lochar Moss evidently retained fen communities locally, perhaps along marginal 'lagg' streams that define the edges of unmodified raised bogs. Galloway mires with mildly basic conditions locally contain plants of western and southern distribution in Britain, such as marsh St John's-wort, lesser skullcap and bog pimpernel.

The lower-level Wigtown flows, which are intermediate between raised and blanket bogs, have plant communities hardly differing in any significant degree from those just described. As blanket bog is predominantly an upland type, it will be dealt with in Chapter 7.

VEGETATION HISTORY

Several of the Borders mires that formed in deep basins have proved to be underlain by lake deposits (clay, mud, marl) of Late-Devensian (Late-glacial) age, corresponding to Zones I to III of the pollen sequence devised by Godwin (1975), beginning around 13,000 years before the present (BP). Mitchell (1948) was the first to investigate this early vegetation history, at Whitrig Bog in Berwickshire, a much cut-over mire where the underlying clay was used for brick and tile making. An exposed face of clay beneath marl and above a lower marl contained leaves of dwarf and net-leaved willows, dwarf birch, crowberry and alpine meadow-rue, and stems/leaves of several northern mosses of wet habitats. The base of the lower marl evidently represented the first phase of open tundra vegetation following the retreat of the ice sheets (Zone I), while the upper layer contained fruits of downy birch, suggesting that it belonged to the temporary warm period that followed the retreat of the ice sheets 13,000 to 11,000 years ago (Zone II). This was succeeded by another cold phase (the Loch Lomond Readvance, Zone III) from 11,000 to 10,000 years ago, when the arctic–alpine plants of the clay again grew on the surrounding bare slopes, and were carried into the lake basin by frost–thaw movements. The upper marl was judged to be of Post-glacial age, but pollen in all these layers was too sparse to allow statistically valid analysis.

Macroscopic plant remains in the Late-glacial deposits at Whitrig Bog were examined further by Conolly (1961), who confirmed the presence of the vascular species named above and added thrift, alpine bistort, mountain sorrel, spiked woodrush, hoary whitlowgrass, mossy saxifrage, either Highland or drooping saxifrage and an arctic poppy. She also found pollen of Iceland purslane and *Ephedra distachya*, a plant unknown in modern Britain.

A detailed study of the early history of Beanrig and Blackpool Mosses was made by Webb & Moore (1982), by analysis of both pollen and macrofossil remains in the bottom sediments, which proved to represent Zones II and III of the Late Devensian. In the earliest period the indications are of a sparse willow and tree birch scrub, with dwarf shrub heaths of dwarf birch and mountain avens, grasslands with rock-rose and bare-ground communities. Juniper was plentiful and increased later, evidently to form scrub, while damp ground had tall herb 'meadow' grading into fen and short-turf calcareous marsh with the 'brown mosses' named above. Open water was rich in aquatics such as pond-weeds, milfoils, water-lilies and charophytes. Falling temperatures during the ensuing colder period saw a retreat of the open woodland and scrub and a re-expansion of alpine-type communities and species which must have been more abundant during the first phase of deglaciation, with bare-ground vegetation and abundance of plants such as dwarf willow, purple saxifrage and Norwegian mugwort. After the cold passed away again there was reversion to a park tundra of open birchwood with juniper scrub, marking the onset of the Post-glacial (Flandrian) period.

When broadleaved woodland of the succeeding Boreal phase took over the dry land surrounding the fens, the tundra and open-ground vegetation retreated to the higher levels of the hills, where the arctic–alpine element became depleted over the millennia to the remnant montane flora that persists in the Moffat–Tweedsmuir Hills today. The communities of wet ground – fen, wet meadow, short-turf marsh and willow scrub – persisted to this day, but the open water of the former lakes was lost by infilling of the basins and valleys through plant succession.

A fascinating discovery of these studies was that in Late-glacial times there grew in the Whitlaw Mosses area several plants which are quite unknown in the wild in Britain today: they include an arctic poppy, *Swertia perennis* and species of *Gypsophila*, *Hedysarum* and *Ephedra*. There were others which persist in Britain only as extreme rarities, such as Norwegian mugwort, Iceland purslane, Highland or drooping saxifrage, mountain sandwort, and the mosses *Scorpidium turgescens*, *Tortella fragilis* and *Paludella squarrosa* (in Ireland, but believed extinct in Britain). The macrofossil evidence set beyond doubt the Late-glacial occurrence near Selkirk of montane plants such as dwarf birch, mountain avens, dwarf willow, mountain sandwort, purple saxifrage and mountain sorrel. While pollen analysis showed the presence of a much larger number of taxa, there was the usual problem with this technique, that uncertainty in pinning down the identity of the exact species led to tantalising doubts about what may have been there. These possibles could have included spring gentian, northern rock cress, alpine milk-vetch, alpine catchfly, alpine cinquefoil, alpine bartsia, alpine mouse-ear, moss campion and Norwegian scurvy-grass. But in several cases they could also have been closely related lowland species with quite different distributions and ecological needs, e.g. *Silene acaulis* and *S. nutans*. Pollen analysis has the advantage that it collects evidence over a fairly wide area around the site being studied; whereas examination of macrofossils is limited by the chance of what a few narrow coring samples have happened to capture, so that a great deal must be missed.

Julie Tight (1987) investigated the late Quaternary history of Wester Branxholme and Kingside Lochs, near Hawick, and found the full Late-glacial sequence at both, with basal deposits showing the open tundra conditions of

Zone I, radiocarbon dated at 12,770 years BP (onset) and 12,180 years BP (close). These gave way to the dwarf shrub tundra, with birch trees and juniper, of the warmer period (Zone II) before the Loch Lomond Readvance, when open tundra again returned (Zone III), but ended at 10,340 years BP. The Post-glacial pattern was of the spread first of birch woodland with juniper, followed later in the Boreal period by replacement by hazel as the dominant tree. During the ensuing Atlantic period, alder, elm and oak became abundant in lowland woods, but hazel continued to dominate the upland landscape. Elm then showed a conspicuous decline, dated to 5,210 years BP at Kingside Loch, and this was followed by the spread of blanket bog within adjoining catchments. The later appearance of cereal pollen at both sites pointed to Neolithic agricultural activity.

Tight found that the succession of lake communities at her two sites had varied in different places: reedswamp was only where there was silting, while carr development was restricted to mineral-rich areas or those supplied by base-rich ground water. In general, open-water aquatic communities were succeeded by reedswamp or reedswamp-carr, and then by fen or fen-carr. Tratt (1997) believed that vegetation development depended partly on the past extent of peat and marl extraction, which has affected most sites. But at the few uncut sites (Brown Moor Heights, Blind Moss, Branxholme Wester Loch, Long Moss) there is a continuous stratigraphic sequence back to the early Late-glacial. Many cutover sites later developed floating rafts of vegetation with luxuriant bryophyte cover, such as at Nether Whitlaw and Beanrig Mosses. The wet-ground communities that have persisted at the Whitlaw Mosses include many of the plant species that were present in the Late-glacial. Some have never been seen in recent times, such as the moss *Paludella squarrosa*, which Tratt (1997) found in at least four different sites, and only 35–40cm below the present surface in Long Moss.

FAUNA

Mammals

Beginning with rivers, the otter is the most notable mammal of this habitat in the region (Fig. 122). Once widespread on all the major streams and on many lochs, it declined seriously after around 1960, as happened over much of southern Britain, evidently as a result of contamination by the dieldrin group of insecticides, which accumulated through the aquatic food chain (Jefferies, 1996). It has made a slow but fairly steady recovery and is once again quite widespread on the bigger rivers and lowland lakes, as well as the Solway shore (Chapter 3).

FIG 122. Otter: this animal is still recovering from its severe decline in the 1960s. (Bobby Smith)

The water vole is another animal described as common by earlier authors (Evans, 1911; Gladstone, 1912), but it has declined here as in many parts of its British range. Its habitats formerly ranged from coastal marsh creeks, farmland ditches and lowland ponds, to bigger rivers and alluvial or peaty runnels at up to 600m or more in the hills. The introduced and unwelcome American mink is a prime suspect in its disappearance, but other factors may have contributed, such as loss and deterioration of its riparian habitat. There is local recovery, however, and a flourishing colony has lately been reported at the confluence of the Esk, Ewes and Wauchope Water in the town of Langholm. Black varieties were said to be frequent in earlier times, especially in the uplands. Daubenton's bat, which hawks insects especially over rivers and lakes, was said by Gladstone (1912) to be common in Dumfriesshire, but Evans (1911) noted that it was very local within the Tweed catchment. I have not been able to ascertain its present status. The water shrew was also described as common in Dumfriesshire by Gladstone but as somewhat local in Tweed by Evans; and there is a dearth of recent information on its occurrence.

Breeding birds

Of the birds, the dipper was once almost ubiquitous on the streams of southern Scotland, from the slower lowland sections to the brattling hill burns, where nests are often placed beside or even behind a cascade (Fig. 123). Some nest sites were known to be occupied over a very long period, such as one on a burn at Corsemalzie with a history of over 100 years (Dickson, 1992). Gladstone (1910, 1923) gave another instance, where the same rock outcrop on the Capel Burn in the hills west of Langholm had held a nest in every year for 137 years from 1785. They bred up to at least 500m at Loch Enoch. By 1987 there was an appreciable decline in breeding population within heavily afforested catchments, where some upland watercourses lost their dippers, at least along certain sections. Vickery (1991) studied 18 streams in Dumfries & Galloway, and found that the enhanced acidification of those within extensively afforested catchments had much reduced the abundance of important dipper prey such as caddisfly larvae and mayfly nymphs. Dipper breeding density (measured by territory length, which varied from 0.60 to 2.05km) was significantly lower along streams of low pH (within forests). The Forestry Commission (undated pamphlet) has reported a recovery of dipper range on the Galloway River Cree and Water of Minnoch by 2002, attributable to large-scale clear-felling and streamside improvement along affected reaches. It is unclear whether numbers and breeding success are also back to 1970 levels, but the bird remains less numerous than fifty years ago.

FIG 123. Dippers nest on streams across the region. (Bobby Smith)

The grey wagtail, a bird less dependent strictly on stream-life for food, has remained widespread in its waterside haunts, breeding up to 670m at Midlaw Linns in the Moffat Hills (Fig. 124). Common sandpipers have also maintained their numbers in both lowland and upland situations, except where there has been excessive disturbance by fishermen, as along the west side of Loch Ken between New Galloway and Mossdale, and at Loch Skene. They reach moderately high density on streams draining from richer catchments, with pairs spaced at 400m or less, and breed up to over 500m beside high-lying lochs. In Galloway, Vickery (1991) found a lower breeding density along the River Cree, with 1.12 pairs per kilometre of stream. Oystercatchers breed along the rivers, though in the lowlands they are common on farmland as well. In the hills, pairs occupy stream shingle beds for nest sites far up the remote glens, such as the Water of Ken, Hermitage Water and Liddelhead.

The kingfisher prefers the flat courses of lowland rivers, where the steep faces of alluvial banks allow the birds to excavate their nest tunnels (Fig. 125). There is a cluster of breeding records for the lower Nith, Lochar Water and Annan in Dumfriesshire, and another along lower Tweeddale in the Borders. Sand martins are more widespread, nesting from salt-marsh creeks and all along rivers into the hills where moraine banks afford nesting sites, and many sand-pits are also used. Large colonies occur in the Borders at Horseburgh near Peebles (510 active burrows) and Hendersyde Island, Kelso (430 burrows).

FIG 124. Grey wagtail: a widespread bird on upland streams. (Bobby Smith)

FIG 125. Kingfisher: a local bird of the lowland rivers. (Bobby Smith)

Islands in moorland tarns have held fluctuating colonies of black-headed gulls, up to several hundred pairs strong. In the capricious way of these birds, they have come and gone without obvious reason from Loch Enoch, Loch Macaterick and Loch Moan, but have persisted more regularly at Loch Urr and Lochinvar. A modest colony (47 pairs in 2000) has developed on the banks of the Megget Reservoir. Common gulls first occupied islets in Loch Skene in 1961, when a pair bred on the reputed old sea eagle site, and there were three pairs in 1985. A few pairs have nested on the shores of St Mary's Loch, but a strong colony has built up at the Megget Reservoir, with 85 pairs in 2000. In Galloway they nest on some of the moorland lochs in small numbers, including Loch Enoch, where they have replaced the black-headed gulls.

The most celebrated of the lake-island breeders is the cormorant, which has a long-established inland colony at the Castle and Mochrum Lochs in the Wigtown Machars. Between 1909 and 1947 the colony averaged 200–220 pairs, but was subject to some persecution by fishermen during the earlier years. Latterly it was protected by the loch owner Lord David Stuart, and numbers increased to 418 nests in 1986, and 518 pairs evenly split between the two lochs in 1991 (Dickson, 1992). Gray (1871) recorded that there was in earlier times a large cormorant colony on islands in Loch Moan, west of the Merrick, but it vanished long ago. Robert Service recorded five pairs of cormorants nesting in trees on the island in Castle Loch, Lochmaben in 1898–1903 (Gladstone, 1923).

The history of the sea eagle as an earlier occupant of hill loch islands is dealt with in Chapter 8. Ospreys once nested on 'sugarloaf' rocks in Loch Skerrow and the Glenhead Lochs in the Stewartry, reputedly up to 1871, while Paton & Pike (1929) said that they often fished in Loch Doon and nested on an islet in a small Wigtownshire loch around 1854. They had all disappeared well before the end of the nineteenth century. An enigmatic second-hand claim of breeding during the 1930s (Pullen, 1937) cannot be accepted in the absence of further information, but the possible coastal record is a little stronger (see Chapter 3). With the increasing number of osprey sightings in spring and summer across southern Scotland in recent years, the return of the bird as a breeder to the region was a keenly anticipated event. Rather surprisingly, in view of its earlier history, the first pair to breed was in the Borders, in 1998. They returned in 1999, rearing two young. The next year two pairs were present, and numbers continued to increase: by 2005 nests there were five breeding sites in the Borders, which between them fledged ten young (P. Gordon, RSPB). In Galloway, a pair built a nest in Wigtownshire in 2001; no young were reared that year, but the same site produced one fledged chick in 2002 and 2003, with two fledged in 2004 and 2005 (C. Rollie).

The waterfowl of southern Scottish lochs include several breeding species of duck. Loch Ken in Galloway is a favoured wildfowl haunt throughout the year, where Maxwell (1950) had 11 species of duck in view at once. He observed that goldeneye were especially numerous here, appearing to gather before their northward spring migration. Although he regularly saw courtship display at the end of March and a few goldeneye often linger on the hill lochs of Galloway into late April, they have only once been known to nest in the region, at Mochrum Loch, Wigtownshire, in 1899, when eggs were laid in the hollow of a decayed ash tree (Dickson, 1992). Mallard and teal are the most numerous breeding duck on Loch Ken, along with smaller numbers of shoveler, wigeon, pochard, tufted duck, goosanders and red-breasted mergansers.

Wigeon were discovered nesting in 1893 at a cluster of moorland lochs in the area of Craik at the head of Ettrick in the west of Selkirk and Roxburgh (Fig. 126). Chapman (1912a) reported breeding at nine of these lochs, several of which had a single pair, others two or three, while 'certain larger sheets boast considerable numbers'. Most nests were in long grass or stunted heather. Wigeon were at six of these Craik lochs on 18 May 1947, when E. Blezard and R. Laidler saw a total of 27 birds, mostly drakes, which probably had sitting mates (a nest with eggs was found). More recently, Thompson & Dougall (1988) made complete surveys of the area, counting 30 pairs at 10 lochs in 1978 and 39 pairs at 17 lochs in 1987, so that this stronghold has been maintained, though only 12 pairs were confirmed breeding in both years. Many of these lochs have become engulfed by the conifers

FIG 126. Wigeon drake: a local breeding duck on moorland. (Bobby Smith)

of Craik Forest, and the wigeon, which nest on the surrounding moorland up to 400m back from the water, have evidently suffered some decline compared with pre-1950 numbers, as their breeding habitat has been lost. Efforts have been made to restore their ground by clearing the trees some way back from the loch margins, and with some success, as increased numbers of the duck are now reported. The heathery islet near the head of Loch Skene was the regular breeding place of a single pair of wigeon up to the late 1930s, but was forsaken by 1946. In Galloway a pair bred at Lilies Loch up to the late 1940s, and nesting is shown in three Stewartry 10km squares in the *New Atlas*.

Chapman (1912a) knew nine breeding places of pochard at Border lochs: six in Roxburgh, two in Berwick and one in Selkirk. Their favourite nest site was in a tall clump of sedge or flags on the outer edge of the most dangerous squashy bog, next to open water. He found tufted ducks more numerous, nesting on 'half the lochs and mosses of the Borders', yet all but unknown in 1889. Some nests were in sedge swamp with open water, but others were in heather or dry vegetation on peat mosses, sometimes adjoining small pools. Shovelers were also fairly evenly distributed on most suitable mosses and lochs, nesting often in swamp, though not as far out on floating rafts as pochards. The recent status of pochard and tufted duck in the Borders remains much the same, but the shoveler is now much less widespread. Mallard are numerous and teal widespread breeders across the region, but the other surface-feeding ducks, pintail, gadwall and garganey, are only rare and sporadic breeders anywhere within the south of Scotland. Most ducks prefer eutrophic waters, but teal and wigeon are often on nutrient-poor and acidic moorland tarns.

Around 1930, eggs from the wild population of greylag geese on South Uist were brought to Lochinch and hatched there, with the later addition of young birds. Introductions were also made in 1933 at Monreith. From the original nuclei at these two Wigtownshire sites, greylags proceeded to spread eastwards and colonise a whole series of mainly low moorland Galloway lochs with islands that provided breeding refuges (Young, 1972). The *New Atlas* shows them as breeding in 20 different 10km squares in southwest Scotland, and this feral population is well established. Only about ten pairs are reported breeding in the northeast district, though larger numbers occur in the Lothians. The introduced Canada goose has also established itself at many places in Dumfries & Galloway, on lochs and tarns and beside rivers, but remains scarce in the Borders. The exotic mandarin duck, introduced to Berwickshire, has become a rare and elusive breeder along the Eye Water and Whitadder. An even more successful colonist has been the ruddy duck, which reached Scotland from its Slimbridge origin in the 1970s and first bred in the Borders in 1989. In 2000 there were 15–20 pairs at 10 sites, with over half the breeders at Bemersyde and Folly Loch.

The little grebe is widespread across the southern Scottish lowlands, nesting mainly on mesotrophic to eutrophic standing waters from the main lochs down to large ponds. The great crested grebe is much scarcer, having colonised the region only since the late 1800s, and only 3–8 pairs are reported from the Borders. Its breeding places extend onto moorland lochs, and include St Mary's Loch. Numbers are higher in the southwest, with seven pairs at Lochrutton Loch, four pairs at Carlingwark Loch and three pairs at Lochinvar in 1999. Both species need shallow lake margins with emergent vegetation in which to build their floating nests. The black-necked grebe has bred in Dumfries & Galloway, and the *New Atlas* records that the Slavonian Grebe was seen at a possible breeding place in the northeast during 1988–91.

During the mid-1950s, both black-throated and red-throated divers appeared on the hill lochs of Galloway and Carrick, and bred sporadically, usually separately, but in one year together at the same site. The known nesting places were Lochs Bradan and Finlas, but Loch Dungeon was probably another, and there could well have been others. These birds added to the Scottish Highland element of the region's wildlife, but then dropped out from the mid-1970s and are not known to have bred since then, though the *New Atlas* has single possible breeding records for both in this district. Increasing acidity of lake waters and loss of food supply is a possible explanation for their failure to maintain this southernmost British foothold.

The grey heron occurs across the region and depends largely on streams and lakes for feeding, though it is exclusively a tree-nester here and so is regarded equally as a woodland bird (see Chapter 4). In the Borders there are 350–380 pairs in about 40 colonies, only two of which reach double figures. In the southwest, Duncan & Duncan (1939) listed 11 colonies with 1–35 nests in Dumfriesshire, and 10 colonies with 1–15 nests in Kirkcudbrightshire. I have been unable to find any recent figures for these counties, though five heronries are named for 1999–2001 (Norman, 2001, 2002). Dickson (1992) said there was only one regular colony in Wigtownshire, at Lochinch, with up to 20 pairs (55 nests in 1914). The bird is still subject to some persecution by fishing interests, but this is probably less than in earlier years.

The larger swamps of earlier times, such as Billie Mire and Huntlywood Moss in Berwickshire, were the haunt of bitterns up to perhaps 1830, but these have long been extinct as breeding birds and their occurrence is limited to occasional winter visitors. Evans (1911) gives a melancholy list of bitterns shot later in the nineteenth century, mostly in winter. The marsh harrier was another inhabitant of extensive reed-beds, and also disappeared as these were drained out of existence during the early nineteenth century, but the species made a surprising comeback when a pair bred successfully in 1990 in a quite small fen near Maybole, just outside our limits in south Ayrshire. It was a one-off occurrence. The hen harrier was also said by Muirhead (1889–95) to have bred annually at Billie Mire up to 1830–35.

In addition to their numerous and scattered upland colonies (see above), black-headed gulls also occupy the fen surrounds to some lochs, and the most consistent of these is at Bemersyde Moss, near St Boswells. This colony was mentioned by Evans (1911), and has recently numbered up to 14,000 pairs – one of the largest colonies in Scotland. By 2004, however, it had declined to 8,000 pairs, after suffering total breeding failure in each year since 2000, with abandonment of eggs and young in mid-June. The presence of otters gives a suspected cause, though predation has not been witnessed (*Scottish Bird News*, March 2005). At least two other moderate colonies, each of several hundred pairs, have been lost since their loch surrounds were smothered in conifers: one at Kingside Loch in Craik and a second at the Black Lochs of Kilquhockadale in Wigtownshire.

Water rails are probably widespread in fens across the region, but overlooked through their secretive ways. A survey in the Borders during 1999–2000 gave an estimate of 150 pairs, with Hare Moss (eight pairs), Hoselaw Loch (three pairs), St Leonard's Pond (three pairs) and Synton Moss (two pairs and two singles) as notable localities (Murray, 2000). Chapman (1912b) recorded the spotted crake breeding in the swamp surrounding a Roxburgh loch, and Service (in Gladstone, 1910) said that nests had occasionally been found in Annandale. The 1968–72 *Atlas* showed a cluster of possible and one confirmed breeding record in south-west Scotland, but there were none for the region in the *New Atlas*. Moorhens nest commonly in the wetter fens and swampy edges of lakes. Coots were once widespread on the richer lake waters, but usually with less than ten pairs at any one locality, and they were always scarce in moorland areas. They showed a dramatic decline during 2001 and 2002. Between 1992 and 1999 casual records gave 52–158 broods annually, with up to 440 young, whereas 2002 had 16 broods and 31 young. Planned survey showed a decline in breeders on 65 per cent of sites selected, and breeding success was poor. Both loss of adults and impaired breeding output were involved. As with the black-headed gulls at Bemersyde, the only relevant factor seemed to be a marked increase in otters. These were surveyed at 279 constant sites throughout the Borders, and signs of their presence increased from 31 per cent of sites in 1977–9, to 39 per cent in 1984–5, to 63 per cent in 1991–4, and this trend has evidently continued (*Scottish Bird News*, March 2005).

Of the small birds of fen, the reed bunting and sedge warbler are widespread though rather sparse breeders: in 2000 both were recorded in over 60 Borders localities, and the Ettrick Marshes were the best locality for both. Grasshopper warblers nest in some of the drier fens, but are not common. The reed warbler was known to breed only on rare occasions prior to 1990, but nesting was confirmed in a Galloway reed-bed from 1993 to 1996, and the species may be regular in this locality (Bruce, 1997).

As on the Cumbrian Solway Mosses, birds such as golden plover, dunlin, short-eared owl, merlin and even hen harrier formerly bred sparingly on the Lochar Moss complex, but disappeared early in the twentieth century. Golden plover nested on Merkland Moss here up to 1921 (Gladstone, 1910, 1923); they have persisted in reduced numbers on some of the intermediate bogs of south Wigtown, such as those around Mochrum Loch. Red grouse remained on Lochar Moss for much longer, but seem to have gone, as have the colonies of lesser black-backed and black-headed gulls that once flourished here and on other large peat mosses. In 1938, lesser black-backs on the Racks Moss sector numbered up to 200–300 pairs, but black-headed gulls were at greater strength with 3,000 pairs, whose effects locally destroyed the bog vegetation and introduced an assortment of lowland 'weeds' such as rosebay willowherb, common sorrel, bramble, chickweed, common rush and various grasses (Pullen, 1942). Geoffrey Matthews studied navigational ability in the mixed colony of lesser black-backs and herring gulls on Anabaglish Moss in Wigtownshire, but this also was

FIG 127. Incubating snipe: a bird which has declined greatly in the lowlands, through draining of fens and 'improvement' of its wet meadowland breeding habitats. (Bobby Smith)

banished by afforestation. Curlews are probably the most notable birds remaining, but even these have declined in recent decades. Snipe and redshank nest in small numbers, but prefer the marshy grasslands (Fig. 127). Meadow pipits are common, reed buntings frequent and grasshopper warblers breed on the rushy ground reclaimed from the bog edges. Stonechats occupy the drier edges, but nightjars seem to have gone – they were still on Kirkconnell Flow in 1960, but there are no recent reports of them.

Winter waterfowl

Some of the wetlands are important for their winter populations of wildfowl. The Borders are an important wintering area for pink-footed geese, but the largest roost lies outside our boundary, at the West Water Reservoir in the Pentland Hills, where up to 56,000 birds have been counted in recent years. Hule Moss in Berwickshire is the next biggest roosting site for pinkfeet, with a maximum number of 25,700 birds recorded in October 1989 (Pritchard *et al.*, 1992). Smaller roosts with hundreds to low thousands occur at Bemersyde, Hoselaw Loch and Fala Flow (which has Gladhouse Reservoir as an alternative site). During the five-winter period 1985–6 to 1989–90 Hoselaw Loch was an important roost for

Icelandic greylag geese, with average peak counts of 2,680 birds (Pritchard *et al.*, 1992). It has since declined to uncertainty as a roost, though 525 birds were seen at the nearby Yetholm Loch in March 2000 (Murray, 2002). Small numbers of whooper swans appear on many of the Borders lochs during winter, but their main haunts are the Tweed and Teviot Haughs, where 150–200 birds are present in most winters.

Of the ducks, modest numbers (100–200) of wigeon, teal and mallard occur in winter on the Borders lochs and marshes, while pochard, tufted duck, goldeneye, goosander and shoveler are in smaller numbers (mostly less than 50). Smew, gadwall and pintail are only occasional. The most favoured lochs are at Bemersyde, Hirsel Lake, Hoselaw Loch, Yetholm Loch and Whitrig Pond. Ruddy ducks assemble after the breeding season on Hule Moss, to a peak of 52–53 in autumn 2000, but few winter in the region.

In the southwest, the Castle Loch at Lochmaben, with its smaller satellites of Hightae, Kirk, Mill and Upper Lochs, and old oxbows at Broomhill, are the most important inland wildfowl haunt (Fig. 128). Pink-footed geese reached a maximum of 13,400 with a mean of 4,270, while greylags (including an unknown proportion of feral birds) peaked at 2,850 with a mean of 1,240 during 1985–6 to 1989–90 (Pritchard *et al.*, 1992). Canada geese and mute swans can reach over 100, and whooper swans just under this figure. Mallard and wigeon each number

FIG 128. Hazy sunrise over Castle Loch, Lochmaben, Dumfriesshire: the most important wildfowl loch in the southwest. (Bobby Smith)

around 500, teal slightly less, and pintail have been up to 900 strong (though usually less). Tufted duck, goldeneye, pochard and goosander can all top the one-hundred mark, but there are usually fewer than twenty shovelers. The next most important site is the long and complex Loch Ken–River Dee with its associated marshes between New Galloway and Bridge of Dee. Its most important item is the flock of Greenland white-fronted geese, usually of around 350 birds, which replaces the pinkfeet here. All of the Castle Loch geese, swans and ducks occur here also, though mostly in smaller numbers.

The outlying section around Threave Island is often the most productive, and was formerly the regular haunt of a flock of bean geese, which had a favourite site on the hillock of Hightae Drum. Donald Watson followed this flock over many years and watched it decline from 400–500 birds during the 1940s to virtual extinction by the 1990s (Watson, 1994). In the 1950s, when it still numbered over 200, there was sometimes the odd lesser whitefront keeping company. Watson, who noted that it was occasionally possible to see eight different kinds of geese on Hightae Drum, thought that the disappearance of the bean geese was most probably caused by changes in farming practice, especially the drying out of marshy ground in the area. Other factors, such as decline in the Fennoscandian breeding stock, and competition from the increasing greylags, could also have been involved.

The third important wildfowl site in the southwest is at Lochinch (White Loch) near Stranraer. A second flock of Greenland whitefronts winters here, to an average number of 505 birds during 1985–6 to 1989–90. The geese roost on the loch or on the foreshore of Torrs Warren (sometimes known as West Freugh) a few kilometres away, and feed on adjoining farmland. Large numbers of greylags (average peak 1,500 birds) also frequent the site, although a large proportion are feral birds originating from the releases made here long ago. Other notable duck sites are Carlingwark Loch at Castle Douglas, and Milton and Auchenreoch Lochs near Crocketford, where there are usually good numbers of pochard, tufted duck and goldeneye. Ruddy ducks are only occasional late summer or autumn visitors to this district.

An interesting winter use of wetlands is as communal roosting places for hen harriers. Donald Watson discovered a major roost south of New Galloway in 1960. The site was a fen-like expanse of peatland adjoining a sluggish stretch of river (a Galloway 'lane'), with sedges, reeds and scattered willows. By the late 1960s the site was used by 20–30 birds, with the numbers coming to roost usually greatest on windy evenings. The excitement of watching the birds assemble at dusk is well described by Donald, who followed this roost for some forty years (Watson, 1994). The birds dispersed during the day, and some at least appeared to travel fair distances from the roost. The roost had declined noticeably by the 1980s, and ten years later it was almost abandoned, though odd birds still occasionally appear there. Another similar-sized harrier roost with up to 32 birds was found around the same time in Wigtownshire by R. C. Dickson (1994). The demise of the Stewartry site corresponded with the finding of other widely scattered roosts with only a few or even single birds in each. Four more were found in Wigtown but with widely varying numbers between years: the main roost here keeps going though with much reduced numbers – six were seen on 5 March 2001. Dickson found that 'brown' harriers (females and immature males) were nearly twice as numerous as grey birds.

Other animals

Adders are common on the peat mosses, which are a favourite habitat, and the Lochar Mosses were a noted haunt. Service (1901) said that when the farm of Tinwald Downs was reclaimed from the north end of this bog complex, a record was kept of the number of adders killed. The average was 100 per hectare. Nothing like this number would be found nowadays, though dozens may occupy the same hibernation den and remain in high density after emerging and before dispersing for the summer. Common lizards are frequent, though mainly on the drier parts of the lowland bogs.

Frogs and toads are still widespread, though perhaps less numerous than in earlier years. Of the newts, the great crested is the rarest, and found mostly along the Galloway coast, though it occurs also on the northeast coast and has a cluster of inland locations in the Selkirk–Hawick area (Beebee & Griffiths, 2000). The palmate newt is scattered across the region, and occurs in more 10km squares than the smooth newt, though both are local.

Peter Maitland wrote a valuable account of the freshwater fish of southwest Scotland in 1970. The brown trout is the most widespread species, but eels also occur in most waters: these two are often the only fish present in hill lochs. Many lowland lochs with nutrient-rich water are dominated by pike, perch, roach, minnow and three-spined sticklebacks, and these are found also in the slower-flowing reaches of lowland rivers. More local fish are the grayling, stone loach and chub, present in some of the main rivers. Rarer species are the bream, in Castle Loch at Lochmaben and the River Annan; rudd, formerly in several lochs in lower Nithsdale but recently only in Culzean Castle Pond to the north of our limits; ten-spined stickleback, once widespread but now uncommon; and the bullhead, with few recent records. The char was found in three oligotrophic hill lochs – Loch Doon, Loch Dungeon and Loch Grannoch – and the vendace was formerly in the Mill and Castle Lochs at Lochmaben. The migratory fish which spend part of their lives in the sea, and the estuarine or wholly marine species, are dealt with in Chapter 3.

Some of the hill lochs have lost their fish populations (mostly brown trout) as a result, it is believed, of the continuing acidification of their waters, which began with atmospheric pollution during the Industrial Revolution. The trout of Loch Enoch were once famous for their truncated caudal fins and rounded lower tail fins, presumed to be caused by abrasion from the sharp granite sand which overlay the loch bed. They were already extinct by the early twentieth century (Dick, 1916). Their deformities and their demise are now both thought to have resulted from the acidification of the loch water. Most of the Galloway granite lochs eventually lost their fish or suffered huge decreases in their abundance. When I visited Loch Skerrow in 1971, numerous fishermen were plying their rods from its shores, but by 1984 not a single angler was to be seen: the fish had become too few to be worth trying for, even if there were any left at all. This factor is thought to explain the loss of char from Loch Grennoch. Conversely, the disappearance of the vendace from its Lochmaben lochs is attributed to nitrogen and phosphate enrichment, especially from farmland runoff and sewage. Peter Maitland has attempted reintroduction of the vendace, first to some of the Glentrool hill lochs, where it has not been seen again, and to the more mesotrophic Loch Skene in the Moffat Hills, where the species was subsequently re-caught.

There has recently been a worrying appearance on the Ettrick tributary of the River Tweed of the American signal crayfish (MacDermid, 2004). As well as being a dominant competitor with the native freshwater crayfish, this intruder is a serious predator of trout and salmon eggs and fry, competes with them for food, removes aquatic vegetation, damages the spawning grounds by erosion of river banks, and carries a harmful fungal parasite. Its release is illegal and stands to put at risk the SSSI quality of the Tweed.

The large heath is a notable butterfly of the acidic bogs, and occurs almost everywhere that has a patch of level flow bog with hare's-tail cotton-grass, the main larval food-plant. It is under-recorded and probably occurs in every 10km square in Galloway and Carrick. During June its dun-coloured form may be seen flitting restlessly across the bogs on sunny days, sometimes in numbers. Here, in Scotland, the prevailing type of this variable butterfly is that with the 'eyelets' on the wing undersides much reduced or even nearly absent: it is distinguished as subspecies *scotica*. The Scotch argus overlaps from its typical habitat on *Molinia* grassland to the peaty moorlands of the west, and the small pearl-bordered fritillary often strays onto the bogs from breeding places with marsh violet in adjoining flushed mires.

The acidic peatlands are significant habitat for moths. Many of the widespread day-flying species of dwarf shrub moorland occur there, such as emperor, fox, northern eggar, silver Y, scarce silver Y, golden Y, clouded buff, ruby tiger, wood tiger, beautiful yellow underwing and true lover's-knot. The Manchester treble-bar is often found on raised bogs in Dumfriesshire, the four-dotted footman is fairly frequent in these habitats, and the dingy shell has recently been recorded from Kirkconnell Flow, which is the only known Scottish site for the bilberry pug (Richard Mearns, personal communication). The only Scottish locality for the bog bush-cricket and a micro-moth, the sorrel pygmy, are at Aucheninnes Moss near Dalbeattie, now threatened by landfill development.

Both standing and running waters are the main habitats for dragonflies, which have been more closely studied in the southwest than the northeast in recent years. The large golden-ringed dragonfly breeds in running waters and is especially common in Galloway, along the streams of the granite uplands, but is less often seen in the Borders. The common hawker is widespread from sea level to small peaty pools on the high tops where Barbara and Richard Mearns have found it breeding at 710m in the Moffat Hills. Lake margins, wet fens and lowland peat mosses are productive habitats for dragonflies and damselflies: their common species include the common hawker, four-spotted chaser, black darter, and the large red, emerald, common blue and blue-tailed damselflies. The variable damselfly is confined to the southwest but is quite widespread there, recorded from 32 lochs, ponds and slow-flowing ditches, mostly at low elevations. The hairy dragonfly has a northern outpost in Galloway near Colvend, Palnackie and Gatehouse of Fleet on the Solway coast, at small lochs with fairly eutrophic waters and fringing growths of reed and common club-rush.

In 1949, I discovered the azure hawker dragonfly on moorland beside Loch Twachtan under the Merrick, and also beside the Cooran Lane, where immature and newly emerged specimens showed it to be a resident breeder (Fig. 129). This boreal–montane species is common on Fennoscandian bogs, but was previously unknown south of the Highlands in Britain. Its Galloway population has proved to be fairly stable over many years, the Silver Flowe being an important breeding site, and another locality was found later in the Cairnsmore of Fleet area. Interestingly, The National Museums of Scotland have a specimen of another boreo-alpine dragonfly of acid bog pools and soakways in the Highlands, the northern emerald, labelled 'Silver Flowe', but without details of date or collector (David Clarke, personal communication). The habitat would seem right, and it could be there.

As evidence of climatic warming, southern dragonflies have been appearing for the first time in southwest Scotland in the last few years (David Clarke,

FIG 129. Azure hawker male: a Highland dragonfly which breeds in moorland pools and tarns among the Galloway Hills. (David Clarke)

personal communication). The first was the surprising occurrence of the vagrant emperor at Caerlaverock on 3 November 1996, when Dave Patterson caught a male of this long-distance migrant. An ordinary emperor dragonfly was seen by Tristan Reid at Craigencallie in 2003, and two others later at Caerlaverock and near Loch Skerrow. Richard and Barbara Mearns recorded the first migrant hawkers at Mill and Castle Lochs, Lochmaben, in September 2004, and saw a southern hawker near Canonbie that same month. The banded demoiselle, previously unknown in Scotland, was found breeding on a stream near Dalbeattie also in 2004. The above records are mostly from Mearns (2005).

In a study of invertebrates on the Silver Flowe, Nelson & Theaker (1982) found the three northern flies *Hydrophorus albiceps*, *Campsicnemus compeditus* and *Phaonia consobrina*. They noted that J. D. Curtis found 77 species of spider here in 1979, and regarded these bogs as having considerable invertebrate interest.

CHAPTER 7

The Southern Uplands: Vegetation and Flora

GRASSLANDS AND HEATHS

THERE ARE GEOGRAPHICAL variations in hill vegetation within the region, reflecting local differences in climate, geology and land management. As elsewhere in the British uplands, much of the vegetation up to the climatic tree limit has been derived from former broadleaved forest, through extensive clearance to create grazing range for domestic animals. Sometimes the resulting communities are recognisably the field–ground layer of woodland, with change in dominant species' abundance according to subsequent land use, as in the case of heather and bilberry heaths, fescue/bent, purple moor-grass and great woodrush grasslands.

The wettest ground was evidently treeless and occupied by open bog. Extensive draining and burning have dried many of these peatlands and, by creating conditions where trees can now grow, have perhaps exaggerated the apparent earlier extent of forest. Bog and underlying peat are most strongly developed under the wetter climate of the southwest, and cover large areas of the gently contoured Wigtownshire moors. The glacial drift smothering the lower levels of the steeper hills of the Stewartry and Carrick has a large extent of peaty gley soils with deep raw humus above the mineral horizon. These mostly highly acidic wet substrates carry a vegetation that may be regarded as shallow bog or wet heath, where there was originally probably a mixture of alder, birch and willows rather than the oak, elm, ash and hazel of dry ground. Flying bent is now dominant here, forming a community monotonous in its botanical poverty, and of little value as pasturage, since its summer greenery soon turns to useless straw. The vast spreads of this *Molinia* on lower slopes and broad valley floors are (or, rather, were) a distinctive feature of the Galloway and Carrick uplands, on both the granite and sedimentary rocks. Where there is marked waterlogging, but with some lateral water movement and transport of mineral particles, there is often a markedly tall, tussocky growth of this grass – dreadful stuff to have to cross on foot (Fig. 130). It is highly combustible in the winter condition, and has been burned a good deal, which maintains or increases its botanical poverty.

The more original state, after loss of the tree or tall shrub cover, appears to be a mixture of *Molinia* with ling heather and/or bog myrtle (M25), but repeated burning, combined with grazing, destroys the shrubs and leaves an almost pure growth of the grass. The flora is extremely limited. Sometimes there are other moisture-loving plants, such as deer sedge, hare's-tail and common cotton-grasses, bog asphodel and cross-leaved heath, mixed with the flying bent. Bog myrtle is the most typical associate and often co-dominant, but burning and heavy grazing first keep it poor in growth and finally suppress it altogether. Tormentil is often plentiful, and there may be devil's-bit scabious and carnation sedge. Pale butterwort is an occasional member of this community in open muddy places. A western plant, it has a curious absence from Britain between Pembrokeshire and Galloway except for the Isle of Man. Bog-mosses may be abundant, and the western species *Sphagnum strictum* occurs widely in the

FIG 130. Tussocky *Molinia* grassland on river alluvium, beside Big Water of Fleet, Dromore, Kirkcudbrightshire.

FIG 131. The *Molinia* moors of the Black Water, looking to Cairnsmore of Carsphairn. Typical haunt of the curlew, a declining species. North of Lochinvar, Kirkcudbrightshire.

Molinia/Myrica community; south of Galloway it occurs only as a rarity in west Wales. Flying bent communities are also widespread in the Moffat and Border Hills, but are never as extensive as in the west, and are there sometimes associated with a flow of richer drainage water, and so tend to have greater species diversity. On the sedimentary formations, flying bent is often mixed with abundance of both common and sharp-flowered rush (M23), as on the moors north of Dalry (Fig. 131).

On dry ground, heather-dominated vegetation is widespread but occurs extensively mainly in the east, particularly the Lammermuirs, where rainfall is lowest. On the Moorfoot Hills it is mainly on steeper slopes, and gentler ground is largely covered with blanket bog The steep-sided Eildon Hills above Melrose are mostly heather-covered, though the common gorse takes over at lower levels. Bell heather, bilberry, cowberry and, on damper ground, cross-leaved heath are common associates (H10 and H12), and one or the other may increase after fire. Of two frequent associates farther south, the western gorse is uncommon on moors north of the border, and seen mainly on crag faces in the Galloway uplands (though also as thickets locally in rough lowland ground), while petty whin is rarer still: both species have evidently retreated through moor-burning. Mosses such as *Pleurozium schreberi, Hylocomium splendens, Hypnum cupressiforme, Plagiothecium undulatum* and *Dicranum scoparium* often form a layer beneath the dwarf shrubs, and on damp ground or shady slopes, bog-mosses such as *Sphagnum capillifolium, S. quinquefarium, S. russowii* and *S. girgensohnii* may be plentiful (H21). Heather communities with abundant bog-moss on fairly steep slopes are the typical habitat of the lesser twayblade, a diminutive orchid. Open places among heather on dry ground, or during recovery after fire, are often lichen-grown, either with crustaceous species, especially of *Cladonia*, or with the frothy 'reindeer moss' types such as *Cladonia portentosa* and *C. arbuscula*.

Grouse-moor management aims at maintaining heather dominance, and involves rotational burning of the heather, usually on a ten-year cycle, so that the grouse have a continuous supply of the young and nutritious growth at four to six years old. Managed moors are thus at any one time covered with a patchwork of different age-classes of heather, from newly burned ground to moderately tall and dense stands (Fig. 132). Seldom is the heather allowed to attain its full stature and to die of old age, so that young growth can regenerate naturally below, as happens when the shrub is left completely alone. Repeated burning also impoverishes the community, by eliminating other dwarf shrubs and herbs that do not recover readily from fire, such as bearberry, petty whin and wintergreens (H16). The effects of fire (Fig. 133) depend on the intensity of the burn (i.e. temperature), which in turn is influenced by the conditions at the

FIG 132. Management of moorland for red grouse, showing pattern of rotational burning of heather. Tarras Water, Langholm, Dumfriesshire.

FIG 133. Muirburn, to encourage a new and nutritious growth of heather for red grouse. (Bobby Smith)

time. Where grazing by sheep is kept low, heather-dominated communities regenerate sooner or later after fire to form a stable climax vegetation.

One of the immediate effects of burning the vegetation is to produce a top-dressing of ash which releases to the soil or peat the elements that plants need, causing an early flush of growth. The effect is dramatically shown by the vigorous flowering of hare's-tail cotton-grass on lowland raised bogs after fires. In theory, this mobilisation of nutrients may also promote their loss by leaching. It has indeed been claimed that long-repeated muirburn causes a net loss of nutrients from the soil–plant system, but the evidence is equivocal. One study which purported to show this effect had neglected to measure the input in precipitation, so that data on the nutrient budget were incomplete.

Although heather tends to flourish best in the drier east of Britain, where plant competitors (mainly grasses and their allies) have less advantage than under a wet climate, the surviving grouse moors of the region are well scattered and include some in the west, as at Cairntable near Muirkirk, and Braid Fell north of Stranraer. There are some in the centre, at Wanlockhead on the Mennock Water, Spango near Sanquhar, and at the head of Daer. The Langholm moors revived for a time under intensive management, but have deteriorated in their grouse stocks again recently. Probably the best remaining grouse moors are on the more northerly Moorfoot Hills and Lammermuirs, but even here there is a good deal of watershed blanket bog as well as dry heather ground, and most areas with high grouse numbers have this mixture of dry and wet habitats. This was true of the ground where the record bag for Scotland was made (see Chapter 8).

Heather moorland has been very widely converted to fescue/bent grassland (U4) by the combination of fire and heavy grazing by sheep, red deer and goats, with massive invasion by bracken as a common end result on dry ground. The intermediate successional stage of blaeberry (bilberry) heath (H18) is frequent in the east but much less so in the west (Fig. 134). From its growth form, blaeberry is less susceptible to grazing than heather, but is eventually suppressed if too heavily cropped. It fruits less well as grazing increases. In the Victorian heyday of grouse-shooting, the moors were sacrosanct to the needs of this bird, and the sheep graziers were kept at bay, but later economics often led to attempts to have the best of both worlds. The result has been the widespread degradation and loss of heather moorland across the Southern Uplands. Many of the photographs in this book show examples of the retreat of heather communities, mostly in the later stages (Figs 135 & 136; see also Fig. 178).

The replacement of heather moorland by acidic grassland under sheep management was first noted by Robert Service (1901), albeit in a rather terse

FIG 134. Blaeberry (bilberry) in fruit: one of the commonest dwarf shrubs of the uplands.

FIG 135. Bare, sheep-grazed hills with circular stell (sheep-pen) below. Devil's Beef Tub, Annanhead, Moffat, Dumfriesshire.

FIG 136. The steep hills of Manorhead, showing shelter woods and dwindling heather patches on the sheepwalks. Peeblesshire.

statement. The change was described in rather more detail in the 1930s by E. Wyllie Fenton, who worked at Boghall Glen in the Pentland Hills of Midlothian, but he appeared not to recognise its full significance as a widespread and ongoing process of change in the Scottish uplands generally. I found that the same pattern of deterioration under heavy grazing and repeated burning was widespread in the hills of north Wales, Lakeland, the Southern Uplands and even parts of the Highlands during the 1950s, but it had gone largely unrecognised up to that time. Even Professor W. H. Pearsall, in his acclaimed *Mountains and Moorlands* (1950) appeared to overlook its importance. It is only in more recent decades that the loss of dwarf shrub heath has become such a matter of importance to ecologists and conservationists concerned with the uplands.

The swards of sheep's fescue, common bent and velvet bent derived through heather loss often have abundant wavy hair and vernal grasses, and are spangled with the tiny white, yellow and blue flowers of heath bedstraw, tormentil and heath milkwort (u4). On slightly moister but sloping ground the dwarf shrub heaths have been extensively replaced by coarse mat-grass swards (u5) and, where drainage is still more impeded, by heath rush (u6). Both mat-grass and heath rush are vigorously competitive plants which reduce or exclude smaller species, producing communities that are botanically impoverished. This range of acidic grassland is virtually identical with that so widespread in the hills of northern England and Wales. Dull habitat everywhere, both biologically and scenically, it is the biotic climax resulting from centuries of exploitation by humans and their animals, and is the typical though unproductive grazing range of sheep. It occupies large areas of the Moffat, Lowther and Galloway hills. The soils are a range of leached and podsolic types in the pH range 4.0–5.0, varying from skeletal brown earths on steep, freely drained slopes to deeper podsols with increasing gleying as drainage deteriorates. The wet *Molinia* grasslands described previously occur mainly on low moorlands, gentler lower hill slopes, and on valley bottoms where drainage is not so impeded as to produce real bog.

On the sedimentary hills there are frequent patches of a rather unusual upland community, with almost pure patches of great woodrush from a few up to hundreds of square metres in size (U16). They occur especially at the middle altitudes, but may be seen up to at least 700m, and are often in hollows which must be presumed to be both damper and more sheltered than the surrounding slopes, and also inclined to hold snow. Great woodrush is locally dominant in lowland oakwoods on acidic soils, but only where these are fenced against stock. Yet, while they seldom produce flowers, the hillside woodrush patches appear stable under the grazing regime.

BLANKET BOGS

As waterlogging increases in the *Molinia* and *Nardus/Juncus squarrosus* grass heaths, the surface peat horizon deepens and moisture-loving plants increase, to the point where the system may be regarded as bog. Where this peatland receives virtually all its water and nutrient input from precipitation and covers more gently contoured landscape in large expanses, it is known as blanket bog. In the west this occurs at all altitudes wherever drainage is seriously impeded, and typically has abundant deer sedge, flying bent, cotton-grasses and bog asphodel, with variable amounts of heather and cross-leaved heath (M17). Bog-mosses vary in cover according to drainage and incidence of muirburn, which often kills them, but on the less disturbed blanket bogs there can be abundance or even dominance of *Sphagnum*, with greater variety of species in the west. In the east, blanket bog is more characteristic of broad hill watersheds and is usually dominated by a mixture of heather and hare's-tail cotton-grass (M19). Common sundew is in both types, but great sundew mostly in western bogs and cloudberry in those of the east.

The Silver Flowe in the upper Dee valley (the Cauldron of the Dungeon;

Fig. 137) is the most extreme example of the western type of blanket bog in the region and has features otherwise confined to flow bogs in the Scottish Highlands. Its chain of eight separate bogs appears as a graded series. The southernmost, Craigeazle, has the domed shape of a raised bog, with steep edges and marginal streams, but merges into shallow hillside bog at the inner edge across a narrow saddle, and has been regarded as blanket bog. With distance north this convexity declines, until on the watershed of the tongue near the Dungeon Lochs, the last three bog patches appear merely as especially wet flow in a general expanse of ordinary blanket bog. Many flow bogs have wet hollows or pools, but here they have developed into intriguing surface patterns varying in detail from one bog patch to the next. Craigeazle has mainly small, *Sphagnum*-filled hollows and flat lawns with rather low intervening hummocks and ridges, representing the most active phase of bog growth. Next to the north, Snibe has a mixture of these vegetated hollows and deeper pools with open water and less vegetation, while there are some taller and drier hummocks (Fig. 138). Though the change is not regular with distance north, the frequency of deep and elongated pools with eroding and enlarging margins, and dry inactive hummocks crowned with mosses and lichens, tends to increase towards the watershed

FIG 137. The Silver Flowe, with a canal-like stretch of stream, 'deep enough to drown you two or three times over' (C. H. Dick). Cooran Lane, Cauldron of the Dungeon, Kirkcudbrightshire.

FIG 138. An active phase of bog growth, with *Sphagnum*-dominated pool and hummock complex on Snibe Bog, Silver Flowe.

flows. From higher levels on the surrounding hills, the elongated pools on some bog patches can clearly be seen to have their long axes arranged parallel to the surface contours of slope (Fig. 139). Only on the flat watershed do the pools lack this orientation. While it could be decidedly tricky crossing these pool systems in the dark, they present little hazard in daylight, and the sinister reputation of the Silver Flowe was a fiction of the novelist S. R. Crockett, to add colour to his tales.

The vegetation shows a mini-zonation in relation to the water table. Open water pools have emergent growths of bogbean and common cotton-grass, and submerged wefts of least bladderwort. Pool bog-mosses that grow first as lax floating forms expand to cover the water surface and then rise slightly above it are *Sphagnum cuspidatum* and *S. auriculatum* (M1 and M2). Lawns of these species become invaded by white beak-sedge, bog asphodel and great and round-leaved sundews, and then invasion by low hummock-forming *Sphagna* such as *S. papillosum*, *S. magellanicum* and *S. subnitens* gradually builds the surface above water level. The tall hummock-formers then appear, with *S. capillifolium*, *S. fuscum* and *S. austinii* forming, respectively, red, brown and orange mounds of compact growth. Other vascular plants appear, albeit sparsely at first: deer sedge, flying bent, hare's-tail cotton-grass, ling and cross-leaved heath (M18). These higher plants form more vigorous growths on the taller hummocks and crowberry sometimes occurs, while the bog-mosses decline and other mosses and lichens increase. The frequency of bog myrtle on some of the Silver Flowe bogs, the abundance of the purple-red leafy liverwort *Pleurozia purpurea* (Fig. 140) and the numerous hummocks of woolly fringe-moss are features typical of west Highland flow bogs, as well as the numerous pools. The bare-edged bogbean pools are the same as the 'dubh lochans' (black tarns) so characteristic of the Flow Country of Sutherland and Caithness. Some bog plants are unaccountably local or absent on the Silver Flowe. Few-flowered sedge is irregularly scattered and bog rosemary and *Sphagnum pulchrum* are only on the Brishie Bog, while cranberry, mud sedge and tall bog-sedge appear to be missing, though all occur on other Galloway blanket bogs.

Similar patches of pool and hummock bog formerly occurred at intervals alongside the River Dee as far as Clatteringshaws. Ellergower Knowe at the eastern foot of Craiglee is a drier version, and there is a small enclave within forest northeast of Craigencallie. A network of large pools in front of Craigencallie House was damaged by forestry ploughing but has recovered, though Raploch Moss beside Clatteringshaws Loch was degraded, with dried-out pools, even by 1947, and then disappeared under conifer forest. To the north, there were

FIG 139. Deep, bare and elongated pools that are not infilling and are arranged parallel to the contours. Long Loch Bog, Silver Flowe.

FIG 140. An Atlantic liverwort, *Pleurozia purpurea*, widespread in the western Highlands and locally common in Galloway bogs and on wet rocks, but absent south of the border.

small patches of pool and hummock bog beside Gala Lane, but these too have gone through afforestation. While the extensive flows of Wigtownshire and south Ayrshire once had a good deal of actively growing *Sphagnum* surfaces with hummock and hollow pattern, these were not in the well-defined systems shown by the Silver Flowe, and open-water pools were mostly few or absent, though there were occasional peaty tarns. The bog vegetation had a similar species composition, but usually a less clear vertical zonation from hollow to hummock. Kilquhockadale Flow was a good example of these low-lying (at 100–150m) Wigtown flows that are really intermediate between true lowland raised bog and hill blanket bog. It has been destroyed, but many good areas remain, for example on the Kirkcowan moors north of Eldrig Loch, and on Kilhern Moss, southeast of New Luce.

The eastern plateau and watershed bogs are less varied. Some of them have infilled *Sphagnum cuspidatum* pools, as on Roan Fell and the Moorfoot ridges, but not in any regular pattern (Fig. 141). Some also have a general abundance of bog-moss (mainly *S. papillosum* and *S. capillifolium*), which indicates continuing active growth of the bog surface (M19). More often they show degrees of erosion by gullying, in the manner so widespread on the extensive Pennine blanket bogs. Incipient channels gradually cut down to expose bare peat, which is removed by wind and water, especially after frost has heaved and loosened the surface. The gullies eventually deepen down to the underlying mineral soil and stones, widen laterally and creep forward into the peat mass. Interconnecting systems of gullies which dissect the bog may form over much of a watershed, and the process can be seen on the Watch Knowe above Loch Skene on Moffat Water, where the Megget Water catchment begins (Fig. 142). Occasionally there is wastage of the whole peat mass, with sheet erosion as the final stage. Regrowth of bog sometimes occurs in the erosion channels (Fig. 143), or on ground entirely denuded of its peat cover, and the colonisation of redistributed peat by mat-grass on the Moorfoot Hills was described by Smith (1918). The drier types of high-level blanket bog often have abundance of bilberry, cowberry and crowberry, and on some eastern moors there is a profusion of cloudberry, as on the Langholm and Newcastleton Hills, and the Moorfoots. By contrast, bog myrtle, so constant on the western bogs, is mostly absent in the east. Some eastern bogs also have abundance of the 'reindeer moss' lichens, especially *Cladonia arbuscula*, *C. portentosa* and *C. uncialis*.

FIG 141. Watershed blanket bogs with hare's-tail cotton-grass, heather and bog-mosses. Breeding habitat of golden plover and dunlin. Moorfoot Hills, Midlothian – Peeblesshire.

FIG 142. Eroding blanket bog on the watershed between the Tail and Winterhope Burns, near Loch Skene, Moffat Hills.

FIG 143. Eroding blanket bog on the watershed of Roan Fell, showing some regeneration. Dumfries – Roxburghshire.

FLUSH BOGS

Where lateral water seepages emerge diffusely at the ground surface, there is bog of a different kind, more localised than blanket bog, but varying in size from a few square metres to many hectares. They are especially characteristic of gently sloping valley floors and lower hillsides where a deep layer of impermeable glacial drift impedes drainage from higher ground. Sometimes they occupy the channels among moraine systems. The water is more aerated than in blanket bog, and it may contain dissolved base nutrients removed from soils higher in the catchment. From the term 'flushing' given by Pearsall (1950) to this process, they are best called flush bogs. The *Molinia/Myrica* communities of acidic seepages are one response to such enrichment, but a more distinct type is where rushes become dominant. In the east the common rush is the most usual species, but in the west the sharp-flowered rush tends to be more prominent, though the two may be mixed (M23). *Sphagnum* species associated with moving water, especially *S. recurvum*, *S. palustre*, *S. inundatum* and *S. squarrosum*, are usually abundant and hair moss *Polytrichum commune* is often present in quantity. *S. affine* is frequent in Galloway flush bogs and in wider expanses of peat influenced by moving water, such as the boggy ground west of Stroan Loch. This bog-moss has the cell-wall comb-fibrils of *S. austinii*, but a laxer growth form and a grey to green colour. Small herbs such as marsh willowherb, marsh violet, heath bedstraw and tormentil are typically present, with water forget-me-not, bog pondweed and lesser spearwort in especially wet places. These rushy flush bogs are widespread and locally extensive over the lower moorlands on both sheep-walks and grouse moors. In places where a high water table is maintained, these types grade into spongy 'poor fen' similar to that noted in the lowlands, with a carpet of the above bog-mosses but a more varied selection of *Carex* species, including bottle, star, white and tufted sedges, with bog pondweed, lesser spear-wort, marsh cinquefoil and bogbean (M4). Mud and slender sedges are occasional, but tall bog-sedge is rare.

More restricted sites of emergent water, as flushes and rills, have spongy carpets and hummocks of moss and liverwort. On the granite (Fig. 144), *Sphagnum auriculatum* is especially common, and on dripping rocks it forms colourful patches of red, brown, yellow and green, while the dense black cushions of *Campylopus atrovirens* grow profusely on irrigated slabs and in gravelly seepages. Muddy flushes with bog asphodel, white beak-sedge and many-stalked spike-rush are also widespread in the west, and lousewort is a common plant of such places. Vascular plants such as blinks, bog stitchwort, golden saxifrage, starry

FIG 144. Rugged granite hills: Craignaw and the Dungeon, Minnigaff, Kirkcudbrightshire.

saxifrage, kingcup and tufted hair-grass are usually present (community intermediate between M21 and M32). Butterwort is a common plant of flushed places, especially in the Galloway Hills, where its violet-purple flowers make a fine show in June. The pale butterwort occurs sparingly in very open places among these western hills, but is inconspicuous and easily overlooked, even when in flower. Marsh St John's-wort is sometimes associated with it in low-level localities. Where the water contains slightly more base nutrients but is still acidic, there are bryophyte springs and flushes with *Philonotis fontana*, *Dicranella squarrosa*, *Drepanocladus exannulatus*, *Acrocladium sarmentosum*, *Scapania undulata*, *Jungermannia exsertifolia* ssp. *cordifolia* and *Riccardia pinguis* (M32).

THE INFLUENCE OF LIME

On the granite hills, such as Cairnsmore of Fleet (Fig. 145), the range of plant communities described above covers most of the variation likely to be encountered within the former forest zone. The same is true of much of the metamorphic aureole of the Merrick and Kells ranges, but on the unaltered greywackes and shales of the sedimentary hills, the presence of lime-rich strata (Chapter 1) widens the diversity of hill vegetation. The prevalence of leaching limits the effects of localised calcareous rocks mainly to flushed areas. Ground where this enrichment is intermittent and mainly during wet weather, when even steep slopes may become saturated, carries a herb-rich grassland probably derived by grazing from taller herbaceous vegetation. It represents an upland variant of the types of grazed herb-rich sward described in Chapter 5. Patches of such grassland occur widely in such situations but are seldom continuously extensive in large stands. Their soils are base-rich brown loams with pH 5.5–7.0. Distinctive plants of the close-grazed swards are red fescue, crested dog's-tail, wild thyme, fairy flax, heath violet, common milkwort, meadow buttercup, self-heal, eyebright, spring sedge, carnation sedge and glaucous sedge (CG10). Occasional members of the community are carline thistle, limestone bedstraw, mountain pansy, meadow oat-grass, hairy oat-grass and rock-rose. These swards are heavily grazed by sheep, and some taller species persist as non-flowering rosettes, though they will reach normal stature and flower again if protected from grazing.

Where the enriched water supply is more continuous, there are base-rich equivalents to the acidic flushes. Cushions of golden moss *Cratoneuron commutatum* form where calcareous springs emerge (M37), and on the most lime-rich rocks sometimes form mounds of tufa. They feed the flushes, which have

FIG 145. The abrupt granite crags at the Clints of Dromore in 1960. The heather has since disappeared from the ground below. Cairnsmore of Fleet, Kirkcudbrightshire.

other mosses such as *Drepanocladus revolvens, D. cossonii, Campylium stellatum, Scorpidium scorpioides, Cratoneuron filicinum, Ctenidium molluscum* and *Bryum pseudotriquetrum.* Such flushes are often open and muddy or gravely, with an incomplete plant cover which includes vascular species such as yellow, flea, tawny and dioecious sedges, jointed rush, marsh arrowgrass, quaking grass, butterwort, self-heal, grass of Parnassus, red rattle and least clubmoss (M11, but *Saxifraga aizoides* is absent). Sometimes they occur as closed communities with a higher cover of mosses and small herbs, the counterpart of small acidic flush bogs (M10). An intermediate type has bog-mosses of base-rich habitats such as *S. teres, S. contortum, S. subsecundum* and *S. warnstorfii*, but with the sedges and herbs of the acidic kinds, such as bottle sedge and marsh violet (M8). Uncommon plants of these basic flush bogs are broad-leaved cotton-grass, alpine rush, alpine meadow-rue and the mosses *Tomentypnum nitens, Hamatocaulis vernicosus* and *Sphagnum platyphyllum.*

MONTANE COMMUNITIES

In the Highlands, heather becomes steadily dwarfed with altitude, and near its upper limit has a prostrate form, flattened to the ground, with its growing apical shoots directed away from the prevailing wind. This prostrate heath has other dwarf shrubs such as bearberry, crowberry and dwarf azalea (H13), and occurs at 760–915m in the central Grampians and even higher in the Cairngorms. In the Southern Uplands, where heather communities have lost ground so widely, these alpine dwarf shrub heaths have been especially sensitive to fire and grazing, and have been almost entirely eradicated, so that the upper limits of *Calluna* heath are artificially depressed, to around 600m. In a very few places, short, prostrate heather mats have survived, with crowberry and short bilberry but lacking bearberry and dwarf azalea, as impoverished remnants of this former alpine heath. They occur at 670m on Cairnsmore of Fleet and at 715–760m on the Carrifran Gans and White Coomb in the Moffat Hills. A low growth of heather approaching this type also occurs on the summit of Dun Rig east of the Manor Water on the Selkirk–Peebles border.

The vegetation that has replaced the high-level *Calluna* heath is either short bilberry heath with some cowberry and crowberry, or transitions from this to short grassland of fescue/bent or mat-grass differing little from the types so widespread at lower levels (close to H19). Rigid sedge begins to appear at about 550m and is generally common above this level, and there are sometimes alpine and fir clubmosses (Fig. 146). Where snow lies late on the Moffat and Tweedsmuir

FIG 146. Fir clubmoss and dwarf willow growing in woolly fringe-moss on high plateau. Corserine, Kells Range, Kirkcudbrightshire.

hills, in north- to east-facing hollows, there are patches of a heath in which the crowberry is the larger hermaphrodite form, and bilberry is locally dominant. This approximates to the crowberry/bilberry or bilberry heaths of late snow beds in the Highlands (H19). The stage associated with still later snow-lie in that region, the dominance of mat-grass (U7), occurs also in these places, and is well developed as a strip in the shelter of walls across the highest summits. These highest hills of the Southern Uplands are the most southerly part of Britain (besides the Big Cheviot at the same latitude) with clear examples of vegetation influenced by prolonged snow cover. A few mosses associated with late snow-lie, such as *Kiaeria falcata* and *Pohlia wahlenbergii* var. *glacialis*, occur sparingly high in north-facing corries, but vascular plants of such habitats, such as sibbaldia and least cudweed, are absent or were lost long ago.

On some high plateaux and broad ridges of the Moffat–Tweedsmuir hills, at around 750m, are patches of cotton-grass blanket bog over rather shallow peat (up to two metres) where heather seems naturally to be replaced by crowberry, cowberry and bilberry (M19, high-level variant). Bog bilberry and rigid sedge may also be present and cloudberry is usually plentiful, while both hummock-forming bog-mosses (which may include *Sphagum fuscum*) and 'reindeer moss' *Cladonia* lichens are sometimes abundant. It is almost identical with high-level crowberry/cotton-grass bog in the Highlands.

On the highest and most exposed plateaux, these montane grass heaths of upper slopes formerly gave way to dominance of woolly fringe-moss in more or less continuous carpets (U10) (Fig. 147). Least willow was often present, especially on stony ground, rigid sedge was constant, and dwarfed shoots of bilberry and cowberry grew up through the moss. This *Racomitrium lanuginosum* heath was widespread on the higher Galloway Hills, from 700m on Cairnsmore of Fleet to the summits of the Kells and Merrick massifs at 845m. In the offat–Tweedsmuir ranges there was a good area on stony ground on Lochcraig Head above Loch Skene, and it occurred extensively on the crowns of the vegetated soil hummocks that covered most of the summits of Carrifran Gans, White Coomb, Broad Law, Cramalt Craig and Dollar Law. Yet, even in 1951, there were clear signs that the woolly fringe-moss cover was receding. Randomly measured hummocks on White Coomb summit that year gave only 28 per cent average woolly fringe-moss cover, though stony flats on Lochcraig Head had more continuous areas of *Racomitrium*. In the following year, Cramalt Craig and the tops immediately to the north still had a good deal of woolly fringe-moss on the hummocky summit ground, while Broad Law was better still. Also in 1952, Hart Fell summit had smaller areas of *Racomitrium*-capped hummocks, but was mostly covered by montane grassland with fescue/bent, mat-grass and heath rush. By the time (1962)

FIG 147. Plateau of Corserine with extensive woolly fringe-moss heath, from Carlin's Cairn, Kells Range, Kirkcudbrightshire.

FIG 148. The hummocks have mostly lost their woolly fringe-moss cover. 22 May 1962, with late snow patches lingering. Cramalt Craig from Dun Law, Peebles – Selkirk.

I took my photograph of hummock ground on Dun Law (Fig. 148), the woolly fringe-moss had almost disappeared and had been replaced by a short turf of sheep's fescue, wavy hair-grass and bents. Cramalt Craig and White Coomb had similarly lost their *Racomitrium*. The Merrick still had a good area of woolly fringe-moss heath in 1949, but it had almost gone by 1976, being again replaced by grasses.

The woolly fringe-moss community has disappeared from all but two hill ranges in the region, leaving short fescue/bent sward in its place. As in Cumbria and Snowdonia, where exactly the same loss has occurred, this change results from the high numbers of sheep which now graze the hill tops in summer, and which by their cropping, treading and manuring suppress the moss in favour of grasses. This effect of sheep was first pointed out by Pearsall (1950). In places, as on Cairnsmore of Fleet, they have eliminated dwarf willow also, but the grazing-resistant rigid sedge survives abundantly on some hill tops, albeit mostly in non-flowering form. It is on the summits of the Kells Range where the woolly fringe-moss heath has survived, and in 1989 it was probably in even better condition than before (Fig. 149). The explanation is that conifer forests encircle the Kells tops up to 610–700m, and the sheep were removed from the unplanted higher ground long ago, so that this is ungrazed except by feral goats and red deer, which are kept in check by the foresters. The *Racomitrium* heaths on

FIG 149. Dense carpets of woolly fringe-moss on rocky summit of Carlin's Cairn, Kells Range, Kirkcudbrightshire.

Corserine and Carlin's Cairn are now almost as good as those of the Highland summits, with dense carpets of the moss, abundant least willow, rigid sedge flowering freely, alpine and fir clubmosses and the dwarf form of goldenrod. There could hardly be a more convincing demonstration of the benefits of removing sheep from the high ground. Yet the build-up of feral goat numbers here threatens to reverse the recovery, and needs to be kept in check. The other place where *Racomitrium* heath has survived is on steep northeast slopes above and around Hartfell Craig, Moffat Hills, which sheep probably avoid. The woolly fringe-moss carpets extend a short way onto the hummocky plateau, but soon pass into grass and dense growths of other mosses in which *Rhytidiadelphus squarrosus*, an enrichment indicator, is abundant.

Where the woolly fringe-moss summit heath is well developed, it acts as nature's compass, for the moss stems have unidirectional growth, away from the prevailing wind, here from the west-south-west. With a little practice this orientation can be recognised – check it against a real compass if you wish, but only where the moss is growing on fully wind-exposed ground.

THE MOUNTAIN FLORA

As on the Cumbrian fells, the prevalence of acidic rock types and base-deficient derived soils determines that the mountain flora of the Southern Uplands is mainly of calcifuge or tolerant species. These are few in number, and it is the more limited occurrences of base-rich rock that boost variety through supporting the more diverse calcicole element. Compared with the Scottish Highlands, it is not in total a rich flora, and lacks even some of the species present on the northern English hills. The region has a scarcity of the steep, open rock habitats with base-rich substrates that are the most productive for mountain plants in Britain. The alpine lady's mantle and yellow saxifrage, so plentiful on the Lakeland fells to the south, are two especially notable absentees. Myrtle willow is the only species not known south of the border. Even so, a total of 40 species which may be termed 'alpine' is not an unworthy figure for a region with only a handful of tops above 750m and none reaching 900m. Indeed, considering that 37 of these occur within the single 10 × 10km grid square which covers Moffatdale, this may be regarded as a productive area.

The studies of both pollen and macrofossils in Late-glacial deposits in the Selkirk fens (see Chapter 6) have shown that tundra-type vegetation existed in the lowlands of the region from 13,000 up to 10,000 years ago, with a rich flora of what are now regarded as alpine or montane species. With the later advance of forest during the Post-glacial, this vegetation retreated up the hills and was eliminated from all but the highest ground, where it persisted as a montane zone. Various adversities – unfavourable climate, plant disease, rock-falls and the grazing of domesticated animals – then whittled down the remnants, so that they survive only in much-depleted form, as regards their species content. Mountain avens and dwarf birch were clearly abundant in the Late-glacial, but the first has entirely disappeared and the second is only doubtfully reported, yet could well occur on little-trodden moorland, for it has two good colonies not far south of the border, on shallow blanket bog of the Kielder moors (Fig. 150) and Spadeadam Waste. Purple saxifrage and moss campion were two probably widespread species that remain common in the Highlands: the first has two small colonies left and the second has become extinct.

The profuse cloudberry of the watershed blanket bogs is probably the most abundant of the calcifuge alpines, though there is a sharp cutoff in occurrence westwards from the Dumfries border and it occurs only in the northeast corner of Galloway. Fruit is produced copiously in some localities, though some populations of this dioecious plant appear to be entirely male and so have none.

FIG 150. The Black Needle Burn, Kielderhead. The border follows its bed. Northumberland on the left, Roxburghshire on the right.

FIG 151. Parsley fern: a common plant of screes in the higher hills of the Southern Uplands.

It is locally abundant at above 400m, but occurs as low as 240m above Newcastle-ton. Parsley fern (Fig. 151) is the next commonest of this group, and grows profusely on screes, crags and drystone walls in the Galloway, Lowther and Moffat Hills (U21), though it thins out markedly east of the last area. It is perhaps more abundant in the Southern Uplands than in any part of the Highlands, which are mostly too cold for it and cause its restriction to the shelter of late snow beds. Two other northern ferns, mountain male fern and northern buckler fern, have been recognised as distinct species only in relatively recent times. The first occurs widely on rock outcrops, especially in the eastern hills, and the second is in block screes of the Moffat and Galloway hills. The fern relatives, fir and alpine clubmosses, are locally common across the main hill ranges, especially in heaths and grasslands at higher altitudes, though the first is often on bogs also. Bearberry is rare in the region. Apart from a large colony on a partly scree-covered hillside in Tweedsmuir, it is confined to scattered small patches on Moffat Water and in the Galloway Hills. As in northern England, it has evidently lost ground through the nearly universal muirburn, which leaves – by pure chance – only a few rocky places unscathed, mostly on the ledges or tops of crags. Dwarf juniper is a similar case: on the Galloway granite, small forms of juniper have survived the conflagrations on certain crag faces, and in places they approach the true dwarf subspecies *nana*. The most convincing of these was a single prostrate patch with short, curved needles that had persisted on a granite pavement above Loch Enoch. Patches on the south crags of Kirriereoch Hill also appeared close to the *nana* form.

Northern crowberry has been found in some quantity but very locally in late snow areas of the Moffat–Tweedsmuir hills, and is reported also from the Galloway Hills. Dwarf cornel (Fig. 152) is associated with it on the White Coomb, and also grows in blaeberry beds on Cramalt Craig and Dollar Law, but it is not abundant. Bog bilberry is inexplicably rare, since its habitats are widespread. It grows in at least two high-level patches of blanket bog and on two dry heathery crags in the Moffat Hills, and is probably overlooked in the area. There is a much lower station with at least four patches at 120–180m on the Newcastleton Fells, and this is closer to its occurrences in lowland peat mosses in north Cumbria. The least willow and rigid sedge in the summit communities are usually stunted in growth, but both attain their full stature when out of the reach of sheep, on steep rocks, with the willow showing leaves 2cm across and the sedge inflorescences up to 20cm tall.

Some mountain plants of wet, open habitats need only slight nutrient enrichment. Starry saxifrage is a fairly widespread plant in the higher Galloway and Moffat hills, where it grows on wet rocks and in springs, rills and flushes

FIG 152. Dwarf cornel: a rare plant of high-level heaths in the Moffat–Tweedsmuir Hills. White Coomb, Dumfriesshire.

over a wide range of altitude (M32). At higher levels, the little alpine willowherb is characteristic of these acidic flushes in the Moffat Hills, and there is a form of thyme-leaved speedwell which approaches the subspecies *humifusa* of such habitats in the Highlands. The rarest plant of these places is the alpine fox-tail grass, first found on the White Coomb in 1956 and later on Cramalt Craig and Hart Fell. It is probably widely scattered in high mossy springs in the area, but sheep crop the silky inflorescences, so that it tends to pass unnoticed as 'grass' in the vegetative state. On the Cross Fell range in Cumbria, removal of sheep during the 2001 foot-and-mouth epidemic caused an unprecedented flowering of alpine fox-tail in 2002, showing it to be far more abundant than anyone had realised (Roberts, 2002). Associated with it in the main Moffat locality are distinctive bryophytes in the bright red *Bryum weigelii, Dicranella squarrosa, Drepanocladus exannulatus, Philonotis fontana, Splachnum vasculosum* and *Jungermannia cordifolia*. The small mountain form of kingcup is plentiful here, too.

The inland form of thrift grows abundantly in moist seepages on the northern cliffs of the Merrick, which are slightly basic, but this is its only locality away from the sea. Sea campion in its mountain form is plentiful on several of the Moffatdale cliffs, on dry and rather acidic rocks, and its showy white flowers compensate for the lack of some other alpines. Scott-Elliot (1896) gives a record by James M'Andrew of alpine hawkweed for Meikle Millyea on the Kells Range, but it has not been seen in recent times. This plant has two habitats: the steep bare crevices of dry acidic cliffs, and the gravelly, unstable, frost-heaved surfaces of barren fell-fields, both of which occur in the named locality, and it could still be there. The long shaggy hairs on all parts of the plant except the petals are distinctive.

The most famous plant of the Moffat Hills is the little fern, oblong woodsia, which is probably best regarded as a calcifuge, though it can also grow on basic rocks (see Fig. 32). It is a plant unaccountably rare in Britain, though quite common in Scandinavia and parts of North America, on rocks both within and above the forest zone. It has only ever been found in twelve of the 10km grid squares in Britain, and is now known in just six of these. Moffatdale once shared with the Lake District fells the distinction of being the British headquarters of this very rare fern. Scott-Elliot (1896) listed five separate stations, in all the main side valleys of Moffat Water and at Annan Head, between 300 and 630m, but ominously remarked that 'of the hundreds of plants said to exist fifty years ago, only two remain, the rest having been eradicated by the ravages of the Innerleithen Alpine Club'. There were undoubtedly other colonies and more than a bunch of local gardeners were involved in the destruction, for its occurrence here became widely known, and Victorian fern-hunters came from afar for this special trophy. John Sadler of the Royal Edinburgh Botanic Garden, having uprooted four out of five tufts that he found in 1857, a few years later castigated 'an English nurseryman' for digging up 14 plants for sale at half-a-guinea a time. G. C. Druce was shown the supposedly last remaining tuft, on Carrifran, in 1911, but could not resist helping himself to a frond for his herbarium. As far as I know, it was not seen again until 1954 when, after a long search, I found a colony of 25 plants, on crumbling dry rocks with little else but parsley fern and sea campion. The British Pteridological Society then found another group of six plants in a different locality in 1972. John Mitchell monitored these two colonies and watched them decline, evidently as the result of a series of prolonged spring droughts. By 1999 the larger one was down to three plants and the smaller one to a single tuft.

In the mid-1990s, Edinburgh University botanists Adrian Dyer, Stuart Lindsay and Phil Lusby began a restoration project by cultivating spores from surviving Moffatdale plants. Numerous prothalli were produced and these grew into mature sporophytes (fern plants). In September 1999 these were transplanted back into appropriate habitats in a locality once known to have had the fern. The two colonies of 1954 and 1972 were on dry, acidic crags, one of them loose and unstable, and the transplants were placed in dry crevices, especially where a little soil, moss or lichen had collected, and in stable scree (which is a frequent habitat in Norway). In June 2000, 119 out of 129 transplants here were still alive and in September there was still over 90 per cent survival (Dyer *et al.*, 2001) – but by summer 2004, only 75 plants could be found (Dan Watson, personal communication). Of the surviving plants accessible to sheep, or more especially goats, eight showed grazing damage.

The population of Britain's rarest fern has thus been partly restored here in a promising restocking exercise, though its long-term success remains to be seen. Purists may assert that such interference is wrong and that Nature should have been left to take its course. But it was humans that directly brought it to such a low ebb, and the chances of the plant recovering of its own accord – except during another ice age – were so remote that it would have become irrevocably extinct. Although most of the known British populations produce spores in abundance, woodsia seems unable to reproduce itself naturally in the wild here – presumably because present conditions are unfavourable in some respect. Many people would prefer to be able to see the celebrated fern still in its native haunts. I only hope that none of its seekers of today feels impelled to repeat the history of Victorian depredations, and that it will be left to grace the bleak rocks where it belongs, as a reminder of the last Ice Age, and the subsequent millennia of change.

The calcicole alpine flora is best represented in the Moffat Hills, where lime-rich rocks occur most extensively at high levels, but a few species occur more widely (ov40). Mossy saxifrage is probably the most widespread, growing plentifully on basic rocks of all the higher ranges, as well as some of the lower outlying hills – Langholm, Hermitage, Spango and the Scaur. In dry places, as among screes, it forms tight cushions that have led the inexperienced to mistake it for tufted saxifrage, but the sharp points of its leaf segments are diagnostic. In moist sites it tends to straggle in laxer growth, with long stoloniferous shoots. Northern bedstraw is quite widespread, usually on ungrazed ledges, but occurs down to low levels on the rocky banks of rivers, or sometimes in grassland kept for hay, and is perhaps best regarded as subalpine. It is grazing-sensitive and only grows tall where it is protected against the sheep. Nor have I seen it in large quantity anywhere in the region.

Only three mountain plants grow more abundantly on lower uplands than amongst the highest hills. The first is the pink-flowered hairy stonecrop, which is widespread in the middle and eastern Southern Uplands and has many localities on the hills of the Dumfries–Roxburgh border, in open basic flushes, though it has declined in afforested areas. This district is its British headquarters, and it is a curiously local plant nationally (Preston *et al.*, 2002). The second is the delicate alpine rush, a national rarity, which is found in open calcareous flushes in a few central upland stations and in the rich fens around Hawick and Selkirk (see Chapter 6), all at quite low altitudes. The third is the mountain pansy, which occurs over a wide range of altitude, from 100 to 750m, and prefers soils of intermediate base-richness. While widespread, it is sparse in most places and small, evidently through sheep-grazing that has greatly reduced its abundance and stature. Up to the 1960s, at least, it grew in great quantity and luxuriance at the old mining villages of Leadhills and Wanlockhead, in herb-rich grassland that had colonised lead-mine debris and ground affected by it (Fig. 153). This huge population of mountain pansy along roadsides and adjoining ground was

FIG 153. Mountain pansy luxuriates on lead-mine spoil in ungrazed places. Leadhills, Lanarkshire.

one of the finest botanical sights of the region. Its copious flowering was the result of excluding sheep from the lead spoil areas, no doubt for fear of toxic effects. The pansy is generally purple-flowered with yellow eyes in southern Scotland, but here occurred every colour form from deep purple to pure yellow, and all manner of mixtures between the two. When I was last at these localities, in 1987, it seemed much less profuse, for the sheep had been allowed access to many of its best sites. Mountain pansy also grows abundantly on the spoil of the Alston Moor and Upper Teesdale lead-mines, and evidently has a tolerance, if not a preference, for soils with high levels of lead. It also appears to need the modest levels of lime that come from the calcite in these heavily mineralised rocks. Surprisingly, neither of the other plants so typical of Pennine lead-mine waste tips, spring sandwort and alpine pennycress, grows on such habitats in southern Scotland. Their only localities here are on the low-level serpentine south of Girvan.

Roseroot sprouts its glaucous, fleshy stems (Fig. 154) from many of the basic crags in Moffatdale and a few of those in Galloway, though it also grows on sea cliffs on both coasts. Mountain sorrel, with its kidney-shaped leaves, is often in its company. The white-flowered crucifer, alpine scurvy-grass, makes shiny-leaved cascades on wet rocks, and grows large on sheltered faces. Lesser meadow-rue also inhabits some of the same cliffs, with some claim to be a mountain plant, though it is equally at home on stony lake shores, riversides and coastal sand dunes. It is one of the few Borders mountain species rare on the mountains of the Highlands. The Moffat Hills are its main upland area, but it has been found on the Merrick. These relatively tall plants sometimes grow on bigger ledges where a good soil cover has developed, supporting a community with affinities to the herb layer of ungrazed upland woods, with wood cranesbill, water avens, meadowsweet, valerian, lady's mantle, marsh hawk's-beard, devil's-bit scabious, knapweed, bush vetch and early purple orchid (fragmentary MG3). Rarer plants of these basic ledges are globeflower, melancholy thistle, wood vetch, stone bramble and spignel, while dry crevices on a few cliffs have hairy rock-cress, upright bitter-vetch and mountain melick grass. Most of the lady's mantle is the common *Alchemilla glabra*, but in the Moffat Hills the cliffs also have *A. filicaulis* and *A. wichurae*. Columbine grows in a native-looking locality in the ravine of Garpol Linn, west of Moffat, but has been regarded by some as an introduction.

Alpine meadow-rue flourishes locally on wet flushed rocks and slopes: it is as abundant on high grassy slopes of the Merrick and Kells ranges as on those of the Moffat–Tweedsmuir massifs, and its small size may protect it from grazing to some extent. In some stony flushes and rills of the Moffat Hills chickweed willowherb is common, but it also accompanies its smaller relative, the alpine

FIG 154. Roseroot grows both on the high crags of the mountains and on the sea cliffs. Above Loch Skene, Moffat Hills, Dumfries-shire.

willowherb, in more acidic springs up to high levels. In similar habitats there is sometimes the pale forget-me-not (Fig. 155), a short-leaved stoloniferous plant once thought to be a British endemic, but later found in the Iberian mountains. It is quite widespread in the eastern Southern Uplands, and also grows in waters only slightly enriched with base nutrients, over a wide range of altitude.

All the remaining 'alpines' are uncommon. Alpine saw-wort has several good Moffatdale colonies, on high, sheltered and ungrazed ledges, and grows also on the Merrick and other Galloway cliffs. Viviparous bistort has a similar

FIG 155. Pale forget-me-not: a local plant of hill flushes in the eastern Southern Uplands.

distribution and habitats, but is in only small amount in most localities. Alpine cinquefoil (Fig. 156) survives on at least two Moffatdale crags, on Carrifran and Black's Hope, and has a strong colony at Cairnbaber, in the Lamachan Hill group of Galloway, where calcareous rocks occur quite extensively. Purple saxifrage is surprisingly rare, given the abundance of suitable habitats. It has long been known at the Grey Mare's Tail in Moffatdale, where it still grows in moderate amount on north-facing rocks beside the main fall but has mostly been collected out from accessible places. Its bright pink-red blooms enliven the dark rocks in early April, when hardly anything else is in flower. While this distinctive alpine grows abundantly at the Falls of Clyde, this locality is outside our boundaries. Its only other certain Southern Upland locality is in basic flushes high on the Merrick, where it was discovered in 1973 by Hugh Lang. A mysterious record for rocks in Glendeans Banks, Traquair, might have been an introduction, but the plant has evidently disappeared.

Downy willow hangs on high on the north cliffs of the White Coomb and the Merrick, representing a last remnant of mountain willow scrub (W20) that probably once had a wider distribution above the forest limits in ancient times, before the sheep flocks began their onslaught on our uplands. It is a pitiful fragment of this distinctive vegetation, which covers huge areas of the Scandinavian mountains, which remain in a virtually natural state. People wishing to see what Scottish mountain vegetation was once like should go to Norway and Sweden. The myrtle willow that has recently been reported as still on the first hill belonged also to this fragile type of vegetation that the graziers destroyed long ago. Another Highland species, the mountain willow, was also reported from the area and from hills farther west in Dumfriesshire, but has not been seen in recent years. The northern but mainly lower-level tea-leaved willow also grows on the high crags above Loch Skene.

Three mountain sedges are present in small amount. Nodding heads of black alpine sedge are scattered about the walls of a ravine near Loch Skene, and on the same faces are dainty tufts of the delicate hair sedge. I found two flowering plants of the first high on Black's Hope, and there is an old record of the second from the same area. Sheathing sedge, which needs only slight enrichment, occurs with other *Carex* species in elevated flush bogs on Hart Fell, and on wet rocks of White Coomb, but it is easily overlooked, especially in grazed situations where flowers may be suppressed, and it has proved to occur beyond the Moffat Hills. In gullies of the Carrifran glen and near Loch Skene are tufts of a grass resembling the glaucous meadow-grass, a widespread Highland alpine, but more robust and less blue-green. It belongs to the plant once called *Poa balfourii*, which the botanical pundits have since reduced to a form of wood meadow-grass, a distinctly lowland

FIG 156. Alpine cinquefoil: a rare mountain plant of lime-rich rocks in both the Moffat and Galloway hills.

species. The mountain form of yellow-rattle, *Rhinanthus minor* ssp. *borealis*, grows on rock ledges of Black's Hope and Carrifran.

All the remaining alpines are single-station plants, hovering on extinction at the end of their Post-glacial retreat in the Southern Uplands. The white flowers of alpine mouse-ear still adorn the dark rocks of a Black's Hope crag, though there are no recent reports of it from the White Coomb locality given by Scott-Elliot (1896). About thirty plants of holly fern still persisted in 1954 over a limited area of steep, mossy, basic rocks in an unfrequented spot, where they eluded the Victorian fern maniacs, but I do not know its present status. Pyramidal bugle is a puzzling plant (see Fig. 35). Always in small quantity on dry basic rocks in its southernmost British stations, it becomes quite common in Ross-shire, Sutherland and Caithness on a much wider range of substrates and habitats, which there include earthy roadside banks. It was discovered on Black's Hope by J. T. Johnstone, who, on different occasions, gave the altitude as 380 and 535m. Rediscovered by John Mason and John Mitchell in 1976, and then independently by R. J. Birkett the same year, its single known locality is at about 600m, which suggests there may have been different patches of the plant (Fig. 157). The habitat is widespread and nondescript, and the species could turn up almost anywhere. Alpine saxifrage (see Fig. 34) is the rarest of all, and another discovery by

FIG 157. The crags of Black's Hope: habitat for arctic–alpine plants of basic rocks. Moffatdale, Dumfriesshire.

Thorburn Johnstone, who remarked that it 'will not number over a dozen plants'. I found probably the same – and perhaps only – colony in 1956, when there were 29 plants (about a dozen in flower) within one square metre of mossy, overhanging rocks. By 1973, a piece of rock had fallen, reducing the colony to seven plants, and that is the last I know of it. This seems to be an example of how natural events gradually reduce such last vestiges of a plant population towards extinction. The species also seems to be fading out of its own accord in northern England, though it was over-collected here in the past. Should we be justified in keeping these relics going by intervention when this is possible? I think we should, but each case has to be decided on its own merits.

Some of these high-level plants are able to persist away from cliff faces, as grazed-down rosettes unable to flower in the close-cropped turf, and often remaining unseen. If grazing is removed, they may regain vigour rapidly, both by increasing their vegetative growth and by flowering again. Roderick Corner discovered such persistent remnants of alpine saw-wort, alpine bistort, alpine meadow-rue, northern bedstraw and sheathing sedge within young conifer forests at the head of Ettrick Water, growing in grassland from which the sheep had been removed. They may have had only a temporary respite, since growth of the trees will before long overshadow and exclude them altogether. Appeal to foresters to help their survival has so far not had much effect.

The slightly lower (745m) massifs of the Lowther Hills in Dumfries and Lanark, and Culter Fell in Peebles and Lanark, are much poorer in montane plants than the Moffat–Tweedsmuir and Merrick–Kells ranges. Lack of rock habitats that would have provided refuges for many species is probably the main reason, for their sedimentary rocks are quite basic in places, as in the Dalveen Pass. Between them, they muster only starry and mossy saxifrages, hairy stonecrop, alpine meadow-rue, alpine saw-wort and stiff sedge, though submontane species are quite well represented.

One important plant has evidently been lost from the region. The yellow marsh saxifrage was recorded from three places on the Lammermuirs during the nineteenth century. Experienced botanists have searched for it repeatedly in recent years, but without success, and conclude that it has gone. One of its localities was said to have been destroyed by drainage. There is a large and well-known colony of the species in the Pentland Hills, outside our boundaries to the north, and another lower-lying station was once known at the western foot of this range. Its habitat is basic, mossy flushes and flush bogs of the kind widespread in the Moffat–Tweedsmuir hills and elsewhere, but the plant has never been found for certain in that area, although there is an old rumoured record. It is an Annex II species under the European Union Habitats and Species

Directive, and its rediscovery in our region would be a find of some significance. The bird's-eye primrose of the northern English limestone was once known in the Lammermuirs and Pentlands, but seems to have disappeared from the region. Its last known locality was near Balerno on the north side of the Pentlands, around 1950 (Miss Oliphant).

Several other mountain plants recorded from the region, mainly from the Moffat Hills, have never been seen in recent times and are not represented by any herbarium material, so they are mostly regarded as errors. Most come from a list compiled by Dr Singer in the *New Statistical Account of Scotland* in 1843. They include yellow saxifrage, Scottish asphodel, sibbaldia, rock and alpine speedwells, russet sedge, rock sedge, chestnut rush, three-flowered rush, three-leaved rush, interrupted clubmoss and dwarf birch (Scott-Elliot, 1896). The last of these would be the most likely to occur, as its blanket bog habitats are extensive and little trodden by botanists. Hoary whitlowgrass appeared in a recent Moffatdale list, but must be regarded as doubtful until more evidence of its presence is forthcoming. A record of alpine woodsia seems likely to be a mistake for the other species.

There are some other plants typical of the mountain areas which either occur only within the potential forest zone, or are found as commonly at low as at high elevations. They may be regarded as subalpine or northern species rather than real alpines, though this is an arbitrary distinction. Mountain everlasting is one of the most widespread – never common, but scattered in dry rocky places and banks, and on fairly acidic as well as basic substrates. In basic flushes the tiny least clubmoss is a very widespread plant, all over the hill country. It is the only one of our native species of *Selaginella*, which run to medium fern-like dimensions in the tropics. Green spleenwort (Fig. 158) is a calcicole present on most basic crags, and its occurrence on granite at the Door of Cairnsmore shows that this rock can contain significant amounts of lime in crushed zones. Seldom abundant, it has perhaps never recovered from earlier collecting, and some of its best colonies are on secluded outcrops of basalt and Old Red Sandstone in the Langholm–Newcastleton hills. Often with it, in dry rock crevices of basic rock, is brittle bladder fern. In the Moffat Hills, where it was sometimes mistaken for woodsia, there is a wide variety in the form of the fronds, but the delicate texture is constant, and it lacks the abundant scales and more compact growth of the other species. By contrast, the serrated wintergreen grows mainly on rather acidic or leached basic rocks in dry places, especially in ravines. Scott-Elliot (1896) reported it for six of the Moffatdale glens and it is still in at least two of them, in small quantity. There is an outlying western locality in Glen Trool and an eastern one on Ewes Water. The shady horsetail is a rare plant of low levels

FIG 158. Green spleenwort: a local upland fern confined to calcareous rocks. Hermitage Water, Roxburghshire.

in open places in Dumfriesshire glens. The widespread crowberry and cowberry of the upland heaths could be included in the subalpine mountain flora, as could tall bog-sedge and few-flowered sedge of the blanket bogs.

Hawkweeds in the Moffat–Tweedsmuir hills attracted the interest of earlier botanists, including J. T. Johnstone (1891) and the *Hieracium* specialists W. R. Linton and E. S. Marshall (1908). Among the species they recorded were *Hieracium iricum, H. pallidum, H. prenanthoides, H. argenteum, H. centripetale, H. lasiocarpum, H. saxorum, H. orimeles, H. pictorum, H. crocatum, H. pseudonosmoides, H. sarcophyllum, H. dupicatum, H. stenophyes, H. strictiforme, H. auratum, H. sparsifolium* and *H. subcrocatum.* Martin (1985) gives a fuller list of taxa for Dumfriesshire, and Stewart (1990) does likewise for Kirkcudbrightshire. Some of these hawkweeds appear to grow on fairly acidic though often friable rocks, but others have an evident need for at least a modest amount of lime in their substrate. Other hill areas in the region are less productive for them.

Of the other 'critical' genera, the eyebrights have received some attention, and noteworthy species on the hills are *Euphrasia scottica, E. curta, E. frigida, E. rostkoviana* ssp. *rostkoviana, E. rostkoviana* ssp. *montana, E. confusa, E. micrantha* and *E. nemorosa.* Eyebrights in general need moderately basic soils and so are most common on the sedimentary hills.

Northern mosses and liverworts are fairly well represented on the high ground and especially the basic crags. Besides the species mentioned above are the mosses *Amblyodon dealbatus, Amphidium lapponicum, Andreaea alpina, Anoectangium aestivum, Arctoa fulvella, Bartramia hallerana, Blindia acuta, Calliergon sarmentosum, Coscinodon cribrosus, Cynodontium jenneri, Ditrichum zonatum, Dryptodon patens, Encalypta ciliata, Grimmia atrata, G. donniana, G. funalis, G. montana, G. torquata, Kiaeria blyttii, Meesia uliginosa, Oedipodium griffithianum, Oligotrichum hercynicum, Orthothecium intricatum, Plagiobryum zierii, Plagiopus oederi, Pohlia elongata, Pseudobryum cinclidioides, Pterygynandrum filiforme* and *Racomitrium ellipticum.* Upland liverworts are *Anthelia julacea, Gymnomitrion concinnatum, G. obtusum, Hygrobiella laxifolia, Jungermannia cordifolia, J. paroica, J. subelliptica, Leiocolea bantriensis, L. heterocolpos, Marsupella adusta, M. alpina, M. emarginata, M. sprucei, Nardia compressa* and *Radula lindenbergiana.*

Northern and upland mosses with distinctly western affinities are *Breutelia chrysocoma, Campylopus atrovirens, C. schwarzii, C. setifolius, Hylocomium umbratum, Hypnum callichroum* and *Rhabdoweissia crenulata,* while comparable liverworts are *Anastrepta orcadensis, Bazzania tricrenata, Gymnomitrion crenulatum* and *Herbertus aduncus* ssp. *hutchinsiae.*

Mountain lichens found in the Moffat–Tweedsmuir hills include *Cladonia rangiferina, Ochrolechia frigida* and *Cetraria islandica.*

CHAPTER 8

The Southern Uplands: Fauna

MAMMALS

THE RED DEER (Fig. 159) is the largest wild animal, once present on the Annandale hills but now restricted to those of Galloway and Carrick. Herds occur from Cairnsmore of Fleet to Loch Doon, on terrain closely resembling west-Highland deer 'forests', but they have become partly dwellers in the new conifer forests as well as on the treeless hills. The foresters control their numbers because of damage to young trees and marauding onto cultivated land, but regard them as a major wildlife feature of their forests and have established viewing facilities for visitors to see the animals in places, such as near Clatteringshaws. There is a local belief that the Galloway red deer originated from escapes in the Cumloden deer park, but others regard them as natives which spread with the other Post-glacial fauna through these uplands.

Wild goats are a distinctive feature of the Southern Uplands, but all are feral animals from originally domesticated stock. They live wild and are mostly tolerated by shepherds, partly because they do not obviously compete with sheep or show much tendency to increase, but also because of their reputation for killing adders by trampling on them. Foresters do not like them, because they damage young trees, and have kept their numbers down in planted areas. Goats are widespread in the higher Galloway Hills, and other herds are in Moffatdale and Tarras Water in the Langholm Hills. Most animals are a dark greyish colour but some are piebald. Patriarchal billies can carry impressive horns, which may be either swept back in ibex style or widely spreading (Fig. 160). Many people admire them as charismatic ornaments to a region largely depleted of its more spectacular fauna, and the re-foresters of Carrifran soon ran into trouble locally

FIG 159. Red deer stag challenging rivals during the rut. (Bobby Smith)

FIG 160. Wild billy goat with a fine spread of horns. Glen Trool, Kirkcudbrightshire.

when they proposed fencing goats out from their property, to protect the young trees. Goats are undeniably a threat to the more uncommon upland flora, because they can reach and graze crag ledges that are inaccessible to sheep, and so cause even greater restriction of sensitive species. But perhaps they long ago caused all the damage of which they are capable.

Bullock *et al.* (1976) surveyed the goats on the Cairnsmore of Fleet National Nature Reserve that year, and counted 650 animals, not uniformly distributed, but showing a tendency to concentrate in eight different areas. There was a daily movement and return between feeding and resting areas, amounting to a home range for each group. In summer, the goats often moved to open hill tops when biting insects were troublesome at lower levels. There was a preponderance of animals in the older age classes, but females exceeded males by a considerable margin, evidently through higher male mortality. Billies were usually in groups separate from the groups of nannies and kids, while goats and sheep seldom consorted with each other, except during bad weather. The high density of goats appeared to stem from the encroachment of surrounding forests onto former goat range, and was accompanied by a reduction in fecundity. Food studies showed that goats tended to eat more *Calluna* and less *Molinia* and broad-leaved grasses than sheep on the same ground.

The mountain hare is widespread over the Southern Uplands, though much less numerously than a century ago. Service (1901) believed its presence was the result of three introductions, beginning around 1846 in Manor, Peeblesshire. Its best areas were always the heathery grouse moors, perhaps because of predator control as much as favourable habitat for food. As the red grouse have declined on many moors, so have the mountain hares, though the animal was always prone to cycles of abundance. They were extremely abundant on the Langholm Hills in the 1920s, but had become sparse by the 1950s and have remained so. Mountain hares still occur widely from the Galloway Hills to the Lammermuirs, but are now scarce in most parts. Their best ground nowadays is probably the Moorfoot Hills of Peebles and Midlothian. They are favourite prey of foxes and golden eagles, and the leverets are often taken by stoats and weasels. Their winter coat of white renders them conspicuous on freshly burned and blackened heather ground in the early spring.

Rabbits are widespread in the hills but patchy, and mainly on the steeper, drier and often rocky ground. They favour good brown soils with nutritious grass where they can also excavate burrows easily, and occur up to at least 500m in suitable places. Isolated colonies sometimes have a high proportion of black individuals. Moles also occur widely on base-rich brown earths with earthworms, and their mounds may often be seen in isolated places up to well over 600m.

Foxes are the chief predator and occur all through the hill country, but their fastnesses are in the rocky hills of Galloway and Moffatdale, where numerous block litters and deep rock crannies provide abundant breeding dens ('yirds' locally). They are almost universally detested and an endless war is waged against them by shepherds and gamekeepers. One Galloway shepherd I knew, who treated fox control as a life's mission, in one year killed 112 of them, young and old, by shooting and trapping. While such inroads may have reduced the fox population locally, they were difficult to sustain, and numbers soon recovered by the infilling of animals from adjoining ground where destruction was less. Doubtless a ceiling on numbers was maintained by the species' own territorial behaviour, but it is probably a valid argument that reduction in number of adults and litters even during one year will lower the food demands of the population and, hence, the amount of predation. The numbers of healthy lambs taken by foxes are unknown, and probably vary according to circumstances, especially the availability of alternative wild prey, such as rabbits, hares and small rodents. Field voles are freely taken, particularly during times of abundance, and may then deflect attention from other prey. Foxes are considerable predators of ground-nesting birds, and often take the sitting bird as well as the eggs. They may well be implicated in the decline of the curlew and perhaps other birds on the remaining moorlands of the region.

Voles and vole 'plagues'

The short-tailed field vole is one of the most important upland mammals (Fig. 161). Towards the end of the nineteenth century, an unprecedented phenomenon was reported from the central Southern Uplands, in the rise in numbers of field voles to 'plague' levels. The animals were described as swarming in the years 1875–6 on upland farms of certain areas, notably at the head of Borthwick Water in Roxburghshire; the watershed between Teviotdale, Eskdale and Liddesdale; upper Nithsdale; and, to a lesser extent, the main Cheviot range (Evans, 1911). Gladstone (1910) said that upper Eskdale, Tynron, Penpont and Durisdeer in Dumfriesshire were particularly affected. Still bigger peaks occurred again later, especially in Dumfriesshire, where low-lying pastures in Closeburn parish had vast numbers of voles in 1889–91, while from 1891 to 1893 'there raged a devastating plague on the upland pastures'. Gladstone (1910) estimated that in Eskdalemuir and the northeast of the county some 8,000ha were affected, in upper Annandale 4,800–6,000ha, and from Queensberry to Thornhill another 6,000ha, making a total of c. 20,000ha in Dumfriesshire alone, over an area 95km long by 15–30km wide. Northeast Kirkcudbright and south Carrick were also affected.

FIG 161. Short-tailed field vole: a key mammal in the ecology of uplands. (Bobby Smith)

These population explosions were immediately followed by a huge increase in numbers and productivity of vole predators: 'This remarkable visitation caused an altogether marvellous immigration of short-eared owls, buzzards and other birds of prey.' Service estimated that 500 pairs of short-eared owls bred in Dumfriesshire, but Gladstone said that probably three or four times that number were present. The owls began nesting in February and continued 'without intermission' until September, usually laying clutches of 8–12 eggs, and rearing an average of seven young. They hunted night and day and for mile upon mile of the moorlands, and always a dozen or more were in sight at once. Kestrels also increased greatly, bred at unusually high density and laid abnormally large clutches. Breeding colonies were found in certain limited ranges of crag, as at the Devil's Beef Tub, where 18 pairs nested in close proximity (Adair, 1892, 1893), and at Craik 30 kestrels were seen hunting at once. Whether from predation, overcrowding and depletion of food supply, disease or other factors, the voles soon crashed from their peak numbers and were at more normal levels a year later. Deprived of the super-abundance of food, the predators did likewise, some starving while others dispersed from the plague areas, though Service believed that disease was also involved. A few, perhaps the stronger or more territorially active, remained, in apparent balance with the much reduced food supply.

It was found in later years that the voles normally showed four-year cycles in numbers, but the peak numbers were never again as high as during the 'plague' years. Never, that is, until hill ground was extensively afforested during the period after World War I. Elton *et al.* (1935) and Goddard (1935) reported an epidemic of short-tailed voles on the Scottish Borders in 1934, Yeates (1948) noted 'a minor vole plague' in the Cheviots in 1939, and Lockie (1955) studied the late stages of a 1954 vole plague in the Carron Valley, outside our region, and in the Midland Valley to the north. Then, in 1970, Mitchell *et al.* (1974) observed the effects of another vole plague in Eskdalemuir. All of these instances were on ground covered with young conifer plantations, where the predominantly grassy vegetation had grown tall and rank over several years after the removal of sheep. In all cases short-eared owls (Fig. 162) increased markedly, and in the Cheviots and Eskdalemuir, kestrels did so as well, together with smaller numbers of barn and long-eared owls. In the absence of data on vole densities obtained by trapping, it is impossible to know just how these various peak populations compare, and what levels the more recent 'plagues' actually reached compared with the original ones. They can, however, be gauged indirectly by the abundance of their chief predators, especially the short-eared owl, which do not seem to have been quite so numerous during the twentieth-century peaks as in those of the late nineteenth century.

FIG 162. Short-eared owl: the bird which famously responds to vole peaks by increasing in numbers, extending its breeding season and increasing its output of young. (Bobby Smith)

Charles Elton researched the history of the two great Victorian vole plagues, and wrote a detailed account in *Voles, Mice and Lemmings* (1942), in which his prime concern was to unravel the causes of the huge and unprecedented explosions in numbers. The Board of Agriculture had sent inspectors to survey the 1891–2 vole plague areas, and set up a Commission of Enquiry under Sir Herbert Maxwell to investigate the causes: the conclusion was that a succession of mild winters followed by dry springs was responsible, by favouring the voles' breeding success and survival. This sounds an altogether inadequate explanation. Elton concluded that at least 40,000ha of hill country was affected, in a large block from northeast Kirkcudbright around Carsphairn, through the northern half of Dumfries to the south of Lanark, Peebles, Selkirk and Roxburgh. He correlated the area of outbreak with a rainfall of 50 inches (1,270mm) or more, but could not see a direct causal relationship. Elton also spent some time examining the earlier Victorian history of declining predator numbers through persecution, which had led by the 1870s to a scarcity of mammals and birds which could possibly control vole numbers. Yet he realised that, while this was very probably a contributory factor, the initial lack of predators could not really account for the origins of the vole explosions. His essay considered the several explanations offered by those involved, but found them all wanting, and came no nearer to identifying the fundamental cause with any conviction.

The factor which appeared to trigger the recent minor 'plagues' was the marked increase in luxuriance of the ground vegetation in young forest, providing a large boost in both fodder and shelter for the voles. It is difficult to imagine how the earlier plagues could have occurred without a similar increase in vegetation growth, but equally puzzling to envisage this happening while large sheep flocks freely grazed the upland pastures. The most telling observations mentioned by Elton were 'a fairly definite opinion among some observers that the vegetation cover had been unusually heavy during the period of increase', and that 'the farmers had not been burning the pasture sufficiently, so that heavy cover was left for the voles'. I therefore suggest that the trigger for the late-Victorian vole plagues was a much-increased luxuriance of the grass swards on the areas concerned, and that this had followed either removal of the sheep or great reduction in their numbers, through a serious economic downturn in sheep farming.

Symon (1959) said that by 1874 there were signs of decline in Scottish hill farming, particularly where the degraded grazings could no longer support the previous high numbers of sheep. Orr (1982) noted that increasing imports of colonial wool and meat periodically weighed heavily against the profitability of hill sheep in the latter part of the nineteenth century. He said that there was often difficulty in letting grazing tenancies, and that some sheep farms were abandoned, while in the Highlands many were converted to deer forests. It is likely that associated manpower shortages also led to a failure to burn off the old tussocky growths of grass during the winter. By the 1890s, prices of mutton and wool fell to half previous levels, affecting all classes of hill sheep farms, but the higher, more exposed and poorer grazings suffered first. Withdrawal of the sheep from the higher and poorer ground would explain the correlation of the vole outbreaks with heavier rainfall areas. There was at the time much hand-wringing over the alleged impact of the vole plagues on the upland sheep flocks by destroying their grazings. Yet the figures given by Elton (1942) showed that there was less than a 10 per cent drop in sheep numbers in the combined counties of Dumfries, Selkirk and Roxburgh after the first vole plague and one of less than 3 per cent after the second. It seems likely that the rodent destruction of pastures impinged mainly at the interface between the upper and lower hill ground, and that the sheep remaining on the latter were not all that seriously affected. The propensity of farmers to 'talk up' impending catastrophes probably went back to those times and, with possibilities of reduced rents in mind, there was good reason to blame the lack of sheep on the higher ground on the voles, forgetting to mention that there had been few if any there in the first place!

In more recent years, vole cycles have been less marked than hitherto on the heavily sheep-grazed Southern Uplands, which is understandable, in the light of the above discussion. But it is puzzling that even recently afforested ground has often failed to show a dramatic increase in their numbers that could be expected from the greatly increased growth of ground vegetation following removal of sheep.

BIRDS

Eagles

As elsewhere among the British mountains, the Southern Uplands gave refuge to some of the larger predatory birds, whose presence became increasingly unwelcome to humans from the Middle Ages onwards, causing a restriction to the wilder and rockier uplands (Fig. 163). Eagles were foremost among these, and both white-tailed and golden eagle were clearly once present in the region. In the late Middle Ages, Symson (1684) observed that ptarmigan on the Minigaff hills sought refuge in stony hollows 'from the insults of the eagles, which are in plenty, both the large grey and the black'.

FIG 163. Former golden eagle country on the granite of Cairnsmore of Fleet, Kirkcudbrightshire.

The well-known eyrie on the islet (Eagle Isle) in Loch Skene, mentioned
by Sir Walter Scott, was that of the sea eagle, occupied in the early 1800s and
possibly up to 1833. Gladstone (1910) said that William Laidlaw, secretary to
novelist Scott, in 1837 named two nesting places of this species used annually
'not many years ago': one at Loch Skene and the other 'on a remote precipice
of Garvald Grains' in Eskdalemuir. Talla Linnfoots in Tweedsmuir was also
mentioned as a nesting place. The two Earn Craigs, near Queensberry and on
Criffel respectively, may well have been breeding haunts in olden times, as
implied by the name. Definite sea eagle breeding haunts inland in Galloway are
less clear, and Robert Service said that reputed nesting places at Lochs Skerrow,
Grennoch and Urr were so mixed up with ospreys as to be impossible to unravel;
but he mentioned the taking of sea eaglets in 1812 from an island in Loch
Macaterick in Carrick. A notable tale concerns two white-tailed eagle chicks taken
from an eyrie on Cairnsmore of Fleet in 1852, one of which famously lived on in
captivity at Cairnsmore House until the end of that century. In 1964, Donald
Watson met the old gamekeeper, Jimmy Nicholson, who told him of his boyhood
duty of feeding the eagle in its blind old age (Watson, 1972). Apart from this
isolated record, it seems likely that the species had disappeared from the
region by the 1850s.

Service wrote (in Macpherson, 1892) that golden eagles bred in 1833 on the farm of Gameshope, on the Peebles side of the Moffat Hills, and Gladstone (1910) quoted the testimony of David Tweedie, interviewed in 1834 when aged 83, that there were formerly six pairs of this bird regularly nesting on Moffat Water. Jardine said in 1838 that a pair or two had nested on the Scottish Borders, but not for twenty years. They were better known in Galloway but were losing ground rapidly by the mid nineteenth century. The Reverend Dick related the tale of a farmer who in the early 1800s dangled a lighted tar barrel in front of an eyrie on the Loch Dungeon cliffs and drove the birds away. A young bird was taken on Cairnsmore of Fleet in 1850, but the last reported nesting was in Glen Trool in 1876 (Harper, 1908). Golden eagles were also known to breed in the Carrick Hills up to the early 1800s (Paton & Pike, 1929).

There was then a gap in breeding records for golden eagles until 1905, when a pair returned to Cairnsmore and laid three eggs, but this nest failed. Another pair attempted to breed at Mullwharchar in Carrick from 1910 to 1923, but the nest was probably robbed in most years (J. F. Peters, unpublished diaries). Possibly they were never absent thereafter from these hills, and birds were seen about the Merrick in the 1930s, but the certain return of golden eagles to Galloway began in 1945, when a pair reared two young on Cairnsmore of Fleet. These birds laid at four different cliffs until 1951, but in 1952 a separate pair took over the most distant of their alternative crags, and bred there every year (Fig. 164). In the meantime, in 1948 another pair had returned to the Loch Doon hills, and annual nesting occurred here up to 2003, except for the year 1995, when the pair laid in a far-distant rock in the Stewartry. A mysterious nest was built in 1948 near the Laggan of Dee, but there is no proof that eggs were ever laid and certainly no young were reared. It was a one-off, though in 1964 a fourth pair began nesting on a crag in this general area; by 1968 they had moved to a distant shelter wood, where they have since bred regularly, with occasional alternative use of small rocks nearby. Apart from an uncertain report of nesting at Craigencallie in 1966, that is the known total of breeding golden eagles in Galloway in recent times. Rumours of nesting on the Merrick, Craignaw and elsewhere were never confirmed.

The breeding history of these four eagle pairs is set out in Table 3. After twice rearing two young, the first pair (territory A) began to show poor success, with several clutches deserted during the 1950s, and failure to lay eggs from 1975. The second Galloway pair (territory C) fared rather better, but from 1973 they, too, failed rather often to rear young. By 1984 the pair in A had evidently dropped out, and its territory became merged with that of the second Galloway pair thereafter. The last proved breeding in this area was in 1989, and although non-breeders remained for a few more years, and are still occasionally seen, territory C is

FIG 164. Golden eagle feeding small young. The pale head and nape are distinctive adult features. (Bobby Smith)

effectively deserted also. The other two pairs (territories B and D) have kept going with some success, though they have sometimes lost eggs or young, and only in a few years have both pairs brought off young (Fig. 165). The breeding success of these Galloway eagles has been only moderate over the whole period since 1945. Clutches of three eggs were seen in Carrick in seven years in the 1950s, and in six years at territory C over a longer period.

Disappearance of the two Galloway pairs was attributed to the effects of advancing afforestation, in reducing their food supply below the level of viability (Marquiss *et al.*, 1985). The removal of sheep from planted ground deprives the birds of this carrion source, so important to western Scottish golden eagles, and there is insufficient alternative food. When the remaining area of open moorland in the feeding range of a pair becomes too small, they do not continue nesting, though they may hang around as non-breeders for a while, before finally giving up altogether. Although there was some forestry encroachment in the territories of the other two eagle pairs, enough open moorland was left to support them (though pair B clearly had a setback during 1974–83), and one pair could reach lower ground with more abundant live prey. Their dependence on sheep carrion exposed these Galloway eagles to contamination by sheep-dip residues of DDT and dieldrin, and there was eggshell thinning and perhaps other sub-lethal

TABLE 3. Breeding success in four golden eagle territories in southwest Scotland, 1945–2005.

PERIOD	TERRITORY	YEARS EXAMINED	YEARS WITH A PAIR	YEARS EGGS LAID	YEARS YOUNG REARED	YEARS ONE BIRD	YEARS DESERTED
1945–63	A	17	17	≥14	3	0	0
	B	12	12	12	6	0	0
	C	10	10	10	4	0	0
1964–73	A	10	10	10	3	0	0
	B	8	6	6	1	2	0
	C	7	7	7	4	0	0
	D	10	8	≥6	5	2	0
1974–83	A	10	5	2	0	3	2
	B	10	6	1	0	4	0
	C	10	10	10	3	0	0
	D	10	10	10	8	0	0
1984–93	A	10	0	0	0	0	10
	B	10	10	10	6	0	0
	C	10	9	5	1	1	0
	D	10	10	9	6	0	0
1994–2005	A	12	0	0	0	0	12
	B	12	11	10	6	1	0
	C	12	1	0	0	0	11
	D	12	12	10	1	0	0

Territories A–D are listed in order of first occupation, 1945 to 1964. Clutch robberies in all four territories accounted for at least 15 nesting failures. During 1984–93, eagles from C were frequently seen in A, so that these two evidently reverted to a single territory. From 1994, single eagles, usually immatures, were occasionally seen in A and C. From 1996, peregrines and/or ravens usually occupied C, and from 2004, another peregrine pair occupied A.

FIG 165. Nearly fledged young golden eagle in one of the two remaining occupied territories. Kirkcudbrightshire. (Geoff Horne)

effects which may have contributed to poor breeding success. But the organo-chlorine sheep-dips were withdrawn and this threat passed away.

It was more than two decades after their return to Galloway before golden eagles attempted to breed elsewhere in the Southern Uplands. A pair was reported in the Moffat Hills in 1971, and they laid eggs the following year, but the nest failed. In 1973 they were said to lay at the head of Wamphray Water, somewhat to the east, and by 1974 they had moved to the vicinity of Bentpath in Eskdale, where they reared young in a tree-lined glen hidden among the hills. They did not linger here, but were presumed to move far into the Cheviots, where, after nesting for a couple of years on a small rock on the Northumbrian side, they crossed into Scotland and took up residence in a shelter wood. There they have remained in most years, guarded discreetly, and seldom seen by casual visitors. They have evidently survived here, albeit with very poor breeding success, because of the substantial area of open moorland left within the vast Kielder and Wauchope forests, which are otherwise unsuitable habitat. Two more pairs of tree-nesting golden eagles are now reported to be established in the

Borders. Immature golden eagles appear from time to time on the grouse moors, which must be the most attractive ground to them for food, but they do not usually last for long. An immature female settled in the Durisdeer Hills in 1988 and soon attracted a male. Much displaying and calling were witnessed in 1989, but one of the birds was reportedly killed in a crow trap that winter. The other bird disappeared around the same time. A youngster ringed in Galloway in 1956 by Ralph Stokoe was caught in a crow trap on the Moorfoot Hills a year later, and released by an enlightened keeper, but survival chances on most grouse moors are usually negligible.

The king of birds thus retains a rather precarious foothold in the Southern Uplands, in terrain now mostly marginal to its needs. Even with provision of deer and goat carrion by the Forestry Commission in Galloway, its food supply is somewhat uncertain. For all its size, it is a shy and secretive creature that shuns the proximity of humans. Even at the nest it hastens to put distance between itself and intruders with ponderous strokes of its great wings, and does not usually appear again until they are far away. Yet its destruction is all too easily achieved. With the right management its numbers could be boosted again, but that would require greater forbearance among the 'sportsmen' who control so much of the best ground for the bird. Developments in the Borders are encouraging, nevertheless.

Peregrines

The earliest inland record of a peregrine eyrie was at Posso Craigs on Manor Water, mentioned as a source of royal eyases in the fifteenth century. There is otherwise little early history of the bird in the Southern Uplands. The name Falcon Craig appears only once, in the Moffat Hills, but MacGillivray (1837–52) was impressed by the cluster of peregrine eyries in this area. The Grey Mare's Tail was one of them, and was noted again by McGilchrist (1905) in the late nineteenth century. Galloway was less well known for its peregrines. Clutches were taken regularly from Cairnsmore of Fleet and Glen Trool during the early 1900s, and there are records of breeding at six other Stewartry haunts between 1900 and 1921. During 1936–8, R. Laidler, P. S. Day and A. K. Bannister found three pairs each year in the Cairnsmore massif, and two more in the hills to the north. From 1946 to 1955 I located eleven pairs in the Stewartry hills, and later saw another two in the Carsphairn area, and two more in Carrick. The records of Donald Cross and others added another five for south Ayrshire. Wigtownshire had no inland breeders, for crags are almost absent. Nithsdale held another five or six pairs (Fig. 166), and on the Dumfries side of the Moffat Hills four pairs bred in the early 1950s, with another two or three in Peebles. Selkirk, Roxburgh

FIG 166. Peregrine feeding young at a Nithsdale eyrie. (Bobby Smith)

and Berwick (inland) appeared to lack the species as a breeder until late in the twentieth century, and only occasional nesting was attempted in the Moorfoot Hills, but in 1954 a long-deserted haunt in the Langholm Hills was reoccupied. The total inland population for the region was 31–33 pairs up to 1960.

Most of the known breeding haunts were tenanted regularly. In a total of 228 visits to 29 territories during 1946–60, evidence of occupation was found in 206 cases (90 per cent), and 23 of the 29 were occupied every time. The regularly occupied haunts were nearly all in the bigger or more extensive cliffs, the irregular ones were in smaller rocks, and the occasionals were in minor outcrops with easily accessible ledges. Where there was a choice, some pairs switched between different cliffs in their areas, but in no particular order. Irregular use often went with a history of persecution, though some regular places also had this problem, but quickly drew in new birds to replace those destroyed. This gave a relatively stable population which during the 1950s fluctuated by only 7–8 per cent around a mean. In Galloway and the Moffat Hills, where cliffs were plentiful, peregrine pairs were fairly evenly spaced out, with an average distance of 5.4km between each occupied eyrie and the next nearest one. This territorial spacing evidently imposed a ceiling on breeding density, and so limited any further increase in population. The rapid turnover of birds at keepered places suggested that enough surplus peregrines were available to fill gaps in the breeding population, but additional new pairs were excluded by the existing territory-holders. The need for good cliffs with secure nest sites prevented expansion into crag-less areas without this competition.

Territorial behaviour evidently matches the population to its food supply: a more efficient arrangement than a free-for-all where numbers of peregrines increase to the point of eating out their food supply and then crash through starvation. Yet how could the barren uplands of Galloway support this number of peregrines at all, with wild prey species so scarce, especially on the granite hills? Examination of eyries, especially those with young, soon revealed domestic pigeons as the principal prey. Feathers from kills, and the closed metal leg-rings left in the nests, showed that most pairs became independent of the local food supply through this transient source of prey. Some pairs had a more varied diet, including red grouse, golden plover, curlew, snipe, black-headed gull, fieldfare, starling and even meadow pipit, but the bulk of the prey by weight was homing pigeon. It was a seasonal food supply, available mainly between early May and September, and only smaller numbers of feral birds were about outside this period. Strangely, wood pigeons were little taken, despite their abundance in the adjoining valleys and expanding forests.

Peregrines were 'controlled' during World War II – though perhaps not in this region – for potential depredations on military carrier pigeons: with some justification, it would seem. Ernest Blezard found a message container complete with coded message in a Galloway eyrie dating from about 1945, and I found the special leg-ring, but without the message container, that had lain in a Moffatdale eyrie from the war years.

The Southern Upland peregrines had poor breeding success during the 1950s. The activities of at least four Ayrshire egg-collectors seemed an obvious reason: Donald Cross of Maybole alone took at least 30 clutches during 1950–60 from Galloway, Carrick and Nithsdale. Yet I was also finding frequent egg-breaking in nests, beginning in 1949, and egg-eating by parent birds was evidently sometimes involved. The population itself held up until 1960, and the serious decline in England and Wales revealed by the national BTO peregrine enquiry of 1961–2 did not affect southern Scotland as badly. Of 26 territories occupied during 1955–60, only eight were deserted during 1961–5, but non-breeding and breeding failure became prevalent among the rest, and in 1962 only one brood was reared. The crash in peregrine population was caused by the organochlorine insecticides, with the dieldrin family as the chief culprits in lethally poisoning birds. In 1966 I connected the widespread egg-breaking with marked eggshell thinning, which began in 1947 coincident with the appearance of DDT as a new factor in the peregrine's world (Fig. 167). I had kept homing pigeon rings from eyries, and one taken in 1947 from a Glentrool nest proved to have minute traces of DDT and its derivative DDE in the remains of gut material adhering to the regurgitated metal. This proved contamination of the parent peregrine, and an advertisement in the *Racing Pigeon* for March 1946 for DDT dusts to control ectoparasites on homers confirmed an obvious contamination pathway. But organochlorine residues from agricultural seed-dressings soon became the main source of bird of prey contamination.

After the Pesticides Advisory Committee had grudgingly accepted the evidence for harmful effects on wild raptor populations, the use of organochlorines was progressively reduced, beginning in 1962. Foot-dragging by the agricultural establishment delayed their final removal until the 1980s. Improvements in the peregrine situation had begun even by 1966, and recovery was clearly under way by 1971. By 1980 the Southern Upland population was back to pre-1961 levels, and that on the sea cliffs was also restored by the following year.

In 1977, Richard Mearns began to study the turnover in the peregrine population, with guidance from Ian Newton. This involved intensive ringing of young, and snaring adults at the nest to ring them also – a difficult task. Adult females (64) naturally proved easier to catch than males (23). Although seven recaptured females had moved to different territories, the estimated annual mortality was 9 per cent among females, and 11 per cent in both sexes combined (Mearns &

FIG 167. Peregrine clutch in a soily scrape. Thin-shelled eggs are especially vulnerable to damage against projecting stones such as the one visible here. Peeblesshire, 1971.

Newton, 1984). While showing a remarkably low mortality in an established adult peregrine population, the study was valid only for this district and over the particular period. Peregrines in the late 1940s would have shown a shorter average life span, for keeper persecution then clearly caused a rapid turnover at some Galloway eyries.

Only the annual checking of breeding territories for occupation and outcome can reliably monitor population behaviour. Two indefatigable peregrine searchers kept this programme going, and enthused bands of helpers, who eventually took over the work. Dick Roxburgh and his team covered Galloway, south Ayrshire and west Dumfries, while George Carse did the same for all ground from Annandale eastwards. Their efforts over more than three decades laid a solid foundation of reliable data on the southern Scottish peregrine population that has continued to grow through the work of the two Raptor Study Groups that evolved from these beginnings.

This information was vital in tracking not only the recovery of peregrine numbers up to 1980, but also its continuing increase to new heights. While the pre-1961 total of breeding territories was around 35, by 2003 it had risen to the astonishing figure of 134, an increase of 283 per cent. Even allowing that many more observers have been active in recent years, compared with the period before 1961, the population explosion is beyond doubt. It closely parallels but even exceeds that in Cumbria to the south (Ratcliffe, 2002). While it has sometimes involved the splitting of former territories into two or even three, it has more often occurred through adaptation to nesting in inferior cliffs, broken banks or even on the ground. Dick Roxburgh found two genuine ground nests, one among rushes on quite flat terrain, which he described as a curlew-type site. It was above a face left by a land-slip within a young conifer plantation, and this perhaps simulated a sheer drop below. The other is shown in Figure 31. At least three more ground nests and one on a grouse butt are reported from the Borders (G. Smith). Nests have become established on buildings, including a church tower in Galashiels and a reservoir dam, and there are at least 19 in quarries, several of which are still being worked. One pair has reared at least three broods from an old raven tree-nest in a Roxburgh moorland glen. Many new nesting places are in lowland situations, below 300m, and include riverside cliffs.

Withdrawal of the organochlorines allowed full recovery in peregrine numbers, but the continuing increase after 1980 must have involved other factors. First, an enhanced output of young birds creating extra pressure for entry to the breeding population is implied. The recruitment of young peregrines built up gradually, with a greater success rate of eyries, compared with the pre-1961 period, reflecting a decrease in both egg-collecting and keeper persecution. The keepers have gone from some nesting grounds, and even on remaining grouse moors at least some keepers were persuaded by the wave of publicity about this endangered species. In the Langholm–Newcastleton area, where only one pair of peregrines was known before 1961, there were seven or eight pairs by 1999. Counties where breeding was unknown until recent years had by 2003 shown a similar increase. There has been more evidence of a surplus of peregrines during autumn and winter, with birds frequently seen in the lowlands, besides the paired adults in established breeding territories, where they mostly remained throughout the year. Second, there had to be an increase in food supply in areas where breeding *density* had risen above its previous ceiling, and this was provided by the increased popularity of pigeon-racing that occurred during the 1970s and 1980s. Third, the expansion of breeding *distribution* through increasing use of easily accessible nesting sites or those close to people must reflect a relaxation of the species' tolerance of disturbance, combined with a reduction in deliberate interference.

This huge increase may not be sustained indefinitely. Pigeon fanciers are reported to be changing their race routes and shortening the racing season in order to reduce predation on their birds, and any contraction in food supply can be expected to affect the extra-high density that has built up in some areas. One territory that had come to hold three pairs up to 2000 was down to a single pair again in 2004, and numbers have dropped slightly in Dumfries & Galloway. Yet in the Borders, new breeding haunts continue to be found annually, and distribution is still expanding. Not all the easily accessible haunts are occupied every year, and on some grouse moors keeper persecution is clearly again causing desertions. The examples of building, ground and tree nests open the possibilities for expansion very widely indeed, and it will be most interesting to watch the future trend of the peregrine population.

Although peregrines and ravens are so typically found nesting in close company with each other, on the same crags (Fig. 168), and often using the same nest ledges in different years, neither will tolerate the proximity of golden eagles. When the returning eagles in Galloway took up residence on three different peregrine and raven cliffs, these two birds promptly withdrew to other nesting places at least two kilometres away, and pairs of each dropped out altogether. When two of the eagle pairs eventually disappeared again, peregrines and ravens once more reoccupied their old haunts. On the other hand, peregrines often displace kestrels and merlins to safe distances. Orchel (1992) found that the mean distance between five regular merlin nesting sites and the nearest peregrine eyries was 1.85km.

FIG 168. A traditional breeding place of peregrine and raven on granite crags. Kirkcudbrightshire.

Other birds of prey

During the middle part of the twentieth century, buzzards were, as upland birds, restricted largely to the Galloway hills, where some 30 pairs bred, mainly on crags. Apart from a one-off nesting on Carrifran in 1948, they were hardly ever seen in the Moffat Hills and the ranges farther east. Probably there had been a decline in Victorian times, since MacGillivray noted several circling over upper Moffatdale in 1832. Since 1960, the Galloway hill population has almost disappeared, in contrast to the astonishing increase in the tree-nesting buzzards in the lowlands and foothills across the whole region (see Chapter 4).

The hen harrier (Fig. 169) was widespread on the moorlands of Galloway and the Borders up to around 1850 (Service, 1901; Evans, 1911; Bolam, 1912), but the game-preservers relentlessly reduced its numbers until it was believed extinct here by 1900. On Lord Ailsa's estate in Ayrshire, 351 hen harriers were killed during 1850–54, and the Duke of Buccleuch's keepers were said to have destroyed 'some hundreds', frequently shooting both male and female from the same nest (Gladstone, 1910). As was said, 'what birds could stand such persecution?' Not long after, the species was regarded as banished from the British mainland and surviving only in the remoter Scottish islands, especially the Outer Hebrides and Orkney, and little was heard of it as a breeding bird in our region for many years. It seems likely now that sporadic attempts at recolonisation were made but quietly terminated. A gamekeeper destroyed at least three broods of young on the moors of Tarras Water near Langholm in the 1920s (E. Blezard). Grouse moors have a fatal attraction for hen harriers, and in the days of intensive keepering their lives on such ground were very short. By the mid-1950s, however, it was clear that the species was making a comeback on the mainland of the Scottish Highlands, and gradually working south, aided by the wartime relaxation from persecution and the expanding young plantations of the Forestry Commission (Watson, 1977). So its reappearance in the Southern Uplands was keenly anticipated.

In April 1949 I had a distant view of a pair of large hawk-like birds, one light and the other dark, flying over moorland near Carsphairn. What else could they have been but harriers? But, as both hen and Montagu's had been reported breeding on the moors of County Durham not long before, their identity remained clouded. The next and also tantalising report was in 1956 from Will Murdoch, shepherd at Palgowan near the head of the Minnoch Water, that all the previous summer a grey, gull-like bird had been frequenting the newly established conifer plantations nearby, beating about low to the ground. Again, a male harrier was the obvious candidate, but which species? Breeding by hen

FIG 169. Hen harrier: the most persecuted of all the birds of prey, by game-preservers who blatantly flout the law. (Philip Newman/Nature Photographers)

harriers was first proved in 1959, when Donald Watson found a nest on the heather moors in the south of the Stewartry, from which young were reared. This was the beginning of a solid recovery, with a core group of four to six pairs establishing in young conifer forests, where they mostly bred successfully, though attempts at nesting on heather moorland elsewhere in the county were dogged by persecution. Breeding also became regular in Wigtownshire from 1965, increasing to a peak of nine pairs in 1979, but falling back to one to four pairs since then (Dickson, 1992). At least three or four pairs bred in south Ayrshire, and nesting was attempted in the west of Dumfriesshire (Watson, 1977).

The pattern of breeding success was the same everywhere: good in young forests, poor on grouse moors. Although some pairs clung to their established forest haunts until the trees were quite large (wind-throw usually made gaps large enough for them to use), they eventually had to move to younger growth, so that breeding distribution changed. Eventually, numbers in the Stewartry dwindled away and the species had disappeared by the mid-1990s, even though young and apparently suitable forests had been planted or replanted in the district. Evidently not all young forests were attractive to harriers, and Donald Watson concluded that even where they nested in this habitat they needed a good area of productive open moorland adjoining the forest, over which to hunt, as well.

By 1970, it was clear that hen harriers were appearing in early spring on the grouse moors of the eastern Southern Uplands, but being mopped up by keepers almost as fast as they arrived. Tales of the destruction of nests and birds began to circulate, and attention focused in particular on the moors around Langholm and Newcastleton. There had earlier been build-up of a breeding group of at least six pairs in the Kielder Forest on the Northumbrian side of the Border in the 1960s, but this had faded out by the mid-1970s, and there was no similar colonisation of new plantations on the Scottish side. I shall return to the fraught subject of hen harriers and grouse moors after dealing with the red grouse.

Kestrels breed widely across the uplands, where they feed mainly on field voles and other small rodents, though the wing cases of large dung and ground beetles appear frequently amongst the small mammal fur in their castings. Their favourite nesting places are in old crow nests in trees (Fig. 170) and on rock outcrops, which are often small and may be little more than a broken bank. They are given to regular fluctuations in breeding strength in parallel with the population cycles of *Microtus*, but I have dealt with this bird in Chapter 5.

The merlin, although widely distributed over the hill country, is concentrated on the heather moors (Fig. 171). A local migrant, it leaves the high ground in early autumn and returns the following March or April, following the movements of

FIG 170. Carrion crow nest in the last scattered willows among the hills. Blackcraig Hill, Kirkcudbrightshire.

FIG 171. Female merlin at a tree-nest with young: a widespread raptor on heather moorland. (Bobby Smith)

its small bird prey, chiefly meadow pipits, skylarks and wheatears. During the breeding season it catches and eats many of the large day-flying moths, emperor, fox and northern eggar, whose caterpillars depend on the dwarf shrub heaths. This may go some way to explaining its preference for the heather moorlands, for its favourite nest site is on the ground amongst tall heather, typically in a steep-sided cleuch (small valley) with projecting rocks on which it can pluck its prey. Merlins also lay on crag ledges and on large detached blocks crowned with heather, but more often in old crow nests in trees. The Langholm–Newcastleton hills are a good merlin area, with a breeding density of 5–6 pairs per 100km². Other grouse moors with good numbers are the Moorfoots and Lammermuirs, but they are sparse on the grassy sheepwalks, such as the Moffat and Lowther hills. Even until quite recently they have been persecuted on some grouse moors, such as those near Langholm, although most game-preservers have long accepted that they are innocuous to grouse and their chicks.

Orchel (1992) studied the western Southern Upland merlin population, where there were once moderate numbers amongst the more heathery hills. During 1960–76, most pairs nested in heather on hillsides and low crags at 100–400m, though 25 of 31 territories were on or close to recently afforested heather and grass moorland. From 1970 to 1985, as the conifers matured and more land was planted, traditional nesting territories inside the forests were abandoned, though some open moorland territories were also deserted. Of the 31 territories occupied during 1960–76, 24 (77 per cent) had apparently been vacated by 1986–7. Desertion of 11 territories inside plantations occurred when the trees were at thicket stage, 3–10m high, and the total area of potential moorland foraging habitat within a 4km radius (c. 50km²) had decreased to a mean of 12.7km² (25 per cent). Orchel found that, by 1986–7, ground-nesting had generally been replaced by tree-nesting near the edge of closed canopy plantations, mostly of Sitka spruce, with the merlins using mainly old stick-nests of carrion crows. The net decline in breeding population since 1960–76, at about 30 per cent, was thus lower than at first seemed likely. Breeding density was measured at nearly 2 pairs per 100km² over the best-studied district of 700km².

Of 17 tree-nests in 1986–7, 15 were close to large areas (mean 26km²) of grass/heather-dominated moorland, and the same number were also within 400m of the moorland–forest edge, so that the merlins evidently depended on the survival of areas of open ground big enough for their hunting outside the forests. Examination of the food of four pairs nesting in heather within young conifer plantations confirmed this: 89 per cent of their prey was of open-country species (with meadow pipit accounting for 66 per cent) and only 11 per cent was of scrub and woodland species. Orchel concluded that long-term conservation of merlin populations in the district would best be achieved by sensitive management of remaining moorland foraging areas and nearby forest nesting habitats.

Murray (2002) says that 40–50 pairs of merlins nest annually in the Borders, though numbers were down in the Lammermuirs and Moorfoots during 1999 and 2000. In the Lammermuirs only nine nests were found in 28 previously used nesting areas, while in the Moorfoots only three nests were known in at least 12 earlier breeding places. The extensive moorlands south of the Tweed were only partly surveyed in 2000: four certain nests were seen and a fifth pair may have nested.

Short-eared owls complete the list of upland birds of prey. Other than during the special conditions when huge vole peaks occur (see above), they are little to be seen on the sheepwalks, but have maintained a low though fairly constant density on the grouse moors, where they are mostly tolerated nowadays. They have, however, declined here of late, and there is now concern over the nationally low breeding population of this owl.

Ravens

The raven shares many of its crag-nesting haunts with the peregrine in an age-old relationship, but – as with this neighbour – its earlier history in the region is not well documented. The Raven Craig in Moffatdale lies at the head of the Carrifran glen, which it is tempting to see as a direct link with the Welsh *carreg fran*, meaning crag of the raven. There are, however, hardly any other rocks named after the bird. Raven Nest on the Dryfe was perhaps a tree site, as there are no suitable rocks. As elsewhere, the raven was once widespread through the lowlands, nesting in trees, but had retreated to the hill country by around 1850 or a little later. Two Moffat nesting places recorded in 1898 by McGilchrist (1905) are still tenanted to this day. Gladstone (1910) said there were 12–16 regular breeding pairs in the Dumfriesshire hills, with as many other places less constantly occupied, though he knew of only one post-1900 tree-nest. Evans (1911) and Bolam (1912) spoke of a very few pairs in Peeblesshire, uncertain nesting in Selkirk and Roxburgh, and extinction inland in Berwickshire. Figures for Galloway were vague, but the bird was evidently widespread among the higher hills. Paton & Pike (1929) said that 11 pairs nested annually in Ayrshire, mostly in the south.

During 1949–65, I knew nine pairs of ravens to nest regularly in the Moffat–Tweedsmuir hills, six of them in Dumfries and three in Peebles, with two more irregular haunts. A tenth pair bred on the west side of upper Annandale. Elsewhere in Dumfries, Ewes Water above Langholm had a single age-old raven haunt (Fig. 172), and I found a single regular pair in a remote part of Eskdalemuir.

FIG 172. An ancient raven nest site, also used by peregrines, below the left-hand skyline rowan on the overhanging nose. Langholm Hills, Dumfriesshire.

Scarcity of suitable crags was the main problem for ravens in these eastern hills. New pairs attempted to establish tree-nests after or perhaps during World War II, but were usually within keeper reach and came to an untimely end. I knew three such near Langholm during 1946–55, and a fourth in a glen above Newcastleton in 1947, as the first confirmed breeding for Roxburghshire. None lasted for a second year. I failed to find the species nesting in Selkirkshire, where crags are few, but suspect occasional tree-nesting was attempted. The Moorfoot Hills had a single pair nesting, usually in Midlothian, but this dropped out in 1977 through increasing persecution.

The Lowther–Queensberry hills and upper Nithsdale, Dumfriesshire, had at least six pairs, three using trees as alternatives to small rocks. The Stewartry had the largest inland population, and during 1946–70 I saw 30 territories with rock-nesting ravens, of which the majority were held regularly, mostly in the main massifs from Cairnsmore of Fleet to the Merrick–Kells ranges. In the central granite hills, three pairs nested within a circle of 1.6km diameter, but the average closest distance between neighbouring pairs of this strongly territorial bird was 3.4km. Southern Ayrshire held at least another 12 mostly regular territories. Only occasional inland pairs were known in Wigtownshire. By 1970 tree-nesting appeared to be increasing on the lower moorlands and marginal lands of Galloway, with pairs occupying shelter belts or tree-grown gullies, and this added at least another five pairs. Near Carsphairn a pair bred on a tall electricity pylon in 1969. The total inland population was thus at least 65 pairs, and with another 45 pairs on the coast (Chapter 3), southern Scotland had some 110 pairs of ravens up to 1970 (Fig. 173).

By 1975 the steady advance of afforestation across the Galloway hills appeared to be displacing ravens, for once-regular pairs had dropped out in the most heavily planted areas. This decline was easily understandable, since sheep carrion was the raven's staple food here, as in most inland districts (Ratcliffe, 1997), and when the trees were planted, the sheep were removed. Voles and other small fry were insufficient to keep the birds going, and so they gave up. Repeating Mick Marquiss's 1974–6 survey of breeding ravens across the whole of southern Scotland and the Cheviots, Richard Mearns found that by 1981 at least 31 pairs had been lost through afforestation, representing 34 per cent of the former 90 pairs. Some of these lost pairs have subsequently returned as large areas of forest were clear-felled, and carrion was provided locally.

When I first knew Galloway, the ravens appeared to have few problems. The occasional pair was destroyed by keepers, and shepherds put down poison, which accounted for a few birds, but the ravens in remoter areas were mostly left alone. But by 1951 egg-collectors appeared. During my April visits I found robbed nests, and sometimes a second, representing loss of the repeat clutch as well. Some birds succeeded with repeats, but if their first clutch was well incubated when taken, they would not try again that year. This problem continued, and affected all parts of the region, so that by 1975 my records showed that about half the raven nests I had inspected had been robbed. The eggers were mostly from within the region, especially Ayrshire; their identity was well known, but the scale of robbery was not generally appreciated and there was little concern to try to stop it. The continued occupation of established territories seemed unaffected, but egging probably limited the raven breeding population in the region. The indiscriminate use of poison by keepers and farmers to control foxes and crows also evidently increased, to cause higher adult mortality. The lack of communal autumn–winter roosts at that time may also have indicated that there was a critically small surplus of non-breeding and immature birds. The first sizeable roost, of 30+ birds, was reported in 1996 near Killiegowan, Wigtownshire.

In recent years a much higher success rate of nests has been found, and the raven appears to have a considerable potential for rapid increase across the Southern Uplands in areas where it is left alone (Fig. 174). When Buccleuch Estates banned the killing of such predators on the Langholm Hills in 1991, the raven breeding population increased from one pair to four pairs, plus two others

FIG 173. Raven nest, a deep bowl thickly lined with sheep's wool in a stick basket. Near Moffat, Dumfriesshire.

FIG 174. Raven feeding well-grown young at a Southern Upland nest. (Bobby Smith)

FIG 175. Raven nest in a birch-grown gill. Tree-nesting has increased in recent years. Langholm Hills, Dumfriesshire.

not known to nest, by 1996. A survey organised by Chris Rollie in 1994 showed that 67 pairs of ravens bred in southern Scotland (including the coast), 19 of them in trees. A second survey of the same area in 1999 gave 127 pairs, including 40 nests in trees. Chris Rollie tells me that during the last few years ravens have become widepread tree-nesters in shelter woods across the lower moorlands and marginal lands of Dumfries & Galloway, and there are reports of increases in the Borders and Cheviots (Fig. 175). I have little doubt that this expansion is the result of reduced persecution, and especially the decline in the use of poison. There is no reason why the population of the species should not rise to a much higher level across the region through tree-nesting becoming general, as it is in central and southern Wales.

Red grouse

The red grouse is the most important upland bird of the region in economic terms (Fig. 176). The record bag of grouse in Scotland was made on Roan Fell at the head of the Tarras Water (Fig. 177): on 30 August 1911 a party of eight guns shot 2,523 birds, and then another 1,266 eight days later (Gladstone, 1930). A total of over 20,500 grouse were shot on these Langholm moors before the end of October in that year. Bags of this size are a thing of the past. Redpath and Thirgood (1997) have a graph showing that the greatest number of grouse shot on Langholm moor between 1949 and 1996 was 5,300 in 1978, while it was quite often under 1,000, and had declined virtually to zero by 1996. Probably it was only an absurdly intensive degree of management that raised stocks of grouse to

FIG 176. Red grouse: our southern form of the circumpolar willow grouse, adapted to treeless moorland and feeding mainly on heather.

FIG 177. The grouse moors where the Scottish record bag was made in 1911. Heather has dwindled even here over the last 80 years. Roan Fell and Tarras Water, Dumfriesshire.

such artificial levels, by suppressing all possible competitors and maximising conditions favourable to the grouse. This degree of intervention evidently continued through the 1930s, but during World War II grouse management was abandoned virtually everywhere, and afterwards it never reached the previous intensity, except perhaps in a few heavily keepered areas. Grouse numbers continued to show the cyclical fluctuations that are characteristic of the species, but the peaks were never as high as those of the early twentieth century.

A new factor had also appeared on the moorland scene – the inexorable rise in sheep numbers from around the end of the war. This increase affected many grouse moors, with the result that the sheep began to out-compete the grouse for the more nutritious growths of heather as food. Moreover, heavy grazing by sheep, in combination with moor-burning, suppresses dwarf shrubs and causes their replacement by grasses, and also bracken on dry ground. The sheep probably do better on the derived grasslands, but the grouse depend on dwarf shrubs, especially ling heather, and as it dwindles and disappears they, too, decline and fade away. Many once-productive grouse moors have suffered heather loss in some degree, with consequent reduction in stocks of this bird (Fig. 178). As we walked on the moors of Tarras Water in 1959, Ernest Blezard told me that there was not the extent of heather ground that he remembered from the early 1920s,

FIG 178. Fence-line effect, with conversion of heather moor to acidic grassland on the more heavily grazed and burned side of the wall. Whita Hill, Langholm, Dumfriesshire.

and a later study showed a 48 per cent loss of heather from this area between 1948 and 1988 (Redpath & Thirgood, 1997).

The history of destruction of predators on grouse moors in this region is probably as bad as anywhere in Britain, and the Langholm Hills provide an example. The years of the record bag on Roan Fell saw a ruthless suppression of all predators that was only temporarily relieved by the Great War. Ernest Blezard's acquaintance with the area began in 1923, when the head keeper of the estate arrived at taxidermist Robert Raine's shop in Carlisle with a female peregrine newly shot from the nest by an under-keeper. As the eggs had been left in the nest in the hope of a shot at the male, Raine took his young assistant to see the under-keeper, who conducted them to the site to secure the clutch, which is now in the Carlisle Museum. The same keeper, one George Little, was responsible for the hen harrier destruction mentioned above. During the 1930s estate records show that, amongst numerous other 'vermin', estate keepers killed an average of 107 'hawks' annually (Redpath & Thirgood, 1997). World War II gave some respite to the birds of prey, but hostilities were resumed soon afterwards, and in 1948 a shepherd told me of the killing of a golden eagle in the Tarras valley during the previous winter. Immature golden eagles appeared in the area subsequently, and one was established in a rocky gill in the spring of 1984, but they did not last long enough to reach adulthood and have a chance of breeding.

Matters came to a head with embarrassing press revelations from a disaffected under-keeper, who claimed that the estate factor and head keeper expected him to enact an illegal policy of killing all birds of prey and that he was supplied with poison by the estate, to be used to this end. 'He estimated that as many as three hundred birds of prey were killed on the estate each year, mostly sparrowhawks and owls but also merlins, peregrines, harriers and occasional eagles' (Macrae, 1990). Buccleuch Estates decided that the situation had to change, and ordered their keepers to adhere to the bird protection laws, while continuing to kill predators which could be legally destroyed, especially foxes and crows. They also began discussions with other parties about a programme of research into the facts of predation on red grouse by raptors, the hen harrier and peregrine in particular. This Joint Raptor Study was set up under the joint sponsorship of seven different organisations and one individual, supervised by Professor Ian Newton and conducted by Drs Steve Redpath and Simon Thirgood of the Institute of Terrestrial Ecology and the Game Conservancy Trust. I had the pleasure of calling on the researchers at their base in Tarras Lodge, and was amused to see their computers, data files and learned journals in the very place where the dour George Little used to sally forth with his twelve-bore to wage war on his employer's enemies.

The outcome of this intensive study during 1992–6 was to confirm what every gamekeeper has always believed: that hen harriers and peregrines kill grouse, and in sufficient numbers to reduce appreciably the 'bag' available to shooters (Redpath & Thirgood, 1997). The critical and damning conclusion was that in the absence of breeding raptors, grouse breeding numbers would have increased by 1.3 times and post-breeding numbers would have increased by 2.5 times. Interested readers should obtain this important report and read the salient facts for themselves. The choice of principal study area was perhaps unfortunate, in that it evidently represented an atypical situation for harriers. The Langholm moors had deteriorated over the past half-century under increasingly heavy sheep grazing, by extensive loss of heather and expansion of grassland in its place, causing a long-term decline of grouse numbers here. The estate, concerned to restore the moors as a grouse shoot, drastically reduced the numbers of sheep. After a few years, the vegetation had become ranker, but without any appreciable re-expansion of heather. The dense grassland, in particular, allowed field voles to increase, and also encouraged a high breeding density of meadow pipits. Both these species are the preferred prey of the harriers, and it was supposed that their abundance allowed this predator to reach high breeding density, which then impacted heavily on the grouse as secondary prey. On five more typical moors elsewhere in Scotland, with dominant heather over much of the ground, and fewer voles and pipits, the harriers stayed at lower density and took fewer grouse.

The ban on killing of raptors at Langholm had rapid results. From virtual zero in 1990, hen harriers increased to 20 pairs by 1997, and peregrines from three to six pairs. As the researchers predicted, grouse numbers continued to decline and reached a level too low to justify continued shooting. Experimental feeding of the harriers with dead chicks of domestic poultry and rodents showed that predation on young grouse could be appreciably reduced by this provision of an alternative food supply. Yet grouse numbers have remained low and the harriers have also dwindled away, to only two pairs in 2004. Moreover, the correlation between meadow pipit/vole density and harrier numbers has also disappeared, so that some other factor appears to be limiting the latter. It looks as though either insufficient harriers are arriving in the area in early spring, or there was greater dependence on grouse for food than was realised, or there is fox predation on harriers, or surreptitious persecution has resumed. Killing of hen harriers elsewhere on grouse moors in the region, including in northwest Dumfriesshire, continues to cause ineffectual protest.

Grouse moors may be a stage nearer the habitat that remained after the forests were cleared, but their vegetation has less diversity and they nearly always lack the full complement of birds of prey that would inhabit such ground in the absence of persecution. For these reasons, they are not – as is sometimes claimed – the ideal wildlife habitat on the British uplands, but a degraded derivative.

Black grouse and ptarmigan

The black grouse was formerly a widespread species across the Southern Uplands (Fig. 179). Abel Chapman (1907, 1924) described the tributary valleys of the North Tyne, just across the Northumbrian side of the Border, as the best area he knew for the bird, which occurred there in quite large numbers. He noted that it favoured the 'white' (i.e. grassy) ground rather than the 'black' (heather) moor, though much of its habitat was of a mixed type, with a good deal of heather and bracken on dry areas, rushes and flying bent in damp places, and streamside willow, birch and alder. The Dumfriesshire hills were also a notable area for black grouse in earlier days. Gladstone (1910) said that the record one-day bag of blackgame was of 247 birds shot at Glenwharrie, near Sanquhar, on 4 October 1869. Watson (1994) noted that they abounded over most of Dumfries & Galloway in those times. On the Langholm Hills, Ernest Blezard found the species

FIG 179. Blackcocks sparring at the lek: now much less common in southern Scotland. (Bobby Smith)

numerous in the mid-1920s, and even meriting the description of 'swarming' in some years: he once found three nests in one afternoon. Numbers here held up through the 1930s but then crashed around 1940, and during the period 1946–75, when I visited the area annually, it remained in low numbers. Five blackcocks in a party was the most I ever saw. Eskdalemuir was evidently a favoured area in earlier years, but the bird declined there also. In Galloway, blackgame increased markedly in the young conifer plantations, which suited them very well, to the point where the foresters waged war on them for damaging the young trees. They were numerous around Clatteringshaws in 1948, and the bubbling calls of displaying males could be heard widely in the new plantations. As the young forest closed into thicket and so became unsuitable for them, the blackgame moved into younger growth, which was continually being established.

They were not all in the conifer forests, and a favourite area where bird-watchers went to see blackgame was the area of tall willows along the upper alluvial course of the Water of Ken, from Strahanna to Holm of Dalquhairn. Some time in the late twentieth century there was a change: much of the new forest had become unsuitable and the species dropped out, but even the newly planted ground failed to help it as before and numbers declined quite markedly. It is now quite sparse across the region, though still widely distributed.

The history of ptarmigan in the region is obscure and rests mainly on the early remarks of Symson (1684):

In the remote parts of this great mountain [the Merrick] are very large red deer; and about the top thereof that fine bird called the Mountain Partridge, or, by the commonalty, the Tarmachan, about the size of a Red-cock, and the flesh much of the same nature; feeds, as that bird doth, on the seeds of the bull-rush, and makes its protection in the chinks and hollow places of thick stones, from the insults of the eagles, which are in plenty, both the large grey and the black, about that mountain.

Maxwell (1901) said that 'a shepherd . . . told me that he had last seen ptarmigan on the Merrick in 1826'. They are quite likely to have been present, but died out long ago, probably through extensive loss of high-level dwarf shrub heath, which is their essential habitat, caused by heavy grazing and burning. Maxwell also referred to unsuccessful attempts to reintroduce the bird to the Galloway hills. More recent proposals for reintroduction have been made, and possibly attempted, but stand little chance of success unless the habitat can first be restored.

Waders

Lapwings were always characteristic birds of the lower moorlands and sheepwalks across the region, but especially the improved grasslands of the marginal and 'inbye' land around the hill farms and shepherds' cottages, where there were base-rich brown soils with plentiful earthworms. They had a mention in R. L. Stevenson's nostalgic poem 'To S. R. Crockett' – 'hear about the graves of the martyrs the peewees crying' – and their voices were, along with those of the curlews, feared by the old Covenanters as betrayers of their hiding places from the pursuing dragoons.* Their local name of deil's plover doubtless came from this reputation. When I stayed at Dregmorn near Talnotry (see Fig. 6) during the 1950s, the lapwings announced my return as I crossed their field by the cottage in the evening. As they were common then, nobody ever counted their numbers or took much notice of them, other than to enjoy their lively presence as messengers of the spring. In recent years they have become objects of concern as they have declined so markedly across these foothill nesting grounds (Watson, 1986). At one time, many of the remoter shepherds' dwellings had a few pairs of the 'peewees' nesting close by, but the birds have dropped out on a large scale from these places and they now occur unpredictably in only rather widely scattered pairs or even more occasional groups. The *Molinia* moors with

---

* The refusal of adherents to the Presbyterian covenants to accept the Anglican church of the Crown in the late seventeenth century led to brutal persecution and martyrdom for many lowland Scots.

improved 'greens' around Lochinvar and Fingland always had a good number of pairs, but they have declined almost to extinction, and there is only sporadic nesting by the odd pair now. Some of the once-favoured bottom-lands are now so highly improved, with enormous numbers of sheep, that lapwing (or other wader) nests could hardly survive the trampling, and they are lost as nesting habitat. A few pairs here and there nested on blanket bog, as on the Moorfoot Hills plateau, but this was unusual habitat.

Some earlier writings described the golden plover as common and implied that it nested very widely and abundantly across the Southern Uplands. While it was no doubt more numerous a century ago than in more recent times, some of the earlier accounts probably gave an exaggerated idea of its former numbers. In my time the best areas for the bird have been the grouse moors of the region: not only is the habitat especially favourable, but the nest predators are destroyed fairly comprehensively. I had a study area on the Moorfoot Hills where, from 1963 to 1973, there were regularly 20 pairs in an area of 372ha, with a mean spacing between adjoining pairs of 433m and an overall density of 5.4 pairs per km². Most pairs bred on cotton-grass/heather blanket bog, but some were on moist or dry *Calluna* heath, including ground where this had been burned. Almost identical ground on the Langholm Hills farther south was less good for the species, for reasons that were unclear. Possibly the Lammermuirs were also good golden plover ground, but I never worked this area. There were evidently other good areas on the grouse moors of Spango Water and Cairn Table in the northwest of Dumfriesshire, but on the sheepwalks the numbers were variable and often low. These plovers breeding on acidic moorland showed the habit (Ratcliffe, 1976) of commuting to the improved inbye grasslands of the upper hill farms to feed, until the young were hatched. On the Moorfoots, W. Brotherston noted that fields at Garvald farm were a favoured feeding place for birds newly returned to the moors in spring, or later off-duty spells from incubation.

On the high tops and ridges on the north side of Megget Water, pairs were up to 800m apart, while on the Moffat Hills they were still more widely spaced. Yet some of the territories were remarkably constant. McGilchrist (1905) remarked on the pair of plovers 'abune the linns' on Midlaw Burn near Loch Skene, and I saw an isolated pair here whenever I passed that way, from 1949 onwards. Numbers were said to be greater on the ridge between Moffatdale and the head of Ettrick, and Ernest Blezard noted moderate numbers on moorland around Kingside Loch in Selkirkshire in 1947.

In Galloway, Donald Watson knew two good areas, one on the moorlands drained by Grobdale Lane, west of Laurieston, where some 20 pairs bred over about 600ha of wet *Molinia* ground, and the other on similar habitat at the head of the Water of Ken, east of Carsphairn. They were sparse but constant on the moors around Lochinvar and Mackilston. The lower granite moorlands had very few, though up to ten pairs bred along the higher watersheds of Cairnsmore of Fleet. A thin scatter of pairs nested along the high tops of the Kells Range, but the Merrick had rather more, especially on the slopes towards Palgowan. On the Wigtownshire flows the species appeared to be widely scattered, and I noted a fair density on Kilquhockadale Flow in May 1952. On some of the south Ayrshire moors there also appeared to be moderate densities.

The golden plover (Fig. 180) has declined sharply across the Southern Uplands, especially through afforestation of its moorland nesting grounds. Partly this was by obliteration of the breeding habitat, but the lack of burning on remaining open moorland adjoining the forests caused even unplanted ground to become rank and unsuitable for the bird and its chicks, and the surrounding forests harboured nest predators (foxes and crows). The losses have been particularly heavy in the western part of the region, and the species is reduced to probably under 50 pairs in the Stewartry. To be fair, this is not the only cause of decline, and golden plover have dropped out on many still extensive areas of sheepwalk beyond the influence of new forests. They seem almost to have gone from the massif of Blackcraig Hill east of Dalry, and the single pair that survived on the flow west of Loch Urr has finally gone. Whether this is through uncontrolled increase in predators or general deterioration of the ground under

FIG 180. Golden plover: a declining bird of the moorlands. The amount of frontal blackness on this individual is fairly typical of Southern Upland birds. (Bobby Smith)

massive increases in livestock grazing, or some other reason, is unclear. Even the good population on the Moorfoot Hills is evidently in decline (D. Thompson), which suggests that it may be factors affecting winter survival which are crucial, since breeding success on this keepered ground was usually good. The Game Conservancy Trust has suggested that increasing infestation by sheep-ticks, and the diseases they carry (e.g. louping ill) may be another factor in the decline of moorland waders such as this.

The dunlin was always more localised than the last species in the Southern Uplands. Apart from its former nesting places on the salt marshes of the Nith estuary on the Solway, it was confined to inland blanket bogs. In the east, Bolam (1912) mentioned breeding on the mosses of upper Liddesdale, at Saughtree Grains and Wormscleugh; at the heads of the Teviot, Kale, Bowmont and Jed waters; around Yetholm and Hoselaw lochs; and in the Lammermuirs at the heads of Lauderdale and the Whitadder and on Hule Moss. Evans (1911) said it occurred in some numbers on the broad peaty watersheds between Eskdalemuir, Ettrick head and Teviotdale, including Moodlaw Loch, which Tweeddale shared with Dumfriesshire. Dunlin were present on the wet moors around Kingside Loch in this area in 1947 (E. Blezard). It bred sparingly on the golden plover grounds of the Moorfoot Hills, where there were good *Sphagnum* pools on the high watersheds. I never saw it on exactly similar terrain in the Langholm Hills, but Steve Redpath told me he had found dunlin nesting on the Roan Fell ridge in the 1990s. On the high tops of the Moffat–Tweedsmuir hills I saw it only once, near the summit of Cramalt Craig, where there are patches of peaty ground.

In Galloway, dunlin were scattered and mainly at lower levels. There was a little colony of at least six pairs on the dried-out Raploch Moss beside Clatteringshaws Loch in 1947, and the Silver Flowe had several pairs along its chain of bogs in 1951. Donald Watson observed birds feeding regularly around Loch Skerrow and along Grobdale Lane, and deduced that they had mates with nests on the surrounding peatlands. Gladstone (1910) mentioned Loch Urr and Closeburn parish as Dumfries breeding places. On the Wigtown flows they were probably once quite widespread: I saw scattered pairs on Kilquhockadale Flow in 1952 and near Eldrig Loch in 1978. In south Ayrshire, Donald Cross found several nests by Linfern Loch.

Very few of these dunlin survive today. The Galloway and Carrick breeding grounds have mostly been obliterated by afforestation, though the Silver Flowe has also lost its dunlin. A few pairs may survive on the Wigtown flows, and the south Ayrshire blanket bogs probably still have a scattering of them. In the east some of the good areas mentioned for earlier times are now submerged under conifers, and only a few groups are known still to be present. At a conservative estimate, some 200 pairs have been lost to the forests in this region – a substantial proportion of the former total. Across the region, the *New Atlas* shows a net loss of twenty-four 10km squares with breeding records in 1968–72.

The curlew is *the* wader of the Southern Uplands (Fig. 181). When I first visited Galloway, from 1946 onwards, some of the lower moors around New Galloway, Dalry and Carsphairn seemed alive with the bird. On fine, sunny days in April, the air was filled with their liquid trilling and bubbling calls as the territorial males displayed to each other, and rose on rapidly beating wings to glide down in graceful descent. No sound was more characteristic of the wide moorlands of flying bent that stretched for miles in all directions around those upland villages. Regrettably, I never counted their numbers then and – as far as I am aware – neither did anyone else; so there is nothing to back my claim that this was some of the best curlew ground in Britain. They remained abundant as far west as Clatteringshaws, but then farther up the Dee their numbers rapidly fell away, until there were only a few in the Cauldron of the Dungeon. On the granite generally they were sparse or absent: there was usually a couple of pairs about the moraines near the railway below the Clints of Dromore, but they were rather few in the Cairnsmore of Fleet massif. On the eastern moors they were at variable density – equal in places to the best Galloway areas, but elsewhere

FIG 181. Curlew incubating: once the most numerous large bird of the sheepwalks, it has declined greatly across the region.

at much lower levels. Gladstone (1910) noted that the species was common on the Dumfriesshire moorlands, and he said that a pure white curlew bred for 12 consecutive years from 1904 at the head of Shinnel Water. Duncan (1947–8) said that the curlew had greatly increased as a breeding bird over the previous 20 years, but this was probably on lowland farmland, as was the case in Cumbria.

Philipson (1954), who watched curlews over many years on the moorlands of Northumberland, reckoned that in the best areas, in the west of the county near the Scottish border, each pair occupied 8ha, equating to a density of 12.5 pairs per km^2. He also believed that the species had declined from a peak around 1920 to barely half the numbers by 1954. On Moffat Water shepherds also told me in 1951 that curlews were far less numerous than in their earlier years. On the Moorfoot Hills, where I observed them while studying golden plovers during 1963–75, curlews were widely spaced, at a mean of about 800m, but apparently stable in numbers. In 1990, I began to monitor a segment of the breeding population on the moors north of Lochinvar in Galloway. There were at least 25 pairs in the area I selected, spaced at an average distance of 480m between neighbouring pairs. If this spacing occurred in a regular geometric pattern, it would give a mean density of 5.2 pairs per km^2, but the actual distribution gave a mean density of 4.5 pairs per km^2. The Lochinvar population was the densest I have known in recent times, but I felt that the species was not as numerous as when I first knew the district.

The main cause of curlew decline over the last half-century is only too obvious. The bird has the great misfortune to favour for its nesting precisely that type of ground that the foresters have so coveted for planting their conifers – the low-level, gently inclined moorlands with flying bent, heather, cotton-grass, bog myrtle and bog-mosses. While not all planted ground would have been curlew habitat, a great deal of it was. Allowing only a modest 2 pairs per km^2 as the previous overall density on afforested ground, with a total recent plantation area of around 2,500km^2, an estimated 5,000 pairs of curlews have been lost across the region from this cause, mainly since World War II. While much larger numbers of passerines such as skylark and meadow pipit must have been lost also, this massive reduction is probably the most serious loss of any animal species to afforestation. Yet it has gone largely unremarked.

Unhappily, even the remnant curlew population of the Southern Uplands appears to be in trouble. The Lochinvar group soon began to decline. Numbers held up until at least 1993, but the 25 pairs that I counted up to then were down to twelve in 1997, nine or ten in 1999, four in 2003, five in 2004 and only two in 2005. Elsewhere in Galloway, I have been able to find only scattered pairs since 2000, and many former breeding places appear deserted. I know of no breeding concentrations now. Casual observation suggests that this decline is general across the lower moorlands and marginal land of the whole region, and that the curlew is in serious trouble in this part of Scotland. The decline appears to have affected some parts of the northeast also, though Des Thompson saw several pairs on Whita Hill at Langholm in May 2005.

What has happened on these open moorlands that could explain such a decline? While I was not able to follow the Lochinvar group through the whole nesting season, it was clear that nest failure was high. Nests that I had found would often be predated within a day or two, and it seemed clear that some of the many pairs whose behaviour was puzzling had already lost their eggs before I watched them. The culprits were evidently foxes and carrion crows. Although curlews will repeat at least once and probably twice, it seemed likely that later nests would have a high failure rate also, and local observers who went over the same ground reported that few pairs behaved as though they had young. It looked as though the breeding output was insufficient to maintain the population.

Foxes and crows are nothing new to this area, though there has been a general decrease in keepering, and fewer are killed than in earlier years. Most of the curlew grounds are close to new forests, which act as breeding refuges to foxes and crows, but provide them with little food, so that they have to forage over open ground outside. While often called 'hoodies', especially in Galloway, the crows of the region are all carrion crows, and common throughout the hill country, except on the grouse moors, where the keepers wage relentless war upon them. They are largely invertebrate feeders, and the eggs and young of other birds form only a minor part of their diet, though they will mop up whatever comes their way and appear deliberately to search for nests. One noticeable feature in recent years is the number of non-breeders scattered over the moors, often in pairs, so that almost all parts of the curlew grounds have crows searching for food. My feeling is that the widespread application of NPK fertilisers, and the widespread provision of mineral supplements, both of which allow still heavier stocking of these marginal lands and lower moors with sheep and cattle, has boosted carrying capacity in invertebrates and promoted an increase in the crow population, which then impacts on the other nesting birds. Foxes may nowadays be short of preferred alternative food such as rabbits and voles. Some of the highly improved bottom-lands are so densely stocked with sheep and cattle now as to be no longer suitable for the curlew. Whatever the case, it looks as though the wonderful abundance of this most distinctive of moorland birds across the region is something we shall not see again.

Gladstone (1910) noted that the redshank was once mainly a coastal bird but spread inland from around 1880. It was widespread on the lower moorlands in the 1960s, though rather sparsely. Little groups bred here and there, as on the ground west of Lochinvar in Galloway. This bird also has decreased and is now much less often seen. Snipe were always present widely on the lower uplands, and nested up to fairly high elevations, but their numbers were difficult to assess and seemed to vary from year to year. Drumming birds were often to be heard, and the sound came eerily though the dark on moonlit nights, while their 'chip-er, chip-er . . .' on the ground was an equally familiar sound. Feeding snipe would rise from many a little marsh in the hills, yet I found only three nests during my wanderings in the Southern Uplands, and perhaps actual breeders were fewer than the number of birds seemed to indicate.

The dotterel (Fig. 182) is the most elusive of the upland waders, and the only truly montane breeding bird in the Southern Uplands. Service (1905–6) said that it probably 'breeds extremely sparingly all along the range of mountains from Moffat to Minnigaff'. Not all the nesting places were on the highest tops: Gladstone (1910) gave records for Queensberry (697m) and Corriedow (470m) at the head of Scaur, and McConachie (1910) mentions an old nesting haunt near Blythe Edge (460m) in the Lammermuirs. The sporadic nesting records during

FIG 182. Dotterel incubating: a true mountain bird which nests irregularly on the higher tops of the Southern Uplands. 1975, Kirkcudbrightshire.

the last forty years include several on different hills at only 650–700m. No one site seems particularly favoured, and breeding in the region probably does not occur every year. In the nineteenth century Lamberton Moor on the Berwickshire coast was a regular stopping place for spring dotterel 'trips', but in more recent years, passage birds are mostly seen on the high ground, with Lowther Hill and Green Lowther one of the most reliable locations. Returning passage birds in the late summer are seldom seen.

Other breeding birds

Of the smaller passerines, the meadow pipit is ubiquitous in its presence on the treeless hills, and equally at home on the grasslands and heather moors, breeding up to the highest levels. The 'moss cheeper' is favourite host to the cuckoo, and also principal prey species of the merlin. Skylarks are common over the uplands generally and breed up to 760m. Wheatears are widespread on the grasslands with rocks and walls for nest sites, and also breed up to the high tops, where a nest that Donald Watson and I found had rusty dotterel breast feathers in the lining. Usually the first of the spring visitors to arrive, they vary in numbers between years.

Whinchats are widespread on the lower uplands, especially on the bracken-infested grasslands, while the resident stonechats tend to favour heathery ground. Stonechats were once more frequent in the milder west, but even there suffered high mortality in severe winters, which left their numbers depressed for several years. But after the recent run of mild winters their numbers have grown and they are now quite frequent all over the Southern Uplands. In the first half of the twentieth century the nightjar was a widespread breeder on the bracken and heather-clad lower hillsides, especially in the southwest, but it had declined seriously even by 1960, and the few recent records are mainly from young conifer forests or open ground within these (Fig. 183).

Up to the 1970s, ring ouzels called from almost every crag and many a rocky slope and little cleuch all over the Southern Uplands, but especially on heather moorland (Fig. 184). Today, they have almost vanished from Galloway, but remain widespread and even numerous from the Dumfriesshire hills eastwards. Burfield (2002) has recently studied the ring ouzel population of the Moorfoot Hills and has concluded that the earlier figure for breeding density of 34 pairs per km^2 (Poxton, 1987) 'is clearly erroneous'. The bird is strongly territorial, and with a mean nearest-neighbour distance of 678m over 40km^2, the true figure may reach 4 pairs per km^2, but is usually rather less. Burfield found that ring ouzels have declined since the 1960s in some parts of the Moorfoots, but have remained stable in other parts; and the proportion of sites holding birds decreased further

FIG 183. Female nightjar feeding young: they have declined seriously across the region, and most of the remaining pairs nest in young forest or on clear-fells. (Bobby Smith)

FIG 184. Male ring ouzel feeding young: a bird that has mysteriously declined, especially in Galloway. (Bobby Smith)

between 1998 and 2000. While afforestation has caused some loss of ouzel habitat in the Moorfoots, the cause of continuing decline remains puzzling. Breeding success is still as good as in an area of the southeast Highlands, where the population remains stable. Decline affects several other regions of Britain, and is under investigation by a Ring Ouzel Study Group, which is looking at breeding biology widely, and has also been to Morocco to search for possible changes in the main wintering haunts of the species, so far with inconclusive results. Burfield confirmed the importance of earthworms in ring ouzel diet (69 per cent of dry weight), and thus the dependence of the bird on grassy 'greens' with good, base-rich soils within its nesting habitat.

Winter birds

Many birds, including some normally regarded as residents in Britain, are only summer visitors to the uplands. Most of the waders have already begun to move out by the end of June, and only a few late repeat-nesters remain in July. Snipe are to be seen there all the year, and there may be an autumnal influx from Fennoscandia, as there is of woodcock, some of which travel through the hills. Most of the smaller passerines leave by the early autumn, and the dipper, wren and stonechat are among those that remain. The larger raptors and scavengers – golden eagle, peregrine, buzzard, raven and carrion crow – stay and hold their territories, but merlins mostly depart to the lowlands and kestrels variably

FIG 185. Redwings arrive in the autumn to feed on rowan and other berries on the uplands. (Bobby Smith)

occupy winter territories on the lower moorlands and marginal land according to the severity of the winter weather. October usually sees the arrival of large flocks of fieldfares and redwings, which frequent the uplands while crops of rowan and hawthorn berries last, but then move on elsewhere (Fig. 185). The vegetarian grouse, red and black, stay on their moorland haunts, though heavy snowfalls can drive them down to lower ground. Waterfowl may continue to frequent the upland lochs, and mallards remain widespread on streams and tarns.

OTHER ANIMALS

Frogs are widespread on the hills and breed in pools up to a fair elevation, as at the Lochans of Auchniebut on the Kells Range (650m). They may be one reason why herons sometimes follow the higher ground, and patches of frogspawn occasionally found on dry ground probably denote the activities of this and other predators. The adder is more numerous in the Galloway hills than in any other uplands I have visited in Britain. Some of them lie out on banks and ledges of cliffs – even near peregrine eyries – and it is as well to remember this when scrambling about steep vegetated places. Farther east their distribution is more patchy. The shepherds did not know them in Moffatdale and I never saw one in many visits there, but the Megget valley immediately to the north is quite a hot-spot for them. They are common on the lower part of Tarras Water, but seldom seen in the upper reaches. Ravens and buzzards will take them as prey, and wild goats are reputed to stamp on them. Viviparous lizards are widespread and fairly common, especially on the heather moors.

Among the insects, the Scotch argus (Fig. 186) is a distinctive butterfly of the lower moorlands in the west, where the larval food-plant, flying bent, is so abundant. It occurs widely over the Galloway moors, and in some years its restless dark form is constantly to be seen on sunny August days over the *Molinia* ground. Farther east, in Dumfries and the Borders, its occurrence becomes much more patchy, and there are no recent records for Berwickshire. The large heath has a similarly wide distribution on the acid peatlands so extensive in the west of the region, but thins out eastwards as this habitat becomes more restricted. Its main larval food-plant is the hare's-tail cotton-grass, and there are scattered colonies of the butterfly on the blanket bogs of the Cheviots up to 500m, though these are mainly on the Northumbrian side. The small heath is almost ubiquitous on the dry hill grasslands, but the mountain ringlet is unknown in the region, despite the widespread occurrence of its habitat, *Nardus* grassland.

FIG 186. Scotch argus butterfly: common on the Galloway moorlands.

Where marsh violets are common among the wet grasslands and flush bogs of
the lower slopes of the western hills, there are many colonies of the small pearl-
bordered fritillary. The more mobile butterflies of the lowlands – vanessids and
whites, in particular – often appear among the hills, and immigrants sometimes
pass through in good numbers.

Among the moths, the large day-flying species, emperor, fox and northern
eggar, are common on the lower moors, though in varying numbers between
years (Fig. 187). Heather moorland is their main habitat, with abundance of
dwarf shrub larval food-plants, and their flowers attract a variety of other species:
silver Y, scarce silver Y, golden Y, pale eggar, ruby tiger, wood tiger, beautiful
yellow underwing, heath rustic and true-lover's knot. The antler moth is
common on the acidic grasslands and sometimes swarms in favourable years.
Rarer moorland moths in the southwest are the argent and sable, tissue, grey-
scalloped bar, northern rustic and brindled ochre. Immigrants appear in
summer, notably the silver Y, and I once found a hummingbird hawk moth
at rest on the wall of a ravine in the Dalveen Pass, but this species can turn
up almost anywhere.

The broad-bordered white underwing, a day-flying arctic–alpine moth,
appears to reach its southern British limits in the Southern Uplands and
Cheviots. Having become familiar with it on the montane heaths of the Scottish

Highlands, I found it on the Moffat and Tweedsmuir hills in 1962, and then on Cairnsmore of Fleet and the Corserine in 1978. Another montane species, the northern dart, is said by Waring *et al.* (2003) to occur in the Southern Uplands, but no localities are given. It has been recorded from the Lake fells, the Crossfell range and the Cheviot, so might be expected in the Moffat Hills or higher tops in Galloway. Richard and Barbara Mearns discovered the northern arches near Wanlockhead and on Lowther Hill, Dumfriesshire in August 2003. It was previously known from southern Scotland only in Midlothian. Considered to be an endemic subspecies of the exile (a moth confined to Shetland), it is widespread in the Highlands and, as a presumed grass-feeder, habitat is hardly the limiting factor in its distribution. The great brocade has been found around New Galloway, and the Mearns regard it as a resident breeder, rather than an immigrant.

FIG 187. Emperor moth female: one of the common diurnal moths of moorland.

CHAPTER 9

Afforestation

A TRANSFORMATION OF SCENE

N O ONE CAN travel through Galloway and the Borders without becoming aware of the huge extent of plantations of coniferous trees in the hill country and even, locally, in the lowlands. Most of them have been created since 1940, and have transformed the character of these previously almost treeless uplands. There is no more appropriate part of Britain in which to examine the pros and cons of this major land-use change. This chapter will catalogue its ecological effects, and try to illuminate briefly the policies and politics that have driven it

The Forestry Commission was established in 1919 as a state agency to develop a strategic reserve of timber in a country severely depleted of its forest cover – down to only 5 per cent of its surface area. Constrained by strict financial rules, the Commission proceeded to acquire the cheapest land available, in areas where competition with farming was least – sandy heaths in the East Anglian Breckland and then unproductive sheep farms in the uplands of northern and western Britain. Its new forests expanded steadily until around 1980, when changing political philosophy allowed private forestry companies increasingly to take over new planting. By 2004 Britain had a total of 2.7 million hectares of forest, covering 11.3 per cent of the land surface, and more than double the forest area of 1919. Of this area, 1.59 million hectares are coniferous, mostly established since 1940 (Fig. 188).

Galloway was one district where this afforestation expanded first. Many of its hill sheep farms were on poor land and becoming unviable, so that selling for forestry was inviting to some landowners. The Ordnance Survey maps of 1925

FIG 188. The advancing tide of new forest, 1984. View from Culreoch to Loch Skerrow, Shaw Hill and Fell of Fleet, Kirkcudbrightshire.

showed only a 300ha block of conifers north of Stroan Loch, and two smaller ones of 100ha each above the south end of Loch Ken and west of Woodhall Loch. When I first visited these hills, in 1946, their general treelessness was still striking (see Figs 1 & 2). Glen Trool had three small patches of old oakwood, and there was a scattering of other fragments elsewhere around the margins of the hill country. There were also a few minor plantations and shelter belts here and there, but the only new Commission forests were along the Palnure Glen and above the west side of Loch Ken. By 1947 new planting was proceeding on the moors west of New Galloway, and in the same year the Commission came to Glen Trool, established a village for forestry workers and began to afforest the surrounding hills. The process rolled on inexorably, and there are now 140,000ha of new forest within Galloway and south Ayrshire alone (Fig. 189).

The Forest of Ae in Dumfriesshire is one of the older forests, established in 1927. With extensions into the Lowther Hills, it covers about 20,000ha. Eskdalemuir in the same county was another largely treeless area when I first knew it, but afforestation here has created another 35,000ha, extending over the watershed with Selkirk into the head of the Ettrick Water and Teviotdale (Craik Forest), mainly through the efforts of private forestry companies. And farther east, on the Scottish slopes of the Cheviots and Liddesdale Hills, Wauchope–Newcastleton Forest covers another 20,000ha. At first, the afforestation was

FIG 189. Recently planted and older forest in 1986. Near Clatteringshaws Loch, Kirkcudbrightshire.

mainly of mineral soils, albeit often the infertile wet gleys so characteristic of these uplands. When techniques for planting deep peats were later developed, attention turned to the raised bogs of the lowlands, such as the huge Lochar Mosses complex near Dumfries and the Moss of Cree near Newton Stewart, and to the extensive flows (flat peat bogs) that grade into blanket bog at low levels in Wigtownshire. The sand dunes of Torrs Warren also received attention. In total, the region has about 2,500km² of forest created since 1919. The trees consist almost entirely of non-native conifers – at first Norway spruce (but with Sitka spruce later preferred), larch and lodgepole pine. Smaller amounts of Scots pine were planted in places, but very few broadleaves.

At face value, this is a great success story and a rare attainment of government long-term aims. Forest cover in this especially unwooded (or deforested) part of Britain has increased dramatically. Those responsible, or their successors, have every right to feel proud of their results, which many of them see as an entirely positive achievement, of great value to the nation. But it is one that has had a profound effect on the wildlife and scenic character of the region, and some others are less persuaded of its unmitigated blessings. An extreme opposite view was that of the late Sir Arthur Duncan, who remarked to me in 1985 that 'what the Forestry Commission has done to Galloway is absolutely criminal'.

The ongoing debate arouses strong passions on both sides, and it is very difficult for any involved and knowledgeable commentator to remain neutral. I shall state my position by saying that I believe afforestation in Galloway and the Borders would have been acceptable in more moderate amounts and located after listening to other interests; but that it has over-stepped the boundaries of acceptability by a fairly wide margin. I shall attempt to justify this view by presenting a rational case.

THE EFFECTS ON HABITAT AND WILDLIFE

First, we should consider the evidence for the effects of afforestation on habitat, plants and animals. The methods of establishing new forests have come increasingly to resemble those of modern agriculture, to the point where the foresters themselves have described them – with evident satisfaction – as 'tree-farming silviculture'. Grazing animals are removed and the ground fenced against their re-entry. The area to be planted is then deep-ploughed, with furrows two metres apart. On wet, peaty ground this has the effect of lowering the water table, drying out the surface horizon and aerating the rooting layer of the young trees. But it is also practised on dry ground, and there provides a competition-free rooting medium. In places, individual turves are dug out and overturned, instead of furrows. The young trees are grown in nurseries from seed of desired provenance, and transplanted at two or three years old to the upturned ridges and turves, where each is given a little ground rock phosphate to encourage establishment and early growth in a usually nutrient-poor habitat. If regrowth of other vegetation appears to threaten heavy competition to the transplants, it is suppressed by herbicide, and if there is a risk of infestation by specific insect pests, such as pine beauty moth on lodgepole pine, there may be spraying of insecticide.

The forest is divided into square or rectangular compartments by leaving a system of rides unplanted, for access and as fire-breaks. Some of the rides are surfaced with compacted earth, gravel and crushed stone to form forest roads for vehicles. At low altitudes, only the very wettest ground, not amenable to ploughing, is left unplanted, but steep screes and crags often have to be left treeless, and severity of climate imposes an upper limit to planting. In many places this is as high as 500m, and experimental plantations have been as high as 620m on the Kells Range. Here and there, inbye fields still needed for domestic stock on farms left within the forest holdings are left unplanted, but typically, as much as possible of the available ground is afforested. Formerly, it

was normal for plantations to approach closely to the edges of streams flowing
through the forest, but since around 1980 planting of stream banks has ceased
and open corridors have been left along watercourses. Before silvicultural
techniques became so successful, there were often gaps where the trees had
failed, or patches of poor growth: these were usually replanted (beating-up).

After about 10–15 years, depending on site quality, the enlarging individual
bushes close into a continuous growth of trees. There is little if any management:
on poorer sites there is often a spraying with calcium phosphate, but otherwise
the young plantation needs little attention. Nowadays, in upland forests, there
is seldom a removal of the lower dead branches of the developing young trees
(brashing), or even thinning of older stands, because of the risk of increasing
their vulnerability to wind-throw during severe gales (Fig. 190). The result is that
the young plantations grow into dense, impenetrable thickets, which eventually
self-thin, but produce trees of slender, pole-like form. These can be felled at
around 20 years as 'small round-wood', which can be converted into particle
board, but are more valuable as timber if left to reach 40–60 years before felling.
The forest is felled in blocks (coupes), usually of less than 150ha, and the
fallen trees are stripped of branches and cut into logs by mechanical harvesters,
before being loaded onto lorry trailers and taken to the pulp and saw mills.
Felling through a forest is usually more staggered in time than the planting

FIG 190. Windblow in spruce forest. 1984, Forest of Ae, Dumfriesshire.

FIG 191. Luxuriant growth of ungrazed bog myrtle. Near Mackilston, Lochinvar Moors, Kirkcudbrightshire.

stages, giving a wider distribution of tree age classes. The clear-fells are usually replanted, and the forest cycle renewed into the second generation. Between planting and harvesting, forest management is often mainly deer and fox control.

During the first few years, before the young trees become dominant, there is typically a flush of ground vegetation, as the previous fodder plants, freed from grazing and burning, put on vigorous growth. Grasses quickly become tall and tussocky, dicotyledonous herbs (forbs) begin to flower freely and dwarf shrubs put on new growth, showing re-expansion where they were being suppressed (Fig. 191). But this state does not last long, unless the young trees die. The developing trees steadily overwhelm the residual community by shade and litter fall, and by 10–15 years the previous vegetation has virtually been extinguished. Fragments survive, as linear ribbons, along rides and roadsides, and on stream banks or any other unplanted ground, or places where trees have died or remained stunted.

Effects on plants

The botanical impact of afforestation is very considerable. Extensive areas of the previously widespread plant communities of the area, with their characteristic species, are obliterated. Most of them are the prevailing grasslands and heaths, with widespread and abundant plants, that remain extensive outside the planted areas, so that it can be argued that the losses do not matter. The flora remains well represented along rides and other open places, and often in a better condition than under the previous grazing regime: for example, bog asphodel flowers freely and bog myrtle grows tall. On wet ground the losses tend to be more significant. The large-scale draining operations dry out the ground extensively, destroying bog communities and flora even in the remaining open places. Raised and blanket bogs support some rare and local plants that are at risk, and this is even more true of the more localised flushes and flush bogs. Raised bog and active blanket bog are now regarded as priority habitats for conservation in the Habitat and Species Directive of the European Union. The Lochar Mosses and Moss of Cree were important examples of raised bog that would once have been automatic choices as sites for protection, but have largely been ruined by afforestation. Many important examples of intermediate and blanket bog in Wigtownshire and south Ayrshire have also been destroyed, and probably the best active blanket bog in Selkirkshire, a flow near Goose Loch in Craik, was obliterated.

The losses to vegetation and flora are, arguably, the most serious of the biological impacts, for there is little if any compensatory gain within the new forests. The plant communities of the planted ground are almost totally excluded when the young forest closes into thicket and, where the trees remain unbrashed and unthinned, the visible plant life is nil. No doubt there are soil fungi and bacteria in the ground below, but green, photosynthetic plants are absent. Even in thinned stands of spruce there is often only a sparse and patchy growth of common ferns and bryophytes (Fig. 192). These increase with openness of the forest, where management has favoured thinning, but in most upland forests the amount of ground vegetation is usually derisory.

Smothering by the trees and drying out of wet ground are not the only problems for plant life. The general lack of grazing also produces rank growths of sharp-flowered rush, tufted hair-grass and creeping soft-grass, eliminating small herbs which might otherwise have survived within the forests. Hairy stonecrop and the rare alpine rush have lost a number of stations within fenced-off forest areas, through the coarse growths of tussocky grasses, and the latter has also been reduced by the scouring of river banks during the flash floods that have followed extensive draining for forestry. The physical effects of afforestation can also affect lake margins and their flora, by the washing-in of silt and gravel producing changes in water chemistry and clarity, and by drying where the trees are planted right up to the edges (Corner, 1989).

FIG 192. There is little ground vegetation even in brashed and thinned older forests. 1986, Cairn Edward Forest, Kirkcudbrightshire.

It is true that there can be a fairly rapid redevelopment of a vegetation cover after clear-felling, partly from buried seed that has survived in the soil, but it is seldom the same as that originally planted. Grasses tend to be dominant, especially the coarse tufted hair-grass, and recovery of moorland dwarf shrubs such as heather and bilberry is usually patchy. Rapid invaders such as gorse, bramble and bracken may appear, but brash from the felled trees is often left in thick, indestructible piles, and reduces the cover of living vegetation (Fig. 193). Moreover, any ground cover is purely transitory, for in another ten years or so, regrowth of the second-generation forest eliminates the open phase again (Fig. 194). Copious natural regeneration of conifer seedlings, especially Sitka spruce, also reduces open ground along plantation edges, such as roadside verges.

So the botanical value of the forest comes down to whatever ground has been left unplanted within the forest fence: rides, roadsides, streamsides, very wet ground, rocky places and any failed areas of trees. In a number of places remaining open, or on ground above the forest limit from which sheep were removed, there are instructive changes within what have come to represent grazing exclosures (Fig. 195). As they are no longer burned either, the process of vegetation recovery is often well shown. On the north face of Black Craig of

FIG 193. It looks like a battlefield. Clear-fell in forest near Laurieston. 2003, Kirkcudbrightshire.

FIG 194. View from Benniguinea across Clatteringshaws Loch to the Merrick, 1994. Second-generation forest in the foreground. Kirkcudbrightshire.

FIG 195. Ground no longer grazed or burned within or above the forest has often become more heathery. 1989, Craignelder, Big Gairy and Cairnsmore of Fleet, Kirkcudbrightshire.

Dee, above the A712 road west of New Galloway, there has been quite a spectacular recovery of heather, which has extended and become luxuriant after being in severe recession, and has scattered birches and rowans; while on unplanted ground alongside this road, bog myrtle forms dense stands two metres tall. Perhaps most striking of all, along the high tops of the Kells Range, there are in places continuous carpets of the woolly fringe-moss, forming *Racomitrium* heath almost as good as that of the Grampian tops, whereas just about everywhere else in the Southern Uplands the high numbers of sheep have eliminated this community. Deer and goats still occur within most of these open places, and limit the scope for full natural recovery of vegetation.

There are a few botanical gains along rides and tracks: the clubmosses spread by tiny windblown spores and the three widespread species, stag's-horn, fir and alpine, have colonised forest verges quite widely in Selkirk and Roxburgh. Trailing St John's-wort is also a frequent colonist of earthy tracks, the slender-leaved variety of sheep's sorrel is almost confined to this habitat, and bird's-foot was found new to Selkirk on a forestry track (Corner, 1989). A variety of mosses and liverworts find congenial conditions here and on the sides of furrows and ridges. The North American moss *Campylopus introflexus* often becomes dominant on the upturned ridges of ploughed ground, where the soil is peaty, forming a grey felt like mouse-fur.

The less common plants extinguished by afforestation in one place or another are listed in Table 4.

TABLE 4. Plants extinguished by afforestation.

VASCULAR PLANTS

Antennaria dioica

Andromeda polifolia *

Blysmus compressus

Botrychium lunaria

Carex curta

C. dioica

C. hostiana

C. lepidocarpa

C. limosa

C. magellanica *

C. pauciflora

Carum verticillatum

Dactylorhiza purpurella

D. incarnata ssp. incarnata

Drosera anglica

D. intermedia

Dryopteris carthusiana

Eleocharis quinqueflora

Eriophorum latifolium

Euphrasia scottica

Gentianella amarella

Isoetes lacustris

Isolepis setacea

Juncus alpino-articulatus *

Meum athamanticum *

Ophioglossum vulgatum

Parnassia palustris

Pinguicula lusitanica

P. vulgaris

Rhynchospora alba

R. fusca *

Rubus chamaemorus

TABLE 4. – *cont.*

VASCULAR PLANTS – *cont.*

Sagina nodosa
Schoenus nigricans
Sedum villosum *
Selaginella selaginoides
Utricularia intermedia
Viola lutea

MOSSES

Entodon orthocarpus
Sphagnum affine
S. austinii
S. balticum
S. fuscum
S. magellanicum
S. pulchrum
S. strictum
S. warnstorfii

LIVERWORTS

Pleurozia purpurea
Radula aquilegia

* rated as a scarce plant in Britain (Stewart *et al.*, 1994).

Effects on animals

The fauna also shows quite profound changes after afforestation. The much-increased luxuriance of ground vegetation following planting provides a great increase in forage and cover for small rodents, notably the short-tailed field vole, which often shows a marked increase in population, occasionally to 'plague' levels. This in turn provides a marked increase in food supply for some carnivorous birds and mammals: the short-eared owl, kestrel, stoat, weasel and fox, in particular, and is followed by marked increases in numbers of the first two. This aspect was discussed at length in Chapter 8, and I shall not repeat it here.

Some of the open-moorland birds do not tolerate the abrupt changes caused by afforestation. The numerous drains probably discourage species with young

292 · GALLOWAY AND THE BORDERS

that leave the nest at an early stage, and those that avoid tall vegetation, and so golden plover, lapwing, dunlin and redshank disappear almost immediately. So do ring ouzel and wheatear, which feed on short grassland, and the raven, which depends so largely on sheep carrion and loses this food supply at once. Pairs in extensively planted territories usually stop breeding and, although they may hang around for some time, they eventually disappear. Golden eagles have lost two of their four Galloway territories for the same reason (see Chapter 8). Red grouse and curlew may linger for a few years, but they, too, fade out as the young trees close in.

The breeding population losses of some birds are substantial. The curlew has suffered a massive decline across the region since 1950 and, while not all of this is the result of afforestation, a large part of it undoubtedly is. Curlew nesting habitat is especially that marginal land and gently contoured lower moorland that have been so extensively consumed by the conifers. Of the 2,500km² planted across the region, a very large proportion would previously have been the nesting grounds of this bird. Breeding density would vary within this terrain, from perhaps only 1–2 pairs per km² to at least 10–15 pairs per km² in the best areas. Allowing a conservative mean of 2 pairs per km² would give an estimate of at least 5,000 pairs of curlews lost to the region from this cause.

The golden plover has in recent times had a patchy breeding distribution across the Southern Uplands. Its best areas were, and still are, grouse moors that have remained unplanted. Elsewhere it was from sparse to locally frequent, and there were more on the gentle moorlands of Wigtownshire and south Ayrshire than on the more rugged hills of the Stewartry. Most of these Galloway breeding grounds have been planted and the bird has virtually gone from the moors around Carsphairn, Lochinvar, Grobdale and Clatteringshaws, where there were once modest numbers. Scattered groups still occur on the unplanted flows of Wigtown and south Ayrshire. In Tweeddale, Eskdale, Ettrick and the Cheviots it has lost ground also. Small numbers survive on the higher hills above the planting limit, as on Cairnsmore of Fleet, the Merrick and Kells ranges and the Moffat–Tweedsmuir hills. Probably around 300 pairs have been lost.

Snipe are widespread breeders on the marginal lands and lower moorlands that have been so extensively planted with trees. Their numbers evidently fluctuate between years and are difficult to estimate at the best of times, so that it is not possible to assess their losses from afforestation, but these must have been considerable. Redshanks were more local and in smaller numbers, but they too have suffered a widespread loss of breeding habitat. The dunlin has probably suffered more than any other species. Always a very local bird in the region, its scattered inland breeding haunts are listed in Chapter 8: they have nearly all been lost to afforestation, and the species may be extinct as an inland nester in the Borders, Dumfriesshire and Kirkcudbright. Small numbers still survive on the Wigtown moors and possibly in south Ayrshire.

The waders have the additional problem that even their unplanted nesting grounds may be adversely affected by adjoining forest. Golden plover and dunlin, in particular, need short vegetation in which to nest, and this was maintained by grazing and even more by the frequent muirburn. When upland is afforested, shepherds on the adjoining sheepwalks dare not burn the moor any more for, if the fire ran out of control and through a forest, it would be their liability. And so the vegetation tends to become rank and unsuitable for these ground-nesting birds. This factor may explain the decline to virtual extinction of the once healthy golden plover population on the open moorlands of Grobdale, which abut extensive recent forests west of Laurieston. Another effect of the forests is to provide a secure refuge for those major predators of ground nests, the fox and crow, which find very little food within the forest and have to forage mainly outside. They inevitably pay attention to any birds nesting on immediately adjoining land.

Dippers usually decline or even disappear from streams flowing from afforested catchments, because their waters become acidified and the food supply much reduced, as Juliet Vickery showed in her studies in Galloway. Some recovery of dipper numbers on affected streams under more sympathetic management has since been claimed (see Chapter 6).

Some other birds were viewed as beneficiaries of afforestation. Black grouse were in earlier years seen in this light, and certainly increased in the young Galloway forests. They were there regarded as a considerable nuisance, from their habit of cropping the leading shoots of young trees, and some effort was made to control their numbers. However, blackgame cannot live in dense forest devoid of ground vegetation and, as the plantations matured, their numbers declined dramatically. Several other species undoubtedly benefit – for a time – from the initial increase in luxuriance of vegetation and the cover this affords. The whinchat and stonechat are open-moorland species that often increase, and there is colonisation by willow warblers, tree pipits, and, at lower levels, grasshopper warblers. The increase in short-eared owls and kestrels (where suitable nesting places occur), through growth in their vole food supply, has been noted, and the return of the hen harrier to Galloway was attributed at least partly to the new forests, where they found good feeding and secure nesting places (Watson, 1977). These predators disappear again when the young trees close into dense forest and, so far, only the occasional pair has been noted breeding on restocks. While merlins have adapted to nesting in trees along the forest edges, they depend for hunting on the persistence of extensive open moorland beyond, and in southwest Scotland have suffered a net population decline through afforestation. Nightjars, once widespread on the lower moorlands, also appeared in a few places, but they depend on residual open areas or pre-thicket stages.

For several years after the first planting there is often a flourishing bird community, in which even some open moorland species linger, such as red and black grouse, curlew and meadow pipit, though passerines have largely replaced waders. This happy state of affairs does not last long. As the trees close in to form thicket growth, the open-ground birds drop out, one by one. They are steadily replaced by woodland species mostly absent from the open moorland: song thrush (Fig. 196), blackbird, chaffinch, robin, dunnock, redpoll, goldcrest, jay, wood pigeon, woodcock, sparrowhawk and tawny owl. The numbers of most of these depend on the amount of thinning and brashing. In thicket stands, breeding birds are limited to canopy-nesting species, and to those able to nest in forest edges or rides and other places where tree growth has remained open. The goldfinch and bullfinch do well where conifers are mixed with broadleaves, and in plantations of mixed age-class. The colonising species are mostly woodland birds common over the whole region and, indeed, over much of Britain, and some are also familiar garden birds. The bonus is the small group of birds formerly rare or unknown in the region. In years when the conifers produce an

FIG 196. Song thrush: one of the commonest birds in the new forests. (Bobby Smith)

FIG 197. Female crossbill incubating: one of the gains from afforestation. (Bobby Smith)

abundance of cones, the crossbill (Fig. 197) and siskin may nest quite numerously, but in poor cone years they are sparse or absent. The other notable gain is the reintroduced goshawk, which first established itself in the larger plantations but has also spread to some of the bigger broadleaved woods (see Chapter 4).

What of the other animals? The rodents have been mentioned previously, but the vole cycles are limited to the open-ground phase of forest growth, and these animals become restricted later to whatever treeless ground remains within the forest. Both red deer and roe deer find shelter within the forest, but the tree compartments have little food for them, and unplanted ground could satisfy the needs of only a very few animals. So both species usually feed outside the forest a good deal and, when pressed by severe winter weather, they may create a marauding problem on farmland and the gardens of those living nearby. Deer control is one of the important tasks of the forest rangers. The widespread feral goats are also culled to keep numbers within reasonable bounds, but there has not been the attempt to exterminate them that removed wild goats completely from the adjoining moorlands in north Cumbria. Red squirrels are one of the few beneficiaries of the new forests, because they are at home in coniferous woods that the ever-expanding grey squirrels cannot exploit. The predators – fox, stoat and weasel – find refuge aplenty in the dense forests, but have to seek their food mainly outside the trees. The fox, as a wide-ranging animal, is little inconvenienced by the situation, and maintains its numbers despite incessant persecution, but the other species are probably limited to the forest edge. The Forestry Commission deliberately introduced the pine marten to their Galloway forests, and have claimed that their venture has been successful, but there is no recent information on the status of this animal.

Adders find good basking sites along rides and any other unplanted ground, and lizards are frequently to be seen, though both have lost an enormous amount of ground to the forests. In the days before the adder was protected, large numbers were killed by the men planting the young trees, who regarded them as a constant hazard in their daily work. But shepherds also killed them widely and the moorland conflagrations that raged relentlessly in the spring must have destroyed countless numbers also.

Butterflies take advantage of the shelter that the trees give from wind, and the more freely flowering herbs along the rides are encouraging to the adults seeking nectar. In the spring, orange-tips, green-veined whites and small pearl-bordered fritillaries are often to be seen, followed later by small tortoiseshells, peacocks, red admirals and painted ladies, large and small whites, meadow browns, common blues and small heaths. The dark-green fritillary occurs here but rather sparsely. Finally comes the speciality of the region, the Scotch argus, which is common in many of the Galloway forests, along rides and edges. It has, however, lost ground on a massive scale, through the obliteration of its moorland habitat, and this is even more true of the large heath, a notable peatland species which needs larger areas of open bog for survival. The large dragonflies, golden-ringed and common hawker, also hunt the rides and forest edges, resting at intervals on the trees. The Galloway speciality, the azure hawker, may have lost some breeding habitat in pools but its most important localities have escaped afforestation.

I am not aware of any studies on the changes in overall invertebrate faunas produced by afforestation, but these must be considerable, with large-scale loss of moorland species and replacement by a limited selection of woodland forms.

THE EFFECTS ON PHYSICAL ENVIRONMENT

The impact of afforestation is not simply on wildlife, for there are quite serious effects on the hydrology of the catchment, on sedimentation, and on soil and water chemistry. The extensive cutting of parallel drains (Fig. 198) not only lowers the water table, especially on peat bogs, but also accelerates runoff of water. After rain, streams within a drained catchment show an increased tendency to spate, with more rapid rise and fall, and a shorter period at peak flow, than before.

FIG 198. A hill drained for afforestation, and excavation of a road-metal quarry, 1985. Torrs, Polmaddy Glen, Kells Range, Kirkcudbrightshire.

Robinson (1980) showed that in the first seven years after ploughing a Cheviot catchment for afforestation, there were higher flood flows and the time to stream peaks was halved, while annual water yield was increased by 5 per cent. The very marked effect immediately after ground treatment tends to subside as the forest matures, but stream flows do not return to their previous state. Accompanying this change, there is a huge increase in sediment load of streams, in both mineral and organic material, immediately after draining operations, representing soil or peat erosion on the affected ground. While this, too, diminishes as the forest matures, it remains higher than before afforestation. Robinson & Blyth (1982) found that the average sediment loads increased at least fifty-fold in an affected stream during draining operations, and took several years to decline to a new equilibrium, which was four times higher than before the drains were cut. There is a further burst of erosion and sedimentation at clear-felling.

Despite the permanent increase in runoff, another effect of the growing forest is that the dense canopy of conifer foliage prevents all the moisture falling as rain from penetrating to the ground beneath. This 'interception loss' of water varies between locations, but an average figure of 20 per cent is given for typical upland forests (Calder & Newson, 1980). Another effect of the dense foliage, in this region of fairly heavy acid deposition, is to 'scavenge' acidity from the atmosphere and concentrate it in the water which reaches the ground. This then drains to the watercourses and causes their acidification, which in turn affects stream life adversely. In Galloway, Harriman & Wells (1985) reported that stream water in a 60 per cent afforested catchment had mean pH of 4.32, compared with 5.20 for a stream in an adjacent unafforested catchment – an eight-fold increase in acidity. Low pH leads to greater mobilisation of metallic ions, notably aluminium and manganese, in soils and hence their increase in stream waters. Aluminium becomes toxic to fish fry and aquatic insects above a certain concentration. The decline or disappearance of dippers from acidified streams evidently resulted from a marked decrease in their invertebrate food supply (Ormerod & Tyler, 1987; Vickery, 1991). Fish are often badly affected, especially salmon and trout: many afforested streams and lakes have lost their trout, and the Rivers Cree and Fleet in Galloway have declined greatly as salmon rivers.

The application of calcium phosphate to the forest results in some of this fertiliser entering the drainage water and causing its enrichment locally, and this eutrophication can lead to algal blooms in more sluggish sections or pools. Fishermen have complained not only of shorter periods of salmon run, because of the increased flash spates of rivers such as the Cree, but also of greater difficulty in maintaining balance when wading in the stream, because of slippery algal growths on the stones.

Attempts have been made to counter lake acidification by adding lime, and an experimental study of this intervention was set up at Loch Fleet (see Chapter 6).

A QUESTION OF BALANCE

Having weighed the balance sheet for wildlife changes from afforestation in this region, I conclude that the losses have outweighed the gains. It is not just a matter of arguing over the changes to a single area – this or that forest, and what they replaced – but of looking at the total impact over the whole of southern Scotland. Some foresters were fond of picturing the open uplands as useless wildlife habitat, and had a variety of pejorative expressions to convey this impression – sterile wilderness, ecological desert, and so on – whilst claiming that their creations had greatly diversified the habitat and enriched its wildlife. Now, it is self-evidently true that planting of woodland on treeless moorland will add a woodland fauna (though not a flora) to the whole, thereby increasing total biodiversity. But this point cannot be used as a simplistic argument for creating a forest anywhere, let alone everywhere. It is necessary to look at the detail of what is being lost and gained.

All too often, the debate has been limited to changes in animal, and especially bird, populations, and the impact on vegetation and flora has been ignored. This impact is usually a near-total disaster, as I have tried to show above: almost everything is lost and hardly anything gained. There have been no critical studies of the botanical effects of afforestation and, in the absence of baseline and monitoring work, assessment is limited to a rather subjective listing of species and localities that have been lost. But it is indisputable that a number of local and uncommon species have declined. When it comes to vegetation considered in its own right, the argument has been that these were widespread and commonplace plant communities which still remained extensive outside the new forests. Leaving aside for the moment the question of for how long this dictum would continue to apply, in the face of ever-expanding afforestation, it blatantly denies the loss of special and rare habitats that are destroyed in the process. Important areas of bog that should clearly have been protected have gone under trees. In Galloway the Moss of Cree, Mindork Moss and Kilquhockadale Flow (the last two earlier notified as sssIs); in Dumfriesshire most of the Lochar Moss; and in Selkirkshire the flow near Goose Loch and boggy surrounds to Moodlaw Loch – all of these important active raised or blanket bogs were drained and converted to forest, of the most ordinary kind, devoid of compensatory gain.

Foresters have claimed that their work was *re-forestation* on land that had been denuded of its original woodland. Some have gone further, in asserting that they are reconstituting the Boreal forest – but this simply will not wash. Apart from the fact that the new forests are almost entirely of non-indigenous trees, the real Boreal forest is almost everywhere distinguished by a field layer of dwarf shrubs, herbs and pteridophytes, and a ground layer of mosses and lichens, which are so conspicuously absent from the British plantations. They are tree farms, quite literally.

What of the 'ecological desert' slur on treeless moorland? I would claim that, over the centuries since their creation through forest clearance, the range of semi-natural dwarf shrub heaths and grasslands of the uplands has acquired considerable wildlife value in its own right. These are types represented little if at all on mainland Europe, and have become the habitat of distinctive assemblages of plants and animals. Many continental wildlife biologists enthuse about them, and about the range of treeless peatlands into which they merge. As agricultural intensification has proceeded apace in the lowlands, they have gained in nature conservation importance as the great reservoir of wildlife remaining in Britain. Their more spectacular birds of prey, golden eagle, peregrine, hen harrier and raven, and the red fox, are all that remain to represent a vanished fauna of large predators that roamed the land at the end of the last Ice Age.

Of the animal groups, birds merit special concern, as they are the one showing the greatest changes and are also the most closely studied. It is necessary to assess the balance sheet of losses and gains by first weighting the relative importance of the species concerned. Probably most ornithologists would regard rarities such as the golden eagle and local or decreasing species such as raven, golden plover, dunlin, curlew, snipe, red grouse, ring ouzel and wheatear as more important than the common birds of woodland and garden that mostly replace them. Species such as woodcock and sparrowhawk might be regarded as fair compensation, while crossbill, siskin and goshawk are more convincingly so, but the temporary colonists of the first open phase can hardly qualify. Here, again, it is the total scale of replacement that has to be looked at: the almost complete loss of dunlin, and the severe declines of other waders. Had it been possible to hold the losses at a lower level, smaller gains of the less common forest species might have been a more acceptable exchange.

THE CRUSADE FOR MORE FOREST

To understand the scale and impact of afforestation across the region, one has to look at how a broad government policy of 85 years ago led to a transformation of land use over such a huge area, with massive effects on the wild flora and fauna, and its habitats. Such an examination is the more relevant because this process is far from ended, but creeps onwards in never-ending expansion. Foresters' confidence that they had control of the whole game, and would cease their quest for more forest only when they ran out of plantable land, was expressed by a Fountain Forestry employee at a conference on Trees and Wildlife in the Scottish Uplands (Ogilvy, 1986):

> I foresee the continuing expansion of forests on all cultivatable land below the commercial tree limit . . . In the year 2026 I do not foresee blocks of forest on a moorland landscape, but the stark moorlands of SSSIs and common grazings isolated within a forest scene.

While Mr Ogilvy's apocalyptic vision received a severe dent only three years later, as I shall relate, his remarks well illustrate the scale of foresters' ambitions, and the style in which some of them promote these.

Steve Tompkins (1989) has well said that forestry is a religion to its practitioners. Having been given a virtually open-ended remit to plant trees by government, courtesy of the taxpayer, many of them went about the job with an almost Messianic belief in its virtues. Perhaps there is nothing wrong with that, and some would applaud such commitment to a public cause. But, after 85 years, it is fair to ask whether the taxpayers' money has been well spent in their interests. The original objective, of creating a strategic timber reserve, was abandoned in 1957. When World War II came, the new forests then established were far too young to be of any use, and with the advent of nuclear weapons it seemed unlikely that Britain would ever again be involved in prolonged conflict that would require a strategic reserve of timber. Various commentators have noted that as one argument after another for planting more trees collapsed, the foresters have always managed to find a new and plausible one for continuing as before. Import savings is still a favourite for, as economist John Bowers has said, it has great appeal to the economically illiterate. Another is creating rural employment.

Two government scrutinies of the Forestry Commission, by the Treasury in 1972 and the National Audit Office in 1986, both dismissed the economic arguments as invalid, and concluded that most upland afforestation failed by a wide margin to meet the accepted rate of return for public sector investment. Forestry jobs were also found to be an especially expensive way of creating employment in the countryside. Most of the planting and harvesting of forests is now done by contract labour, producing a peripatetic workforce that creates problems of its own. The forestry village of Glen Trool now consists mainly of holiday lets. Of the import savings plea, the Comptroller and Auditor General wrily said that any business in the country could argue for receiving public subsidy in order to out-compete overseas suppliers.

None of this criticism had much effect in depressing the rate of new planting. The forestry industry has the backing of an extremely influential lobby in Parliament, especially in the Lords, where heated rhetoric and angry vehemence have often won the day, along with old-boy sympathies of ministers. The 'government's annual planting target' or, rather, the shortfall in meeting it, was brandished like some holy writ to urge the maintenance of the level of Exchequer support. This target, like nearly all official forestry policy, was concocted by the Forestry Commission and its clients and rubber-stamped by government. The appearance of several private forestry companies, and their enthusiastic jumping on the afforestation band-wagon, owed much to a loophole in the tax laws that allowed wealthy individuals to make quite rapid and large tax-free capital gains from investments in new plantations. They were favoured also by the Thatcher government preference for private enterprise, so that the Forestry Commission did little more than replace its existing forests as they were felled, while nearly all new afforestation was done by the forestry companies for their customers, albeit largely at taxpayer expense. Private forestry has never received an official financial scrutiny comparable to those imposed on the Forestry Commission, but other parties diagnosed that, with its wealthy clients and tax loopholes, this sector was engaged in a scandalous rip-off of public funds.

The private forestry bubble burst after one of them, Fountain Forestry, pushed its luck too far, through a gold-rush onslaught on the Flow Country of Sutherland and Caithness, a previously unknown moorland wilderness comprising probably the largest system of blanket bogs in the world, and one of the few parts of Britain that had remained almost treeless since the Ice Age. As a result of fierce campaigning by conservationists, the then Chancellor of the Exchequer, Nigel Lawson, removed forestry from the tax system in March 1988, and put a stop to this legalised racket. Cases already in the pipeline were given a five-year period in which to go forward, and the financial support was transferred to direct grant-aid for tree-planting and, later, forest management. The level of taxpayer support stayed almost the same, at an average of 70 per cent of overall costs (Tompkins, 1989), but the change meant that it applied only to those who owned or leased land and could find the remaining 30 per cent costs from their own pockets. This greatly restricted the field of applicants, and so the overall rate of new planting dropped very considerably, to howls of protest from the forestry lobby.

The current position in southern Scotland is that new planting still continues, though fewer sheep farms have turned over to this land use in the last few years. So much hill land is already under trees that the planting rate must have slowed, regardless of the changed regime of taxpayer support, but a further gambit was the introduction of regional 'Indicative Forestry Strategies' (IFS), purportedly to achieve a more planned and less controversial allocation of yet more land to afforestation. Adam Watson (1995) well described them as 'a costly con trick', for they appeared to be a ruse to ensure that the planting went on. Even in already heavily afforested districts, such as the Galloway uplands, the question was not whether forestry should continue at all, but where best to locate yet more plantations. In 1985 the Forestry Commission was instructed by government to ensure that it achieved 'a reasonable balance' with other land use interests, including nature conservation. This was at once interpreted by the Commission not as requiring some limits to the amount of afforestation within any area, but as how they might make concessions to other interests within their forest holdings. The area occupied by roads, rides and unplantable ground was treated as a concession to the maintenance of open ground! And when asked what would happen if planting applications were submitted for areas allocated as a priority for other uses, the foresters replied that, 'Ah, but the strategy is only

indicative.' In Dumfries & Galloway, the Forest Authority refused to accept IFS
and continued to approve controversial schemes. If the Nature Conservancy had
tried tactics like these, there would have been endless complaints and a
ministerial hauling over the coals, but forestry has always been allowed special
favours.

A new factor that must call into question the earlier confidence with which
the forestry lobby pushed the policy of open-ended afforestation is the lately
depressed timber prices when the crop is realised. Parts of the former Soviet
Union, notably the Baltic states, have been raising hard currency by heavy cutting
of their vast boreal coniferous forests, and this has forced world softwood timber
prices down. Garforth & Dudley (2003) stated that 'timber prices and hence
revenues have fallen by 50 per cent'. I am informed on good authority that while
timber prices fluctuate wildly in the short term, the long-term trend is downwards. The situation further undermines the attempts to claim economic validity
for the afforestation industry. One wonders what the authors of the report by the
Centre for Agricultural Strategy at Reading might have to say now, since their
case in 1980 for another 1.9 million hectares of new forest was based partly on
predictions of increases in timber prices of 30–150 per cent by 2025 (Tompkins,
1989). Now that there has to be a hard eye on the value of the end product of
afforestation, the incentive to private planters has been somewhat reduced. With
so large a dependence on the public purse, the economics of private forestry
must be as suspect as those of the state sector.

The latest argument for planting more conifers is carbon sequestration, to
reduce the impact on global climate of carbon dioxide output by industrialised
Britain. Oliver Rackham remarked that this was rather like asking people to
drink more water in order to reduce sea-level rise.

WHAT PRICE NATURE CONSERVATION?

The Nature Conservancy had a hard time trying to persuade the Forestry
Commission not to plant areas that it wished to remain in a treeless condition.
In our 1951 report to the Nature Conservancy on the Silver Flowe, Donald Walker
and I recommended that the whole chain of bogs from Craigeazle in the south
to the Round Loch in the north be established as a National Nature Reserve,
together with as much as possible of the surrounding catchment, to protect the
hydrology of the system (Ratcliffe & Walker, 1958). Because of the interesting
differences between the separate bogs of the chain, it seemed essential to treat
them as an indivisible unit. When the Conservancy opened negotiations in the

mid-1950s with the Forestry Commission, who by then owned the whole valley, it was soon clear that senior foresters were unpersuaded by this argument. The Conservator declared that he could grow prime Sitka spruce on Craigeazle Bog, and intended to do so. Only after some lengthy arguments did the Commission finally back down and grudgingly concede the inclusion of Craigeazle in the reserve. But they drew the line at ideas of catchment protection, and the reserve boundary was drawn close to the hillside edge of the bog series. In the event, the Commission planted the hillside draining to Craigeazle Bog, but left the entire slopes of Craignaw and the Dungeon Hill to the west unplanted, as a central wilderness area (Fig. 199).

Later, as a member of the Nature Conservancy staff in Scotland, I recommended that the small surviving blocks of ancient semi-natural hill oakwood in the area be notified as SSSIs. The largest of these was the Wood of Cree on the east side of the River Cree. I had also been noting the inexorable advance of blanket afforestation over the hill country of Galloway (Fig. 200), and suggested that one of the least affected areas be set aside as a reserve, to perpetuate at least one good example of the open moorland ecosystem of the district, before it was too late. My preference was for Cairnsmore of Fleet, where there was at the time rather little planted ground, and two pairs of golden eagles were notable

FIG 199. The rugged west side of the Cauldron of the Dungeon has been left unplanted. 1982, Kirkcudbrightshire.

FIG 200. Blanket afforestation in 1979 on the Water of Minnoch, on slopes of the Merrick Range. Kirkcudbrightshire.

members of the resident fauna. This suggestion did not go down at all well within the Scottish HQ of the Conservancy, where there were considerable sympathies with Forestry Commission aims. I was told that the Galloway uplands were ecologically just a southern offshoot of the western Highlands, where this type of moorland covered huge areas and held a large population of golden eagles and other hill birds, so there was no need to make waves over resisting forestry at Cairnsmore. I countered that the Galloway uplands had their own biogeographical identity, and that I was only following the philosophy of the Conservancy's founding fathers in trying to safeguard a network of sites across the national gradients in main habitats. I also pointed out that afforestation was advancing rapidly and reducing similar habitat in many parts of the western Highlands too, especially the southwest, which was nearest to Galloway, ecologically as well as geographically.

The matter was left hanging for some years, though at some point the Regional Officer, Tom Huxley, told me that the Commission had decreed that the Conservancy had to choose between the Wood of Cree (which they planned to coniferise) *or* Cairnsmore of Fleet (where they were acquiring land): they would concede one but not both. It seemed to me that the Commission were simply being greedy, as well as unreasonable. Out of the hundreds of thousands of hectares available to them, on top of the huge area already planted, they begrudged nature conservation a few hundreds. They had been given a blank cheque to create new forests, and became obsessed by annual planting targets. When Donald Watson made a plea for more and larger enclaves to be left unplanted in the new forests, Conservator James gave him the brush-off with the rejoinder that it was his job to grow trees.

The newly reconstituted Nature Conservancy Council decided in 1973 to pursue the Cairnsmore Reserve issue, but new forest was already spreading round the flanks of the area, and it was too late to acquire the whole massif as an entire and intact topographic unit, which should always be the aim in protecting mountain areas. After much wrangling and, finally, an appeal by the NCC Chairman to the Minister, the Commission sold a block of Cairnsmore that was too short of bottom land to be viable for the eagles, and after planting continued here, both pairs disappeared. A reserve was achieved, but it was far less satisfactory than it could have been if determined action had been taken before the foresters had actually moved in. At the Wood of Cree there was a happier outcome, for it was not under-planted and was later acquired by the RSPB, to become one of their important reserves in southwest Scotland. Adjoining, more scattered blocks of older oak were, nevertheless, all under-planted, thereby removing a more natural and mature edge to the main wood.

When in 1969 the Nature Conservancy produced the draft of its *Nature Conservation Review*, to identify the sites of national importance to biological nature conservation in Britain, the Forestry Commission was consulted for its views. Its response was to identify the total area of potentially afforestable land within these sites, and to express displeasure at the prospect of so much land being 'sterilised' against its activities. As the agency for supporting private forestry, by dispensing advice and grant-aid, the Commission also effectively controlled the policy of the private sector too. It championed the planting programmes of the forestry companies as enthusiastically, and challenged any objections to the planting of important wildlife sites as robustly, as if they were on its own estate. Kilquhockadale Flow was a *Nature Conservation Review* site that was planted regardless. Mindork Moss SSSI, also in Wigtownshire, was afforested by a private company after the case was defended by the Commission and approved by the Scottish Secretary. A recent case was the application in 1997 by Buccleuch Estates Ltd for grant-aid to plant 383ha of low moorland at Mitchellslacks under Queensberry in the Lowther Hills, contiguous with the 6,600ha Forest of Ae. Despite the RSPB's argument that this was, amongst other bird interest, the best remaining area for breeding curlews in Dumfries & Galloway, with the highest recorded density of this rapidly declining wader in the district, the supposedly conservation-minded estate pressed its claim. The matter was settled *de facto* at a meeting of Dumfries & Galloway Council's mid and upper Nithsdale Committee, when planning officers were prevailed upon by the estate to withdraw their recommendations for objection, and the application was supported by a clear majority of the Council. Who among local councillors in that area is going to oppose the Duke's company? Faced with this Council view of the proposal, and a lack of objection from other conservation bodies (including SNH), the Forestry Authority naturally gave grant-aid, and the curlews have gone.

The incestuous nature of the relationships between the state and private forestry sectors, with 'revolving door' entry to top jobs in the latter by retiring chairmen and senior officers of the former, was pointed out by Tompkins (1989). The two sectors operated virtually as one, and evidently thought it right and proper that they should do so. Since the outcry against the wave of 'sleaze' that helped to bring down the last Tory government, there was for a time a rather harder eye on these cosy relationships between officials and their client interests, but they have begun to surface again.

Slowly, there has been a change of heart. In 1985, as a result of a House of Lords enquiry, the Forestry Commission adopted its new policy for broadleaved woodland, which involved halting further coniferisation of ancient semi-natural stands. It also accepted the precedence of SSSIs, and undertook to manage those on its own estate according to the wishes of the NCC, and not to seek to acquire others for planting. Still more recently, through retirement of the 'old guard' and the ascendancy of a new generation of young foresters with more enlightened views and, in some cases, a genuine concern for nature conservation, the Commission has been striving to make amends for some of the past. It seems finally to have accepted that timber production can no longer be the undeviating goal of the state forests, and that these have to be managed as a public asset for a range of interests. The ancient semi-natural woods in the ownership of Forest Enterprise are being managed with wildlife and amenity interests as a priority, and some worthwhile stands which had been under-planted with conifers, such as those adjoining the Wood of Cree in Galloway and Craigieburn in Moffatdale, are having these removed. In some places where an extension of open moorland is desirable, felled areas will not be restocked. More broadleaves are also being planted than for many years.

But some of the past mistakes or excesses are probably beyond correction, and everyone just has to live with them. The new forests are there, in huge quantity, and much of the current conservation effort is in the category of making the most of them. There is much talk of diversification, and while this is to be welcomed, the real possibilities appear to be rather limited. Orchel (1992) believed that restructuring of forest in Galloway during felling and restocking was beneficial to several species of raptor and owl, by providing new foraging and nesting areas. The main option is to widen the age-class distribution of trees by a staggered felling of compartments. Greater diversity of species choice in replanting is likely to be rather localised, and increased brashing and thinning, which might allow greater development of ground cover and under-shrubs, must be limited to sheltered, mainly lowland, sites where wind problems are slight. Even if the foresters were prepared to give up land by not replanting trees – and present low timber prices must surely lead to questions about the validity of replanting – it will not be easy to restore what was there before. In south Cumbria the local Wildlife Trust have acquired the afforested raised bog of Foulshaw Moss, and are attempting to restore it to an active state; but this is slow and expensive work, and it remains to be seen how successful it will be. The systems of drainage ditches remain on both wet ground and dry, and are a major hurdle to any programme of restoration. Probably it will take centuries before good open-ground wildlife habitat can be recovered on most sites once under conifers. And still the fundamental problem has not been resolved, since the planting of yet more conifers on open moorland and marginal land continues, in one place or another.

I have assembled some photographs (Figs 201–8) that convey more clearly than any words what has happened to the Galloway moorlands. Figure 201 shows the granite mass of Shaw Hill in 1955 rising behind a completely treeless expanse of moorland, alternating between dark heather ground and pale *Molinia*, with bracken around drier moraines and outcrops. The photograph reproduced as Figure 202 is taken from exactly the same place 23 years later, and shows the solid wall of conifers stretching away to the lower slopes of Shaw Hill. The upper part of the hill has been left unplanted, and illustrates the recovery of heather on ground above the forest limits where sheep are absent. Figure 203 is another once treeless scene in 1955, looking across the Laggans and Loch Dee to the Cauldron of the Dungeon and Corserine, while Figure 204 shows the same view in 2004, with extensive forest all around the loch and right up the eastern side of the valley. Figure 205 shows the Silver Flowe in 1956, before the foresters arrived, but Figure 206, taken in 1984, shows a large expanse of young trees on the lower slopes of the Kells Range. Figures 207 and 208 show the same cottage at Backhill of the Bush, in 1961 and 1988.

Readers will have to judge for themselves which state – before or after – they prefer, but should remember that these pictures conceal the detailed character of the forests, with their impenetrable thickets of trees and geometric systems

FIG 201. Shaw Hill from a moving train near Loch Skerrow in 1955. Tree-planting was soon to begin. Kirkcudbrightshire.

FIG 202. Precisely the same view in 1978. Forest extends to the lower slopes of Shaw Hill.

FIG 203. Cauldron of the Dungeon and Loch Dee from the White Laggan. 1955, Kirkcudbrightshire. A treeless landscape.

FIG 204. Precisely the same view in 2004. Some forest in the middle and far distance, on the right, has recently been clear-felled. Silver Flowe along the valley bottom.

FIG 205. Southern end of the Silver Flowe. Craigeazle and Snibe bogs, in 1956, before afforestation arrived in the valley of the Cauldron, Kirkcudbrightshire.

FIG 206. The same view as Figure 205, in 1984, after afforestation of the slopes beyond Craigeazle Bog.

FIG 207. Deserted shepherd's cottage at Backhill of the Bush in 1961. Corserine behind. Kirkcudbrightshire.

FIG 208. Backhill of the Bush in 1988. The forest road has since been taken to the house.

of rides and roads. It is not really possible to pass valid opinion without going to see the true nature of the new forests – the reality and not the image. You have to go and walk among them and weigh it all up for yourself. No doubt some will feel that, on balance, the trees are a worthwhile addition to scenery and habitat, and will have no sense of what has been lost. Maybe some will welcome the tracks that give ready access to country once accessible only by hard walking, but enthusiasts for wilderness will find it now greatly reduced in extent.

CHAPTER 10

Conservation and the Future

THE MAIN ISSUES

I T WILL BE CLEAR from the preceding chapters that Galloway and the
Borders have suffered from the wave of development on almost all
kinds of land that has so characterised the period in Britain since
around 1940. Yet this has been only the latest – perhaps final is the better word
– phase of a long period of human onslaught on the natural environment that
began with the Neolithic forest clearances for early agriculture, and later saw the
widespread draining of wetlands for the same purpose. Because we have been
unable to witness it, the scale of the destruction of natural habitat through the
whole period from the late Stone Age up to the nineteenth century is difficult
to appreciate. For northern Britain, a visit to Fennoscandia gives some idea of
what has been lost. Yet it is true that, up to around 1900, many of the new
habitats that replaced the old were also rich in wildlife, and there may even have
been gains in species diversity in exchange for part of the huge populations of
woodland and wetland flora and fauna. The hallmark of development from the
mid twentieth century onwards has been the increasing *net loss* of biodiversity,
especially on farmland and in forest.

The period between the two World Wars was a relatively quiescent time,
when agriculture was somewhat depressed and forestry had not yet taken off.
But even then, within our region, there was the major intrusion of hydroelectric developments in the Ken–Dee valley, with the creation of the loch at
Clatteringshaws and the chain of dams and lochs above Kirkcudbright, and the
enlargement of Loch Doon in Carrick. The subsequently massive impact of
afforestation across much of the region has given the strongest sense of scenic

and ecological transformation, but the workings of the post-1940 agricultural revolution, though less dramatic, have been another pervasive cause of change, in both the lowlands and uplands.

To give an example of well-documented change over the last half-century, Emma-Jane Ahart has recently led a group to survey the flora and fauna of Glencairn parish, for comparison with the detailed checklist of plants and animals made by John Corrie in 1910, in his history of the parish, *Glencairn: the Annals of an Inland Parish*. This is a fairly typical upland area in the west of Dumfriesshire, of 12,030ha, with valley-bottom farms and hill sheepwalks reaching some 550m, and includes the village of Moniaive. It has experienced most of the adverse land-use changes I have described earlier, and its wildlife has declined accordingly. The new *Glencairn Environmental Audit Report* found that of the 112 species of rare plants recorded in 1910 only 59 were found within the decade before 2001: a loss of nearly 50 per cent. Many of the surviving 59 had also become much rarer. The populations of many species of birds and mammals had also shown serious declines, though to a lesser extent than plants, as they are more mobile and better able to adapt to change. The most affected birds were those associated with open ground, especially in their nesting, and they had been displaced by afforestation: conifer plantations now cover about 23 per cent of the parish. There had, however, been a large increase in populations of animals that were much persecuted in the early twentieth century, especially the birds of prey and badgers (Ahart, 2001).

I have dealt with most of these development impacts under the appropriate habitats, and given afforestation a chapter to itself. What are the portents for more? Hill-top radar navigational stations have despoiled the summits of Broad Law and the Lowther Hills, and intrusive power lines have been taken through the Galloway Hills, but the march of the masts may be just starting. A mobile-phone tower has just appeared on the watershed at Birkhill, between Moffat and Yarrow Waters, and a high-level wind farm whirls its gleaming blades high on the hills east of Cairnsmore of Carsphairn. Numerous other wind-farm applications lie on Scottish government desks. A list in *The Herald* for 11 January 2005 gives twelve for the Scottish Borders (plus another five already approved), nine for Dumfries & Galloway (plus another five already approved), and several more for those parts of Ayrshire and Lanarkshire lying within our region. The Galloway proposals include one for 45 turbines on the ridge of Blackcraig Hill at Troquhain – a familiar skyline to those entering the Galloway moorlands from the Corsock road. It is to be hoped that there is truth in the rumour that no wind farm can be allowed within 30km of the seismological station in Eskdalemuir. The proposal for a massive array of windmills at Robin Rigg, a sandbank in the

Solway Firth, is not without potential problems for both wildlife and scenic beauty. Little is known about the hazards for birds, but the finding of a peregrine dead under a tower in Ayrshire is worrying, and in mid Wales a red kite was found with its wing sheared off beneath a turbine.

The nuclear power station at Chapelcross, Annan, has closed and is to be decommissioned, but with the nuclear lobby again becoming vocal, in response to the demand for 'clean' energy, and refusing to face the seemingly insoluble problem of radioactive waste disposal, one should not assume that we have heard the last of their claims on land for new constructions. Our polluting nuclear installations not only deposit dangerous radionuclides around our own coasts, but also export them to other countries, such as Ireland and Norway.

Water demands increase all the time. The most recent addition to the numerous water-supply reservoirs was the Megget, where the dam was completed in 1984, after minimal protest from defenders of scenic beauty (Figs 209 & 210). This will hardly be the last of the water engineers' claims on the Southern Upland valleys, but at least hydro-power has not repeated its ambitious project in Galloway. There is official encouragement, nevertheless, for small-scale hydro projects which could affect interesting stream ravines. Proposals to dam the upper Solway with barrages for either water supply or tidal energy came to nothing, and the lunatic proposal in 1996, resuscitating a scheme conceived

FIG 209. The Megget valley in 1972, before the reservoir came. Selkirkshire.

FIG 210. The Megget Reservoir drowned a stretch of moorland valley in 1984.

in 1795 for a canal from the Solway to the Tyne, seems also to have faded away (Ratcliffe, 2002). But never underestimate the capacity of entrepreneurial types and engineers to bounce us with great plans that are seductive in their promise of wealth and job creation, but hugely threatening to the natural environment and wildlife.

Quarrying continues at numerous sites, but has been mostly beneficial in creating new breeding sites for certain birds of prey, especially peregrines. Mining for coal and minerals has virtually ceased within the region, unless one includes the continuing commercial exploitation of lowland bogs for horticultural peat. The military have commandeered the dunes of Torrs Warren, and there is a long-standing tank gunnery range on the coast from Torrs Point to Port Mary southeast of Kirkcudbright, but the region has so far escaped fairly lightly from so-called defence needs.

PROTECTED AREAS

Nature reserves are the foremost category of area for wildlife protection, with management aimed primarily at this goal. The National Nature Reserve (NNR) was formerly regarded as the strongest form of official designation, but other 'approved bodies' were later allowed to bestow this title on areas regarded as nationally important for wildlife or geological features. Moreover, Scottish Natural Heritage (SNH) has shown its waning concern for NNRs by de-declaring 20 of them, including one in southern Scotland, the Tynron Juniper Wood in Dumfriesshire. The region's NNRs are the Silver Flowe, Kirkconnell Flow, Cairnsmore of Fleet and Caerlaverock in Dumfries & Galloway, and the Whitlaw Mosses, St Abbs Head and Cragbank Wood in the Borders. A much larger number of places has been notified as Sites of Special Scientific Interest (see Appendix 1 for a full list) but, even with the strengthened powers under the Countryside and Rights of Way Act 2000, the safeguards are weaker than for NNRs, and nature conservation interest is usually secondary to management for other purposes. Some of the NNRs and SSSIs have been proposed by the UK Government as Special Protection Areas (SPAs) under the European Union Birds Directive and Special Areas of Conservation (SACs) under the Habitats and Species Directive, to contribute to the European network of protected areas in the Natura 2000 programme. These Directives require not only that the Natura 2000 sites receive adequate protection, but also that they be restored to 'favourable conservation status' where this does not obtain at present.

The NGOs (non-governmental organisations) have also established nature reserves in our region. The Scottish Wildlife Trust (SWT) has reserves at over twenty sites (Fig. 211), the Royal Society for the Protection of Birds (RSPB) has six reserves (Fig. 212), the Wildfowl & Wetlands Trust (WWT) has a reserve at Caerlaverock, while the National Trust for Scotland (NTS) manages four properties (Fig. 213) and the Woodlands Trust has seven. A list of all these is given in Appendix I.

While protected areas might hopefully be safe from damage into the distant future, this does not necessarily follow, even on NNRs. The Silver Flowe had benefited from the removal of sheep and abandonment of moor-burning that resulted from the surrounding afforestation, and the plant communities were in excellent condition, but in 1993 a disastrous fire – whether malicious or accidental – ran across much of the reserve and set back the improvements. The Whitlaw Mosses are small basin and valley mires, and it was not foreseen when the reserve was established that continued farming of the catchments would result in inflow of fertiliser and eutrophication of the ground water. To protect such places it is preferable to acquire the whole catchment and prevent this kind of surrounding influence, or to make management agreements with the landholders to curtail fertiliser applications. The interest and character of Cragbank Wood have been seriously reduced by the uncontrollable scourge of Dutch elm disease, which has killed all the wych elms. Cairnsmore of Fleet has

FIG 211. Hill oakwood at Doon of Castramont, Fleet Valley, Kirkcudbrightshire. Scottish Wildlife Trust reserve.

FIG 212. The Wood of Cree, Kirkcudbrightshire. RSPB reserve.

FIG 213. Loch Skene, a high loch on sedimentary rocks where vendace have been introduced. Moffat Hills, Dumfriesshire. A property of the National Trust for Scotland.

suffered from the self-inflicted wounds of a disastrous fire, substantial loss of heather moorland and decline in bird numbers under enthusiastic management for sheep by NCC and SNH. Sometimes it appears that the fundamental objective of having a nature reserve becomes forgotten, and that management can become an end in itself, instead of the means to an end: the tail wags the dog. On Cairnsmore it appears that the wish of Edinburgh HQ to win good marks from other farmers overrode any consideration of wildlife needs, and has left present SNH staff with a serious problem in restoration. The RSPB often seems more in tune with management requirements, and their early action in raising water tables on their recently acquired Mersehead reserve had rapid results in increasing breeding bird populations.

SSSIs are notoriously vulnerable to damage, by neglect as well as inappropriate management, and many of those in the region are in a less good condition than when they were first notified. Woodlands have been coniferised, over-grazed or allowed to grow into high forest. Grasslands have been 'improved' by fertiliser addition (Fig. 214), and fens enriched by nutrient runoff. The intermediate and blanket bogs of Mindork Moss and Kilquhockadale Flow were destroyed by afforestation, despite their SSSI status, while upland sites have continued to lose their dwarf shrub heaths under heavy grazing and repeated fires. On some, protected birds of prey continue to be persecuted.

Yet it has to be said that, without these designations, nature conservation in Galloway and the Borders would be decidedly worse off. Many of the protected areas would have fallen to the relentless march of agricultural intensification and modern silviculture, and to the multifarious ways in which human use degrades the natural environment. Many of the reserves are well managed and gaining in wildlife interest. Caerlaverock Merse and its adjunct, East Park Farm, and the RSPB reserve at Mersehead, are a success story, with a steadily growing population of barnacle geese and several other wildfowl.

Seabird breeding colonies in several places, such as the Mull of Galloway and St Abbs Head, have increased considerably in size. Protected areas are effective at safeguarding especially important sites of limited extent, or dense wildlife aggregations, such as seabird colonies; but they can cover only a small part of any region (about 4 per cent in Galloway and the Borders), and so are much less good at conserving widespread but ordinary habitats and widely dispersed species, such as birds of prey.

FIG 214. Emerald green of upland grazings improved by fertiliser addition. Laghead, looking to Cairnsmore of Fleet, Kirkcudbrightshire.

INFLUENCING LAND-USE POLICIES

Nature conservation in the generality of the environment must therefore rely on inputs to policies which express other concerns, but impinge strongly on wildlife and its habitats. Much depends on how far the main land users can be persuaded to take account of wildlife needs in pursuing their rightful objectives, but the approach has to begin with central government and its various departments. This has been a hard battle, and no less in Galloway and the Borders than in other parts of Britain. Farming has been slavishly supported by the Department of Agriculture for Scotland (or whatever it is called now), and for many years there was little sympathy for any protests or pleas from the nature conservation side. Much of the damage has already been done, and it would take a very long time to restore what has been lost, by way of flowery grasslands, pastures and lower moors once rich in wading birds, dwarf shrub heaths destroyed by heavy grazing and indiscriminate muirburn, and montane communities also degraded by sheep.

Given the now wide recognition that much upland farming is completely uneconomic and kept alive by endless taxpayer subsidies, the time is ripe for an attempt to reverse the tide. There is already a whole raft of agri-environment schemes that aim to pay farmers for backing off from the goal of maximum crop production (both plant and animal), and for introducing management practices intended to benefit wildlife and scenic interest. These have been greeted with much enthusiasm in some circles, but should be judged according to their visible results, which – so far – I find frankly unimpressive. There has been much talk, over quite a long time, of reform of the EU Common Agricultural Policy, with reduction or phasing out of the subsidies that have been so damaging to nature conservation interests. I shall believe this when it has actually happened and there are results to see. The reality appears to be that, despite all the talk, the agricultural lobby manages to keep putting off the evil day of meaningful change.

The problem is also that so many of the wildlife losses are so difficult to reverse, especially the changes to habitat that are so widespread. Herb-rich meadows and pastures have been lost on a massive scale, and the realistic prospects for restoration can be on only minuscule (Fig. 215). Lowland wetlands have widely been converted to farmland, and many of the remnants are eutrophicated. Even if the conifer forests could be removed from peatlands and moorland, as is happening in a few places, there would not be a rapid reversion to former conditions. Farmland birds in general are in serious trouble but, if

FIG 215. Rush-grown wet pastures: an important habitat for breeding lowland waders, now much reduced through 'improvement'. (Bobby Smith)

the adverse factors can be removed, they are mobile creatures and will often make their own way back without human assistance. The spread of the buzzard back through most of its lost ground across southern Scotland is perhaps the most astonishing wildlife gain of recent time, followed by the super-recovery of the peregrine population after it was first restored by pesticide restrictions. The raven also shows signs of welcome expansion of range and numbers. All of these must reflect a considerable reduction in persecution, through the spread of enlightened attitudes, itself the result of an educational campaign by conservation bodies.

The same applies to many other animals, though some are sedentary and may have to be reintroduced. Plants are on the whole more difficult, especially when considered as communities. Some will spread freely and re-colonise suitable habitats of their own accord, but many have only limited powers of spread, and some of the rarities are particularly immobile. An old herb-rich meadow representing hundreds of years – perhaps more – of ecological history can be destroyed by ploughing in a few hours. Restoring its botanical character could take many long years of dedicated effort and cost a huge sum of money. Thus, even with relatively benign management programmes in place over whole farms, there will seldom be any rapid changes in the floristic value of land that has lost virtually the whole of this interest. Unless farmers can be persuaded –

and paid – to grow wildflower crops, there will be little change on their land. The requirement to control 'weeds' on setaside land removes any possibility of allowing arable or intensive pasture to show a natural succession back to some more interesting state. Unless conservationists can get involved in the definition of the rules regarding these management options, there will be little more than a wish-washy maintenance of essentially dull farmland.

Forestry is a rather similar case. While further hand-wringing over the wholesale loss of hill ground may be futile, it seems to me important to understand how this catastrophe for nature conservation happened. When one compares the situation with that in the Lake District, not far away, there is no avoiding the conclusion that it was largely because so few voices were raised against the foresters' onslaught. The Friends of the Lake District was a campaigning body founded largely to fight the Forestry Commission's obliteration of the Cumbrian fells with conifers, which it did with great success (Ratcliffe, 2002). The Nature Conservancy smiled benignly on the business: not only did it have several ex-foresters among the senior staff, and even practising foresters on its committees, but it was also cowed by the prevailing ethos that government bodies do not fight each other, certainly not in public, and preferably not in private either. Nor do they tread on the corns of the rural establishment and other powerful vested interests. The NGOs were embryonic, and not until much later did they gear up to addressing the major problems of land use. The Southern Uplands had no great contingent of admirers among the public at large, to compare with the numerous defenders of Lakeland. So it was left to a few locals to grumble, and now and then to make ineffective protest to officials they happened to know. Only later – much too late – did sheep farmers and other concerned parties get together with a Campaign for the Border Hills, to try to halt the tide.

I welcome the changed and more sympathetic view taken by the new generation of foresters towards wildlife conservation, but it will be a slow and uncertain business to improve the existing forests significantly for the native flora and fauna. Every effort should be made to identify remnants of ancient semi-natural woodland within the holdings of Forest Enterprise and the private forestry companies, and to urge their protection or restoration. Forest Enterprise has already begun restoration work at sites which had previously seemed a lost cause, and this is excellent. As a voluntary initiative, the Borders Forest Trust has acquired the Carrifran valley in Moffatdale and is planting native broadleaved trees and shrubs with the aim of restoring woodland of the kind which grew there long ago – a wildwood. Even with volunteer labour, including the collection of seeds from ancient woodland remnants nearby, it is expensive and uphill work, and more effort of this kind needs to come from the state forestry agency, instead of continuing to pursue its open-ended policy of expanding coniferous afforestation. With the softwood timber market now in a depressed state, what is the case even for replanting clear-fells with yet more conifers?

The initiative of Dumfries & Galloway Council in sponsoring, with official bodies and NGOs, a *Local Biodiversity Action Plan* (Barnes, 1999) is a valuable step forward in acknowledging local authority responsibility for nature conservation. The recognition that the first step is to make a comprehensive assessment of the region's diversity of flora and fauna, and their habitats, from as full as possible a database, is praiseworthy and deserves to be supported by information from all concerned. From this assessment, applying stated criteria, 22 habitats have been identified as most in need of conservation action and termed Local Priority Habitats. Action Plans for all of them have been published. Similarly, 123 species have been identified as most in need of conservation action and termed Local Priority Species, and it is intended to prepare Action Plans for all of these. A second, unpublished list of over 450 species of Local Conservation Concern has been prepared for plants and animals whose status needs watching, in case threat to their survival increases to the point where action is required. The Plan should be read by all interested naturalists and conservationists – it is the most encouraging development in recent years.

GAME PRESERVATION

Grouse-shooting today is in a fraught situation. The Joint Raptor Study has given great support to the view that economically viable grouse moors are incompatible with uncontrolled bird of prey populations, and led to a clamour for legalised removal of at least some hen harriers and peregrines from these moors. Bird conservationists object to putting the clock back to Victorian times, as they see it, and giving up the hard-won victories for which they have fought over so many years. Surreptitious persecution continues meantime wherever the keepers feel they can get away with it, reinforced by a feeling of moral authority, that they were right all along about the effects of predators, and that the law is misguided in prohibiting their destruction. As examples, a gamekeeper near Peebles was convicted in August 2004 of killing 25 protected birds of prey, including 22 buzzards and a goshawk (Fairburn & Reynolds, 2004), and a map showed Kirkcudbrightshire to have the biggest concentration of instances of persecution of birds of prey and owls in Britain in 2003 (RSPB, 2004). Illegal poisoning is still rife and has caused the death of 13 reintroduced red kites in Galloway (C. Rollie).

I cannot see that there is any happy solution to this dilemma. Views are polarised and I can only state my own, which is that if grouse-shooting cannot continue without the destruction of such sovereign birds as hen harriers, peregrines, buzzards and golden eagles, then it will have to stop. They like killing birds, we like enjoying the living creature – the argument is as simple as that. The ritual slaughter of large numbers of sentient creatures, for little more purpose than to demonstrate the skill, status and wealth of a select group of people, is in itself increasingly abhorrent to the public at large today. The argument that it is a traditional sport cuts no ice at all: many practices once considered traditional were abandoned as society became more civilised. Game-keepers need not be driven into unemployment. There will be a continuing need for managers of the uplands and, as happened in the state forests and National Nature Reserves, many gamekeepers could become rangers or wardens, if there was sufficient will and money to support the transition.

The most difficult question is about the economic value of the grouse moors. They are always held up as a major source of rural income and employment, though their contribution to the national wealth is derisory. It is true that they attract revenue by virtue of their intrinsic value (i.e. the native red grouse), without any need for the public subsidy that maintains uneconomic farming and forestry in the uplands. If well-off people are willing to pay the sums necessary to sustain grouse-shooting as a viable proposition to the moor owners or lessees, why should they not be allowed to do so? This is where the argument comes full circle, because the answer is that they cause unacceptable conflict with the wishes of the rest of society. And it will not do to dismiss this as arrogant interference by outsiders who do not understand what is involved, or who have no right to intrude on the lives of others. We all live now in one interconnected society, and no one group can claim exclusivity for its affairs. Freedom is a slippery concept, for it so often involves trampling on the freedoms of others.

It is a fair point to ask if the defenders of the birds of prey are prepared, or able, to compensate for the lost income if grouse-shooting were to be abandoned. Taken as a group, they lack the individual wealth of the shooting fraternity, and would, in any case, object to paying directly for what they have always regarded as something that should be free. Their effect is more indirect and diffused, as part of the growing body of recreational and tourist interest that has become a major economic force in the countryside over the last half-century. The uplands and their human inhabitants need to be considered as a whole, and their future evaluated as a recreational resource and as service providers, which the public should support financially as users. It could hardly happen under New Labour on present form, but it should not be beyond the wit of humankind to devise some system of modest levy and readjustment of existing subsidies which would provide sufficient income to sustain the resident population at a decent standard of living. Grouse moors occupy a lesser area of the uplands than sheepwalks or hill forests, and as potentially superior habitats for wildlife than either of these, I see no reason why they should not also receive public subsidy for a different kind of use in future – as areas for the wider enjoyment of nature.

THE FUTURE

Prophesies mostly have one thing in common – they nearly always turn out to be wide of the mark if not hopelessly wrong. So I do not intend to indulge in any. Global warming is the most dire of the prospects that loom in the coming years, and could eclipse everything else in its impact on wild nature. The loss of 'soft' coastal habitats, especially salt marshes, and of the montane biota, are widely predicted, if temperature increase and sea-level rise continue at even the less apocryphal estimates. We all know where present thinking to combat 'green-house' emissions is leading – endless proliferation of inefficient wind farms and more nuclear energy. Government pays scant heed to the needs for energy conservation or reducing vehicle emissions. Speed limits are ignored by about 90 per cent of the population, while fashionable suvs consume more than their fair share of fossil fuels, and the roads are clogged with heavy goods vehicles. If they wish to avoid a land ruined for wildlife, as well as much larger social and economic problems, it is up to concerned people to raise their voices and put pressure on the politicians to take more realistic action.

Protected Areas

NATIONAL SCENIC AREAS

Dumfries & Galloway Region
Nith Estuary
East Stewartry Coast
Fleet Valley

Borders Region
Upper Tweeddale
Eildon and Leaderfoot

SITES OF SPECIAL SCIENTIFIC INTEREST (SSSI) – BIOLOGICAL

Principal habitats for which sssis were notified: C = coastland, W = woodland, G = lowland grassland, We = wetland, U = upland grasslands and heaths, R = rock; (M) = Mixed biological and geological interest.

An asterisk * denotes area shared with England.

Dumfries & Galloway Region

SSSI	HABITAT	AREA (HA)	GRID REFERENCE
Abbey Burn Foot to Balcary Point	C	186	NX790469
Airds of Kells Wood	W	28	NX679706
Ardwall Hill	U	219	NX575573
Auchencairn and Orchardton Bays	C	179	NX818532
Auchrochar Wetlands	We	25	NX094605
Back Bay to Carghidown	C	237	NX400367
Backwood	W	14	NS995986
Bailliewhirr	G	35	NX427414
Bell's Flow	We	72	NY320760
Black Loch	We	37	NX991875
Blood Moss	We	10	NX272725
Borgue Coast	C	749	NX610457
Burrow Head	C	244	NX450360
Cairnbaber	U	36	NX486762
Cairnsmore of Fleet	U	3,559	NX515665
Carrick Ponds	We	45	NX581506
Carsegowan Moss	We	50	NX429588
Castramont (Carstramon) Wood	W	86	NX592605
Castle Loch	We	109	NY087815
Chanlockfoot	W	19	NX803990
Cleugh	G	54	NX611867
Coshogle Wood	W	20	NS863047
Cotland Plantation	W	15	NX411545
Cree Estuary	C	3,457	NX465545
Dirskelpin Moss	We	125	NX265588
Dowalton Loch	We	125	NX402467
Dryfe Water	We	13	NY178943
Ellergower Moss	We	35	NX482796
Flow of Dergoals	We	172	NX245580
Glen App and Galloway Moors	U	8,942	NX123718
Glentrool Oakwoods	W	79	NX400788
Hannaston Wood	W, G	26	NX596824
Heart Moss	We	22	NX770480
Kenmure Holms	We	154	NX638765
Kilhern Moss	We	123	NX200628
Killiegowan Wood	W	56	NX584574

SSSI	HABITAT	AREA (HA)	GRID REFERENCE
Kirkconnell Flow	We	142	NX970700
Kirkcowan Flow	We	777	NX255705
Lag Meadow	G	5	NX885783
Lagganmullan	G	29	NX557556
Langholm–Newcastleton Hills	U	7,679	NY435915
Laughenghie and Airie Hills	U	2,309	NX620660
Loch Wood	W	10	NY084972
Lochmaben Lochs	We	36	NY062838
Longbridge Muir	We	514	NY050690
Lower River Cree	We	156	NX413649–448619
Mennock Water	We	48	NS815082
Merrick–Kells	U	8,925	NX450840
Milton Loch	We	73	NX840715
Mochrum Lochs	We	460	NX295535
Moffat Hills	U	2,858	NT155135
Mull of Galloway	C	104	NX115315
Newlaw Moss	We	9	NX733479
North Lowther Uplands	U	7,833	NS800200
Penton Linns	W	9*	NY433774
Perchhall Loch	We	10	NY110879
Port o'Warren	C	6	NX876534
Raeburn Flow	We	65	NY295718
Ravenshall Wood	W	44	NX520525
Ring Moss	We	52	NX332672
River Dee (Parton–Crossmichael)	We	517	NX710685
Royal Ordnance, Powfoot	We, G	37	NY165657
Salt Pans Bay	C	29	NW966614
Scare Rocks	C	2	NX258333
Skyreburn Grasslands‍	G	41	NX544585
Stenhouse Wood	W	19	NX795931
Threave and Carlingwark Loch	We, G	309	NX743625
Torrs Moss	We	15	NX781618
Torrs to Mason's Walk	(M) C	168	NX710437
Torrs Warren–Luce Sands	C	2,409	NX140545
Upper Solway Flats and Marshes	C	29,951*	NX160610
Water of Ken Woods	W	73	NX595809
White Loch–Loch Inch	We	60	NX107609

SSSI	HABITAT	AREA (HA)	GRID REFERENCE
Wood of Cree	W	145	NX382712
Woodhall Loch	We	130	NX670675

Borders Region

SSSI	HABITAT	AREA (HA)	GRID REFERENCE
Airhouse Wood	W	15	NT477537
Akermoor Loch	We	16	NT407210
Alemoor West Loch and Meadow	We, G	36	NT389148
Allan Water Hillhead	G	18	NT460100
Ashkirk Loch	We	5	NT476192
Avenal Hill and Gorge	W, G, R	48	NT522374
Bemersyde Moss	We	25	NT612330
Berwickshire Coast (Intertidal)	C	205	NT834702–979575
Blind Moss	We	8	NT458184
Branxholme Easter Loch	We	8	NT434118
Branxholme Wester Loch	We	12	NT420109
Buckstruther Moss	We	4	NT540120
Burnmouth Coast	C	169	NT960610
Catshaw Hill	G	6	NT540233
Clarilaw Grasslands	G	44	NT561274
Coldingham Common, Long Moss	We	47	NT856685
Coldingham Loch	We	17	NT895685
Colmsliehill Junipers	W	35	NT508409
Cragbank and Wolfehopelee	W	21	NT590073
Craigdilly	W	22	NT184208
Din Moss and Hoselaw Loch	We	46	NT306315
Faldonside Loch	We	6	NT505328
Foulden Burn	(M) W, R	6	NT921549
Gattonside Moss	We	5	NT548368
Gladhouse Reservoir	We	187	NT299535
Glenkinnon Burn	W	37	NT424336
Gordon Moss	We	45	NT635425
Greenlaw Moor	We	1,175	NT705500
Henderland Bank	W	5	NT240232

SSSI	HABITAT	AREA (HA)	GRID REFERENCE
Hermanlaw and Muchra Cleuchs	W	6	NT221165
Hummelknowes Moss	We	5	NT515127
Jedwater Woodlands	W	27	NT673147
Kielderhead Moors: Carter Fell–Peel Fell	U	948*	NT650030
Kingside Loch	We	13	NT342134
Kippilaw Moss	We	1	NT492154
Kirkhope Linns	W, R	8	NT382239
Kirkton Burn Meadow	G	5	NT535141
Langton Lees Cleuch	W	14	NT740523
Lindean Reservoir	We	14	NT502291
Long Moss–Drinkstone Hill	G, We	32	NT480185
Longnewton Cutting	G	4	NT587266
Lurgie Loch	We	12	NT677395
Lynnwood–Whitlaw Wood, Slitrig	W	11	NT499131
Makerstoun–Corbie Craigs to Trow's Craigs	We, R	12	NT662313–685328
Minto Craigs	R	10	NT582208
Moorfoot Hills	U	8,723	NT370460
Mount Bog	We	12	NT103429
Nut Wood	W	3	NT309385
Pease Bay Coast	(M) C	65	NT781718
Pease Bridge Glen	W	12	NT792701
Plora Wood	W	22	NT350368
Redden Bank Lime Works	G	2	NT789369
Riskinhope	W	9	NT234190
River Tweed	We	2,598	NT052139
Selkirk Racecourse Moss	We	4	NT498278
St Abbs to Fast Castle	C	257	NT880699
St Mary's Loch	We	256	NT250228
The Hirsel	W, We	93	NT825413
Threepwood Moss	We	54	NT518424
Tweedsmuir Hills	U	8,848	NT165265
Tweedwood–Gateheugh	W, R	30	NT583342
Westwater Reservoir	We	51	NT117523
Whiteadder Water	We	103	NT787568–921546
Whitlaw Bank to Harden Hill	W, G	7	NT505131
Whitlaw Mosses	(M) We	21	NT506286

SSSI	HABITAT	AREA (HA)	GRID REFERENCE
Whitlaw Rig	G	6	NT518293
Whitmuirhall Loch	We	12	NT499273
Williamhope	W, G	69	NT427343
Woodhead Moss	We	13	NT613262
Yetholm Loch	We	22	NT803280

South and East Ayrshire Districts

SSSI	HABITAT	AREA (HA)	GRID REFERENCE
Aldons Hill	G	236	NX183900
Auchalton	G	6	NS336037
Ballantrae Shingle Beach	C	34	NX080818
Bennane Head Grasslands	G	74	NX110880
Craig Wood	W	24	NX134829
Craighead Quarry (M)	R	3	NX234013
Feoch Meadows	G	83	NX270821
Knockdaw Hill	G	392	NX155883
Knockdolian Hill	G, R	68	NX113848
Littleton and Balhamie Hills	G	243	NX130867
Pinbain Burn to Cairn Hill	(M) G	524	NX165925

SITES OF SPECIAL SCIENTIFIC INTEREST (SSSI) – GEOLOGICAL

Dumfries & Galloway Region

SSSI	AREA	GRID REFERENCE
Bigholms Burn	2	NY316812
Carron Water & Hapland Burn	10	NS887022
Clatteringshaws Dam Quarry	10	NX547754
Corsewall Point to Milleur	60	NX000729
Cruggleton Bay	1	NX479448

SSSI	AREA (HA)	GRID REFERENCE
Grennan Bay	7	NX074438
Isle of Whithorn Bay	4	NX476363
Lagrae Burn	10	NS705145
Lea Larks	10	NX564691
Leadhills – Wanlockhead	50	NS880141
Locharbriggs Quarry	4	NX990810
Morroch Bay	12	NX017524
Penton Linns	9	NY433774
Pibble Mine	8	NX527606
Polhote and Polneul Burns	34	NS694114
Port Logan	5	NX092402
River Esk, Glencartholm	4	NY376796
River Nith at Drumlanrig Bridge	3	NS858000
Shoulder o' Craig	1	NX663491
Talnotry Mine	9	NX478703
West Burrow Head	2	NX452341

Borders Region

SSSI	AREA (HA)	GRID REFERENCE
Grieston Quarry	2	NT314362
Hareheugh Craigs	8	NT688400
Kershope Bridge	7	NY499834
Lennel, Charlie's Brae	6	NT857411
Lintmill Railway Cutting	6	NT733463
Lynslie Burn	24	NT130572
Old Cambus Quarry	2	NT806705
Oxendean Burn	4	NT772561
Palmers Hill Railway Cutting	2	NY548964
Siccar Point	6	NT811709
Thornylee Quarry	1	NT420363
Whiteadder Water	103	NT787568–921546

South & East Ayrshire Districts

SSSI	AREA (HA)	GRID REFERENCE
Afton Lodge	3	NS417259
Byne Hill	9	NX180945
Girvan to Ballantrae Coast Section	89	NX153935
Knockormal	6	NX134885
Laggan Burn	3	NX202945–206946
Millenderdale	1	NX177905
Sgavock	6	NX073808

NATIONAL NATURE RESERVES (NNR)

An asterisk * denotes also SSSI.

Dumfries & Galloway Region
Caerlaverock *
Cairnsmore of Fleet *
Kirkconnell Flow *
Silver Flowe *

Borders Region
Cragbank Wood *
St Abbs Head *
Whitlaw Mosses *

LOCAL NATURE RESERVES (LNR)

Castle Loch LNR *
Wigtown Bay LNR

NATURE RESERVES OF OTHER BODIES

An asterisk * denotes also SSSI.

Royal Society for the Protection of Birds (RSPB)

NAME	AREA (HA)	GRID REFERENCE
Ken–Dee Marshes *	120	NX699684
Kirkconnell Merse	300	NX990690
Mersehead *	1,084	NX928566
Mull of Galloway *	12	NX156305
Scare Rocks	2	NX258333
Wood of Cree *	266	NX383715

Scottish Wildlife Trust (SWT)

NAME	AREA (HA)	GRID REFERENCE
Auchalton Meadow		NS335036
Bemersyde Moss *	25	NT614340
Blackcraig Wood	17	NX440641
Carsegowan Moss *	50	NX425587
Carstramon Wood *	80	NX592605
Dowalton Marshes	57	NX405467
Drummains Reedbed	6	NX984610
Duns Castle	78	NT778550
Feoch Meadows *	83	NX270821
Gordon Moss *	56	NT635425
Greyhill Grasslands *		NX181941
Hare and Dunhog Mosses	10	NT471247
Hoselaw Loch and Din Moss	26	NT808317
Knowetop Lochs (Lowes Lochs)	23	NX706786
Pease Dean *	33	NT790704
Southwick Coast	19	NX910558
St Abbs Marine Reserve		NT919674
Stenhouse Wood *	19	NX795930
Thornton Glen		NT735741

SSSI	HABITAT	AREA (HA)	GRID REFERENCE
Whitlaw Wood *		9	NT500132
Woodhall Dean			NT681728
Yetholm Loch *		26	NT803275

Wildfowl and Wetlands Trust (WWT)

Caerlaverock		NY018652

National Trust for Scotland (NTS)

NAME	AREA (HA)	GRID REFERENCE
Grey Mare's Tail and White Coomb *	922	NT182150
Murray Isles		NX571501
Rockcliffe & Rough Island	19	NX843532
Threave *	607	NX746620

Woodland Trust

NAME	AREA (HA)	GRID REFERENCE
Aldouran Glen, Wigtownshire	13.2	NX007635
Drumlea, Dumfriesshire	0.3	NY243775
Plora Wood, Peeblesshire	19.7	NT344365
St. Ronan's Wood, Peeblesshire	27.1	NT327368
Jacob's Well, Berwickshire	1.0	NT847400
Fairbairn Copse, Berwickshire	0.9	NT779718
Pressmennan Wood, East Lothian	86.2	NT630729

Conservation Organisations

Government responsibility for nature conservation was vested in the **Nature Conservancy** in 1949, and passed to its successor the **Nature Conservancy Council** in 1973. The organisation was devolved in 1990 and the Scottish part amalgamated with the Countryside Commission for Scotland in 1991 to form **Scottish Natural Heritage** (SNH). Its headquarters was until recently in Edinburgh, and there are regional offices in the south at Dumfries and Galashiels, covering the Dumfries & Galloway and Borders sectors. The main functions of the organisation are to establish and manage National Nature Reserves, notify Sites of Special Scientific Interest for wildlife and geological features and guide their management accordingly, give advice to ministers and the public on nature conservation, conduct appropriate research, and disseminate knowledge about the natural environment. SNH is more directly under the control of the Scottish government than was the erstwhile Nature Conservancy Council. It is thus subject to political and policy changes, such as the recent decision to move most of its HQ staff from Edinburgh to Inverness, and also to input from advisers and administrators within government.

Local authorities (LAs) exert a powerful influence on wildlife conservation through their control of the legal planning process for proposed developments on SSSIs, though this excludes farming and forestry. Planning decisions are influenced by guidelines issued by central government. Local authorities are required to have regard to the needs of nature conservation, and have power to set up Local Nature Reserves, of which there are two in the region. Some LAs are more enthusiastic about nature conservation than others, and undertake a variety of helpful initiatives in support.

The **Forestry Commission** (FC) is the government body in charge of state forestry. It was split in 1996 into the **Forestry Authority**, which advises government on forestry policy and deals with advice and grant-aid to private foresters; and **Forest Enterprise**, which owns and manages the state forests. Under the last Conservative Government, Forest Enterprise was obliged to sell off some of its woodland estate to the private sector, but this policy stopped in 1997. The state forestry policy was for many years after its inception in 1919 driven by the commercial need to plant rapidly growing softwood conifers, both in restocking existing woodland and in afforesting treeless ground. The Commission was also required to limit afforestation to land of the lowest agricultural value, but was then given a virtual blank cheque from the taxpayer to plant conifers on such open heath, moorland and bog as it could acquire. After many years of controversy, including two highly critical reviews by the Treasury and National Audit Office, the Commission and its two arms have recently softened the hard-line policy on conifers. It has undertaken to manage and restore ancient semi-natural woodlands and SSSIs to maintain their landscape and wildlife value, and is making serious efforts to pursue nature conservation initiatives of its own. The recent fall in softwood timber prices has also undermined purely commercial objectives. The Commission has always adopted an open-access policy to its forests for the public, when there are no reasons to deny it.

The **Royal Society for the Protection of Birds** (RSPB) is the premier non-governmental organisation for wildlife and has a Scottish HQ in Edinburgh, and regional offices near Castle Douglas and in Galashiels. It also establishes and manages nature reserves (including six in the region), gives advice and promotes land-use policies sympathetic to wildlife, but is independent of government and can afford to be more assertive than the official side. It is more concerned than SNH with enforcement of bird protection law and regularly brings prosecutions for infringements. As a charity it is legally responsible to the public at large, but has a special interest in fostering the wishes of its own membership, now over one million strong.

The **Scottish Wildlife Trust** (SWT) is the leading exclusively Scottish conservation NGO, with over 20 reserves in the region (see Appendix 1). It aims to enhance and preserve habitats and wildlife, by establishing and managing protected areas, and by influencing environmental policies, e.g. through inputs to legislation, as in the Nature Conservation (Scotland) Act 2004, which contains a legal commitment to conserve Scotland's diversity of wildlife. SWT campaigns for change in land use, such as the move to environmentally friendly farming.

The **National Trust for Scotland** (NTS) has over 260,000 members and is the largest conservation charity in Scotland, though its responsibilities include the ownership and care of historic houses and gardens, and the commercial management of farms and woodland, as well as the care and protection of landscape and wildlife. Some of its large upland properties are important to nature conservation, such as the Grey Mare's Tail and White Coomb, and these are managed with a view to enhancing their wildlife interest.

The **Woodland Trust** is a charity concerned with the conservation of ancient and semi-natural woodland throughout Britain. To this end it has launched an open-ended programme of woodland acquisitions, and it now manages over 1,000 woods, with the aim of achieving the desired tree composition and structure, and maximum wildlife content, in the longer term. Exotic conifers are gradually removed and replaced with native trees, for instance. Many of the Trust's woodlands are small, but some are SSSIs and even Natura 2000 sites. The Trust also aims to re-establish woodland of native trees in areas of deforested upland, as at Glen Finglas in the Trossachs area. There are over 130,000 members, but policy is to make Trust woodlands open for the public at large to enjoy.

Plantlife International was founded in 1989 to promote the conservation of wild plants in their natural habitats, in Britain, Europe and across the world, and its goal is to halt the loss of wild plant diversity. Its early efforts in this country were by influencing government policy and legislation, and supporting European Union Directives on wildlife site protection. Plantlife in the UK has a growing membership which exceeds 10,000, and it has emphasised educational work to raise the level of public awareness and support. High-profile projects have concerned rescuing especially endangered species ('Back from the brink'), and the identification of symbolic flowers for each county of Britain. Latterly an expanding suite of nature reserves has been acquired, especially floral meadows and grasslands but also a Caithness flow. On the international front, a prime objective is to identify areas of major botanical importance, such as centres of endemism, across the world, as the first step towards their protection. Plantlife has a Scottish Officer based in Stirling, though it does not yet have any reserves in southern Scotland.

The **Borders Forest Trust** was set up around 1990 to re-create the Wildwood – 'a place where plants and animals natural to the area could flourish undisturbed, and where people could come to gain inspiration and increased understanding'. In 1990 it bought the Carrifran valley in Moffatdale and has steadily been planting a variety of trees and shrubs native to the area, through the voluntary efforts of its supporters.

The **Heather Trust** is an independent charity dedicated to the promotion of high standards of moorland management. Working with a wide range of other organisations throughout the UK, the Trust seeks to improve moorland habitat for the benefit of wildlife, domestic stock, game and all people with an interest in moorland areas. It is based in Dumfries and its supporters are especially game-shooters.

The **Botanical Society of the British Isles** (BSBI) is largely a body of amateur botanists concerned especially with the taxonomy, distribution and status of the flowering plants, ferns and fern-allies of Britain and Ireland. It has a countrywide network of Recorders, one to each Watsonian vice-county, and a panel of referees in plant identification. The combined membership has twice been mobilised in field recording to produce data for compilation of atlases of the British flora, with dot distribution maps for each species, and the first of these, in 1962, was the prototype for all other mapping schemes for various groups of plants and animals. Its journal *Watsonia* has shown an increasing preoccupation with micro-species (e.g. of *Rubus fruticosus*), hybrids and alien species, and it is, in my opinion, over-inclined to accept nomenclatural changes. While its information, especially in the atlases, is valuable to other bodies, some felt that there was still need for a more serious approach to plant conservation and this led to the setting up of Plantlife.

The **Botanical Society of Scotland** (formerly the Botanical Society of Edinburgh, founded in 1836) is a parallel Scottish body to the BSBI, and the two hold annual joint meetings in Scotland. It deals with all groups of wild plants and publishes the *Botanical Journal of Scotland* and a newsletter, which contain material dealing with our region.

The **British Pteridological Society** (BPS), **British Bryological Society** (BBS), **British Lichen Society** (BLS) and **British Mycological Society** (BMS) aim to promote knowledge of, respectively, ferns and their allies, mosses and liverworts, lichens, and fungi. They have been concerned especially with the taxonomy of their various groups, and with the distribution and status of species, but in more recent years their journals have increasingly reported research at a deeper level of study.

The **Berwickshire Naturalists' Club**, founded in 1831, is the oldest natural history society in Britain, with a mostly amateur membership, and has operated over the whole of the eastern Borders. Its *History* is the Club's journal for publication of papers and notes on the flora, fauna and geology of the district.

The **Dumfries & Galloway Natural History and Antiquarian Society** was founded in 1862, and its objects were to collect and publish the best information on the natural sciences and antiquities (including history). Its *Transactions* have been the main vehicle for publication of papers on the natural history of Dumfries & Galloway.

The **Scottish Ornithologists' Club** (SOC) was founded in 1936. It headquarters have recently moved from Edinburgh to Aberlady, and it has 14 separate branches, of which four are in the south – at Stranraer, Dumfries, New Gallo-way and Melrose – and a fifth is just outside, in Ayr. It publishes the journal *Scottish Birds* and the annual *Scottish Bird Report*, supports research projects in ornithology, and maintains close links with the BTO. While not a campaigning organisation, many of its members are active in nature conservation, through other bodies and individual or group initiatives. Its Borders and Dumfries & Galloway Branches produce valuable annual bird reports.

The **British Trust for Ornithology** (BTO) is a research organisation that aims to provide objective data on British birds to government, its agencies, conservation NGOs and any other parties who need such information. It is not a campaigning organisation and remains neutral on conservation issues. The BTO relies on external funding by customer bodies, but is able to give good value for money by using the large, unpaid labour force of its members to gather field data under the leadership or guidance of its staff, or the representatives of the numerous regions into which it has divided the whole country. Its Enquiries are especially surveys (often repeated at suitable intervals) of numbers, abundance and distribution of wild birds, either of individual species (e.g. rook, nightjar, peregrine) or of all species, as in the case of the surveys which led to the two breeding bird atlases. Some of its member-supported projects are continuous, and thus provide even more precise monitoring information on status, such as the surveys of garden birds and estuarine waterfowl. The BTO also runs the national bird-ringing scheme, on which migration studies are based and which informs work on population dynamics. The BTO has a Scottish office with six staff on Stirling University campus, and works closely with the SOC.

The **Wildfowl and Wetlands Trust** (WWT) was set up by Sir Peter Scott in 1946 at Slimbridge on the Severn estuary to promote wildfowl conservation. Its early main feature was the captive wildfowl collection at Slimbridge, but the Trust broadened out by setting up visitor centres in several parts of the country, including one at Caerlaverock on the Solway, and by the appointment of research staff to study particular species or groups and their problems. It runs a monitoring scheme of wildfowl counts, to observe changes in status. Its mission is now the broader one of conserving wetlands and their biodiversity.

The **South-west Scotland Raptor Study Group** and **Borders Raptor Study Group** are composed mainly of amateur bird of prey enthusiasts, who spend much of their spare time checking the breeding territories and nests of their favourite species, and providing data to organisers who compile annual reports from these returns. Some members conduct ringing projects or engage in other work, including putting up nest-boxes for kestrels and barn owls, and making nest-ledges and scrapes to attract peregrines to unoccupied rocks. Their contacts with farmers, shepherds, keepers, etc. help to build up a body of local interest which helps to support the conservation goals.

The **British Association for Shooting and Conservation** (BASC) and the **Game Conservancy Trust** (GCT) see themselves as conservation bodies, though their basic purpose is the shooting of wildfowl and game-birds by members, and their conservation activities are a means to this end. BASC owns properties, such as Priestside Merse near Annan, and manages them to the benefit of habitat, flora and other birds besides wildfowl. Some of its members have been involved in translocations of wildfowl in the interests of their sport, and were a factor in the spread of feral greylag geese in southwest Scotland. GCT is a privately funded research organisation which investigates population declines in game-birds (e.g. grey partridge and red grouse) or other problems detrimental to shooting interests. It was one of the parties involved in the Joint Raptor Study of bird of prey predation on red grouse on the Langholm Moors.

Butterfly Conservation has a Scotland team of four based in Stirling. Its activities include butterfly distribution and abundance recording, research on individual species, and establishing reserves. Butterfly Conservation published *The Millennium Atlas of Butterflies in Britain and Ireland* (Asher *et al.*, 2001), and one of its important concerns is monitoring the northward spread of certain species in evident response to warming climate.

Fungi

Roy Watling

Unfortunately, in parallel to many Scottish areas, the Southern Uplands over the decades have not been well documented for fungi. It is true that some very early records exist for fungi, including the marsh-loving rare *Agaricus* (*Omphalia*) *belliae*, now placed in the genus *Mycena* (Johnston, 1853), from the southernmost limit of the area, and *Phyllotopsis nidulans*, the only known record from Scotland, from near Penicuik at the northern limit, but generally records are limited. Unlike the Scottish Highlands, Western and Northern islands and Perthshire, the southern parts of Scotland have been visited only occasionally by mycologists, resulting in a rather poor coverage (Watling, 1986). Between the years 1883 and 1983 there were 19 formal forays (Watling, 1983), including visits by the Cryptogamic Society of Scotland, before its incorporation into the Botanical Society of Scotland. The British Mycological Society has only visited the area a handful of times over its hundred-year history, although interesting lists have nevertheless been generated. A spring foray in 1986, based at Newton Stewart, was held to examine the mycota of policies at Castle Kennedy, Torrs Warren, Logan Botanic Garden, Glen Trool etc., and an upland foray in 1999, based on Melrose, visited several sites including Glentress, Mellerstain, Floors Castle and the Eildon Hills. Records from the end of the nineteenth century for the Southern Uplands are found scattered under the entries 'Tweed' and 'Solway' in Stevenson's *Mycologia Scotica* (1879).

Recently several projects have stimulated interest in the fungi south of the Southern Uplands Fault, and these have added many records. The projects include an in-depth study over a ten-year period in a wood near Stobo, resulting in 9,499 records covering 954 species (Watling, 2005) and a survey of meadow fungi over a wide swathe of country (Newton *et al.*, 2003). With the growing popularity of foraying the Borders have become a focus, spurred on by local NGOs and the Borders Recording Centre. At least one foray has been held annually at Dawyck for the past 15 years. The necessity to have fungal input to make a complete biological inventory of an area has often stimulated fungal studies in areas otherwise not examined. Thus, during the survey of the heritage of Glencairn (Ahart, 2001) even after only a few visits the presence of a significant number of fungi was demonstrated. Visits to Mellerstain, Floors Castle and Bowhill have over the years produced interesting records in part because of the exotics planted therein. Unfortunately many of the records generated, although available, are not easily accessed, so those of the author and the husband/wife team of Adrian Newton and Lynn Davy have been placed on a CD-ROM, work sponsored by SNH. Many voucher specimens have been deposited in the Herbarium of the Royal Botanic Garden in Edinburgh, but some records lack adequate documentation and many need to be reassessed.

In order to place the Southern Upland mycota into some context it is probably useful to examine the results from the Heron Wood project based at Dawyck, an abandoned beech plantation on Silurian gravels, invaded some twenty years ago by a birch front. It and the surrounding more formal gardens have been studied extensively for ten years but with records reaching back to the beginning of the twentieth century (Watling, 2005). In general the background macromycota is much the same as that of the Lothians (Watling, in Smith *et al.*, 2002). Thus the same common wood-rotting fungi such as *Hypholoma fasciculare* and *Mycena galericulata* are to be found; leaf-litter rotters such as *Mycena galopus*, *Clitocybe fragrans* and some species very specific to their host substrate (e.g. *Mararsmius setosus* and *Mycena capillaris* on *Fagus*, *Mycena pterigena* on fern rachii), and grassland litter rotters such as *Marasmius oreades* and *Calocybe gambosa*, are common and widespread. In addition there are mycorrhizals such as the ubiquitous *Amanita rubescens*, *Boletus chrysenteron* and *Russula ochroleuca*, and pathogens such as *Armillaria gallica*, especially on *Betula*, and *Xerula radicata*, especially on *Fagus*. In the same way, exceedingly widely distributed are *Russula fellea*, *R. mairei* (= *nobilis*), *Lactarius blennius*, *Tricholoma ustale* and *Oudemansiella mucida* on woody debris, all tied to *Fagus*, and *Suillus grevillei* and *Gomphidius maculatus*, both tied to *Larix*. Common denominators between the Southern Uplands and adjacent areas also occur amongst the brackets such as *Trametes versicolor* and the crusts (resupinate fungi) such as *Stereum hirsutum*, both to be found on fallen branches and stumps. Amongst the more obvious micro-fungi are the lignicolous *Xylaria hypoxylon* and *Mollisia cinerea*, and *Dasyscyphus virgineus* on herbaceous debris, in addition to *Diatrype disciformis*, *Quaternaria quaternata* and *Hypoxylon fragiforme* etc., tied to *Fagus* – so there are no surprises here. From the text above it becomes clear that the presence of *Fagus* is crucial for the existence of a whole array of fungi. Beech, although widely distributed, is not native to the area.

As one has come to expect, intensive studies always throw up interesting records which are new to an area and possibly also to adjacent areas, but the significance of these sightings, because of poor ongoing collecting, is really un-known. Larger fungi are notoriously erratic fruiters: fruiting bodies may appear literally in hundreds in some years whilst in other years there may be only one or two, or even none at all. The recorder must be there at the right time when such small numbers appear as they are putrescent and soon leave little or no trace of their former presence.

Nevertheless *Leucopaxillus rhodoleucus* has been found at Dawyck, growing in a ring under *Chamaecyparis nootkatensis*, at which time it was only the second British record. The ring has expanded and the colony split into at least three enlarging sectors, so the population appears strong. Close by, amongst moss by the stream some ten years earlier, *Dendrocollybia* (= *Collybia*) *racemosa*, with its unusual asexual structures adorning the stem, occurred; this is a rare nitrophilous agaric but despite being found amongst *Sphagnum fimbriatum* at Bean Rigg Moss it is generally rarely recorded, perhaps because of its small size and drab colours. A second fungus with asexual spores on its stem is *Squamanita paradoxa*, which in fact turns out to be a dual organism, uniting the *Squamanita* and the widespread and common *Cystoderma amianthinum*. Only previously known before these sightings from single records from the south of England and from Mull, during 2004 it was collected at several other sites in the UK. *Clitocybe truncicola*, found on the Glen SSSI at Selkirk, is an important addition to the Scottish mycota. Torrs Warren requires further attention, as several unusual fungi were collected there growing in the dunes.

Amongst the micro-fungi, *Cornutispora triangularis* on the lichen *Pertusaria pertusa* was a first for the United Kingdom and the small disc fungi *Pyrenopeziza kolaensis* and *Cistella stericola* are seldom seen and hardly ever recorded; similarly *Unguicularia tityri*, which is found on deer and rabbit pellets. All grow at Dawyck on other fungi, the last on *Schizothecium vesticola*, a minute flask-fungus. This emphasises that the right collector has be around to recognise such critical finds. However, *Spathularia flavida*, although a disc fungus, is a bright yellow macro-mycete and a Red Data List species; a single site under a *Taxus* hedge is known at Dawyck. Forest pathogens have been widely studied in the Southern Uplands and the region holds the type locality for such micro-species as *Phomopsis pseudo-tsugae*, a needle cast fungus, and in parallel *Lophodermium vagulum*, described new to science from a whole spectrum of Chinese rhododendrons in the Borders.

Amongst the other significant finds are *Mycena pelianthina*, an agaric tied to *Fagus* with a southern distribution in Scotland: it is decidedly uncommon but good populations are known from the Borders. A feature of Dawyck is the large troops of the elegant *Phaeolepiota aurea* which occur in the autumn; this is a rather rare fungus nationally. Both these species also occur in the Lothians, unlike the little *Hohenbuehelia cyphelliformis*, which has been found on a rotten *Abies alba* trunk. It has probably been overlooked, but it is an important member of the reticulate pattern which fungi play in the community; it preys on nematodes, as do many of the pleurotoid agarics. This species was on the same substrate as the uncommon *Lentinellus castoreus*; some of the *Abies* were planted at Dawyck over a hundred years ago. The spread of the use of woodchips for flowerbed mulch has extended the range of many fungi, including some previously more frequent in remnants of the Caledonian forest, e.g. *Chrysomphlaina grossula* (= *Omphalina wynniae*), and woodland-margin fungi such as *Macrocystidia cucumis*. They now often occur in huge troops just as *Psilocybe aurantiaca* at Logan; in this last case it has almost certainly been introduced from Australia, possibly with plant material. Similarly, *Schizophyllum commune* has spread throughout the region; normally a southern lignicolous fungus, it is colonising silage, the fruiting bodies bursting out of the black polythene bags. The first records in Scotland came from near Stranraer in the late 1960s.

Other uncommon fungi are *Lentinus lepideus* on conifer and *Volvariella bombycina* on fallen *Ulmus*, both at Mellerstain, in addition to *Boletus impolitus*, a bolete with a more southern distribution in the British Isles. Another elm-loving fungus, rare in Scotland as a whole, is *Hypsizygus ulmarius*, found at Traquair House. *Suillus variegatus*, a bolete characteristic of the Caledonian pinewoods, has been surprisingly spotted at Bowhill, and a relative formerly known as *S. neuschii* has occurred at Glentress associated with *Larix*. The first parallels the finding in the western and eastern sectors of *Tapinella* (= *Paxillus*) *atrotomentosa*, *Pholiota flammans* and *Pleurocybella porrigens*, fungi more in keeping with the Scottish pinewoods and some long-established plantations. These species apparently still find a home in the Southern Uplands in the small scattered groups of pines in the area. A good example also is *Suillus granulatus*, a widespread yet not common species in Scotland. The brackets *Fomes fomentarius* and *Inonotus obliquus* both grow on old birches and are more a feature of the glens of the north; they are decidedly rare in the Borders, with a handful of records each. The rather uncommon jelly *Pseudohydnum gelatinosum* is also found at Glentress, and *Calocera pallidospathulata*, unrecognised as distinct until very recently, is now throughout the conifer plantations in the Southern Uplands. The Hirsel has supplied records which include *Rugulomyces* (= *Calocybe*) *ionides*, *Lactarius britannicus* and *L. rubrotinctus*, the last two suggesting a more southern element. With the finding of the unusual *Melanotus proteus* in Dumfries on cut ends of *Picea* stumps, research was carried out by the Forestry Commission to determine its ability to out-compete common pathogenic fungi. This find stimulated the search for other members of this predominantly tropical–subtropical genus.

Boletus pulverulentus, a bolete generally considered to have a southwestern distribution in Scotland, occurs regularly associated with *Tilia* at Dawyck and often in large numbers, but in Glencairn it occurs with its more normal host *Quercus*. Also in the western part of the Southern Uplands there is a slightly wetter, milder overall climate than experienced at Dawyck, and this allows several small *Mycena* species, which occur on mossy trunks, to flourish. Two rare brackets, *Ganoderma pfeiferrei* and *Ischnoderma benzoinum*, the former on an old beech stump, the latter on a wind-blown *Abies alba*, occur at Glencairn and Dawyck respectively. *Aleurodiscus wakefeldiae* on *Fagus* branches is only known in Scotland from a single record from the Peebles area, where *A. amorphus* on *Abies* branches also occurs. The latter is parasitised by the jelly *Tremella simplex*, painted and described by Beatrix Potter from Dunkeld, before it was formally described. These are the only records from Scotland, but they encouraged the Kew mycologists to examine their English exsiccata of *A. amorphus*, on which it was found; it probably has a wide distribution in the UK. The rare *Cytidia salicina* was confirmed not to be extinct from recent collections just south of the Southern Uplands at Kielder Forest, but what were probably old fruit-bodies had been located earlier at Murder Moss. Plora Wood is a site for the very uncommon *Porphyrellus porphyrosporus*, a bolete in Scotland more characteristic of the Tay valley, and also for the reduced agaric called *Rimbachia arachnoidea*, for which there are few UK records. The purple *Clavaria zollingeri*, which is also found in the tropics, is a significant record.

With the many large estates and planted policies of exotic trees and shrubs, the fungi at Dawyck give a good impression of the potential of the Southern Uplands, but there are other elements which need to be considered. The wax-cap survey is a good example, concentrating on semi-natural, undisturbed grassland. During this survey it became patently clear that fungi previously thought to be rare were more widespread, exposing our lack of good recording data. Thus several populations of *Hygrocybe calyptriformis*, a flagship species for conservation, have been identified. During this work several unimproved grasslands were identified that require special conservation attention, not because of the occurrence of a single species of fungus but for a suite of interrelated groups (Newton *et al.*, 2003). These are called wax-cap grasslands and are fast disappearing; indeed Scotland holds the greatest number and most extensive development of these communities in Europe. The Southern Uplands are custodian to a large number of these communities: good wax-cap grasslands include areas around Lindean Reservoir and Blackpool Moss. In the autumn these grasslands glow with the reds, oranges and yellows, and sometimes greens, of the fruiting bodies – meadow jewels. These and other grassland fungi have been the subject of an investigation using monitored plots at Sourhope. The fieldwork is allowing population studies in the non-fruiting stage to be undertaken, and underpinned by molecular work, so that useful management strategies can be developed (Deacon, 2001).

Typical upland and montane fungi might be expected in the Southern Uplands. Thus *Galerina paludosa*, *Phoilota mysostis* and *Tephrocybe palustris*, all so characteristic of *Sphagnum* bogs, are found in sites ranging from the Devil's Beef Tub to the Carrifran glen, in the latter of which re-afforestation with native species is being practised. It will be interesting to see what fungi appear in the future, possibly introduced with planting material, as demonstrated for Kergord in Shetland (Watling, 2002). In peaty areas at higher altitude the basidiolichens *Lichenomphalina hudsoniana* and *L. luteovitellina* are found, both species being more familiar to those collecting in the Cairngorms. The thalloid, non-fruiting form of the former (= *Coriscium viride*) has a wider but patchy distribution south of the fault line. Both species were previously placed in *Omphalina*. As a result of heavy grazing over centuries the dwarf willow communities have all but disappeared from the area but in the few spots of *Salix herbacea* left the ectomycorrhizal alpine *Russula pascua* has been collected. Diligent collecting surely will find additional fungi associated with these islands of willow.

The distribution of micro-fungi is difficult to assess as there are so few mycologists studying this group, but there is a multitude of taxa including the causal agent of Dutch elm disease, *Ceratocystis ulmi*, which has devastated some woodlands in the Uplands, including woods around Newton St Boswells. The rhododendron mildews *Microsphaera azaleae* and *Oidium ericinum* are undoubtedly very recent arrivals but now are widespread. The non-pathogenic *Capnobotrys dingleyiae* is another probable introduction; it forms spongy masses in the crooks and groins of Border *Taxus* and other evergreen conifers, especially in the west. *Rosellinia necatrix*, which damages garden peonies, has been recorded, emphasising that foray lists are not the only source of information, but official horticultural and agricultural reports too. Unfortunately voucher material has rarely been kept or, if it was, has now been lost in the many reorganisations which have overtaken our advisory services. There are similar examples of intro-ductions amongst the macromycetes, including the false truffle, *Hydnangium carneum*, associated with eucalypts, which has been collected at Logan as well as in Lothian sites.

Although only an incomplete inventory is available to us it does suggest that the Southern Uplands play host to some rare and uncommon British fungi – but also that with better collecting, especially in the southwestern sector, some of these might be found to be more widely distributed and other rare ones may appear. The available inventory also suggests that the mycota of the region stands at a similar figure to that of the Lothians, or slightly higher, that is about 2,750, of which 700 are larger forms. The rusts and smuts in the Borders directly linked to vascular plants only approach 50 or so records, so are undoubtedly under-recorded, contrasting with the slime moulds, which are well known with over 70 taxa. Despite the fact there are approaching 125 mitosporic fungi recorded for the region, for a fuller picture there is still a need for more records of these fungi, and of oomycetes and zygomycetes, all of which demand microscopic examination.

References and Further Reading

Adair, P. (1892). The short-eared owl and the kestrel in the vole plague districts. *Annals of Scottish Natural History*, **12**, 219–31.

Adair, P. (1893). Notes on the disappearance of the short-tailed field vole, and on some effects of the visitation. *Annals of Scottish Natural History*, **13**, 193–202.

Ahart, E. (2001). *The Glencairn Environmental Audit Report*. Privately published and circulated. Moniaive.

Altringham, J. (2003). *British Bats*. New Naturalist 93. Collins, London.

Anon. (2005). Will there be a windfarm near you? *The Herald*, 11 January 2005.

Asher, J., Warren, M., Fox, R., Harding, P., Jeffcoate, G. & Jeffcoate, S. (2001). *The Millennium Atlas of Butterflies in Britain and Ireland*. Oxford University Press, Oxford.

Barnes, A. (ed.) (1999). *Dumfries & Galloway Local Biodiversity Action Plan*. Dumfries & Galloway Biodiversity Partnership, Dumfries.

Battarbee, R. W., Flower, R. J., Stevenson, A. C. & Rippey, B. (1985). Lake acidification in Galloway: a palaeo-ecological test of competing hypotheses. *Nature*, **314**, 350–2.

Battarbee, R. W., Stevenson, A. C., Rippey, B., Fletcher, C., Natkanski, J., Wik, M. & Flower, R. J. (1989). Causes of lake acidification in Galloway, South-west Scotland: a palaeoecological evaluation of the relative roles of atmospheric contamination and catchment change for two acidified sites with non-afforested catchments. *Journal of Ecology*, **77**, 651–72.

Baxter, E. V. & Rintoul, L. J. (1953). *The Birds of Scotland*. Oliver & Boyd, Edinburgh.

Beebee, T. J. C. & Griffiths, R. A. (2000). *Amphibians and Reptiles*. New Naturalist 87. Collins, London.

Birks, H. H. (1972). Studies in the vegetational history of Scotland. II. Two pollen diagrams from the Galloway Hills, Kirkcudbrightshire. *Journal of Ecology*, **60**, 183–217.

Bolam, G. (1912). *Birds of Northumberland and the Eastern Borders*. Frank Palmer, London.

Braithwaite, M. E. (2004). *Berwickshire Vice-County Rare Plant Register*. Privately printed and circulated.

Braithwaite, M. E. & Long, D. G. (1990). *The Botanist in Berwickshire*. Berwickshire Naturalists' Club, Berwick.

Brenchley, A. (1986). The breeding

distribution and abundance of the rook (*Corvus frugilegus*) in Great Britain since the 1970s. *Journal of Zoology, London* (A), **210**, 261–78.

Bridson, R. H. (1978). The natterjack toad: its distribution in south-west Scotland 1976. *Transactions of the Dumfriesshire & Galloway Natural History and Antiquarian Society*, Series III, **53**, 46–56.

Bruce, K. (1997). Reed warblers breeding in south-west Scotland. *Scottish Birds*, **19**, 119–20.

Bullock, D., North, S. & Williams, D. (1976). Feral goats on Cairnsmore of Fleet. Unpublished report to the South West Region (Scotland) of the Nature Conservancy Council.

Burd, F. (1989). The saltmarsh survey of Great Britain: an inventory of British saltmarshes. *Research and Survey in Nature Conservation*, **17**. Nature Conservancy Council, Peterborough.

Burfield, I. J. (2002). The breeding ecology and conservation of the ring ouzel *Turdus torquatus* in Great Britain. Unpublished PhD thesis, University of Cambridge.

Calder, I. R. & Newson, M. D. (1980). The effects of afforestation on water resources in Scotland. In: *Land Assessment in Scotland: Proceedings of the Royal Scottish Geographical Society Symposium, Edinburgh, 1979* (ed. Thomas, M. F. & Coppock, J. T.). Aberdeen University Press, Aberdeen.

Carruthers, W. & Moffat, J. C. (1863). *The Ferns of Moffat*. Moffat.

Chamberlain, D. F. (1971). The Summer Meeting 1971 [at Peebles]. *Journal of Bryology*, **7**, 146–9.

Chapman, A. (1907). *Bird-Life of the Borders*. 2nd edn. Gurney and Jackson, London.

Chapman, A. (1912a). Spring notes on the Borders. *British Birds*. **6**, 107–11.

Chapman, A. (1912b). Spotted crake nesting in Roxburghshire. *British Birds*, **6**, 96.

Chapman, A. (1924). *The Borders and Beyond*. Gurney and Jackson, London.

Clavering, M. (1953). *From the Border Hills*. Nelson, Edinburgh.

Conolly, A. P. (1961). Some climatic and edaphic indications from the Late-glacial flora. *Proceedings of the Linnean Society of London*, **172**, 56–62.

Conolly, A. P. & Dahl, E. (1970). Maximum summer temperature in relation to modern and Quaternary distributions of certain arctic–montane species in the British Isles. In: *Studies in the Vegetational History of the British Isles* (ed. Walker, D. & West, R. G.), pp. 159–223. Cambridge University Press, Cambridge.

Corner, R. W. M. (1979a). The botanist's Scotland. 5. Roxburghshire V.C. 80. *Botanical Society of Edinburgh News*, **29**, 5–10.

Corner, R. W. M. (1979b). The botanist's Scotland. 6. Selkirkshire V.C. 79. *Botanical Society of Edinburgh News*, **29**, 10–12.

Corner, R. W. M. (1981). A contribution to the lichen flora of south east Scotland. *Transactions of the Botanical Society of Edinburgh*, **43**, 307–15.

Corner, R. W. M. (1985). *Flowering Plants and Ferns of Selkirkshire and Roxburghshire: a check-list for vice-counties 79 and 80*. Botanical Society of the British Isles, Lancaster.

Corner, R. W. M. (1989). Monitoring and forestry developments along the Roxburgh and Selkirk border. *BSBI Scottish Newsletter*, **11**, 9–11.

Corner, R. W. M. (1992). *Additions and Amendments to the Flowering Plants and Ferns of Selkirkshire and Roxburghshire*. Privately circulated.

Corrie, J. (1910). *Glencairn: the Annals of an Inland Parish*. Thomas Hunter, Dumfries.

Cunningham, D. (1951). Butterflies and moths of the Solway area. *Transactions of* the *Dumfriesshire & Galloway Natural History and Antiquarian Society*, Series III, **28**, 150–6.

Deacon, L. (2001). Fruitbodies at Sourhope: studying fungal diversity and function at the Soil Diversity field site. N ERC *News*, Autumn 2001, 24–5.

Dick, C. H. (1916). *Highways and Byways in Galloway and Carrick*. Macmillan, London.

Dickson, R. C. (1992). *The Birds in Wigtownshire*. GC Publishers, Wigtown.

Dickson, R. C. (1994). Wintering hen harriers in west Galloway. *Transactions of the Dumfriesshire & Galloway Natural History and Antiquarian Society*, Series III, **69**, 3–6.

Duncan, A. B. (1947–8). List of the birds of the Stewartry of Kirkcudbright. *Transactions of the Dumfriesshire & Galloway Natural History and Antiquarian Society*, Series III, **24**, 129–43; **25**, 44–68.

Duncan, A. B. & Cunningham, D. (1953). Moths taken at light in 1951 in Dumfriesshire and eastern Kirkcudbright. *Transactions of the Dumfriesshire & Galloway Natural History and Antiquarian Society*, Series III, **30**, 166–70.

Duncan, U. (1956). A bryophyte flora of Wigtownshire. *Transactions of the British Bryological Society*, **3**, 353–74.

Duncan, W. & Duncan, A. B. (1939). List of heronries in Dumfriesshire and Kirkcudbrightshire in 1928. *Transactions of the Dumfriesshire & Galloway Natural History and Antiquarian Society*, Series III, **21**, 28–47.

Dyer, A. Lindsay, S. & Lusby, P. (2001). The fall and rise of the oblong woodsia in Britain. *Botanical Journal of Scotland*, **52**, 107–20.

Eckford, R. J. A. (1932). The geology of the Merrick Region. In: *Galloway: the Spell of its Hills and Glens*, by A. McCormick. John Smith, Glasgow.

Elliot, W. (1878). Some account of the plague of field mice in the border farms in 1876–77. *Proceedings of the Berwickshire Naturalists' Club*, **8**, 447–72.

Elton, C. (1942). *Voles, Mice and Lemmings*. Oxford University Press, Oxford.

Elton, C., Davies, D. H. S. & Findlay, G. M. (1935). An epidemic among voles on the Scottish border in the spring of 1934. *Journal of Animal Ecology*, **4**, 277–88.

Evans, A. H. (1911). *A Fauna of the Tweed Area*. David Douglas, Edinburgh.

Fairburn, R. & Reynolds, J. (2004). Gamekeeper escapes prison term for 'worst case of wildlife crime'. *The Scotsman*, 26 August 2004.

Farrell, L. & Miles, C. D. (2003). *Hydrilla verticillata* (L.f.) Royle, Esthwaite waterweed. *BSBI Scottish Newsletter*, **25**.

Flower, R. J. & Battarbee, R. W. (1983). Diatom evidence for recent acidification of two Scottish lochs. *Nature*, **305**, 130–3.

Forestry Commission (1950). *Glen Trool*. National Forest Park Guides. HMSO, London.

Fuller, R. J. (1995). *Bird Life of Woodland and Forest*. Cambridge University Press, Cambridge.

Garforth, M. & Dudley, N. (2003). *Forest Renaissance. The Role of State Forestry in Britain: a Discussion Paper*. Forestry Commission, Edinburgh, and WWF, Godalming.

Gibbons, D. W., Reid, J. B. & Chapman, R. A. (1993). *The New Atlas of Breeding Birds in Britain and Ireland*. Poyser, London.

Gladstone, H. S. (1910). *The Birds of Dumfriesshire*, Witherby, London.

Gladstone, H. S. (1912). *A Catalogue of the Vertebrate Fauna of Dumfriesshire*. Maxwell, Dumfries.

Gladstone, H. S. (1923). *Notes on the Birds of Dumfriesshire: a Continuation of The Birds of Dumfriesshire*. Dumfries & Galloway Natural History and Antiquarian Society, Dumfries.

Gladstone, H. S. (1930). *Record Bags and Shooting Records.* Witherby, London.

Goddard, T. R. (1935). A census of short-eared owl (*Asio f. flammeus*) at Newcastleton, Roxburghshire, 1934. *Journal of Animal Ecology,* **4,** 113–18, 289–90.

Godwin, H. (1975). *History of the British Flora: a Factual Basis for Phytogeography.* 2nd edn. Cambridge University Press, Cambridge.

Gordon, J. G. M. (1919). The Lepidoptera of Wigtownshire. Pt. II, Geometrae, Deltoides & Pyralides. *Transactions of the Dumfriesshire & Galloway Natural History and Antiquarian Society,* Series III, **6,** 156–67.

Gordon, R. S. (1913). A list of the Macro-Lepidoptera of Wigtownshire. Pt. I. *Transactions of the Dumfriesshire & Galloway Natural History and Antiquarian Society,* Series III, **1,** 168–88.

Graham, I. M., Redpath, S. M. & Thirgood, S. J. (1995). The diet and breeding density of common buzzards *Buteo buteo* in relation to indices of prey abundance. *Bird Study,* **42,** 165–73.

Gray, R. (1871). *The Birds of the West of Scotland including the Outer Hebrides.* Thomas Murray, Glasgow.

Greig, D. C., Goodlet, G. A., Lumsden, G. I. & Tulloch, W. (1971). *The South of Scotland.* 3rd edn. British Regional Geology. Natural Environment Research Council. HMSO, Edinburgh.

Griffin, L. R., Skilling, D., Smith, R. T. & Young, J. G. (2004). The rookeries of Dumfriesshire 2003. *Transactions of the Dumfriesshire & Galloway Natural History and Antiquarian Society,* Series III, **78,** 1–29.

Harper, M. McL. (1908). *Rambles in Galloway: Topographical, Historical, Traditional and Biographical.* 3rd edn. Mann, Dumfries.

Harriman, R. & Wells, D. E. (1985). Causes and effects of surface water acidification in Scotland. *Water Pollution Control,* **84,** 215–24.

Harvie-Brown, J. A., Trail, J. W. H. & Eagle Clark, W. (eds) (1893). Report on the plague of field-voles in Scotland. *Annals of Scottish Natural History,* **13,** 129–45.

Hayward, I. M. & Druce, G. C. (1919). *The Adventive Flora of Tweedside.* Buncle, Arbroath.

Hill, M. O., Preston, C. D. & Smith, A. J. E. (1991–4). *Atlas of the Bryophytes of Britain and Ireland.* 3 vols. Harley Books, Colchester.

Hough, T. B. & Scott-Elliot, G. F. (1919). Notes regarding bird life in the Stewartry. *Transactions of the Dumfriesshire & Galloway Natural History and Antiquarian Society,* Series III, **6,** 48–65.

Idle, E. T. & Martin, J. (1975). The vegetation and land use history of Torrs Warren, Wigtownshire. *Transactions of the Dumfriesshire & Galloway Natural History and Antiquarian Society,* Series III, **51,** 1–10.

Jardine, W. (1838–43). *The Natural History of the Birds of Great Britain and Ireland.* 4 vols. Edinburgh.

Jefferies, D. (1996). Decline and recovery of the otter: a personal account. *British Wildlife,* **7,** 353–64.

Jeffrey, A. (1864). *The History and Antiquities of Roxburghshire.* 4 vols. Seaton & MacKenzie, Edinburgh

Jenkins, D. (ed.) (1986). *Trees and Wildlife in the Scottish Uplands.* ITE Symposium, **17.** Institute of Terrestrial Ecology, Huntingdon.

Johnston, G. (1829–31). *A Flora of Berwick on Tweed.* Carfrae, Edinburgh; Longman, London.

Johnston, G. (1853). *The Natural History of the Eastern Borders.* J. van Voorst, London.

Johnstone, J. T. (1891). Notes on the flora of the Moffat district. *Transactions of the*

Dumfriesshire & Galloway Natural History and Antiquarian Society, Series II, **7**, 45–50.

Johnstone, J. T. (1893). Notes on the flora of Moffat district for 1891. *Transactions of the Dumfriesshire & Galloway Natural History and Antiquarian Society*, Series II, **8**, 18–21.

Jones, V. J., Stevenson, A. C. & Battarbee, R. W. (1989). Acidification of lakes in Galloway, south-west Scotland: a diatom and pollen study of the Post-glacial history of the Round Loch of Glenhead. *Journal of Ecology*, **77**, 1–23.

Lewis, F. J. (1905). The plant remains in the Scottish peat mosses. *Transactions of the Royal Society of Edinburgh*, **41**, 699–723.

Linton, W. R. & Marshall, E. S. (1908). Plants observed near Moffat, Dumfries, July, 1907. *Journal of Botany*, **46**, 212–15.

Lockie, J. (1955). The breeding habits of short-eared owls after a vole plague. *Bird Study*, **2**, 53–69.

Lusby, P. (1992). Survey of selected lowland grasslands in the Borders. Unpublished Report to Scottish Natural Heritage.

M'Andrew, J. M. (1882). *List of Flowering Plants of Dumfriesshire and Kirkcudbrightshire*.

M'Andrew, J. M. (1890). Botanical notes: list of mosses [Dumfries & Kirkcudbright]. *Transactions of the Dumfriesshire & Galloway Natural History and Antiquarian Society*, Series II, **6**, 89–101.

M'Andrew, J. M. (1891). List of lichens gathered in Dumfriesshire, Kirkcudbrightshire, etc. *Transactions of the Dumfriesshire & Galloway Natural History and Antiquarian Society*, Series II, **7**, 28–36.

M'Andrew, J. M. (1895). A list of Wigtownshire plants. *Transactions of the Dumfriesshire & Galloway Natural History and Antiquarian Society*, Series II, **10**, 72–111.

M'Andrew, J. M. (1911). Notes on the Hepaticae and mosses of the three south-western counties of Scotland. *Transactions of the Dumfriesshire & Galloway Natural History and Antiquarian Society*, Series II, **23**, 306–9.

McConachie, W. (1910). The birds of Lauderdale. *History of the Berwickshire Naturalists' Club*, **20**, 317.

McCormick, A. (1932). *Galloway: the Spell of its Hills and Glens*. John Smith, Glasgow.

MacDermid, A. (2004). Tweed feels the claws of the alien invader. *The Herald*, 4 December 2004.

McGilchrist, C. R. B. (1905). *Birkhill: a Reminiscence*. 2nd edn. James Lewis, Selkirk.

MacGillivray, W. (1837–52). *A History of British Birds, Indigenous and Migratory*. 5 vols. London.

McGowan, B. (1912, 1914, 1921). A list of Coleoptera of the Solway district. *Transactions of the Dumfriesshire & Galloway Natural History and Antiquarian Society*, Series II, **24**, 271–84; Series III, **2**, 234–44; Series III, **7**, 62–6.

McHaffie, H. (2004). *Woodsia ilvensis* re-introduction programme. *Pteridologist*, **4**, 67.

Mack, J. L. (1926). *The Border Line*. Oliver & Boyd, Edinburgh.

Macpherson, H. A. (1892). *A Vertebrate Fauna of Lakeland*. Douglas, Edinburgh.

Macrae, C. (1990). A poisonous life on the wild side for rare birds of prey. *The Observer, Scotland*, 15 April 1990.

McWilliam, J. M. (1936). *The Birds of the Firth of Clyde*. Witherby, London.

Maitland, P. S. (1970). The freshwater fish fauna of south-west Scotland. *Transactions of the Dumfriesshire & Galloway Natural History and Antiquarian Society*, Series II, **47**, 49–62.

Marquiss, M. & Newton, I. (1982). The goshawk in Britain. *British Birds*, **75**, 243–60.

Marquiss, M., Newton, I. & Ratcliffe, D. A.

(1978). The decline of the raven *Corvus corax* in relation to afforestation in southern Scotland and northern England. *Journal of Applied Ecology*, **15**, 129–44.

Marquiss, M., Ratcliffe, D. A. & Roxburgh, R. (1985). Breeding success and diet of golden eagles in southern Scotland in relation to change in land use. *Biological Conservation*, **34**, 121–40.

Marshall, J. R. (1962a). The physiographic development of Caerlaverock merse. *Transactions of the Dumfriesshire & Galloway Natural History and Antiquarian Society*, Series III, **39**, 102.

Marshall, J. R. (1962b). The morphology of the upper Solway salt marshes. *Scottish Geographical Magazine*, **78**, 81–99.

Martin, M. E. R. (1985). Wild plants of Dumfriesshire (V-C 72 Dumfries). *Transactions of the Dumfriesshire & Galloway Natural History and Antiquarian Society*, Series III, **60**, 21–42.

Maxwell, G. (1950). Wild animals and birds. In: *Glen Trool*, pp 40–5. Forestry Commission National Forest Park Guides. HMSO, London.

Maxwell, H. (1901). *Memories of the Months*. 1st series, 2nd edn. Arnold, London.

Mearns, B. (2005). *The Dragonflies of Dumfries and Galloway*. Unpublished summary sheet for local circulation.

Mearns, R. (1983). The status of the raven in southern Scotland and Northumbria. *Scottish Birds*, **12**, 211–18.

Mearns, R. (2001). Juniper *Juniperus communis* in Dumfries and Galloway. *Transactions of the Dumfriesshire & Galloway Natural History and Antiquarian Society*, Series III, **75**, 1–28.

Mearns, R. & Newton, I. (1984). Turnover and dispersal in a peregrine *Falco peregrinus* population. *Ibis*, **126**, 347–55.

Mercer, J., Waddell, J. & Buckland, R. (2004). *Provisional Atlas of Scottish Borders Butterflies*. Scottish Borders Biological Records Centre and Butterfly Conservation East of Scotland Branch.

Meteorological Office (1952). *Climatological Atlas of the British Isles*. HMSO, London.

Milne-Redhead, H. (1962). The Autumn Meeting at Dumfries, 1961. *Transactions of the British Bryological Society*, **4**, 380–3.

Milne-Redhead, H. (1963). Plant distribution in south west Scotland. *Transactions of the Dumfriesshire & Galloway Natural History and Antiquarian Society*, Series III, **40**, 163–7.

Milne-Redhead, H. (1964). A bryophyte flora of Dumfriesshire and the Stewartry of Kirkcudbright. Part I. Liverworts. *Transactions of the Dumfriesshire & Galloway Natural History and Antiquarian Society*, Series III, **41**, 17–29.

Milne-Redhead, H. (1972). A check-list of the flowering plants, ferns and fern-allies of the vice-counties of Dumfries, Kirkcudbright and Wigtown. *Transactions of the Dumfriesshire & Galloway Natural History and Antiquarian Society*, Series III, **49**, 1–19.

Mitchell, G. F. (1948). Late-glacial deposits in Berwickshire. *New Phytologist*, **47**, 262–4.

Mitchell, J. (2001). *Loch Lomondside*. New Naturalist 88. Collins, London.

Mitchell, J., Placido, C. & Rose, R. (1974). Notes on a short-tailed vole plague at Eskdalemuir, Dumfriesshire. *Transactions of the Dumfriesshire & Galloway Natural History and Antiquarian Society*, Series III, **51**, 11–13.

Moar, N. T. (1969). Late-Weichselian and Flandrian pollen diagrams from south-west Scotland. *New Phytologist*, **68**, 433–67.

Moore, N. W. (1987). *The Bird of Time: the Science and Politics of Nature Conservation*. Cambridge University Press, Cambridge.

Morss, W. L. (1927). The plant colonisation of Merse lands in the estuary of the River Nith. *Journal of Ecology*, **15**, 310–43.

Muirhead, G. (1889–95). *The Birds of Berwickshire*. 2 vols. David Douglas, Edinburgh.

Murray, R. (ed.) (2000). *The Borders Bird Report*, **19**, 1999. Scottish Ornithologists' Club, Edinburgh.

Murray, R. (ed.) (2002). *The Borders Bird Report*, **20**, 2000. Scottish Ornithologists' Club, Edinburgh.

Murray, R. (ed.) (2003). *The Borders Bird Report*, **21**, 2001 & 2002. Scottish Ornithologists' Club, Edinburgh.

Murray, R., Holling, M., Dott, H. & Vandome, P. (1998). *The Breeding Birds of South-East Scotland: a Tetrad Atlas, 1988–1994*. Scottish Ornithologists' Club, Edinburgh.

Nature Conservancy Council (1986). *Nature Conservation and Afforestation in Great Britain*. NCC, Peterborough.

Nelson, J. M. (1980). The invertebrate fauna of a tidal marsh at Caerlaverock, Dumfriesshire. *Transactions of the Dumfriesshire & Galloway Natural History and Antiquarian Society*, Series III, **55**, 68–76.

Nelson, J. M. & Theaker, J. H. (1982). Invertebrates caught on a bog within the Silver Flowe National Nature Reserve, Galloway. *Transactions of the Dumfriesshire & Galloway Natural History and Antiquarian Society*, Series III, **57**, 23–8.

New Statistical Account (1845). *The New Statistical Account of Scotland, by the ministers of the respective parishes, under the super-intendence of a committee of the Society for the Benefit of the Sons and Daughters of the Clergy*. 15 vols. Blackwood, Edinburgh. Originally published in 52 parts, 1834–45.

Newton, A. C., Davy, L. M., Holden, E., Silverside, A., Watling, R. & Ward, S. D. (2003). Status, distribution and definition of mycologically important grasslands in Scotland. *Biological Conservation*, **111**, 11–23.

Newton, I. (1986). *The Sparrowhawk*. Poyser, Calton.

Newton, I. (1991). Habitat variation and population regulation in sparrowhawks. *Ibis*, **133**, Suppl. 1, 76–88.

Newton, I. & Rothery, P. (2001). Estimation and limitation of numbers of floaters in a Eurasian sparrowhawk population. *Ibis*, **143**, 442–9.

Nichols, H. (1967). Vegetational change, shoreline displacement and the human factor in the late Quaternary history of south-west Scotland. *Transactions of the Royal Society of Edinburgh*, **67**, 145–87.

Norman, P. (2001). Birds in Dumfries and Galloway. *Dumfries & Galloway Regional Bird Report*, **15**, 1999–2000.

Norman, P. (2002). Birds in Dumfries and Galloway. *Dumfries & Galloway Regional Bird Report*, **16**, 2001.

North Solway Ringing Group (1973). Breeding birds of the Solway islands. *Transactions of the Dumfriesshire & Galloway Natural History and Antiquarian Society*, Series III, **50**, 5–17.

Ogilvy, R. S. D. (1986). Whither forestry? The scene in AD 2025. In: *Trees and Wildlife in the Scottish Uplands* (ed. Jenkins, D.). ITE Symposium, **17**. Institute of Terrestrial Ecology, Huntingdon.

Orchel, J. (1992). *Forest Merlins in Scotland: Their Requirements and Management*. Hawk and Owl Trust, London.

Ormerod, S. J. & Tyler, S. J. (1987). Dippers *Cinclus cinclus* and grey wagtails *Motacilla cinerea* as indicators of stream acidity in upland Wales. In: *The Value of Birds* (ed. Diamond A. W. & Filion F. L.). ICBP Technical Publication, **6**, 191–208.

Orr, W. (1982). *Deer Forests, Landlords and Crofters*. John Donald, Edinburgh.

Paton, E. R. & Pike, O. G. (1929). *The Birds of Ayrshire*. Witherby, London.

Peach, B. N. & Horne, J. (1896). The geology of Dumfriesshire. In: *The Flora of Dumfriesshire*, by G. F. Scott-Elliot. James Maxwell, Dumfries.

Pearsall, W. H. (1950). *Mountains and Moorlands*. New Naturalist 11. Collins, London.

Perring, F. H. & Walters, S. M. (eds) (1962). *Atlas of the British Flora*. New Nelson, London.

Philipson, M. (1954). North-eastern bird studies: the curlew and black grouse. *Transactions of the Carlisle Natural History Society*, **18**, 14–22.

Poxton, I. R. (1987). Breeding status of the ring ouzel in southeast Scotland. *Scottish Birds*, **14**, 205–8.

Prater, A. J. (1981). *Estuary Birds of Britain and Ireland*. Poyser, Calton.

Preston, C. D., Pearman, D. A. & Dines, T. D. (2002). *New Atlas of the British and Irish Flora*. Oxford University Press, Oxford.

Prestt, I. & Ratcliffe, D. A. (1972). Effects of organochlorine insecticides on European birdlife. In: *Proceedings of the XV International Ornithological Congress* (ed. Voous, K. H.), pp. 486–513. Brill, Leiden.

Pritchard, D. E., Housden, S. D., Mudge, G. P., Galbraith, C. A. & Pienkowski, M. W. (eds) (1992). *Important Bird Areas in the United Kingdom, including the Channel Islands and the Isle of Man*. RSPB, Sandy.

Pullen, O. J. (1937). Some rarer birds of Galloway. *The Gallovidian Annual*, 1936–7, 72–8, Dinwiddie, Dumfries.

Pullen, O. J. (1942). A Dumfriesshire gullery. *Transactions of the Dumfriesshire & Galloway Natural History and Antiquarian Society*, Series III, **22**, 165–9.

Ratcliffe, D. A. (1959). The mountain plants of the Moffat Hills. *Transactions of the Botanical Society of Edinburgh*, **37**, 257–71.

Ratcliffe, D. A. (1962). Breeding density in the peregrine *Falco peregrinus* and raven *Corvus corax*. *Ibis*, **104**, 13–39.

Ratcliffe, D. A. (1976). Observations on the breeding of the golden plover in Great Britain. *Bird Study*, **23**, 62–116.

Ratcliffe, D. A. (1986). The effects of afforestation on the wildlife of open habitats. In: *Trees and Wildlife in the Scottish Uplands* (ed. Jenkins, D.). ITE Symposium, **17**. Institute of Terrestrial Ecology, Huntingdon.

Ratcliffe, D. A. (1997). *The Raven*. Poyser, London.

Ratcliffe, D. A. (2002). *Lakeland*. New Naturalist 92. Collins, London.

Ratcliffe, D. A. & Walker, D. (1958). The Silver Flowe, Galloway, Scotland. *Journal of Ecology*, **46**, 407–45.

Redpath, S. M. & Thirgood, S. J. (1997). *Birds of Prey and Red Grouse*. The Stationery Office, London & Edinburgh.

Riddle, G. (1992). *Seasons with the Kestrel*. Blandford, London.

Roberts, G. & Sutcliffe, R. (1996). Where to watch butterflies in south west Scotland. *Butterfly Conservation News*, **63**, Autumn/winter 1996.

Roberts, J. (2002). After foot and mouth, Cross Fell in bloom. *The Carlisle Naturalist*, **10**, 33–42.

Robinson, M. (1980). *The Effect of Pre-Afforestation Drainage on Stream Flow and Water Quality of a Small Upland Catchment*. Report 73. Institute of Hydrology, Wallingford.

Robinson, M. & Blyth, K. (1982). The effect of forestry drainage operations on upland sediment yields: a case study. *Earth Surface Processes and Landforms*, **7**, 85–90.

Rodger, D., Stokes, J. & Ogilvie, J. (2003). *Heritage Trees of Scotland*. Forestry Commission, Wetherby.

Rodwell, J. (1991–2000). *British Plant*

Communities. 5 vols. Cambridge University Press, Cambridge.

Vol. 1. (1991). *Woodlands and Scrub.*

Vol. 2. (1991). *Mires and Heaths.*

Vol. 3. (1992). *Grasslands and Montane Communities.*

Vol. 4. (1995). *Aquatic Communities, Swamps and Tall-Herb Fens.*

Vol. 5. (2000). *Maritime Communities and Vegetation of Open Habitats.*

Rollie, C. (2004). The Galloway Kite Trail. *Scottish Bird News*, **71**, 13.

Rose, F. & James, P. W. (1976). A survey of the lichens of Galloway and western Dumfriesshire. Unpublished report to the Nature Conservancy Council.

Rowan, A. (1994). Summer Field Meeting, South West Scotland 1993. *Bulletin of the British Bryological Society*, **63**, 15–19.

Rowe, S. M. (1978). An investigation of the erosion and accretion regime on the salt marshes of the Upper Solway Firth, 1949–1975. *Nature Conservancy Council, CSD Report*, **141**. NCC, London.

Royal Society for the Protection of Birds (2004). *Birdcrime 2003. Offences Against Wild Bird Legislation in 2003.* RSPB, Sandy.

Royal Society for the Protection of Birds, British Trust for Ornithology & Wildfowl & Wetlands Trust (2004). *The State of the UK's Birds 2003.* RSPB, Sandy.

Sadler, J. (1857). *Narrative of a Ramble Among the Wild Flowers of the Moffat Hills.* William Muir, Moffat.

Scott-Elliot, G. F. (1896). *The Flora of Dumfriesshire, Including Part of the Stewartry of Kirkcudbright.* James Maxwell, Dumfries.

Service, R. (1901). The vertebrates of Solway: a century's changes. *Transactions of the Dumfriesshire & Galloway Natural History and Antiquarian Society*, Series II, **17**, 15–31.

Service, R. (1905–6). The waders of Solway. *Transactions of the Natural History Society of Glasgow*, **8**, 46–60.

Sharrock, J. T. R. (1976). *The Atlas of Breeding Birds in Britain and Ireland.* Poyser, Berkhamsted.

Shaw, G. (1995). Habitat selection by short-eared owls *Asio flammeus* in young coniferous forests. *Bird Study*, **42**, 158–64.

Shaw, G. & Livingstone, J. (1992). The pine marten: its reintroduction and subsequent history in the Galloway Forest Park. *Transactions of the Dumfriesshire & Galloway Natural History and Antiquarian Society*, Series III, **67**, 1–7.

Silverside, A. J. (1990). *The Flowering Plants and Ferns of Wigtownshire: a Very Provisional Check-List.* Privately printed.

Sinclair, J. (1791–9). *The Statistical Account of Scotland, drawn up from the communications of the ministers of the different Parishes.* 21 vols. Edinburgh.

Smith, P. M., Dixon, O. D. & Cochrane, M. P. (2002). *Plant Life of Edinburgh and the Lothians.* Edinburgh University Press, Edinburgh.

Smith, R.W. J. (1969). Scottish cormorant colonies. *Scottish Birds*, **5**, 363–8.

Smith, W. G. (1918). The distribution of *Nardus stricta* in relation to peat. *Journal of Ecology*, **6**, 1–13.

Solway Firth Partnership (1996). *Solway Firth Review.* Dumfries & Galloway Council, Dumfries.

Stace, C. (1997). *New Flora of the British Isles.* 2nd edn. Cambridge University Press, Cambridge.

Steers, J. A. (1973). *The Coastline of Scotland.* Cambridge University Press, Cambridge.

Stevenson, J. (1879). *Mycologia Scotica.* Edinburgh.

Stewart, A., Pearman, D. A. & Preston, C. D. (1994). *Scarce Plants in Britain.* Joint Nature Conservation Committee, Peterborough.

Stewart, O. M. (1987). Professor Hutton Balfour's botanical visits to Kirkcudbrightshire, 1843 and 1868.

Transactions of the Dumfriesshire & Galloway Natural History and Antiquarian Society, Series III, **62**, 1–4.

Stewart, O. M. (1990). Flowering plants and ferns of Kirkcudbrightshire. *Transactions of the Dumfriesshire & Galloway Natural History and Antiquarian Society*, Series III, **65**, 1–68.

Stewart, O. M. (1992). Scarce plant project survey in Kirkcudbrightshire. *BSBI Scottish Newsletter*, **14**, 21–2.

Stewart, O. M. (1996). Yellow water-lilies in Kirkcudbrightshire. *BSBI Scottish Newsletter*, **18**, 13–14.

Stirling, A. McG. (1960). Kirkcudbright plant notes. *Transactions of the Dumfriesshire & Galloway Natural History and Antiquarian Society*, Series III, **37**, 165–7.

Sutherland, A. (1925). The shore vegetation of Wigtownshire. *Scottish Geographical Magazine*, **41**, 1–.

Symon, J. A. (1959). *Scottish Farming Past and Present*. Oliver & Boyd, Edinburgh.

Symson, A. (1684). *A Large Description of Galloway with an Appendix Containing Original Papers from the Sibbald & McFarlane MSS, Edinburgh (1684)*. Printed for Tait, Edinburgh, 1823.

Taylor, I. R., Dowell, A., Irving, T., Langford, I. K. & Shaw, G. (1988). The distribution and abundance of the Barn Owl *Tyto alba* in south-west Scotland. *Scottish Birds*, **15**, 40–43.

Thom, V. M. (1986). *Birds in Scotland*. Poyser, Calton.

Thompson, D. L. & Dougall, T. W. (1988). The status of breeding wigeon in Ettrick Forest. *Scottish Birds*, **15**, 61–4.

Thompson, J. V. (1807). *A Catalogue of Plants Growing in the Vicinity of Berwick upon Tweed*. London.

Thomson, G. (1980). *The Butterflies of Scotland*. Croom Helm, London.

Tight, J. A. (1987). Late Quaternary history of Wester Branxholme and Kingside Lochs, southeast Scotland. Unpublished PhD thesis, University of Reading.

Tipping, R. (1997). Vegetation history of southern Scotland. *Botanical Journal of Scotland*, **49**, 151–62.

Tompkins, S. (1989). *Forestry in Crisis: the Battle for the Hills*. Helm, London.

Tratt, R. (1997). The Scottish Border fens: controls on vegetation development and composition. Unpublished PhD thesis, University of Sheffield.

Vickery, J. A. (1991). Breeding density of dippers *Cinclus cinclus*, grey wagtails *Motacilla cinerea* and common sandpipers *Actitis hypoleucos* in relation to the acidity of streams in south-west Scotland. *Ibis*, **133**, 178–85.

Village, A. (1990). *The Kestrel*. Poyser, London.

Waring, P., Townsend, M. & Lewington, R. (2003). *Field Guide to the Moths of Great Britain and Ireland*. British Wildlife Publishing, Rotherwick.

Watling, R. (1983). Forays of the Cryptogamic Society of Scotland. *Bulletin of the British Mycological Society*, **17**, 55–60.

Watling, R. (1986). 150 years of paddock stools: a history of agaric ecology and floristics in Scotland. *Transactions of the Botanical Society of Edinburgh*, **45**, 1–42.

Watling, R. (2002). New fungal records from Shetland. *Shetland Naturalist*, **2** (2), 51–6.

Watling, R. (2005). Dawyck Botanic Garden; the Heron Wood cryptogamic project. *Botanical Journal of Scotland*, **56**, 109–18.

Watson, A. (1995). Indicative Forestry Strategies: a costly con trick. *Ecos*, **16**, 52–8.

Watson, A. D. (1972). *Birds of Moor and Mountain*. Scottish Academic Press, Edinburgh.

Watson, A. D. (1977). *The Hen Harrier*. Poyser, Berkhamsted.

Watson, A. D. (1988). *A Bird Artist in Scotland.* Witherby, London.

Watson, A. D. (1994). *One Pair of Eyes.* Arlequin Press, Chelmsford.

Watson, K. & Macpherson, P. (1999). Plant recording in upland Lanarkshire (V.C. 77). *Glasgow Naturalist,* **23**, 26–8.

Webb, J. A. & Moore, P. D. (1982). The Late Devensian vegetational history of the Whitlaw Mosses, southeast Scotland. *New Phytologist,* **91**, 341–98.

Wernham, C., Toms, M., Marchant, J., Clark, J., Siriwardena,G. & Baillie, S. (2002). *The Migration Atlas: Movements of the Birds of Britain and Ireland.* Poyser, London.

Wright, L. (c.1990). *Birds on Scottish Lowland Farms.* Nature Conservancy Council and Scottish Wildlife Trust, Edinburgh.

Yeates, G. K. (1948). *Bird Haunts in Northern Britain.* Faber & Faber, London.

Young, J. G. (1968). Birds of the Scar Rocks: the Wigtownshire gannetry. *Scottish Birds,* **5**, 204–8.

Young, J. G. (1972). Distribution, status and movements of feral greylag geese in south-west Scotland. *Scottish Birds,* **7**, 170–82.

General Index

Species Index